How to Do *Everything* with Your

iPod™ & iPod mini

Second Edition

Guy Hart-Davis

McGraw-Hill/Osborne

New York   Chicago   San Francisco   Lisbon
London   Madrid   Mexico City   Milan   New Delhi
San Juan   Seoul   Singapore   Sydney   Toronto

McGraw-Hill/Osborne
2100 Powell Street, 10th Floor
Emeryville, California 94608
U.S.A.

To arrange bulk purchase discounts for sales promotions, premiums, or fund-raisers, please contact
McGraw-Hill/Osborne at the above address. For information on translations or book distributors
outside the U.S.A., please see the International Contact Information page immediately following
the index of this book.

How to Do Everything with Your iPod™ and iPod™ mini

Copyright © 2004 by The McGraw-Hill Companies. All rights reserved. Printed in the United
States of America. Except as permitted under the Copyright Act of 1976, no part of this publication
may be reproduced or distributed in any form or by any means, or stored in a database or retrieval
system, without the prior written permission of publisher, with the exception that the program
listings may be entered, stored, and executed in a computer system, but they may not be reproduced
for publication.

234567890 FGR FGR 01987654

ISBN 0-07-225452-1

Publisher	Brandon A. Nordin
Vice President &	
Associate Publisher	Scott Rogers
Acquisitions Editor	Megg Morin
Project Editor	Emily K. Wolman
Project Manager	LeeAnn Pickrell
Acquisitions Coordinator	Agatha Kim
Technical Editor	Clint Roberts
Copy Editor	Emily K. Wolman
Proofreaders	Marian Selig, Linda Medoff
Indexer	Karin Arrigoni
Composition	International Typesetting and Composition, Melinda Lytle
Illustrators	International Typesetting and Composition, Melinda Lytle
Series Design	Michelle Galicia
Cover Series Design	Dodie Shoemaker
Cover Illustration	Guy Critenden
iPod Photograph	Doug Rosa
iPod mini Photograph	Davies + Starr

This book was composed with Corel VENTURA™ Publisher.

Information has been obtained by **McGraw-Hill**/Osborne from sources believed to be reliable. However, because of the possibility of
human or mechanical error by our sources, **McGraw-Hill**/Osborne, or others, **McGraw-Hill**/Osborne does not guarantee the accuracy,
adequacy, or completeness of any information and is not responsible for any errors or omissions or the results obtained from the use of
such information.

Dedication

This book is dedicated to the people who gave us MP3, AAC, and the iPod.

Contents at a Glance

Contents

Acknowledgments

I'd like to thank the following people for their help with this book:

- Megg Morin for developing the book and relaying hardware as necessary
- Agatha Kim for handling the acquisitions end of the book
- Clint Roberts for reviewing the manuscript for technical accuracy and contributing many helpful suggestions
- Emily Wolman for editing the manuscript and coordinating the production of the book
- Marian Selig and Linda Medoff for proofreading the book
- Waseem Andrabi for laying out the pages
- Karin Arrigoni for creating the index
- Sue Runfola, Bob Robinson, and Dimitri Proano at Apple for their help and quick turnarounds on the cover elements
- Roger Stewart for lurking in the background, pulling strings as required

Introduction

The iPod is the best portable music player available at the time of writing. Small enough to fit easily into a hand or a pocket, the iPod can hold the contents of your entire CD collection in compressed files and can deliver up to ten hours of music on a single battery charge. You can download a dozen CDs' worth of music from your computer to your iPod in less than a minute, and you can recharge your iPod quickly either from a power outlet or from your computer. And whereas the first iPods worked only with the Mac, the later iPods and the iPod mini work with Windows as well.

The iPod mini, introduced in February 2004, provides almost-full iPod functionality in an even smaller and cuter package. The main disadvantage of the iPod mini is that it can hold less music than the regular iPods.

But you know all this. (That *is* an iPod in your pocket, isn't it? Thought so.) If you're looking at this book in a bookstore, chances are you're wondering why anyone would need a 400-page book to use a simple music player.

Answer: They wouldn't. But the iPod isn't just a portable audio player with terrific sound quality and huge capacity. You can also load it up with your calendars, and display your appointments on it. You can also copy to your iPod all your contact records and all your text notes—anything from a shopping list to a book. By using third-party utilities, you can transfer up-to-the-minute headlines, weather reports, stock quotes, driving directions, and other text from the Internet onto your iPod, swiftly and automatically. You can even transfer information from widely used organizers such as Microsoft Outlook (on Windows), Microsoft Entourage (on the Mac), and Palm Desktop (on both platforms).

So you can use your iPod to carry your essential information with you, and you can check your appointments or display driving directions even while the music keeps thundering. But that's not all. Because the iPod is based around a hard disk and connects to your computer via FireWire or USB, you can transfer to it any files that will fit on the hard disk. So you can use your iPod to carry a backup of your vital documents with you, or even to transfer files from one computer to another. If your computer is a Mac, you can even install Mac OS X or System 9 on your iPod (but not your iPod mini) and boot your Mac from the iPod.

What Does This Book Cover?

To help you get the maximum enjoyment and use from your iPod, this book covers just about every iPod topic you can think of and various related topics into the bargain.

NOTE

This book shows you how to make the most of your iPod on Windows XP (on the PC) and Mac OS X. If you're using Windows 2000 rather than Windows XP, you should be able to follow along just fine, but you'll need to choose slightly different commands in the interface at some points. For example, Windows XP's default configuration is to use a different Start menu layout than Windows 2000, so if you're using Windows 2000, you'll need to make some different Start menu choices. You'll get used to this in next to no time.

Chapter 1, "Understand the Different iPods—and Choose the Right One," explains what an iPod is (okay, you know this), how to distinguish the three different generations of iPod and the iPod mini from each other, and how their capabilities differ. The chapter then suggests how to choose the iPod that's best for you.

Chapter 2, "Get Up and Running with Your iPod or iPod mini," runs you through the steps of connecting your iPod to your computer and installing iTunes and the iPod software on your Mac or PC. It also shows you how to connect your speakers or headphones to your iPod and how to use your iPod's controls.

Chapter 3, "Bring Yourself Up to Speed with AAC, MP3, and Digital Audio," tells you what you need to know about audio quality and compression. This chapter explains what CD-quality audio is and why it sounds good, why AAC and MP3 sound almost as good as CD-quality audio, and what advantages they offer over uncompressed audio. The chapter then discusses how to choose between AAC and MP3, and how to get the best possible results when creating AAC files or MP3 files from CDs or other audio sources. This chapter also briefs you on the basics of copyright law regarding MP3 and digital audio, and explains the copy-protection techniques the record companies are using to prevent people from copying CDs.

Chapter 4, "Load Music onto Your iPod or iPod mini Using a Mac," shows you how to master iTunes on Mac OS X. You'll learn how to set up and configure iTunes, choose suitable settings for ripping and encoding compressed and uncompressed files, and create a music library that you synchronize with your iPod. You'll also learn to use the graphical equalizer to improve the sound of music both on iTunes and on your iPod, share music with other users, and listen to Internet radio.

Chapter 5, "Load Music onto Your iPod or iPod mini Using Windows," is the mirror image of Chapter 4, covering iTunes on Windows instead of on the Mac. In this chapter, you'll learn how to set up and configure iTunes, choose suitable settings for ripping audio to the different file types iTunes supports, and create a music library that you synchronize with your iPod. You'll also learn how to use the graphical equalizer, share music and access others' shared music, add artwork to songs, and listen to Internet radio.

Chapter 6, "Create, Edit, and Tag Your Audio Files," shows you how to work with MP3 files and AAC files in ways that iTunes itself can't manage, by using various Windows and Mac audio utilities. This chapter starts by telling you how to convert other audio file types to MP3, AAC, WAV, or AIFF so you can play them on your iPod. Then it discusses how to create MP3 files or AAC files from cassettes or vinyl records, and how to remove scratches and hiss from audio files created from sources such as these. It also shows you how to trim song files to remove intros or outros you don't like, how to tag your song files with accurate data so that iTunes and your iPod can sort them correctly, and how to save audio streams to disk so you can listen to them later.

Chapter 7, "Buy Music from the iTunes Music Store," explains what the iTunes Music Store is, how to set up an account, how to find music by browsing and searching, and how to buy and download music. The chapter also explains what digital rights management (DRM) is, what its implications are, and why you should think about them even when using the iTunes Music Store. At the end of the chapter, you'll learn how to authorize and "deauthorize" computers for using music bought from the iTunes Music Store.

Chapter 8, "Download Audio Files from the Internet," discusses the various sources of audio files on the Internet and makes sure you understand the dangers of downloading unauthorized copies of copyrighted works. This chapter explores the tension between the music industry and music consumers, explains what the "darknet" is and how P2P networks greatly enlarged it, and shows you sites where you can find authorized, legitimate audio files.

Chapter 9, "Burn CDs and DVDs from iTunes," shows you how to use the features built into iTunes to burn CDs and DVDs. You'll learn the basics of burning and the differences between audio CDs, MP3 CDs, and data CDs and data DVDs; learn to configure iTunes for burning CDs; and learn how to troubleshoot problems you encounter when burning CDs.

Chapter 10, "Put Your Contacts on Your iPod or iPod mini," covers how to put your contact information on your iPod so that you can carry it with you. This chapter explains the vCard format, which is the key to putting contact information—or other text—onto the iPod, and shows you how to create vCards using several widely used applications on both Windows and the Mac. The chapter then tells you how to put contacts on your iPod and how to view them on it.

Chapter 11, "Put Your Calendars on Your iPod or iPod mini," explains how to transfer your calendar information from your Mac or PC to your iPod and view it there. The key to putting calendar information on your iPod is the vCalendar format, which this chapter discusses.

Chapter 12, "Create Notes and Put Other Information on Your iPod or iPod mini," shows you how to put text other than contacts and calendar information on your iPod. This chapter starts by discussing the limitations of the iPod as a text-display device and mentioning types of text best suited to the iPod. Then it explains how to use the iPod's built-in Notes feature before going on to cover a variety of third-party Mac and Windows utilities for putting text on your iPod.

Chapter 13, "Keep Your iPod or iPod mini in Good Working Shape," covers how to keep your iPod in good working shape. The chapter starts by discussing the components that make up your iPod, then moves along to tell you how to maximize battery life and where to get your battery replaced if it fails. From there, this chapter walks you through things that make your iPod unhappy; how to keep your iPod's operating system up-to-date; and how to carry, store, and clean your iPod.

Chapter 14, "Use Your iPod or iPod mini As a Hard Drive," shows you how to use your iPod as a hard drive for backup and portable storage. If your computer is a Mac, you can even boot from your iPod (but not your iPod mini) for security or to recover from disaster; see the second Special Project for details. Along the way, you'll learn how to enable disk mode on your iPod, transfer files to and from your iPod, and optimize your iPod's hard disk to improve performance if necessary.

Chapter 15, "Enhance Your iPod or iPod mini with Accessories," discusses the various types of accessories available for the iPod, from mainstream accessories (such as cases and stands) to more esoteric accessories (wait and see). This chapter also discusses how to connect your iPod to your home stereo or car stereo.

Chapter 16, "Master Advanced iPod Skills," shows you how to perform a variety of advanced maneuvers with your iPod. The chapter starts by walking you through the processes of moving an iPod from Mac OS X to Windows or the other direction. It then shows you how to change the computer to which your iPod is linked—a useful skill when you upgrade your computer. The chapter explains how to synchronize several iPods with the same computer and shows you how to load your iPod from multiple computers. You'll also learn how to transfer song files from your iPod's music library to your computer and how to use your computer to play songs directly from your iPod.

Chapter 17, "Troubleshoot iPod and iTunes Problems," shows you how to work your way through troubleshooting your iPod when normal service is interrupted. You'll learn how to avoid voiding your warranty, approach the troubleshooting process in the right way, learn key troubleshooting maneuvers, and use your iPod's built-in diagnostic tools to identify suspected problems. You'll also learn key maneuvers for making iTunes behave itself when it's unruly.

On the purple-shaded pages, you'll find three Special Projects. The first Special Project shows you how to use the Belkin Media Reader for iPod to turn your iPod (but not your iPod mini) into an indispensable companion for your digital camera. The second Special Project walks you through the process of setting up your iPod (but again, not your iPod mini) as a boot disk for your Mac. The third Special Project discusses how to share your songs with other users of your Mac or PC, and describes how you might want to go about setting up a music server for your household.

Conventions Used in This Book

To make its meaning clear without using far more words than necessary, this book uses a number of conventions, three of which are worth mentioning here:

- Note, Tip, and Caution paragraphs highlight information to draw it to your notice.
- The pipe character or vertical bar denotes choosing an item from a menu. For example, "choose File | Open" means that you should pull down the File menu and select the Open item on it. Use the keyboard, mouse, or a combination of the two as you wish.
- Most check boxes have two states: *selected* (with a check mark in them) and *cleared* (without a check mark in them). This book tells you to *select* a check box or *clear* a check box rather than "click to place a check mark in the box" or "click to remove the check mark from the box." (Often, you'll be verifying the state of the check box, so it may already have the required setting—in which case, of course, you don't need to click at all.) Some check boxes have a third state as well, in which they're selected but dimmed and unavailable. This state is usually used for options that apply to only part of the current situation.

Part I

Enjoy Audio with Your iPod and iTunes

Chapter 1

Understand the Different iPods—and Choose the Right One

How to...

- Understand what an iPod is and what an iPod mini is
- Understand what your iPod or iPod mini doesn't do
- Distinguish the three generations of iPod and the iPod mini
- Choose the right iPod (or an iPod mini) for your needs

If you don't already have an iPod or an iPod mini, you'll need to beg, borrow, or buy one before you can make the most of this book. This short chapter tells you what you need to know about what an iPod (or iPod mini) is and does, and what it isn't and doesn't do. It explains which different types of iPod are available at the time of writing, and shows you how to distinguish among them and how to differentiate them from the iPod mini. Finally, it suggests how to choose the iPod that will best suit your needs.

If you're already the proud owner of an iPod or an iPod mini, you may prefer to skip directly to Chapter 2, which shows you how to get up and running with it.

Saying "iPod or iPod mini" every sentence is a little awkward, so in this chapter (and the rest of this book) I'll use the term *iPod* to cover all iPods, including the iPod mini. Where the iPod mini behaves differently, or there's something you need to think about if you plan to use an iPod mini rather than a regular iPod, I'll tell you. I'll use *regular iPod* to refer to a full-size iPod.

What Is an iPod? What Is an iPod mini?

An iPod—the regular, full-size iPod—is a portable music player with a huge capacity, a rechargeable battery good for eight to ten hours of playback, and easy-to-use controls. An iPod mini is a smaller and cuter version with more modest capacity. Your iPod or iPod mini connects to your Mac or PC via a FireWire cable or USB cable that enables you to transfer large quantities of song files and other files quickly to the player.

Built around the type of hard drive used in small laptop computers, a regular iPod doubles as a contact database, calendar, and note board, enabling you to carry around not only all your music but also your vital information. You can also put other textual information on your iPod so you can carry that information with you and view it on the iPod's screen. With extra hardware, you can extend your iPod's capabilities even further. For example, with a custom microphone, you can record audio directly onto it. With a custom media reader, you can store your digital photos on your iPod's hard disk without using a computer. This capability can make your iPod a great travel companion for your digital camera—especially a camera that takes high-resolution photos.

The iPod mini is built around the type of hard drive used in the tiniest laptop computers and some consumer electronics, such as cell phones that have swallowed a PDA and decided that extra storage would improve their digestion. The iPod mini has most of the capabilities of the regular iPod, but at the time of writing, it doesn't support recording audio or downloading digital photos from third-party devices.

If music, contacts, calendar, notes, and other text aren't enough for you, you can also use your iPod as an external hard disk for your Mac or PC. Your iPod provides an easy and convenient means of backing up your data, storing files, and transporting files from one computer to another. And because your iPod is ultra-portable, you can take those files with you wherever you go, which can be great for school, work, and even play. The iPod mini scores even higher on portability than the regular iPod, but because its capacity is so much lower, it's not so great for carrying around huge quantities of files.

Your iPod supports various audio formats, including Advanced Audio Coding (AAC), MP3 (including Audible.com's Audible files), WAV, and AIFF. Although the iPod doesn't support other formats—such as Microsoft's Windows Media Audio (WMA), RealNetworks' RealAudio, or the open-source audio format Ogg Vorbis—at this writing, you can convert audio files in those formats to AAC, MP3, or another supported format easily enough so that you can put those files on your iPod.

Your iPod contains a relatively small operating system (OS) that lets it function on its own—for example, for playing back music, displaying contact information, and so on. The OS also lets your iPod know when it's been connected to a computer, at which point the OS hands over control to the computer so you can manage it from there.

Your iPod is designed to communicate seamlessly with iTunes, which runs on both the Mac and Windows. If you prefer, you can use your iPod with other software as well on either operating system. If you use your iPod with iTunes, you can buy music from the iTunes Music Store, download it to your Mac or PC, and play it either on your computer or iPod.

What Your iPod *Doesn't* Do

So much for what your iPod does and what it consists of. This section discusses some of the things your iPod *doesn't* do and what its limitations are. Some may seem obvious, but if you're in the market for an iPod, you'll benefit from being clear on all these points right now.

You Can't Enter (Much) Information onto Your iPod Directly

Out of the box, your iPod is strictly a play-and-display device: you can't enter information onto it directly. All the information your iPod contains must come from a computer (a Mac or a PC) across a FireWire cable or USB cable.

This changes if you buy a hardware accessory that's designed to work with the iPod. (The accessory needs to be specifically designed to work with the iPod, otherwise the iPod won't recognize it.) You can then input certain types of data—for example, you can record audio or import photos from a digital camera—without connecting your iPod to a computer. (The iPod mini can't handle these types of input at the time of writing.)

iPod fans and pundits have long predicted an iPod keyboard that will let you type text onto your iPod, but Apple hasn't obliged yet. At this writing, dictating voice memos is as good as text entry gets.

The iPod Isn't the Smallest or Most Skip-Proof Player in Town

Because your iPod is based around a hard drive, it's far larger than the smallest digital audio players around. Some of the smallest players are around the size of a cigarette lighter, while a regular iPod is more the size of a packet of cigarettes, and an iPod mini is the size of a stack of credit cards.

Your iPod is also less resistant to skips than solid-state players that store data on flash memory rather than on a hard disk. But as you'll see in the section "What You Might Want to Know About Your iPod's Internals," in Chapter 13, Apple has done some clever engineering to reduce skipping caused by the hard drive being knocked around. That said, if you need a super-lightweight, super-tough, or wholly skip-proof digital audio player, you should probably look beyond the iPod.

One solution is to use your iPod for most of your music and buy an inexpensive, low-capacity digital audio player for your higher-energy or higher-impact pursuits. That way, if you wipe out while trying to set a new speed record on your street luge, you won't need to buy a new iPod—just a titanium ultraportable player, a pair of Kevlar shorts, and a pack of Moleskin.

Your iPod Supports Only AAC, MP3, WAV, and AIFF Audio Formats

At the time of this writing, your iPod supports only a limited range of audio formats: AAC, MP3 (including Audible.com's AA format), WAV, and AIFF. Your iPod doesn't support major formats such as the following:

- Windows Media Audio (WMA), Microsoft's proprietary format. WMA has built-in digital rights management (DRM) capabilities and is used by several of the largest online music stores (such as Napster 2.0).

- RealAudio, the RealNetworks format in which much audio is streamed across the Internet and other networks.

- Ogg Vorbis, the new open-source audio format intended to provide royalty-free competition to MP3.

Because you can convert audio files from one format to another, and because the MP3 format is very widely used, this limitation isn't too painful. But if your entire music library is in, say, WMA or Ogg format, you'll have to do some work before you can use it on your iPod. Worse, if your songs are in another compressed format, you'll lose some audio quality when you convert them to AAC or MP3.

Distinguish the Three Generations of iPods and the iPod mini

As of March 2004, Apple has released three generations of regular iPods and one generation of the iPod mini:

- The first generation of regular iPods consisted of 5GB and 10GB iPods and worked only with the Mac, to which they connected directly via FireWire. iPod enthusiasts developed ways of making the iPods work with Windows and Linux as well.

- The second generation of regular iPods consisted of 5GB, 10GB, and 20GB iPods. These iPods came in separate versions for the Mac and for Windows (Linux users were still out of luck), but still connected to the Mac or PC directly via FireWire. The 10GB and 20GB models included a wired remote control and a carrying case.

NOTE   *Second-generation Mac iPods were sometimes called MiPods, and Windows iPods were sometimes called WiPods. You could convert an iPod from MiPod to WiPod, and vice versa, if necessary, but because doing so reformatted the iPod's hard disk, it wasn't a great idea even at the best of times.*

- The third generation of regular iPods started with 10GB, 15GB, and 30GB iPods in Spring 2003, then progressed to 20GB and 40GB iPods in September 2003. Third-generation iPods have a slimmer case and sleeker look than first-generation and second-generation iPods, and they work with both the Mac and Windows straight out of the box. Most models include a new iPod Dock for connecting the iPod to the Mac or PC via FireWire, a wired remote control, and a carrying case. You can also connect third-generation iPods to a PC via USB if you buy a custom cable for doing so.

- The iPod mini, released in February 2004, has a 4GB capacity, is smaller than the regular iPods in all three dimensions, is lighter and cuter, and comes in different colors.

As you can see from that list, there's a fair amount of overlap, including three different 10GB iPods and two different 20GB iPods. And by the time you read this, Apple may well have released higher-capacity third-generation iPods or a fourth- or subsequent generation, complicating matters even further.

You can tell the capacity of any regular iPod easily, because it's engraved on the back—for example, "10GB" or "40GB." (The first generation of iPod mini has a 4GB capacity, but it's not written on the player.) You can also tell easily whether a regular iPod is third-generation or not:

- The third-generation iPods are more streamlined and have the four control buttons (Previous, Menu, Play/Pause, and Next) arranged in a backlit line under the screen, as shown on the right in Figure 1-1.

- The first- and second-generation iPods are squarer and have the four control buttons arranged around the scroll wheel, as shown on the left in Figure 1-1.

The differences between third-generation iPods and earlier iPods are also easy to see from the top, as you can see in Figure 1-2:

- The third-generation iPods are shallower in depth than the first- and second-generation iPods.

- The third-generation iPods have a slimmer Hold switch than the earlier iPods.

- The third-generation iPods have a plain headphone socket rather than a headphone socket with an extra ring of contacts for the remote control.

- The first- and second-generation iPods have a FireWire socket on the top, while the third-generation iPods don't.

The differences on the bottom is even clearer: third-generation iPods have a socket for a Dock connector, while earlier iPods have nothing (see Figure 1-3).

Distinguishing first-generation iPods from second-generation iPods requires a closer look. The first-generation iPods have no cover on their FireWire port, while the second-generation iPods'

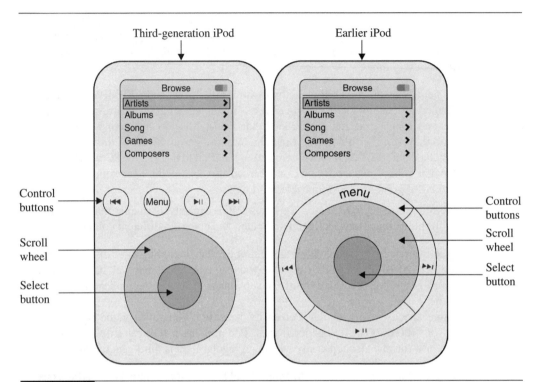

FIGURE 1-1 This illustration shows how to tell third-generation iPods from earlier generations. The first- and second-generation iPods have a squared look, with the four control buttons arranged around the scroll wheel. The third-generation iPods have a sleeker look and the four control buttons arranged under the screen.

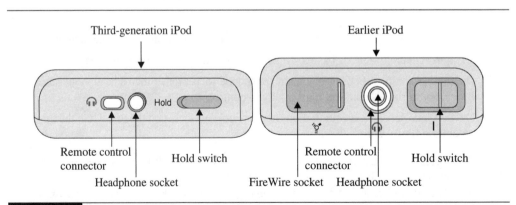

FIGURE 1-2 The top of third-generation iPods is substantially different from the top of earlier iPods.

Did you know?

Why Your iPod's Capacity Appears to Be Less Than Advertised

Forty gigabytes is a huge amount of music—around ten thousand four-minute songs. Even four gigabytes can hold a thousand songs, enough to keep you quiet (if that's the word) for nearly three days of solid listening. But unfortunately, you don't actually get the amount of hard disk space that's written on the iPod.

There are two reasons for this. The first (and eminently forgivable) reason is that you lose some hard-disk space to the iPod's OS and the file allocation table that records which file is stored where on the disk. This happens on all hard disks that contain operating systems, and costs you only a few megabytes.

The second (and much less forgivable) reason is that the hard-drive capacities on iPods are measured in "marketing gigabytes" rather than in real gigabytes. A real gigabyte is 1024 megabytes; a megabyte is 1024 kilobytes; and a kilobyte is 1024 bytes. That makes 1,073,741,824 bytes (1024 × 1024 × 1024 bytes) in a real gigabyte. By contrast, a marketing gigabyte has a flat billion bytes (1000 × 1000 × 1000 bytes)—a difference of 7.4 percent.

So your iPod will actually hold 7.4 percent less data than its listed drive size suggests (and minus a bit more for the OS and file allocation table). You can see why marketing folks choose to use marketing megabytes and gigabytes rather than real megabytes and gigabytes—the numbers are more impressive. But customers tend to be disappointed (to say the least) when they discover that the real capacity of a device is substantially less than the device's packaging and literature promised.

Almost all hard-drive manufacturers give capacities in marketing gigabytes, which has conferred herd immunity on them so far. At this writing, a class-action lawsuit about this double-system of measurements is in the works, and might force manufacturers to state the capacity less ambiguously. A previous class-action lawsuit forced monitor manufacturers to state the viewable screen size of cathode-ray tube monitors as well as the size of the screen itself (part of which is cut off by the monitor bezel). This is why you see monitor ads that state "15" monitor, 13.7" visible"; before the lawsuit, the ads simply claimed "15" monitor."

FireWire port is covered with a flexible plastic plug. Beyond that, try using the scroll wheel: in the first-generation iPods, it is mechanical, while in the second-generation iPods, it uses a sensor (and so doesn't move to the touch).

Understand Apple's Software Improvements to First- and Second-Generation iPods

Design and cosmetic differences aside, the main differences among the various iPod models have been in their system software. As usual with any product that involves software, Apple has patched holes and fixed bugs in the iPod's operating system, the connector to iTunes, and iTunes itself.

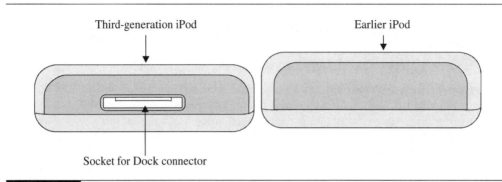

Third-generation iPod   Earlier iPod

Socket for Dock connector

FIGURE 1-3   Bottom line: third-generation iPods have a socket for a Dock connector; earlier iPods don't.

But Apple has also gradually added a slew of features to the first- and second-generation iPods via software updates. These are the major features that Apple has added:

- Contact-management storage that lets you synchronize your contacts with your iPod and view them on the screen
- A graphical equalizer that you can use for changing the sound of the music to suit your tastes
- A Shuffle feature that lets you shuffle playback not only by songs but also by albums
- A feature called *scrubbing* that lets you wind forward or backward through the song you're playing so you can find the part you want to hear
- A Calendar application that can synchronize with calendaring software (such as iCal on the Mac) to transfer your calendar information to your iPod
- A Clock application

If your iPod is not as new as it might be, check if you can update its OS with any features that Apple has released more recently. See the section "Keep Your iPod's Operating System Up to Date," in Chapter 13, for details of how to download and install updates.

Understand the Software Improvements in the Third-Generation iPods and the iPod mini

The third-generation iPods provide substantial improvements in hardware, especially in capacity. But they, and the iPod mini, also offer substantial improvements to their software, including the following:

- **AAC playback**   Third-generation iPods and the iPod mini can play back songs encoded with AAC, a high-quality compression format. See "What Is AAC? Should You Use It?" in Chapter 3, for details on AAC.
- **Alarm Clock**   You can set your iPod to start playing music (or beeps, if you prefer) at a particular time. See "Use Your iPod's Alarm Clock to Wake You Up," in Chapter 2.

How to ...   Check the iPod Software Version

To check which version of software is installed on your iPod, follow these steps:

1. Scroll down to the About item on the main menu on a first- or second-generation iPod, or on the Settings menu on a third-generation iPod or an iPod mini.

2. Select the About item and view the version number displayed at the bottom of the screen.

- **On-The-Go playlist**   On the third-generation iPods and the iPod mini, you can create a temporary playlist by using the On-The-Go playlist. This is a great improvement over having to create all your playlists on your computer. See "Queue a List of Songs on Your iPod," in Chapter 2.

- **Time display**   You can set the third-generation iPods and the iPod mini to display the time in the title bar. See "Display the Time in the Title Bar," in Chapter 2.

- **Ratings**   You can assign ratings (from one star to five stars) to songs from the iPod or the iPod mini, whereas before you could assign ratings only from iTunes. See "Rate Songs on Your iPod," in Chapter 2.

- **Redesigned and customizable menus**   The third-generation iPods and the iPod mini feature some menu changes designed to put the items you need closer to your fingertips. For example, the Backlight item now appears on the main menu, so you can turn on the backlight more easily. Better yet, you can customize the main menu by choosing which items (from a preset list) appear on it. See "Customize the Main Menu for Quick Access to Items," in Chapter 2.

- **Text notes**   The third-generation iPods and the iPod mini can display text notes, so you no longer have to clutter up your Contacts folder with notes disguised as vCards.

- **Games**   The third-generation iPods and the iPod mini also offer three new games: Music Quiz, in which your iPod challenges you to identify snippets of songs against the clock; Parachute, an action game in which you try to shoot down helicopters and parachutists before they overwhelm you; and Solitaire, a one-player card game. You'll find these games under Extras | Games.

Choose the iPod That's Best for You

To accommodate your music library and such other files as you want to carry with you, you'll probably want to buy the highest-capacity, latest-generation iPod you can afford. But if you don't need the iPod Dock, and if it's still the first half of 2004, and if you can pick up a second-generation

20GB iPod at a knockdown price, you might choose to do so. First-generation iPods are now too long in the tooth to be a sensible buy. (This is because rechargeable batteries gradually lose their capacity after they're manufactured, even if they're not being used.) By the second half of 2004, the same will apply to second-generation iPods as well.

If you decide to buy a second-generation iPod, you'll need to choose between a Mac iPod and a Windows iPod. As mentioned earlier, you can convert an iPod between Mac and Windows, but it's better to get the right format from the start. (See the section "Move Your iPod from Mac to Windows—and Back," in Chapter 16, for details on how to convert an iPod from one format to another.)

If you want the smallest and cutest high-capacity player, or if you want your iPod in a color other than white, you're looking at the iPod mini. The iPod mini is great for smaller music libraries, or for carrying only the newest or most exciting songs in your colossal library with you, but its lower capacity makes it poor value alongside the regular iPod.

Table 1-1 shows you how much music you can fit onto the iPod mini and the different models of regular iPod at widely used compression ratios for music. For spoken audio (such as audio books, plays, or talk radio), you can use lower compression ratios (such as 64 Kbps or even 32 Kbps) and still get acceptable sound with much smaller file sizes. The table assumes a "song" to be about four minutes long and rounds the figures to the nearest sensible point. The table doesn't show less widely used compression ratios such as 224 Kbps or 256 Kbps. (For 256 Kbps, halve the 128 Kbps numbers.)

NOTE   *The iPod refers to tracks as "songs," so this book does the same. Even if the tracks you're listening to aren't music, the iPod considers them to be songs. Similarly, the iPod and this book refer to "artists" rather than "singers," "bands," or other terms.*

To decide which model to buy, you'll probably want to ask yourself the following questions:

■   Do I want an iPod mini, or would a regular iPod be a better choice?

■   How much music do I want to put on my iPod, and at what quality? (Usually the answer to the first part of the question is "as much music as possible," and the answer to the second part is "high enough quality that it sounds great on my headphones and speakers.")

iPod Nominal Capacity	iPod Real Capacity	128 Kbps		160 Kbps		192 Kbps		320 Kbps	
		Hours	Songs	Hours	Songs	Hours	Songs	Hours	Songs
4GB	3.7GB	67	1000	54	800	44	667	27	400
5GB	4.7GB	83	1250	67	1000	55	835	33	500
10GB	9.3GB	166	2500	134	2000	110	1670	67	1000
15GB	14GB	250	3750	200	3000	165	2500	100	1500
20GB	18.6GB	332	5000	270	4000	220	3350	134	2000
30GB	27.9GB	500	7500	400	6000	330	5000	200	3000
40GB	37.2GB	664	10,000	540	8000	440	6700	268	4000

TABLE 1-1   iPod Capacities at Widely Used Compression Ratios

■ What other items do I want to put on my iPod, and how much space will they need?

■ Do I need a case, iPod Dock, and remote control for my iPod? (Apple tends to offer the least expensive regular iPod without these items. If you buy these items separately, you'll end up spending more than if you'd bought the next model up, which not only includes the accessories but also has a higher capacity.)

■ How much can I afford to spend?

If you've set your heart on an iPod mini, buy one. Otherwise, if money is no object, buy the highest-capacity iPod available: between your music and the other items you'll probably want to use the iPod for, you'll very likely take up most of its capacity soon enough. But if money is tight, you may need to sacrifice iPod capacity for solvency. Never mind—you may be richer next year, or at least iPod prices will probably have come down.

Chapter 2

Get Up and Running with Your iPod or iPod mini

How to...

- Identify the different components included with your iPod or iPod mini
- Set up your iPod, connect it to your PC or Mac, and install iTunes
- Load music onto your iPod
- Connect your speakers or headphones to your iPod
- Use your iPod's controls
- Navigate through your iPod's screens
- Customize the settings on your iPod

This chapter shows you how to get started using your iPod or iPod mini. The chapter covers a lot of ground, but most of the ground is flat and smooth, so we can move quickly. To keep things moving, I'll also refer you to discussions in other chapters if you need to get up to speed on certain topics.

In case you haven't unpacked your iPod already, we'll start by going through which items you'll find in the box and what they're for. After that, this chapter runs you through how to attach your iPod to your Mac or PC, how to install the software that lets the computer talk to your iPod, and how to get music loaded onto your iPod. Then the chapter takes you on a tour of the iPod's interface, getting you up to speed with the controls and the navigation screens quickly and easily.

As in the previous chapter, I'll use *iPod* to refer to both regular, full-size iPods and the iPod mini. Where one or the other behaves differently, I'll use the term *regular iPod* or *iPod mini,* as appropriate.

What's in the Box?

Depending on the model, your iPod's box probably includes the following components:

- Your iPod.
- An iPod case (not included with the 5GB iPod or with the 10GB or 15GB third-generation iPod). This case has a sturdy belt clip and grips your iPod firmly but provides no direct access to the controls on the front panel. (Third parties offer various other iPod cases; some cases are for general use, and some are for more specialized use. See the section "Cases," in Chapter 15, for a discussion of some of the more interesting types of cases you can get.) The iPod mini comes with a plastic belt clip rather than a case.
- A pair of ear-bud headphones.
- A wired remote control (not included with the 5GB iPod, the 10GB or 15GB third-generation iPod, or the iPod mini) that lets you control the music while your iPod is stowed in its case or your pocket.

- A FireWire cable for attaching your iPod to your Mac, your PC, or your iPod Power Adapter. The iPod mini comes with a FireWire cable for connecting to your Mac or PC via FireWire and a USB cable for connecting to a PC (not to a Mac) via USB.

- A power adapter (formally called the iPod Power Adapter) for the occasions when you want to recharge your iPod from a wall socket. (As you'll see in Chapters 3 and 4, you can also recharge your iPod directly from the FireWire port on your Mac or the FireWire port on some PCs, and you can recharge an iPod mini from a PC via USB.) Depending on the country in which you buy your iPod, the power adapter probably has retractable prongs (to avoid damaging anything else you're carrying it with—or stabbing backward into you from your pocket). It may also have removable prongs you can change to use the adapter in a variety of sockets. The power adapter is built to accept 100 to 240 volts AC, so with the right prongs (or adapters), you can use it to power your iPod most of the way around the world.

TIP   *The Apple Store (store.apple.com) sells a World Travel Kit Adapter for the iPod. You can also get clumsier but less expensive adapters at RadioShack or any competent electrical store.*

- An iPod Dock for the more expensive third-generation iPod models. The 10GB and 15GB models don't include the iPod Dock, but you can buy it separately. You can buy a similar iPod Dock for the iPod mini. First- and second-generation iPods can't use the iPod Dock, because they don't have the necessary iPod Dock connector.

- A CD containing iTunes and the iPod software (for the Mac and PC) and several booklets containing instructions, the license agreement for the iPod, and so on.

NOTE   *If you buy a second-generation Windows iPod, you'll get a CD containing MUSICMATCH Jukebox Plus rather than a CD containing iTunes.*

Set Up Your iPod or iPod mini

After you've unpacked your iPod, turn it on and choose the display language it should use for communicating with you. (Depending on where you bought your iPod, it may be set to display a different language at first than the language you want.) Your choices range from English, German, French, Italian, and Spanish through Norwegian and Finnish to Japanese, Korean, and Simplified and Traditional Chinese.

To turn on your iPod, press any button. Your iPod displays the Apple logo for a few seconds and then displays the Language Settings screen. Use the Scroll wheel to scroll to the language you want to use, and then press the Select button.

To turn off your iPod, press and hold the Play/Pause button for a couple of seconds until the display goes blank.

If you don't turn off your iPod and it's not playing any music, it goes to sleep automatically after a few minutes if you don't press any buttons.

How to ... Reset the iPod to Recover from the Wrong Language

If you choose the wrong language on your iPod, or if a helpful friend changes the language for you, you may find it difficult to navigate the menus to change the language back to your usual language. You can recover by resetting all settings. This option isn't as drastic as it sounds: it turns off Repeat, Shuffle, EQ, Sleep Timer, and Backlight Timer; it puts Startup Volume and Contrast to their midpoints; and it sets the language to its local default. For example, if you bought your iPod in the United States, resetting all settings should return the language to English.

To reset all settings, follow these steps:

1. Press the Menu button as many times as is necessary to return to the main screen. (Five times is the most you should need to press the Menu button to get back to the main screen, even from the deepest recesses of the menus.) You'll see the iPod text at the top of the menu, no matter which language your iPod is using.

2. Scroll down three clicks to select the fourth item on the main menu. This is the Settings item, but you may not be able to recognize the name in another language.

3. Press the Select button to display that menu.

4. Scroll down to the last item on the menu, the Reset All Settings item. This item appears in English, no matter which language your iPod is currently using.

5. Press the Select button to display that menu.

6. Scroll down to the second item. This is the Reset item; again, it appears in English, no matter which language your iPod is using.

7. Press the Select button. Your iPod resets and displays the Language selection menu startup screen.

8. Choose your preferred language.

Get Your Mac or PC Ready to Work with Your iPod

Before you connect your iPod to your Mac or PC, you may need to upgrade some components on your Mac or PC. This section discusses what you need to check and how to bring your Mac or PC up to scratch if it falls short.

Get Your Mac Ready to Work with Your iPod

If you bought your Mac in 2003 or later, chances are it's already all set for working with your iPod; it has one or more FireWire ports, Mac OS X (Panther or Jaguar) with iTunes, plenty of disk space and memory, and a recordable CD drive or a DVD burner. But if you have an earlier

How to ... **Understand FireWire**

FireWire is Apple's name for the Institute of Electrical and Electronics Engineers (IEEE) standard 1394 (IEEE 1394), which defines a high-speed data-transfer technology. The name *FireWire* is widespread for IEEE 1394, but you'll also see devices described as "IEEE 1394" rather than "FireWire." Sony uses the trademarked term *i.Link* for IEEE 1394, so if you have a Sony computer, look for i.Link.

Technically, FireWire is a *bus*—a path for transferring data. It competes with the Universal Serial Bus (USB) for the same area of computer functionality—a fast bus for connecting peripheral equipment to the computer. Apple helped develop and popularize FireWire, so all modern Macs include FireWire ports. PC makers went with USB instead, with the exception of Sony, which chose four-pin FireWire as the connection for its digital camcorders. So almost all recent PCs include USB ports, but only high-end PCs and Sony multimedia PCs include FireWire ports.

When Apple introduced the iPod, FireWire was by far the best technology for loading large amounts of data onto a portable device. At that time, the USB 2.0 standard hadn't yet been implemented, and FireWire blew USB 1 out of the water. Now, USB 2.0 is giving FireWire direct competition.

The first generation of FireWire, which conforms to IEEE standard 1394a, delivers speeds of up to 400 megabits per second (Mbps—about 50MB of data per second), compared to USB 1's 12 Mbps (about 1.5MB of data per second). USB 2.0 provides speeds of up to 480 Mbps, so USB 2.0 devices can be faster than FireWire devices. Some of the Windows-based iPod competitors, such as the Archos MP3 Jukebox and some of the Creative Nomad models, use USB 2.0 for data transfer. However, FireWire has a couple of other tricks up its sleeve, as you'll see in Chapters 12 and 14. And the second generation of FireWire devices, which are called FireWire 800 and conform to IEEE standard 1394b, provide speeds of up to 800 Mbps.

FireWire ports and cables come in two basic types: four-pin and six-pin. Four-pin cables are more compact than six-pin cables. Six-pin cables supply power to the FireWire devices via the cable, whereas four-pin cables don't supply power. Most of Sony's VAIO notebooks have four-pin FireWire/i.Link ports. Six-pin cables can recharge your iPod, whereas four-pin cables cannot.

Mac, or if your recent Mac came with a plain CD-ROM drive rather than a recordable CD drive, you may need to update one or more of these areas. The following subsections briefly discuss what you need.

Add FireWire If Necessary

To use an iPod at all, your Mac must have a FireWire port. Because Apple has been plugging FireWire assiduously for several years now, all current Macs—iMacs, eMacs, iBooks, PowerBooks, and Power Macs—include at least one or two FireWire ports, and the latest PowerBooks and PowerMacs include one or more FireWire 800 ports.

If your Mac doesn't have FireWire, you can add one or more FireWire ports easily enough to most Macs that lack FireWire by using a PCI card (for a desktop Mac) or a PC Card (for a PowerBook). For example, if you have a PowerBook G3, you may need to add a FireWire PC Card.

First, make sure the card is compatible with the version of Mac OS X you're using. Then install the card and any drivers needed to make it work. That's about as difficult as adding FireWire to a fireless Mac gets.

Check Your Operating System Version

Make sure your version of Mac OS is advanced enough to work with your iPod. You need Mac OS X 10.1.5 or later to use iTunes 4 at all, and 10.2.4 or later to share music and burn DVDs; upgrade if necessary. If you're not sure which version of Mac OS X you have, choose Apple | About This Mac to display the About This Mac window, and then look at the Version readout.

NOTE *Because Apple is trying actively to drive users to Panther (Mac OS X 10.3), and because Apple develops patches and updates for Panther before developing them for older versions of Mac OS X, you'll get best results from Panther.*

Check Disk Space and Memory

Make sure your Mac has enough disk space and memory to serve your iPod adequately. In most cases, memory shouldn't be an issue: if your Mac can run Mac OS X and conventional applications at a speed you can tolerate without sedation, it should be able to handle your iPod. Technically, Panther and Jaguar require an absolute minimum of 128MB of RAM, but most users reckon 256MB a practical minimum, 512MB a good idea, and 1GB or more a prerequisite for brilliance.

Disk space is more likely to be an issue because of the vast amount of space you're likely to want to dedicate to your music library. The best situation is to have enough space on your hard drive to contain your entire music library, both at its current size and at whatever size you expect it to grow to in the foreseeable future (or within the lifetime of your Mac). That way, you can synchronize your entire music library easily with your iPod (if your music library fits on your iPod) or just whichever part of your music library you want to take around with you for the time being. For example, to fill a 40GB iPod with music, you'll need 40GB of hard-disk space to devote to your music library. Recent desktop Macs have hard disks large enough to spare 40GB without serious hardship, but if you have an older Mac, a PowerBook, or an iBook, space problems may be looming in your horoscope. For example, the G4 1 GHz iBook comes with a 60GB hard disk—so to fill your 40GB iPod, you'd need to use two-thirds of your hard disk for your music library.

If you have a desktop Mac, you should be able to add another hard drive without undue effort. Typically, the least expensive option will be to add another EIDE hard drive or SCSI drive (depending on the configuration of your Mac) to the inside of your Mac. Alternatively, you can go for an external FireWire, USB, or SCSI drive (again, that's if your Mac has SCSI).

If you have a PowerBook or an iBook, your best bet is probably to add an external FireWire or USB hard drive. Upgrading the internal hard drive on a laptop tends to be prohibitively expensive— and you have to transfer or reinstall the operating system, your applications, and all your data after the upgrade.

Add a CD-R Drive If Necessary

If your Mac doesn't have a CD burner, you may want to add one so you can burn CDs from iTunes and other applications.

For a desktop Mac that has a full-size drive bay free, an internal CD-R drive is the least expensive option. Alternatively, turn to one of the alternatives that suit both desktop Macs and portables: external FireWire, USB, or SCSI recordable CD drives.

> **TIP** *If you add an internal SuperDrive to a desktop Mac, you can burn playlists to DVD as well, which can be useful for archiving your music.*

Get Your PC Ready to Work with Your iPod

If you bought your PC in 2003 or later, there's a fair chance it'll have everything you need to start using your iPod and iTunes:

- A USB 2.0 port (for a third-generation iPod or an iPod mini) or a FireWire port (for any generation of iPod or an iPod mini)
- Windows XP (either Home Edition or Professional) or Windows 2000 (either Professional or Server)
- A 500 MHz or faster processor (you can get away with a slower processor, but it won't be much fun)
- 128MB RAM for Windows XP or 96MB RAM for Windows 2000; much more RAM is much better
- Enough hard-disk space to contain your music library
- A CD burner

If your PC can't meet those specifications, read the following subsections to learn about possible upgrades.

Add USB 2.0 or FireWire If Necessary

Most PCs manufactured in 2003 or later include one or more USB 2.0 ports. Many high-end PCs include one or more FireWire ports—but most low-end PCs don't. (This is because adding FireWire ports costs money and because FireWire isn't part of the basic PC specification.) If you prefer to use FireWire for your iPod rather than USB, you can add one or more FireWire ports to your PC by installing a PCI card (in a desktop PC) or a PC Card (in a notebook PC).

If you're a current PC owner looking to upgrade from USB 1.*x*, choosing between USB 2.0 and FireWire can be tough, particularly if you don't have a clear picture of all the peripherals you're likely to want to connect to your PC during the rest of its lifetime. Your best choice may be to add both USB 2.0 and FireWire to your PC. Various companies make PCI cards that include both USB 2.0 and FireWire ports, so you need sacrifice only a single slot on a desktop PC. On a portable PC, you'll probably need separate PC Card devices for USB 2.0 and FireWire.

TIP

The main advantage of FireWire over USB is that FireWire can provide enough power to recharge your iPod, whereas USB can't (although USB can recharge an iPod mini, which is smaller and less greedy). If you're adding a FireWire card to your PC, choose a card that has six-pin sockets rather than four-pin sockets. Six-pin sockets can transfer power across the cable (for example, for recharging your iPod), whereas four-pin sockets can't.

Check Your Operating System Version

Make sure your PC is running Windows XP or Windows 2000. If you're in doubt about which of the many versions of Windows your computer is running, display the System Properties dialog box (press WINDOWS KEY-BREAK or choose Start | Control Panel | System) and check the readout on the General tab. If you don't have one of these versions of Windows, upgrade to one of them—preferably to Windows XP.

Check Memory and Disk Space

If you don't know how much memory your computer has, check it. The easiest place to check is the General tab of the System Properties dialog box (Start | Control Panel | System).

To check disk space, open a Windows Explorer window to display all the drives on your computer. Right-click the drive in question and choose Properties from the shortcut menu to display the Properties dialog box for the drive. The General tab of this dialog box shows the amount of free space and used space on the drive.

Add a CD-R Drive If Necessary

If you want to be able to burn audio CDs from iTunes, add a recordable CD drive to your computer. Which drive technology is most appropriate depends on your computer type and configuration:

- For a desktop PC that has an open 5.25" bay and a spare connector on an EIDE channel, an internal EIDE CD drive is easiest. (If your desktop PC has SCSI, use SCSI instead, because SCSI requires fewer processor cycles than EIDE.)

- For a desktop PC that has no open 5.25" bay or no spare EIDE connector, or for a portable PC, consider either a USB 2.0 CD drive or a FireWire CD drive.

NOTE

Because USB 1.x is relatively slow, USB 1.x CD recorders can manage only 4X burning speeds. So you'll probably want to use USB 1.x only when you must—for example, if you have a USB 1.x drive available and can't afford to upgrade.

Connect Your iPod to Your Computer

The next step is to connect your iPod to your computer. Your iPod's preferred means of connection is the FireWire cable that came with it. But if you're using a third-generation iPod with a PC rather than a Mac, and your PC doesn't have FireWire, you can connect via USB instead. (More on this in a moment.) Once your iPod is connected to your computer, the iPod acts as a hard drive controlled by the computer.

> **NOTE** *The first step for an iPod mini is to plug it into its power adapter, plug the adapter into a socket, and charge the iPod mini for four hours or until it's sated.*

Connect Your iPod to Your Mac

To use your iPod with your Mac, you connect it using the FireWire cable that came with it:

- First- and second-generation iPods include a FireWire cable that has a regular six-pin FireWire jack at each end. Plug one end into a FireWire port on your Mac (or on a hub attached to your Mac) and the other end into the port on the top of the iPod.

- Third-generation iPods and the iPod mini include a FireWire cable that has a regular six-pin FireWire jack at one end and a wider, flat connector at the other end. You plug the six-pin jack into a FireWire port on your Mac (or on a hub attached to your Mac) and the wider connector into your iPod Dock (if your iPod includes one) or into the port on the bottom of your iPod or iPod mini. The symbol side of the connector goes upward, facing the matching symbol on the iPod Dock, or facing the front of your iPod or iPod mini. If you have an iPod Dock, slide the iPod onto the connector in the iPod Dock to complete the connection to your Mac. If you have a pair of amplified speakers or a stereo input on a receiver available, you can connect it to the Line Out port on the back of the iPod Dock so that you can play music from the iPod through the speakers.

Once your iPod is connected, it starts recharging its battery and (with default settings) automatically synchronizes its contents with the music library on the computer.

> **NOTE** *To be able to use AAC files on a first- or second-generation iPod, you need to update it to version 1.3 or later of the iPod Software. Run Software Update to download the latest iPod Software Updater.*

Connect Your iPod to Your PC

To use your iPod with your PC, install iTunes and the iPod Software, and then connect your iPod via FireWire or USB. The following sections discuss the details.

Install iTunes and the iPod Software

Before you connect your iPod to your PC, install iTunes and the iPod Software from the iPod CD. (If you've lost the iPod CD, or if you'd like to have the very latest version of the software, you can download the iTunes installer and the iPod Software installer from the iTunes area of the Apple web site: www.apple.com/itunes.) Close all other applications before running the installer, because you'll need to reboot your PC afterward.

The iTunes installation routine is relatively straightforward, but you'll benefit from taking in a few details and making a few decisions. Here's what happens:

1. Click through the Welcome screen.

2. Read the license agreement. Accept it if you want to proceed.

3. Read the Information page. This covers system requirements for iTunes, warns you that you won't be able to use MUSICMATCH Jukebox or Audible Manager to transfer music to your iPod after you install iTunes, and tells you that installing iTunes installs QuickTime as well. Click the Next button when you're ready to go on.

4. On the Setup Type page, choose suitable options for your needs:

- Leave the Install Desktop Shortcuts check box selected (as it is by default) if you want to have an iTunes icon on the desktop. Otherwise, clear this check box.

- Leave the Use iTunes As The Default Player For Audio Files check box selected (as it is by default) if you want to use iTunes as your primary audio player. (iTunes associates itself with the AAC, MP3, and WAV file extensions.) Otherwise, clear this check box.

- Leave the Use QuickTime As The Default Player For Media Files check box selected (as it is by default) if you want to use iTunes for playing video files. (QuickTime associates itself with a variety of video, audio, and still image formats, including those formats associated with the following extensions: MOV, QT, SD2, 3GP, 3GPP, 3G2, 3GP2, MP4, MPG4, AMC, PNG, PNT, MAC, PICT, PIC, PCT, QTIF, QTI, DV, and DIF.) Otherwise, clear this check box.

5. On the Choose Destination Location page, either accept the folder in which iTunes offers to install itself (an iTunes folder in your \Program Files\ folder), or click the Browse button and use the resulting Choose Folder dialog box to specify a different folder.

6. Click through the iPod ad that the installer displays next. The installer then installs iTunes and QuickTime, and creates the desktop shortcuts and commandeers the file associations if you allowed it to. It then displays the Installation Successful page, which invites you to restart your computer now:

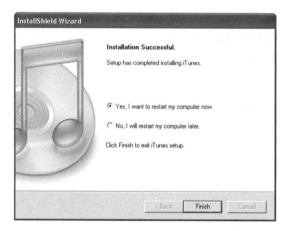

7. Leave the Yes, I Want To Restart My Computer Now option button selected and click the Finish button to quit the installer and let it restart your computer. (If you need to take other actions before restarting, select the No, I Will Restart My Computer Later option button, click the Finish button, and then restart your computer manually when the time is right.)

Here's the procedure for installing the iPod Software:

1. In the Choose Setup Language dialog box, select the language you want to use, and then click the OK button:

The installer prepares the InstallShield Wizard, which displays its Welcome screen.

2. Click the Next button. The installer then displays the license agreement.

3. Read the license agreement, and accept it if you want to install the software. The installer then installs the software and displays the InstallShield Wizard Complete page, which invites you to restart your computer.

4. Leave the Yes, I Want To Restart My Computer Now option button selected and click the Finish button to quit the installer and let it restart your computer.

After Windows restarts, launch and configure iTunes as follows:

1. Launch iTunes in whichever way you prefer:

- Double-click the iTunes icon on the desktop (if you let the installer add it).
- Choose Start | All Programs | iTunes | iTunes.

2. On the Welcome To iTunes page, click the Next button to display the Find Music Files page:

3. To let iTunes search for music files in your My Music folder (the My Music folder inside your My Documents folder), leave the Yes, Find MP3 And AAC Files In My Music Folder option button selected. Otherwise, select the No, I'll Add Them Myself Later option button.

4. Click the Next button to display the Keep iTunes Music Folder Organized page:

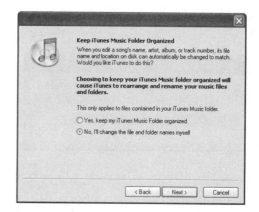

5. Choose whether you want iTunes to automatically change the filenames of song files, and the names of the folders that contain them, when you edit the tag information attached to the files. The default setting is the No, I'll Change The File And Folder Names Myself option button, but you can select the Yes, Keep My iTunes Music Folder Organized option button if you want to have iTunes change the names of the files and folders automatically for you.

6. Click the Next button to display the iTunes Music Store page:

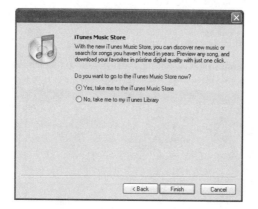

7. Unless you want to start buying music from the iTunes Music Store immediately, select the No, Take Me To My iTunes Library option button instead of the Yes, Take Me To The iTunes Music Store option button (the default). Then click the Finish button to finish configuring iTunes.

The iTunes window appears. If your computer is connected to the Internet, iTunes checks to see if an updated version is available. If one is available, iTunes displays a message box such as this one:

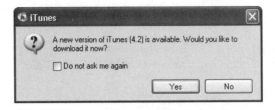

Click the Yes button if you want to download the new version now (bear in mind that downloading it may take a while). Otherwise, click the No button and remember to download the new version later.

After downloading a new version of iTunes, run its setup routine to install it. You'll need to follow through the steps and decisions discussed earlier in this section—and restart your PC once again.

Connecting Your iPod via a FireWire Cable

If your PC has one or more FireWire ports free, connecting your iPod to your PC should be a snap—but it varies a bit depending on which type of iPod you have.

- First- and second-generation iPods include a FireWire cable that has a regular six-pin FireWire jack at each end. You plug one end into a FireWire port on your PC (or on a hub attached to your PC) and the other end into the port on the top of the iPod.

- Third-generation iPods and the iPod mini include a FireWire cable that has a regular six-pin FireWire jack at one end and a wider, flat connector at the other end. You plug the six-pin jack into a FireWire port on your PC (or on a FireWire hub attached to your PC) and the wider connector into your iPod Dock (if your iPod includes one) or into the port on the bottom of your iPod or iPod mini. The symbol side of the connector goes upward, facing the matching symbol on the iPod Dock, or facing the front of your iPod or iPod mini. If you have an iPod Dock, slide the iPod onto the connector in the iPod Dock to complete the connection to your Mac. If you have a pair of amplified speakers or a stereo input on a receiver available, you can connect it to the Line Out port on the back of the iPod Dock so that you can play music from the iPod through the speakers.

Once your iPod is connected, it should start recharging its battery. So when you've connected your iPod to your PC via a FireWire cable, immediately check to see whether your iPod is charging. If it is charging, the battery indicator in the upper-right corner of the iPod's screen will ripple its parts in sequence. If not, your iPod isn't charging. You'll need to charge it via the iPod Power Adapter after synchronizing your iPod with your PC (and perhaps charge it before synchronizing as well).

Connecting via USB

If your PC doesn't have FireWire, you can connect your iPod via USB instead. To do so, buy an Apple iPod Dock Connector to FireWire and USB 2.0 Cable from the Apple Store or a reseller. This is a Y-shaped cable with an iPod Dock Connector at the tail, a six-pin FireWire jack at the end of one branch, and a USB jack at the end of the other branch.

NOTE *The iPod mini comes with a USB cable that transfers not only data but also enough power to recharge its battery. So you don't need to buy an extra USB/FireWire cable for the iPod mini.*

Once you have the cable, connect it as follows:

1. Connect the USB end of the cable to a USB 2.0 port on your PC.

2. Connect the FireWire end of the cable to the iPod Power Adapter that came with your iPod, and plug the power adapter into an electrical outlet. (You do this so that your iPod receives power, which it doesn't get along the USB cable.) For an iPod mini, skip this step.

CAUTION *Don't plug both the FireWire and USB ends of the cable into your computer (or even into two separate computers). Doing so will most likely confuse iTunes, your iPod, or both.*

3. Connect the Dock Connector at the other end of the cable to your iPod Dock (if you have one) or your iPod or iPod mini (if you don't).

4. If you have an iPod Dock, slide the iPod onto the connector in the iPod Dock to complete the connection to your Mac. If you have a pair of amplified speakers or a stereo input on a receiver available, you can connect it to the Line Out port on the back of the iPod Dock so that you can play music from the iPod through the speakers.

5. Your PC recognizes your iPod, displays a series of Found New Hardware pop-ups announcing that it has found a USB Mass Storage Device, an Apple iPod USB Device, and a couple of other moderately accurate descriptions, all of which refer to your iPod.

6. Your iPod appears in the Source pane in iTunes, just as it should.

The process isn't always as simple as it might be. Following are some wrinkles that you might run into.

"USB Device Not Recognized" Warning   On some PCs, when you connect your iPod, Windows claims not to recognize it:

Treat this announcement as a bid for attention rather than something actively wrong. After displaying this pop-up, Windows usually recognizes the iPod. So if you see this message, wait for a minute or two, and see if Windows and iTunes can work out between them what your iPod is and load the appropriate drivers for it. If they do, you'll see the Safely Remove Hardware icon in the notification area. If you click this icon, it will tell you that it thinks your iPod is a USB Mass Storage Device and the drive letter it has assigned to it:

"HI-SPEED USB Device Plugged into non–HI-SPEED USB Hub" Warning   If you plug your iPod into a USB 1.*x* port instead of a USB 2.0 port, Windows displays this warning:

If you click the pop-up, Windows displays a message box giving you more detail. The gist is that USB 1.*x* is much slower than USB 2.0, so file transfers will take far longer. If you're using USB 1.*x*, you're probably aware of this problem but don't want to deal with it just now (for example, by adding USB 2.0 ports to your PC). Click the Close button (the X button) to get rid of the pop-up.

iTunes Helper Message Box   If you've installed iTunes but you haven't yet installed the iPod Software when you connect your iPod, iTunes displays the iTunes Helper message box telling you that you need to install the iPod Software:

> **iTunes Helper**   ☒
>
> An iPod has been detected, but the iPod software is not installed.
>
> Please install the iPod software from the CD that came with your iPod or download it from www.apple.com.
>
> [OK]

Click the OK button to dismiss the message box, install the iPod Software, and then try again.

Complete the iPod Setup Assistant

After you install iTunes and the iPod Software and connect your iPod, iTunes displays the iPod Setup Assistant:

Change the name in the The Name Of My iPod Is text box if you like. Clear the Automatically Update My iPod check box if you want to update your iPod manually from the start.

If you want to register your iPod, click the Register My iPod button and follow through the registration procedure. (You can also register later at www.apple.com/register.) Otherwise, just click the Finish button to close the iPod Setup Assistant and apply your choices to your iPod.

Load Your iPod with Music

If you chose in the iTunes Setup Assistant to let iTunes update your iPod automatically, iTunes performs the first update after you connect your iPod. If you chose to update your iPod manually, follow the instructions in "Synchronize Your Music Library with Your iPod," in Chapter 4 (for the Mac) and Chapter 5 (for Windows).

Even though FireWire and USB 2.0 are two of the fastest connection technologies available to consumers, your first-ever synchronization may take an hour or two if your music library contains a large number of songs. This is because iTunes copies each song to the iPod. Subsequent synchronizations will be much quicker, as iTunes will need only to transfer new songs you've added to your music library, remove songs you've deleted, and update the data on songs whose tags you've changed. (A *tag* is a container on a compressed file that has slots for information such as the song's name and the artist's name.)

If you're using USB 1.*x* rather than USB 2.0 to synchronize an iPod with iTunes on Windows, the first synchronization will take several hours if your music library contains many songs. You might plan to perform the first synchronization sometime when you can leave your PC and your iPod to get on with it—for example, overnight, or when you head out to work.

> **TIP** *To force iTunes to copy to your iPod AAC files and MP3 files that lack the tag information your iPod normally requires, add the tracks to a playlist. Doing so can save you time over retagging many files manually and can be useful in a pinch. (In the long term, you'll probably want to make sure all your AAC files and MP3 files are tagged properly.)*

Connect Your Headphones or Speakers

As you learned earlier in this chapter, your iPod comes with a pair of ear-bud headphones—the kind that fit in your ear rather than sit on your ear (*supra-aural headphones*) or over your ear (*circumaural headphones*). The headphones come with foam covers that fulfill the dual purposes of softening the impact of the headphones on your ears and cleaning from your ears any wax and debris you missed with your latest Q-Tip.

Ear buds are the most discreet type of headphones and could probably be used by longhaired monks without being detected as long as they didn't start rocking out during their devotions. Most ear buds wedge in your ears like the iPod's ear buds do, but others sit on a headband and poke in sideways.

There's nothing magical about the iPod's headphones—they're designed to look good with the iPod, and they're quality headphones with a wide frequency range, but otherwise they're normal headphones. I find they deliver pretty good sound and are tolerably comfortable for short or moderate periods of listening. For extended listening, I prefer circumaural headphones, such as Sennheiser Ovations. In a noisy environment, noise-canceling circumaural headphones such as Bose's QuietComfort headphones are hard to beat. (Like all Bose products, the QuietComfort headphones are so expensive—about as much as an iPod mini, since you ask—that Bose doesn't advertise the price but rather the installment plan they offer. Even more expensive are Shure's E5c ear buds—$499, www.shure.com—and the ER-4 Micro-Pro earphones from Etymotic Research, Inc.—$330, www.etymotic.com.)

If you don't like the sound your iPod's headphones deliver, or if you just don't find them comfortable, use another pair of headphones with your iPod. Any headphones with a standard jack will work; if your headphones have a quarter-inch jack, get a good-quality miniplug converter. You can get better ear buds than the iPod's headphones (but you'll pay for the privilege, even if you don't go for the Shure or Etymotic ear buds) or use another type of headphones. Whichever type of headphones you choose to use, don't turn the volume up high enough to cause hearing damage.

> **TIP** *Given that I've just suggested you refrain from deafening yourself with headphones, this next suggestion may come as a surprise: if you use your iPod often with a high-end pair of headphones, get a headphone amplifier to improve the sound. A headphone amplifier plugs in between the sound source (in this case, your iPod) and your headphones to boost and condition the signal. You don't necessarily have to listen to music louder through a headphone amplifier—the amplifier can also improve the sound at a lower volume.*

Instead of using headphones, you can also connect your iPod to a pair of powered speakers, a receiver, an amplifier, or your car stereo. To make such a connection, use a standard cable with a 1/8" stereo headphone connector at the iPod end and the appropriate type of connector at the other end. For example, to connect your iPod to a conventional amplifier, you need two phono plugs on the other end of the cable.

NOTE   *Powered speakers contain an amplifier so you don't need to use an external amplifier. Many speaker sets designed for use with portable CD players, MP3 players, and computers are powered speakers. Usually, only one of the speakers contains an amplifier, making one speaker far heavier than the other. Sometimes the amplifier is hidden in the subwoofer, which lets you put the weight on the floor rather than on the furniture.*

The iPod headphone jack delivers up to 60 milliwatts (mW) altogether—30 mW per channel. Turn down the volume when connecting your iPod to a different pair of headphones, powered speakers, or an amplifier. Make the connection, set the volume to low on the speakers or amplifier, and then start playing the audio. Turn the volume up as necessary. That way, you won't deafen yourself, blast your neighbors, or blow the speakers or amplifier.

Get Familiar with Your iPod's Controls

To keep the iPod as streamlined as possible, Apple has reduced the number of controls to a minimum by making each control fulfill more than one purpose; on the iPod mini, Apple has reduced the number of controls even further by integrating the buttons into the Scroll wheel. You'll get the hang of the controls' basic functions easily, but you also need to know how to use the controls' secondary functions to get the most out of your iPod—so keep reading.

Read Your iPod's Display

Your iPod has an LCD display that shows up to six lines of text and multiple icons. (The iPod mini's display is a little smaller than that of a regular iPod.) Figure 2-1 shows the display with labels.

The title bar at the top of the display shows the title of the current screen—for example, iPod for the main menu (the top-level menu), Now Playing when your iPod's playing a song, or Artist when you're browsing by artist.

To turn on the display's backlight, hold down the Menu button for a couple of seconds. The backlight uses far more power than the LCD screen, so don't use the backlight unnecessarily when you're trying to extract the maximum amount of playing time from a single battery charge. As you'll see in "Set the Backlight Timer," later in this chapter, you can configure how long your iPod keeps the backlight on after you press a button.

Use Your iPod's Controls

Below the iPod's display are the six main controls for accessing songs (and data) and playing them back. On third-generation iPods, these controls are arranged as a line of four buttons below the screen,

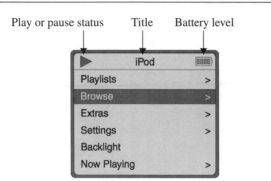

Play or pause status   Title   Battery level

FIGURE 2-1   The iPod's LCD display contains six lines of text and key icons.

while on second-generation iPods, these controls are arranged as a ring of four buttons around the Scroll wheel and the Select button; and on the iPod mini, the buttons are integrated into the Scroll wheel (which is formally called the *Click wheel*) to save space. Figure 2-2 shows the difference.

- Press any button (but not the Scroll wheel) to switch on your iPod. (You *can* press the Scroll wheel on the iPod mini, because the buttons are integrated into it.)

- Press the Menu button to move up to the next level of menus. Hold down the Menu button for a second to turn the backlight on or off.

- Press the Previous/Rewind button and the Next/Fast-Forward button to navigate from one song to another and to rewind or fast-forward the playing song. Press one of these buttons once (and release it immediately) to issue the Previous command or the Next command. Hold down the button to issue the Rewind command or the Fast-Forward command. Your iPod rewinds or fast-forwards slowly at first, but then speeds up if you keep holding down the button.

- Press the Play/Pause button to start playback or to pause it. Hold down the Play/Pause button for three seconds or so to switch off your iPod.

- Press the Select button to select the current menu item.

- Use the Scroll wheel to scroll up and down menus, change the volume, or change the place in a song. Early iPods had a moving Scroll wheel mounted on ball bearings. Later models have a more durable solid-state Scroll wheel that's touch-sensitive. The iPod mini has a solid-state Scroll wheel that tilts to allow clicks on the four buttons incorporated in it. By default, your iPod plays a clicking sound as you move the Scroll wheel to give you feedback. You can turn off this clicking sound if you don't like it.

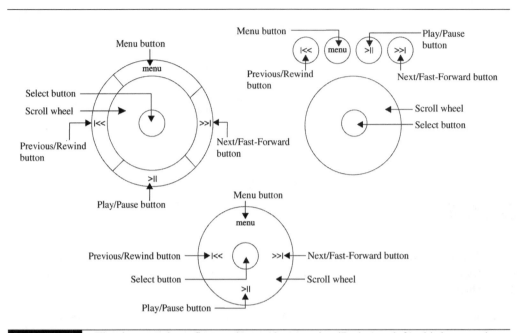

FIGURE 2-2 The six controls on first- and second-generation iPods (top left), third-generation iPods (top right), and the iPod mini (bottom)

> NOTE
>
> *The Scroll wheel adjusts the scrolling speed in response to your finger movements on the Scroll wheel and the length of time you scroll for: when you're scrolling a long list, it speeds up the scrolling as you continue the scroll, then slows down as you ease back on the scroll. This behavior makes scrolling even long lists (such as the Songs list, which lists every song on your iPod) swift and comfortable.*

Browse and Access Your Music

The iPod's menu-driven interface makes browsing and accessing your music as easy as possible on the device's compact display.

Once you've accessed a list of songs—be it a playlist, an album, or a listing of all songs by an artist or composer—you can press the Play button to play the list from the start. Alternatively, scroll down to another song, and then press the Play button to start playing from that song.

> NOTE
>
> *You can customize the main menu on third-generation iPods and the iPod mini (see "Customize the Main Menu for Quick Access to Items," later in this chapter, for details). This section assumes you're using the default menu layout.*

Play a Playlist

To access your playlists, scroll to the Playlists item on the main menu (it's the top item, so it may be selected by default), and then press the Select button. On the resulting screen, scroll down to the playlist you want to play, and then press the Select button.

Browse Your Music

To browse your music, select the Browse item on the main menu. Your iPod displays the Browse menu, which contains entries for Artists, Albums, Songs, Genres, and Composers. Scroll to the browse category you want to use, and then press the Select button to access that category.

- The Artists category displays an alphabetical list of all the music on your iPod sorted by artist. The first entry, All, displays an alphabetical list of all the albums on your iPod. Otherwise, scroll down to the artist and press the Select button to display a list of the albums by the artist. This menu also has a first entry called All, which displays an alphabetical list of all songs by the artist.

NOTE *The artist, album, song title, genre, composer, and other data comes from the tag information on the AAC file or MP3 file. An album shows up in the Artists category, the Albums category, the Genre category, or the Composers category because one or more files on your iPod has that album entered in the Album field on its tag. So the entry for an album doesn't necessarily mean that you have that entire album on your iPod—you may have only one song from that album.*

- The Albums category displays an alphabetical list of all the albums on your iPod. Scroll down to the album you want, and then press the Select button to display the songs it contains.

- The Songs category displays an alphabetical list of every song on your iPod. Scroll down to the song you want to play—it may take a while to scroll that far—and then press the Select button to start playing the song.

- The Genre category displays a list of the genres you've assigned to the music on your iPod. (Your iPod builds the list of genres from the Genre field in the tags in AAC files and MP3 files.) Scroll to a genre, and then press the Select button to display the artists whose albums are tagged with that genre. You can then navigate to albums and songs by an artist.

- The Composers category displays a list of the composers listed for the songs on your iPod. (Your iPod builds the list of composers from the Composer field in the tags in MP3 files or AAC files.) Scroll to a composer and press the Select button to display a list of the songs by that composer.

Play Songs

Playing songs on your iPod could hardly be easier, but here are the details anyway.

Start and Pause Play

To start playing a song, take either of the following actions:

- Navigate to the song and press the Play/Pause button or the Select button.
- Navigate to a playlist or an album and press the Play/Pause button or the Select button.

To pause play, press the Play/Pause button.

How to ...   Use the Composers Category Effectively to Find Music

The Composers category is primarily useful for classical music, because these songs may be tagged with the name of the recording artist rather than that of the composer. For example, an album of The Fargo Philharmonic playing Beethoven's Ninth Symphony might list The Fargo Philharmonic as the artist and Beethoven as the composer. By using the Composers category, you can access the works by composer: Bach, Beethoven, Brahms, and so on.

But there's no reason why you shouldn't use the Composers category to access nonclassical songs as well. For example, you could use the Composers category to quickly access all your Nick Drake cover versions as well as Drake's own recordings of his songs. The only disadvantage to doing so is that the tag information for many CDs in the CD Database (CDDB) don't include an entry in the Composer field, so you'll need to add this information if you want to use it. In this case, you may be better off using iTunes to create a playlist that contains the tracks you want in the order you prefer.

There's also no reason why you should confine the contents of the Composers field to information about composers. By editing the tags manually, you can add to the Composer field any information by which you want to be able to sort songs on your iPod.

Change the Volume

To change the volume, scroll counterclockwise (to reduce the volume) or clockwise (to increase it) from the Now Playing screen:

Change the Place in a Song

As well as fast-forwarding through a song by using the Fast-Forward button, or rewinding through a song by using the Rewind button, you can *scrub* through a song to quickly change the location.

Scrubbing can be easier than fast-forwarding or rewinding because your iPod displays a readout of how far through the song the playing location currently is. Scrubbing is also more peaceful, because while Fast Forward and Rewind play blips of the parts of the song you're passing through (to help you locate the passage you want), scrubbing keeps the song playing until you indicate you've reached the part you're interested in.

To scrub through a song, follow these steps:

1. Display the Now Playing screen.

2. Press the Select button to display the scroll bar:

3. Scroll counterclockwise to move backward through the song or clockwise to move forward through the song.

4. Press the Select button to cancel the display of the scroll bar, or wait a few seconds for your iPod to cancel its display automatically.

Use the Hold Switch

The Hold switch, located on the top of your iPod, locks your iPod controls in their current configuration. The Hold switch is intended to protect your iPod controls against being bumped in active environments—for example, when you're exercising at the gym or barging your way onto a packed bus or subway train. When the Hold switch is pushed to the end so the red underlay shows, your iPod is on hold.

The Hold switch is equally useful for keeping music playing without unintended interruptions and for keeping your iPod locked in the Off position, which prevents the battery from being drained by the iPod being switched on accidentally when you're carrying it.

If your iPod seems to stop responding to its other controls, check first that the Hold switch isn't on.

Attach and Use the Remote Control for Easy Operation

Most second- and third-generation iPod models include a remote-control unit that plugs into the headphone port so that you can pocket the iPod and control the music without continually having to reach into your pocket; for those second- and third-generation models that don't include the remote control, and for the iPod mini, you can buy the remote as an accessory. Your headphones (or speakers) then plug into the socket on the remote-control unit's cable.

The remote control is largely self-explanatory, but two points are worth mentioning:

- The remote control in second-generation iPods connects via a recessed ring around the headphone socket. With these models, you need to push the jack of the remote-control unit firmly into its socket for it to engage. If the remote control seems to stop working, check first that it's plugged in properly.

- The remote control in third-generation iPods and the iPod mini uses a separate connection socket next to the headphone socket. This connection seems to work well, but the different socket means that the remote controls for second- and third-generation iPods aren't compatible. So if you're shopping for a remote control, make sure you get the right type for your iPod. Third-generation iPods and the iPod mini use the same connection, so their remote controls are compatible.

Recharge Your iPod's Battery to Keep the Songs Coming

The battery icon on your iPod's display shows you how your iPod is doing for battery power. Four bars is a full charge; one bar means the gas gauge is nearing empty. Second-generation iPods claim up to 11 hours of battery life, while third-generation iPods and the iPod mini manage more like eight hours on a good day.

You can recharge your iPod by plugging it into your computer (if you're using a Mac or a PC with a six-pin FireWire connector, or if you're using an iPod mini with its USB cable) or by plugging in the iPod Power Adapter.

- The advantage to using the computer is that you don't need to lug around the AC adapter; the disadvantage is that if your computer is a portable, you'll need to lug the computer's AC adapter, because the iPod draws power from the computer's battery when the computer is running on the battery. Another disadvantage is that the hard drive on some iPods can get stuck spinning (so it doesn't stop spinning when it should) when recharging from the computer via FireWire. (If this happens to your iPod, reset the iPod by holding down the Menu and Play buttons for several seconds.)

- The advantage to using the AC adapter is that you can run the iPod from the adapter even while the battery is charging.

The battery in a regular iPod is designed to recharge in about three hours; the battery in an iPod mini requires more like four hours After about an hour of recharging, the battery should be at about 80 percent of its charge capacity—enough for you to use the iPod for a while.

When recharging from a computer, your iPod displays each of the four bars in the battery icon in sequence. When your iPod displays all four bars together, the charging is complete.

When recharging from the AC adapter, your iPod flashes a large battery icon and displays the word *Charging* at the top of the screen. When charging is complete, your iPod displays the battery icon without flashing it and with the word *Charged* at the top of the screen.

> **NOTE**   *See the section "Maximize Your iPod's Battery Life," in Chapter 13, for advice on how to get the longest life possible from your iPod's battery.*

Navigate the Extras Menu

The Extras menu provides access to your iPod's contacts, calendar, clock, notes (on third-generation iPods and the iPod mini), and games.

- To access a contact, scroll to the Contacts item on the Extras menu, and then press the Select button. On the Contacts screen, scroll to the contact, and then press the Select button. See Chapter 10 for details on how to put contacts onto your iPod.

> **NOTE**   *The original 5GB first-generation iPod didn't include the Contacts feature, which was added in the 10GB iPod. If you have one of the original 5GB iPods, you can use the iPod Software Updater 1.1 to add the Contacts feature to your iPod.*

- To use Calendar, scroll to the Calendars item on the Extras menu, and then press the Select button. Calendar displays the list of calendars. Scroll to the calendar you want and press the Select button to display the calendar in month view. Use the Scroll wheel to access the day you're interested in, and then press the Select button to display the events listed for that day. The one-month display shows empty squares for days that have no events scheduled and dots for days that have one or more events. If the day contains more appointments than will fit on the iPod's display, use the Scroll wheel to scroll up and down. See Chapter 11 for a discussion of how to transfer your calendars to the iPod.

- To use your iPod's clock features, scroll to the Clock item on the Extras menu, and then press the Select button. On first- and second-generation iPods, you'll see just the clock itself. On third-generation iPods and the iPod mini, the Clock screen gives you access to the Alarm Clock, Sleep Timer, and Date and Time settings.

- To access your text notes on third-generation iPods and the iPod mini, scroll to the Notes item on the Extras menu, and then press the Select button. Chapter 12 discusses how to put notes on your iPod.

- To play the game or games included with the iPod, scroll to the Game item (on second-generation iPods) or Games item (on third-generation iPods and the iPod mini) on the Extras menu, and then press the Select button. On second-generation iPods, selecting the Game item starts the Breakout game. On third-generation iPods and the iPod mini, it takes you to the Games menu, from which you can choose the Music Quiz, Brick, Parachute, or Solitaire game.

Choose Settings for Your iPod

To choose settings for your iPod, scroll to the Settings item on the main menu, and then press the Select button. The resulting menu offers a list of choices that varies depending on which generation the iPod belongs to. The following sections discuss what you need to know about these items.

Apply Shuffle Settings to Randomize Songs or Albums

Instead of playing the songs in the current list in their usual order, you can have your iPod shuffle them into a randomized order by applying the Songs setting to Shuffle. Similarly, you can have your iPod shuffle the albums by a particular artist or composer into a random order by applying the Albums setting to Shuffle.

To apply a Shuffle setting, scroll up to the Shuffle item on the Settings menu and press the Select button to apply the Shuffle setting you want. The settings are Off (the default), Songs, and Albums.

Repeat One Track or All Tracks

The Repeat item on the Settings menu lets you choose between repeating the current song (choose the One setting), all the songs in the current list (the All setting), or no songs (Off, the default setting). Scroll to the Repeat item, and then press the Select button one or more times to change the setting.

Use Sound Check to Standardize the Volume

Sound Check is a feature for normalizing the volume of different songs so you don't have to crank up the volume to hear a song encoded at a low volume and then suffer ear damage because the next song was recorded at a far higher volume. Scroll to the Sound Check item on the Settings menu, and then press the Select button to toggle Sound Check on or off.

NOTE   *For Sound Check to work on your iPod, you need to turn on the Sound Check feature in iTunes. Press COMMAND-Y or choose iTunes | Preferences on the Mac to display the Preferences dialog box, or press CTRL-Y or choose Edit | Preferences to display the iTunes dialog box on Windows. Click the Effects button to display the Effects sheet on the Mac, or click the Effects tab to display its controls on Windows. Select the Sound Check check box, and then click the OK button to close the dialog box.*

Choose Equalizations to Make Your Music Sound Better

Your iPod contains a graphical equalizer—a device that alters the sound of music by changing the level of different frequency bands. For example, a typical equalization for rock music boosts the lowest bass frequencies and most of the treble frequencies, while reducing some of the midrange frequencies. Typically, this arrangement punches up the drums, bass, and vocals, making the music sound more dynamic. A typical equalization for classical music leaves the bass frequencies and midrange frequencies at their normal levels while reducing the treble frequencies. This arrangement should provide a less shrill and more mellow effect than cat-gut strings being scraped by horsehair bows or woodwind reeds being blasted by powerful lungs might otherwise produce.

Your iPod should include the following equalizations: Acoustic, Bass Booster, Bass Reducer, Classical, Dance, Deep, Electronic, Flat, Hip Hop, Jazz, Latin, Loudness (on third-generation iPods and the iPod mini), Lounge, Piano, Pop, R & B, Rock, Small Speakers, Spoken Word, Treble Booster, Treble Reducer, and Vocal Booster. (You might long for a Vocal Reducer setting for some artists or for karaoke, but the iPod doesn't provide one.)

Most of these equalizations are clearly named, but Flat and Small Speakers aren't entirely obvious:

- ■ Flat is an equalization with all the sliders at their midpoints—an equalization that applies no filtering to any of the frequency bands. If you don't usually use an equalization, there's no point in applying Flat to a song, because it's essentially the same as not using an equalization. But if you *do* use an equalization for most of your tracks, you can apply Flat to individual tracks to turn off the equalization while they play.

- ■ Small Speakers is for use with small loudspeakers, not for audio by small orators. This equalization boosts the frequency bands that are typically lost by smaller loudspeakers. If you listen to your iPod through portable speakers, you may want to try this equalization for general listening.

To apply an equalization, scroll to the EQ item on the Settings menu. The EQ item shows the current equalization—for example, EQ – Rock. To change the equalization, press the Select button. On the EQ screen, scroll to the equalization you want, and then press the Select button to apply it.

You can also specify the equalization to use for any particular song by working in iTunes, as described in "Specify an Equalization for an Individual Song" in Chapter 4. Your iPod then applies this equalization when you play back the track on the iPod. The equalization also applies when you play the track in iTunes.

TIP *Don't take the names of the equalizations too literally, because which of them you find best will depend on your ears, your earphones or speakers, and the type of music you listen to. For example, if you find thrash sounds best played with the Classical equalization, don't scorn the Classical equalization because of its name.*

Change the Contrast to Make the Screen Readable

To change the contrast to make the screen more readable under the prevailing light conditions, scroll to the Contrast item, and then press the Select button to access the Contrast screen. Scroll clockwise to darken the screen, counterclockwise to lighten it.

NOTE *You can change the contrast both when you're using the backlight and when you're not using it.*

Turn Alarms On and Off

Second- and third-generation iPods and the iPod mini can remind you of appointments in your calendar when their times arrive. Third-generation iPods and the iPod mini can also function as an alarm clock (see "Use Your iPod's Alarm Clock to Wake You Up," later in this chapter, for details).

To access the alarms settings on a third-generation iPod or an iPod mini, choose Extras | Clock | Alarm Clock.

Choose the On setting for Alarms to receive a beep and a message on the screen. Choose the Silent setting to receive only the message. Choose the Off setting to receive neither the beep nor the message.

Use the Sleep Timer to Lull You to Sleep

Your iPod's Sleep Timer is like the Sleep button on a clock radio or boom box: it lets you tell your iPod how long to continue playing music, presumably to lull you to sleep. You can set values of 15, 30, 60, 90, or 120 minutes.

Your iPod displays a clock icon and the number of minutes remaining on the Now Playing screen so you can see the Sleep Timer is running. To turn off the Sleep Timer, access the Sleep screen again and select the Off setting.

Choose Extras | Clock | Sleep Timer to change Sleep Timer settings on a third-generation iPod or an iPod mini.

Set the Date and Time

Use the Set Time Zone item on the Date & Time screen to access the Time Zone screen, on which you can set the time zone (for example, US Mountain). Use the Set Date & Time item on the Date & Time screen to access the Date & Time screen, which presents a simple interface for setting the time and date. Use the Scroll wheel to adjust each value in turn. Press the Select button to move to the next value.

Choose Extras | Clock | Date & Time to set date and time settings on a third-generation iPod or an iPod mini.

Choose How to Sort and Display Your Contacts

To specify how your iPod should sort your contacts' names and display them on screen, scroll to the Contacts item on the Settings screen, and then press the Select button to display the Contacts screen.

To change the sort order, scroll (if necessary) to the Sort item, and then press the Select button to toggle between the First Last setting (for example, Joe Public) and the Last, First setting (for example, Public, Joe).

To change the display format, scroll (if necessary) to the Display item, and then press the Select button to toggle between the First Last setting and the Last, First setting.

Most people find using the same sort order and display format best, but you may prefer otherwise. For example, you might sort by Last, First but display by First Last.

Turn the Clicker On or Off

The Clicker item on the Settings screen toggles the clicking sound your iPod plays when you use the Scroll wheel. Press the Select button to toggle the setting between On and Off. (The default setting is On.)

2

Check the "About" Information for Your iPod

From the main menu (on a first- or second-generation iPod) or the Extras menu (on a third-generation iPod or an iPod mini), you can scroll down to the About item and press the Select button to display the following information about your iPod:

- Your iPod's name and serial number
- Your iPod's hard-disk capacity and the amount of space free right now
- The iPod Software version number

NOTE   *In most cases, it's worth updating your software to the latest version available. To do so, download the latest version of the iPod Software Updater from the Apple Software Downloads web site (www.apple.com/swupdates), run the iPod Software Updater, and follow through its screens. First- and second-generation iPods use one version of iPod Software Updater, third-generation iPods use another, and the iPod mini uses yet another— so be sure to get the right one for your iPod.*

Set the Backlight Timer

To customize the length of time that the display backlight stays on after you press one of the iPod's controls, scroll to the Backlight Timer option and press the Select button. Then you can choose from the following settings:

- Choose the Off setting to keep the backlight off until you turn it on manually by holding down the Menu button for a couple of seconds. You can then let the backlight go off automatically after the set delay or hold down the Menu button again for a couple of seconds to turn it off.
- Specify the number of seconds (between 1 and 10 on first- and second-generation iPods, and between 2 and 20 on third-generation iPods and the iPod mini) for the backlight to stay on after you press a control.
- Choose the Always On setting to keep the backlight on until you choose a new setting from this screen. (Even holding down the Menu button doesn't turn off the backlight when you choose Always On.) This setting is useful when you're using your iPod as a sound source in a place that's too dark to see the display without the backlight and when you need to change the music frequently.

NOTE   *When you use the Always On setting, it's best to have your iPod running on main power. Try not to use the Always On setting when running on battery power, because doing so chews through the battery surprisingly quickly. In a pinch, you can use the Always On setting to light your way with the iPod—for example, if you have a power outage at night, or if you happen to get stuck in a cave. But unless you're strapped for light, you'll find your iPod makes a poor substitute for a flashlight, because the light isn't focused into a beam.*

Use the Third-Generation iPod and iPod mini Features

In this section, you'll learn about the features introduced on the third-generation iPods: the iPod Dock, the Alarm Clock, the On-the-Go playlist, and more. The iPod mini shares these features but doesn't include the iPod Dock.

Play Music Through the iPod Dock

If your iPod includes an iPod Dock, you can play music from your iPod when it's docked. Plug a cable with a stereo miniplug into the Line Out connector on the iPod Dock and connect the other end of the cable to your powered speakers or your stereo.

Use your iPod's controls to navigate to the music, play it, pause it, and so on. Use the volume control on the speakers or the receiver to control the volume at which the songs play.

Use Your iPod's Alarm Clock to Wake You Up

Third-generation iPods and the iPod mini include an Alarm Clock feature that you can use to blast yourself awake either with a beep or with one of your existing playlists. (At the time of writing, you can't use an artist, album, song, or composer directly—you need to create a playlist from the songs you want to wake up to.) This feature seems guaranteed to be almost as popular as the Sleep Timer feature.

To use the Alarm Clock, follow these steps:

1. Create a custom playlist for waking up if you like. (Or create several—one for each day of the week, maybe.)

2. Choose Extras | Clock | Alarm Clock to display the Alarm Clock screen.

3. Select the Alarm item and press the Select button to toggle the alarm on or off, as appropriate.

4. Select the Time item and press the Select button to access the Alarm Time screen. Scroll to the appropriate time and press the Select button to return to the Alarm Clock screen.

5. Select the Sound item and press the Select button to display the Alarm Clock listing of playlists available. Select the playlist and press the Select button to return to the Alarm Clock screen.

6. Connect your iPod to your speakers or stereo (unless you sleep with headphones on).

7. Go to sleep (perchance to dream).

When the appointed hour (and minute) arrives, your iPod wakes itself (if it's sleeping) and then wakes you.

Display the Time in the Title Bar

Third-generation iPods and the iPod mini can display the time in the title bar in place of the name of the current screen. When you display a different screen, or when you switch on your iPod, it displays the screen's name for a few seconds, and then switches to display the time.

To make your iPod display the time, follow these steps:

1. Choose Settings | Date and Time to display the Date & Time screen.

2. Scroll to the Time In Title item and press the Select button to turn on the item.

Customize the Main Menu for Quick Access to Items

Third-generation iPods and the iPod mini let you customize the main menu by controlling which items appear on it. By removing items you don't want and adding items you do want, you can give yourself quicker access to the items you use most.

For example, the Playlists item appears by default at the top of the main menu. If you don't use playlists, you may want to remove it so that you don't always have to scroll past it to get to the Browse item. Or you might choose to put the Artists item on the main menu so that you don't have to go through Browse to access it.

To customize the main menu, follow these steps:

1. Choose Settings | Main Menu to display the Main Menu screen.

2. Scroll to the item you want to affect.

3. Press the Select button to toggle the item's setting between On and Off.

4. Make further changes as necessary, and then press the Menu button twice to return to the main menu and see the effect of the changes you made.

To reset your main menu to its default settings, choose the Reset Main Menu item at the bottom of the Main Menu screen and choose Reset from the Reset Menus screen. (Resetting all settings also resets the main menu, as you'd expect.)

Queue a List of Songs on Your iPod or iPod mini

One of the features that iPod users pressed Apple for was the ability to create playlists on the fly on their iPods rather than having to create all playlists through iTunes ahead of time. Third-generation iPods and the iPod mini deliver this capability, enabling you to create one temporary playlist called On-the-Go.

To create your On-the-Go playlist, follow these steps:

1. If you've previously created an On-the-Go playlist, choose Playlists | On-the-Go | Clear Playlist to dispose of it. (Alternatively, keep the existing On-the-Go playlist and add further songs to it.)

2. Navigate to the first song you want to add to the playlist.

3. Press the Select button and hold it down until the song name starts flashing.

TIP   *You can also queue a playlist or album by navigating to it and then pressing and holding down the Select button until the item's name starts flashing.*

4. Repeat steps 2 and 3 for each additional song that you want to add to the On-the-Go playlist.

To play your On-the-Go playlist, choose Playlists | On-the-Go. (Until you create your first On-the-Go playlist, selecting this item displays an explanation of what the On-the-Go playlist does.)

Rate Songs on Your iPod

Third-generation iPods and the iPod mini let you assign ratings to songs from your iPod as well as from iTunes. To assign a rating to the song that's currently playing, follow these steps:

1. Display the Now Playing screen if it's not currently displayed.

2. Press the Select button twice in quick succession. Your iPod displays five hollow dots under the song's name on the Now Playing screen.

3. Scroll to the right to display the appropriate number of stars in place of the five dots, and then press the Select button to apply the rating.

Chapter 3

Bring Yourself Up to Speed with AAC, MP3, and Digital Audio

How to...

- Understand why music needs compression
- Understand lossless and lossy compression
- Learn what AAC is and how it works
- Learn what MP3 is and how it works
- Learn about other key digital audio formats
- Understand ripping, encoding, and "copying"
- Choose an appropriate compression rate for AAC and MP3 files you create
- Load uncompressed WAV and AIFF files on your iPod
- Understand the basics of copyright law with regard to audio
- Understand copy-protection techniques for CDs

You'll almost certainly want to use your iPod extensively for carrying your music and listening to it. That means putting as much music on your iPod as possible, probably in AAC or MP3 format—and keeping the quality as high as you need for all types of playback you perform. (I'll explain what AAC is in "What Is AAC? Should You Use It?" and what MP3 is in "What Is MP3? Should You Use It?," both later in this chapter.)

This chapter discusses the background information that you must understand in order to make the most of digital audio on your iPod. I'm sure your focus is on results rather than theory, but to get the right results with compressed audio, you need to understand a little theory about what compressed audio is and why it works. But don't worry—the chapter moves along briskly, and if your attention strays in one section, you can skip ahead to the next one.

In particular, if your music collection is extensive, you'll need to balance music quality against quantity. You can store pure CD-quality audio on your iPod, but not very much of it. You can store a huge quantity of highly compressed audio on your iPod, but it won't sound too great. Or you can settle for a happier medium that delivers high-enough audio quality but lets you take all your essential music with you. This chapter shows you how, and it starts by explaining why music files are so big that they need compressing.

Why Do You Need to Compress Music?

In short, you must compress music files because they're huge. For music files to sound passable, they need to contain a lot of data. For them to sound perfect to the human ear, they need to contain a *huge* amount of data. (More on what such perfection entails and on the precise quantities of data in "What Does CD-Quality Audio Mean?," later in this chapter.)

As you'll know if you've surfed the Web using a slow Internet connection, different types of content require different amounts of data to represent them. Typically, text requires the smallest amount because of the (relatively) minuscule number of possible characters in the Western European character set: letters (in uppercase and lowercase), letters with modifications signs (such as å and ÿ), numbers, punctuation, symbols, and so on.

So, to represent text, you need to represent only the sequence of letters and any necessary formatting information. For text, basic ASCII uses seven bits of data for each character, giving 128 different permutations (2×2×2×2×2×2×2). Extended ASCII uses eight bits of data for each character, giving 256 different permutations (2×2×2×2×2×2×2×2)—enough for the vast majority of Western languages. (By comparison, Chinese and Japanese—each of which has many thousand characters—require larger numbers of bits. But Unicode takes care of them by using a relatively extravagant 64 bits of data for each character.) Then you need to represent the font name, size, and so on, but this information can be represented in text as well, so it doesn't require much more data.

Graphics, audio, and video require far more data than text because they contain so many more variables. A text character can be any of the, say, 256 characters in the extended ASCII character set. However, a graphic can show anything visible, a moment of audio can represent any sound, and a moment of video can represent a combination of the two.

Some of this data is more compressible than others. For example, high-resolution graphics contain a huge amount of data, but they can be highly compressible. To give a crude example, a compressed graphics format (or a compression program, such as StuffIt or WinZip) can give an instruction such as "use blue of the hue 0,64,192 for the next 2000 pixels" instead of saying "blue of the hue 0,64,192" 2000 times in succession. (Actually, the file just says "0,64,192" because it knows it's talking about colors using Red, Green, Blue [RGB] data—but you get the idea.) The program that opens the compressed file then restores the compressed information to its former state, essentially re-creating the full picture. This is called *lossless* compression—the compressed file contains the information necessary to re-create the complete original file.

But audio is much harder to compress than graphics, because it's less static. (Video is even worse, because it has not only audio but also images changing at 25 to 30 frames per second—but luckily video isn't our problem in this book.) You can perform some audio compression by reducing repeated information to a set of instructions for repeating it—hold this sound for three seconds, and so on. But to significantly reduce the amount of data needed to represent audio, usually you need to discard some of the data. This is called *lossy* compression, because the data discarded is lost. As you'd think, to make compressed audio sound as good as possible, the compression format must discard the data that's least important to the listener. Hold that thought—we'll get back to how encoding schemes such as AAC and MP3 do this in a page or two.

In the meantime, there *is* one means of stripping down music to a minimal set of information— a means other than writing it down as a score on paper. That way is called *MIDI (Musical Instrument Digital Interface),* a music format for representing music as a set of computer instructions. Essentially, MIDI assumes that each particular instrument sounds a given way and provides a set of instructions for how each of the instruments in the song should play.

For example, you can tell a MIDI file to play a piano note for a given time with given attack (how hard the note is struck), given sustain (how long the note is held), and so on. In this way, a minimal amount of data can produce a full-sounding track. Depending on the set of instruments used, the MIDI track will sound different on different equipment—but so will the same score played by the same pianist on a different Steinway, the same Beethoven symphony played by different orchestras (leaving the conductors out of the equation), or the same Beatles instrumental standard covered by different substandard tribute bands.

That all works well enough for music that can use generic instrument sounds—for example, a grand piano, a distorted electric guitar, or a regulation snare drum. But it doesn't work for vocals, because you can't effectively synthesize a voice. Even if you could, you couldn't synthesize the right voice. And even if you could synthesize the right voice, you would need to describe the tone, expression, and delivery. You can't exactly say "just like Bowie doing 'Ziggy Stardust' but with different words" or "Justin Timberlake an octave higher than sounds comfortable" and expect a computer to deliver it. So, compression for music needs to take a subtler approach—knocking out the less important parts of the music while preserving as much as possible.

But we're getting ahead of ourselves here. First, let's consider what audio quality is and what data is required to deliver it.

What Determines Audio Quality?

Having high audio quality means having enough data for your audio equipment to deliver playback that sounds not only recognizable from the original but also good. That's pretty obvious once you think about it, but to get high-quality audio playback, you need several different things, including:

- A high-quality audio signal—for example, an uncompressed audio file (such as a CD track, a WAV file, or an AIFF file) or a compressed audio file (such as an AAC file, an MP3 file, or an Ogg Vorbis file).
- A high-quality playback device, such as your iPod.
- Good speakers or earphones. With speakers, you also need an amplifier, either built into the speakers or separate.
- Ears in tolerable condition. If you've lost hearing in some parts of the audio spectrum, you may need your audio equipment to compensate in order to make the music sound good to you. Even if you have perfect hearing, you still need to get music of a quality you like.

The first two items—the audio signal and the playback device—aren't subjective. Most people can agree whether an audio signal is high-quality or not, because audio quality is measured by the amount of data conveyed rather than by whether you like the audio or not, and you can objectively compare the playback quality of different audio devices.

But the last two items—the speakers or headphones, and your ears—are highly subjective. If you like Limp Bizkit, you probably won't get good mileage out of a system designed to deliver quality Liszt. If you prefer Beethoven, you'll need speakers that can deliver the subtleties and the thunder of classical music rather than speakers designed to crank out country and western. If acoustic folk music is what brings light into your life, speakers or headphones designed to deliver stomach-churning bass and explosions in action games won't do you much good.

Anyway, you get the idea, so enough of that for now. We'll consider all these variables later in this chapter.

What Does CD-Quality Audio Mean?

As you probably know, the human ear is an imperfect audio instrument, capable of detecting (and conveying to the brain) a limited set of audio frequencies that spans the range of experiences that humans evolved (or were designed, depending on your point of view) to know about.

Sound frequency is measured in hertz (Hz) and kilohertz (KHz): 1 Hz is one cycle per second, and 1 KHz is a thousand cycles per second. The typical human ear (let's assume it's yours, even if you've been listening to loud music as much as I have) can detect sound waves from about 20 Hz to 20 KHz. Not surprisingly, most music made by and for humans concentrates on these frequencies, with some (usually unnoticed) overlap at each end. Low-frequency sounds below 20 Hz are called *infrasound,* and high-frequency sounds above 20 KHz are called *ultrasound.* (The ultrasound devices used for physical therapy emit very high-frequency waves to subtly rearrange your tissues. If you hear these waves, you're in trouble.)

> **NOTE** *Animals' hearing overlaps human hearing at both ends of the scale. Typically, dogs' hearing ranges from 50 Hz to about 45 KHz, which is why they can hear dog whistles that most people can't. Bats' ears can hear up to 120 KHz, which is why they can navigate without bothering humans or dogs. Dolphins can hear up to 200 KHz, so bats might be able to annoy them in certain limited circumstances. Elephants can hear infrasound frequencies down to about 5 Hz, so bats don't bother them but earth tremors may.*

CD-quality audio is digital audio that includes the full range of frequencies that humans can hear (again, with some overlap at the high and low ends for the gifted and to annoy susceptible animals). The digital audio is created by using a process called *sampling*—taking snapshots of the audio stream to determine how a particular moment sounds.

CD-quality audio samples audio 44,100 times per second (a sampling rate of 44.1 KHz) to provide coverage with no gaps. Each sample contains 16 bits (2 bytes) of data, which is enough information to convey the full range of frequencies. There are two tracks (for stereo), doubling the amount of data. The data on audio CDs is stored in *pulse code modulation (PCM),* a standard format for uncompressed audio.

CD-quality audio consumes around 10MB (megabytes) of storage space per minute of audio—a huge amount of data even in these days of 250+GB hard drives. So you can see why you need compression to make a large amount of music fit on a device like your iPod.

How Compressed Audio Works (in Brief)

Digital audio data tends to be difficult to compress using lossless compression because it contains so much rapidly changing information. So most methods of compressing digital audio data tend to use lossy compression, discarding the least important parts of the audio while trying to keep everything vital for the sound.

As you'd imagine, the first part of this reduction is getting rid of data on any frequencies that fall outside the hearing range of most humans. There's no point in including any frequency that the vast majority of listeners won't even be able to hear. (Ultrasound and infrasound fall by the wayside here.) But most audio *codecs* (*co*der/*dec*oders) get more subtle than that. Besides taking into account the limitations of the human ear, the codecs use *psychoacoustics,* the science of how the human brain processes sound, to select which data to keep and which to discard. As a crude example, when one part of the sound is masked by another part of the sound, the encoder discards the masked part, because you wouldn't hear it.

How much data the encoder keeps depends on a setting called the *bitrate.* Almost all encoders let you choose a wide range of bitrates. In addition, most MP3 encoders can encode either

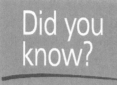

Infrasound Can Affect You Even When You Can't Hear It

Even if your ears can't *hear* infrasound, it may affect you. In summer 2003, scientists in Britain conducted an experiment to gauge the effects of infrasound on the listener. The scientists added infrasound bass lines to modern music works being performed and asked the audience to fill in questionnaires that asked how certain passages of the music affected them, using double-blind techniques to make the results as valid as possible.

The infrasound passages produced unsettling effects such as increased heart rate, feelings of anxiety, shivers on the skin, and fluttering in the stomach. In some participants, the infrasound even evoked sharp memories of emotional losses.

Pipes in some church and cathedral organs can produce infrasound frequencies down to around 16 Hz, which may account for some of the feelings some people experience in such places of worship. It may also explain why elephants tend to avoid churches.

at a constant bitrate (CBR) or a variable bitrate (VBR). The pros and cons of CBR and VBR are discussed in the section "Choose Between CBR and VBR for MP3," later in this chapter.

What Is AAC? Should You Use It?

Advanced Audio Coding (AAC) is a codec for compressing and playing back digital audio. AAC was put together by a group of heavy hitters in the audio and digital-audio fields, including Fraunhofer IIS-A (the German company that developed MP3), Sony Corporation, Dolby Laboratories, AT&T, Nokia, and Lucent. AAC is newer than MP3 (which is discussed in the next section), is generally agreed to deliver better sound than MP3, and is more tightly controlled than MP3. It is one of the key audio components of the MPEG-4 specification, which covers digital audio and video.

> **NOTE** *Some people refer to the Advanced Audio Codec instead of Advanced Audio Coding. The same abbreviation—AAC—applies. In any case, most people stick with the abbreviation rather than using the full name.*

> **NOTE** *The iTunes Music Store (discussed in Chapter 6) uses AAC for its songs, so if you buy songs from it, you won't have any choice about using AAC. If necessary, you can convert the songs to other formats. For example, you might convert a song from AAC to MP3 so that you can use it with an MP3 player that can't handle AAC.*

MPEG-2 AAC and MPEG-4 AAC

At the time of writing, AAC comes in two flavors: MPEG-2 AAC and MPEG-4 AAC. From the names, you'd hazard that MPEG-2 AAC is part of the MPEG-2 specification for digital audio and video, whereas MPEG-4 AAC is part of the MPEG-4 specification—and you'd be right.

MPEG-2 AAC is used for several purposes. It's part of the specification for the DVD-Audio Recordable (DVD-AR) format and is used for some Internet-audio purposes, such as streaming and downloading audio.

MPEG-4 is a newer specification that includes more capabilities and delivers higher-quality sound than MPEG-2. Among other uses (such as in iTunes, QuickTime, and your iPod), MPEG-4 AAC is used as the general audio codec for 3G wireless terminals.

QuickTime 6 includes an AAC codec. If your Mac has QuickTime 6.2 or a later version installed, iTunes uses MPEG-4 AAC as its default encoding format. (If your Mac has an earlier version of QuickTime installed, iTunes uses MP3 as its default encoding format.)

AAC's 48 Channels

AAC can work with up to 48 full-frequency audio channels. This gives it a huge advantage over MP3, which can work with only two channels (in stereo) or a single channel (in mono).

If you're used to listening to music in stereo (in other words, using two channels), 48 channels seems an absurd number. But typically, only a small subset of those channels would be used at the same time. For example, conventional surround-sound rigs use 5.1 or 7.1 setups, using six channels or eight channels, respectively. Other channels can be used for different languages, so that an AAC player can play a different vocal track for differently configured players. Still other tracks can be used for synchronizing and controlling the audio.

AAC Licensing

Dolby Laboratories handles AAC licensing via its independent subsidiary Via Licensing Corporation (www.vialicensing.com). Via charges royalties on the sale of AAC encoders and decoders (either hardware or software), but there are no fees for distributing content in AAC format. So usually the manufacturers or developers of the encoders and decoders take care of the licensing payments and pass along the costs to the end users by including them in the cost of hardware and software decoders. That means you don't need to worry about getting a license for using AAC—Apple has taken care of them for you in iTunes, QuickTime, and your iPod.

The cost of AAC licenses varies depending on the type of AAC (MPEG-4 AAC is a little more expensive than MPEG-2 AAC) and the number of channels used in the implementation. For example, stereo uses two channels (the left channel and the right channel), is widely used in consumer products, and comes at a very affordable cost. (Mono is even cheaper, but few people want to listen to mono sound when they can have stereo instead.) A high-end home-theater product using 7.1 surround sound uses eight channels and costs correspondingly more. Products classed as "professional" rather than "consumer"—for example, video-production equipment—cost more yet.

Advantages of AAC

For music lovers, AAC offers higher music quality than MP3 at the same file sizes, or similar music quality at smaller file sizes. Apple reckons that 128 Kbps AAC files sound as good as 160 Kbps MP3 files—so you can either save a fair amount of space and enjoy the same quality or enjoy even higher quality at the same bitrate. Around 24 Kbps, AAC streams provide quite listenable sound, whereas MP3 streams sound quite rough. (*Streaming* is the method of transmission used by Internet radio, in which you can listen to a file as your computer downloads it.)

Small file sizes are especially welcome for streaming audio over slow connections, such as modem connections. AAC streamed around 56 Kbps sounds pretty good (though not perfect), while MP3 sounds a bit flawed.

The main advantage of AAC for the music industry is that the format supports digital rights management (DRM). This means that AAC files can be created in a protected format with custom limitations built in. For example, the song files you can buy from the iTunes Music Store are authorized to be played on up to three different computers at the same time. If you try to play a song on a computer that's not authorized, the song won't play.

NOTE   *To tell if an AAC file is protected or not, choose File | Get Info and check the Kind readout on the Summary tab of the Song Information dialog box. If the file is protected, the Kind readout reads* Protected AAC Audio File. *If not, Kind reads* AAC Audio File. *Alternatively, check the file extension: the .m4p extension indicates a protected file, whereas the .m4a extension indicates an unprotected file.*

Disadvantages of AAC

AAC's disadvantages are largely acceptable to most users of iTunes and the iPod:

- At the time of writing, AAC files aren't widely used. One reason is that, because AAC is relatively new and hasn't been very widely implemented, few AAC encoders and decoders are available. However, in iTunes (and QuickTime) and the iPod, Apple has provided AAC encoding and decoding for the Mac and for Windows. Because AAC is the default format for ripping (discussed in "Understand Ripping, Encoding, and 'Copying'," later in this chapter) in iTunes 4, its usage is growing rapidly.

- Encoding AAC files takes more processor cycles than encoding MP3 files. But as processors continue to increase in speed and power by the month if not by the week, this becomes less and less of a problem. For example, even relatively antiquated Macs (such as my PowerBook G3/333) and PCs (for example, a Celeron 600) have plenty of power to encode and decode AAC—they just do so more slowly than faster computers.

- For consumers, the largest potential disadvantage of AAC is the extent to which DRM can limit their use of the files. At the time of writing, Apple has delivered a relatively flexible implementation of DRM in the music sold by the iTunes Music Store. However, if Apple and the record companies tighten the licensing terms of the files in the future, consumers may have cause for concern. In this sense, AAC could act as a Trojan horse to wean customers off MP3 and onto AAC, then gradually lock them in to a format that the music industry can control.

What Is MP3? Should You Use It?

Like AAC, MP3 is a file format for compressed audio. That doesn't sound like much, but for music enthusiasts, MP3 has been one of the most exciting developments since the sound card, amplifier-inside speakers, or noise-canceling headphones. This is because MP3 allows you to carry a large amount of high-quality audio with you on a small device and enjoy it at the cost of nothing but the device, battery power, and time.

Among Mac users, MP3 has been overshadowed recently by AAC since Apple incorporated the AAC codec in iTunes, QuickTime, and the iPod. But MP3 remains the dominant format for compressed audio on computers running Windows (where its major competition comes from WMA, Microsoft's proprietary Windows Media Audio format) and computers running Linux.

MP3's name comes from the Motion Picture Experts Group (MPEG; www.chiariglione.org/mpeg/—*not* www.mpeg.org, which you might expect it to be), which oversaw the development of the MP3 format. MP3 is both the extension used by the files and the name commonly used for them. More correctly, MP3 is the file format for MPEG-1 Layer 3—but most people who listen to MP3 files neither know that nor care to know such details.

NOTE *Before you ask, there are also MP1 and MP2 formats (which preceded MP3) as well as an MP4 format (for the MPEG-4 file format, which came later).*

MP3 can deliver high-quality music in files that take up as little as a tenth as much space as uncompressed CD-quality files. For speech, which typically requires less fidelity than music, you can create even smaller files that still sound good, enabling you to pack that much more audio in the same amount of disk space.

MP3 Patent and Royalty Rates

There's a widespread perception that MP3 is an open standard that anyone can use, but the reality is a bit different. Although MPEG oversaw the development of MP3, Fraunhofer IIS-A did most of the work.

Fraunhofer and Thomson Corporation (which describes itself as providing "information workflow solutions that help business and professional customers work more productively") hold patent rights over MP3 audio compression. So anyone who wants to create an MP3 encoder or decoder—whether hardware or software—needs to pay a per-unit royalty to Fraunhofer and Thomson. For example, if you choose to create a hardware MP3 decoder, you need to pay $0.75 per unit; if you create a hardware encoder, the fee is $5 per unit.

You don't need a license to *use* MP3 hardware or software, as long as the hardware or software is licensed. You're also free to stream MP3 audio for "private, non-commercial activities," such as home entertainment. But you do need a license to stream MP3 audio for commercial purposes—for example, if you're using MP3 for webcasting. (See www.mp3licensing.com for details.)

For commercial MP3 software, licensing isn't an issue—whoever developed the software will have paid the licensing fee (and you'll probably have paid them for the software). But for MP3 freeware, licensing is potentially an issue, although the developers of such software are much more likely to be the targets of patent enforcement than users of the software, because the developers are easier and juicier targets.

Understand Other Digital Audio Formats

For most of the music you store on your Mac and enjoy via iTunes or your iPod, you'll want to use AAC, MP3, or whichever combination of the two you find most convenient. Both iTunes and the iPod can also use WAV files and AIFF files.

How to ...   Choose Between MP3 and AAC

Apple's current implementation of AAC in iTunes and the iPods has a lot to commend it. AAC delivers high-quality audio, small file size, and enough flexibility for most purposes. But if you want to use the files you rip from a CD on a portable player that doesn't support AAC, or you need to play them using a software player that doesn't support AAC, choose MP3 instead.

Similarly, if you want to share your music files with other people in any way other than sharing your music library via iTunes, MP3 is the way to go—but remember that you need the copyright holder's explicit authorization to copy and distribute music.

AIFF files and WAV files are basically the same thing—uncompressed PCM audio, which is also referred to as "raw" audio. AIFF files are PCM files with an AIFF header (the *header* is a section of identification information contained at the start of the file), while WAV files are PCM files with a WAV header. AIFF tends to be more widely used on the Mac than on Windows, which favors WAV. If you want the ultimate in audio quality, you can create AIFF files or WAV files from your CDs and store them on your computer or iPod. The problem with doing so is that each full-length CD will take up between 500MB and 800MB of disk space compared to the 50MB to 80MB it would take up compressed at 128 Kbps.

CAUTION   *When you put uncompressed audio files on your iPod, you run into another problem: the battery wears out much more quickly. This is because the uncompressed files tend to be too large for your iPod's memory to cache effectively, so the hard disk is used much more often than for compressed audio files.*

For you as a digital-audio enthusiast, other formats that may be of interest include the following:

- WMA is an audio format developed by Microsoft. It's the preferred format of Windows Media Player, the Microsoft audio and video player included with all desktop versions of Windows.

- mp3PRO is designed to be a successor to MP3, as its name implies. It delivers higher audio quality than MP3 at the same bitrates. For example, mp3PRO files encoded at the 64 Kbps bitrate are similar in quality to MP3 files encoded at the 128 Kbps bitrate. Like MP3, mp3PRO requires hardware and software manufacturers to pay royalties to Thomson Corporation.

- Ogg Vorbis is an open-source format that's patent free. It's relatively new and has yet to catch the public's attention. You can get an Ogg Vorbis plug-in for QuickTime (from www.illadvised.com/~jordy) that enables iTunes to play Ogg Vorbis songs.

Understand Ripping, Encoding, and "Copying"

Audio CDs store data in a format different to that of data CDs (for example, a CD containing software or your favorite spreadsheets). Most audio CDs use a format called Red Book and contain only audio data. Other CDs use a format called CD Extra that lets the creator include a data track as well as the audio tracks. This data track can contain any kind of data—for example, videos, pictures, or text.

Audio CDs store the data for their songs in a format that file-management programs on Windows (for example, Windows Explorer) and System 9 (for example, the Finder) can't access directly. If you put an audio CD in your CD drive and open a Windows Explorer window or a System 9 Finder window, you'll see only minuscule CDA (CD Audio) files rather than the huge uncompressed files that contain the songs. The CDA files are pointers to the song files. These pointers are called *handles.* You can use Windows Explorer or the Finder to copy the handles from the CD to your hard disk, but copying them won't do you much good, because the audio will still be on the CD. By contrast, Mac OS X can access the data on an audio CD seamlessly.

To get the audio off the CD, you need to perform a process called *ripping.* Ripping sounds vigorous but simply means using a program to extract the audio from the CD (by using the handles to access the audio data). You can rip audio to uncompressed files—typically WAV files or AIFF files—or immediately encode it to a compressed file format such as AAC, MP3, or WMA.

TIP	*Mac OS X lets you rip a song to an AIFF file by performing a Copy operation from the CD using the Finder. For example, drag the song from a Finder window to the desktop to rip it to an AIFF file there. However, in most cases, it makes more sense to use iTunes to rip songs and encode them to AAC files or MP3 files.*

In iTunes, Apple uses the term "importing" to cover extracting the audio from CD, encoding it (if you're using AAC or MP3), and saving it to disk. By contrast, in Windows Media Player, Microsoft uses the term "copying." This is both accurate and inaccurate, clarifying and misleading, at the same time. It's accurate because ripping and encoding a WMA file or MP3 file of a song on a CD does create a copy of it, with all the copyright implications involved. The term "importing" skates over the copyright implications of creating the compressed files.

Yet "copying" is inaccurate because, in the computer sense, a Copy operation almost always creates a perfect copy of the file involved, not a lower-quality version in a substantially different format. (For example, if you copy a Word document, you expect the copy to be a Word document with the same contents, not a WordPad or TextEdit document with a minimal amount of formatting and missing some of the less interesting parts of the text—as judged by the computer.) But for users who don't understand how audio is stored on CDs and how compression works, the term "copying" implies creating a perfect copy of the CD audio on the computer's hard disk. And that's not the case.

Learn about CDDB and Other Sources of CD Information

iTunes and many other ripping and encoding applications download CD information from the CD Database (CDDB; www.cddb.com). CDDB is a collaborative project that allows anyone who can connect to the Internet to access its data.

You can look up information manually by using the CDDB interface, but in most cases audio programs look up CD information automatically for you, either when you insert a CD or when you instruct the program to look up the current CD. If the CD you're trying to look up doesn't have an entry in CDDB, you can submit one.

Choose an Appropriate Compression Rate, Bitrate, and Stereo Settings

To get suitable audio quality, you must use an appropriate compression rate for the audio files you encode with iTunes. In the previous chapter, you saw how to set your encoding preferences. Here, you'll learn what effect the different settings have.

iTunes' default settings are to encode AAC files in stereo at the 128 Kbps bitrate using automatic sample-rate detection. iTunes calls those settings High Quality, and they deliver great results for most purposes. If they don't suit you, you can choose custom AAC settings for the files you create. With AAC you can change the bitrate, the sample rate, and the channels.

iTunes' MP3 encoder gives you more flexibility. The default settings for MP3 are to encode MP3 files in stereo at the 160 Kbps bitrate, using CBR and automatic sample-rate detection. iTunes calls those settings High Quality, and they deliver results almost as good as the High Quality settings with the AAC encoder, although they produce significantly larger files because the bitrate is higher.

For encoding MP3 files, iTunes also offers preset settings for Good Quality (128 Kbps) and Higher Quality (192 Kbps). Beyond these choices, you can choose the Custom setting and specify exactly the settings you want: bitrates from 16 Kbps to 230 Kbps, CBR or VBR, sample rate, channels, the stereo mode, whether to use Smart Encoding Adjustments, and whether to filter frequencies lower than 10 Hz.

Test the Sound Given by Different Bitrates to Find Which Is Best

Choosing a compression rate for your music collection shouldn't be a snap decision; making the wrong decision can cost you disk space (if you record at too high a bitrate), audio quality (too low a bitrate), and the time it takes to rip your entire collection again at the bitrate you should have chosen in the first place.

Ideally, you should rip a representative selection of the types of music you plan to listen to using your computer and your iPod. Encode several copies of each test track at different bitrates, and then listen to them over a period of several days to see which provides the best balance of file size and audio quality.

Make sure some of the songs test the different aspects of music that are important to you. For example, if your musical tastes lean to female vocalists, listen to plenty of those. If you prefer bass-heavy, bludgeoning rock, listen to that. If you go for classical music as well, add that to the mix.

This probably all sounds obvious enough—and it should be. But plenty of people don't take the time to find out which bitrate is best for them and their music, although they find plenty of time to complain about the results.

Choose Between CBR and VBR for MP3

After choosing the bitrate at which to encode your MP3 files, you need to choose between constant bitrate (CBR) and variable bitrate (VBR).

NOTE   *This choice doesn't apply to AAC encoding.*

CBR simply records each part of the file at the specified bitrate. CBR files can sound great, particularly at higher bitrates, but generally, VBR delivers better quality than CBR. This is because VBR can allocate space more intelligently as the audio needs it. For example, a complex passage of a song will require more data to represent it accurately than will a simple passage, which in turn will require more data than the two seconds of silence before the massed guitars come crashing back in.

The disadvantage to VBR, and the reason why most MP3 encoders are set to use CBR by default, is that many older decoders and hardware devices can't play them. If you're using iTunes and an iPod, you won't need to worry about this. But if you're using an older decoder or hardware device, you may need to check that it can manage VBR.

Choose Between Normal Stereo and Joint Stereo for MP3

As you'll know if you've browsed through ancient vinyl records, early recordings used *mono*— a single channel that didn't deliver any separation among the sounds. On a song recorded in mono, all the instruments sound as though they're located in the same place. Many mono recordings made by competent recording engineers sound pretty good, but the effect is very different from listening to a live band. In most cases, you'll want to stick with stereo, which produces the effect of different instruments sounding as though they're in different locations. But if your sound source is mono (for example, a live recording with a single microphone), stick with mono when encoding the audio.

Once you've decided to use stereo, your next choice is between normal stereo and joint stereo. If you haven't met these terms before, don't worry: the last few conventional forms of consumer audio—LPs, cassette tapes (including digital audio tapes, or DATs), and CDs—essentially removed this choice from you, so you didn't need to worry about it. But computer audio, and specifically MP3, has reequipped you with this choice. So it's a good idea to understand your options and use them as necessary—even if that means simply choosing the best setting for your needs and sticking with it through thick and thin.

Stereo delivers two channels: a left channel and a right channel. These two channels provide positional audio, enabling recording, and mixing engineers to separate the audio so that different sounds appear to be coming from different places. For example, the engineer can make one guitar sound as though it's positioned on the left and another guitar sound as though it's positioned on the right. Or the engineer might fade a sound from left to right so it seems to go across the listener.

NOTE Surround sound *goes much further than stereo, enabling the sound engineer to make sounds seem like they're behind you, moving through your mouth from molar to incisor, and so on. MP3 doesn't support surround sound, but AAC does.*

Normal stereo (sometimes called plain stereo) uses two tracks: one for the left stereo channel and another for the right stereo channel. As its name suggests, normal stereo is the normal form of stereo. For example, if you buy a CD that's recorded in stereo and play it back through your boom box, you're using normal stereo.

Joint stereo (sometimes called mid/side stereo) divides the channel data differently to make better use of a small amount of space. The encoder averages out the two original channels (assuming the sound source is normal stereo) to a mid channel. It then encodes this channel, devoting to it the bulk of the available space assigned by the bitrate. One channel contains the data that's the same on both channels. The second channel contains the data that's different on one of the channels. By reducing the channel data to the common data (which takes the bulk of the available space) and the data that's different on one of the channels (which takes much less space), joint stereo can deliver higher audio quality at the same bitrate as normal stereo.

TIP *Use joint stereo to produce better-sounding audio when encoding at lower bitrates, and use normal stereo for all your recordings at your preferred bitrate. Where the threshold for lower-bitrate recording falls depends on you. Many people recommend using normal stereo for encoding at bitrates of 160 Kbps and above, and using joint stereo for lower bitrates (128 Kbps and below). Others recommend not using normal stereo below 192 Kbps. Experiment to establish what works for you.*

The results you get with joint stereo depend on the quality of the MP3 encoder you use. Some of the less capable MP3 encoders produce joint-stereo tracks that sound more like mono tracks than like normal-stereo tracks. Better encoders produce joint-stereo tracks that sound very close to normal-stereo tracks. iTunes produces pretty good joint-stereo tracks.

Using the same MP3 encoder, normal stereo delivers better sound quality than joint stereo—at high bitrates. At lower bitrates, joint stereo delivers better sound quality than normal stereo, because joint stereo can retain more data about the basic sound (in the mid channel) than normal stereo can retain about the sound in its two separate channels. However, joint stereo provides less separation between the left and right channels than normal stereo provides. (The lack of separation is what produces the mono-like effect.)

Load Uncompressed Files on Your iPod for Unbeatable Sound Quality

To get the ultimate music quality, you can load uncompressed audio files—either WAV files or AIFF files—on your iPod. If you rip these audio files directly from the CD at full quality, you'll have truly CD-quality files. (You can also create lower-quality WAV files or AIFF files if you choose.) Such files provide the equivalent of carrying your CDs with you on your iPod.

The disadvantages to loading uncompressed files on your iPod are as follows:

- You can't fit as much music on your iPod. You'll be able to fit only about 60 full-length CDs on a 40GB iPod—or 6 full-length CDs on a 4GB iPod mini.

- You'll wear out your iPod's battery much more quickly. This is because the uncompressed files will be too large for your iPod's memory to cache effectively, so the hard disk will be used much more often than if you're playing smaller files.

Copyright Law for Digital Audiophiles

Unless you've created an original work yourself and needed to protect it, you may well never have needed to bother yourself with copyright law. But if you're listening to digital audio on your iPod, knowing the basics of copyright law is a good idea, for two reasons:

- You can make sure you don't take any actions that breach copyright law (or that, if you do take such actions, you do so wittingly rather than otherwise).

- You can be an empowered consumer and defend your rights against companies (as well as lobbyists and lobbied governments) that want to take them away from you for commercial reasons.

 This section discusses U.S. law. If you live in another country, check the laws to make sure your actions with copyrighted works stay within them.

What Copyright Is

Copyright consists of a set of laws designed to encourage authors to produce original works by preventing other people from copying those works without permission. Copyright protection acts as an incentive for authors to put time into creating works in the hope of receiving money from the sales of those works.

For example, say you write the ultimate truck-driving anthem. Copyright ensures Garth Brooks can't make a hit of it and rake in millions of dollars without your granting him (or his record company) the right to record and distribute the song. In exchange for granting those rights, you'll receive money, typically. Without copyright, you might receive nothing.

Copyright applies to almost all original works. There are some limitations: the key one is that you can copyright only the expression of an idea, not the idea itself. For example, you can't copyright the idea of your truck-driving anthem—you have to go ahead and write the anthem. Once you've stored the anthem in a tangible form (for example, by writing it on paper or as a computer file, or by recording it), you have a copyrighted work. You don't even have to register the copyright with the Copyright Office, but doing so is a good idea because it makes dealing with copyright infringements much easier. For works created since January 1, 1978, copyright lasts until 70 years after the death of the author or last surviving coauthor ("life plus 70").

Corporate copyrights last for 95 years, thanks to the Sonny Bono Copyright Term Extension Act of 1998. The extension means that The Walt Disney Company will keep control of Winnie the Pooh and Mickey Mouse until the 2020s. Similarly, Time Warner retains the rights to vast numbers of early music recordings, television episodes, and movies (such as *Gone with the Wind* and *Casablanca*). As you might imagine, Disney was one of the companies that lobbied for the extension. The Copyright Term Extension Act was challenged in 2002 but was upheld by the U.S. Supreme Court in January 2003.

When You Can Copy Copyrighted Material Legally, and Why

Copyright law is sweeping. Basically, it says you need permission from the copyright holder to copy any copyrighted work. But there are various specific exceptions and some gray areas, some of which directly affect copying audio CDs and creating AAC files or MP3 files from them. The following sections run through the key elements in the puzzle.

Time-Shifting and Place-Shifting

The Betamax Decision of 1984, sometimes also called the "Sony Decision" because Sony created the Betamax video form, allows you to time-shift or place-shift a copyrighted work. This decision, handed down by the Supreme Court, established that home taping of broadcasts doesn't infringe copyright.

You're allowed to copy a copyrighted broadcast work to *time-shift* it for personal use so you can experience it later. For example, you may record a radio show so you can listen to it the next day. Similarly, you may *place-shift* a copyrighted work for personal use so you can listen to it somewhere else on different equipment. For example, you may create MP3 files from a copyrighted CD so you can listen to them on your iPod while skiing.

What Personal Use Allows You to Do

The Audio Home Recording Act (AHRA) of 1992 includes a provision called *personal use* that allows you to use what the AHRA terms a "digital audio recording device" to copy a copyrighted work onto a different medium so you can listen to it. For example, you can transfer a CD to a MiniDisc so you can listen to it on your MiniDisc player.

Personal use seems to cover ripping and extracting CDs perfectly—except that the AHRA considers computers "multipurpose devices" rather than "digital audio recording devices." The digital audio recording devices the AHRA covers were digital tapes, such as DAT, and Digital Compact Cassettes (DCCs, a short-lived competitor to DAT).

Fair Use and Why It Doesn't Apply to MP3

Fair use is a copyright provision that causes huge amounts of confusion. Fair use allows you to reproduce part of a copyrighted work without permission but without infringing copyright in limited circumstances. For example, if you're reviewing a book, you might be able to fairly use short quotes from it to illustrate the points you're making. When criticizing a movie, you might be able to fairly reproduce a picture from it. When teaching, you might be able to make multiple copies of a couple of pages from a book so each member of the class could read them.

All those examples say "might" because fair use is judged according to four very fluid factors (which we won't get into here). One person's understanding of fair use may be very different from another's, and fair use issues are frequently taken to court.

In brief, what you need to know about fair use is this: fair use is seldom if ever relevant to copying audio CDs or creating MP3 files. But you'll often hear people using the phrase as justification for illegal copying they've performed.

Burning CDs of Copyrighted Works for Others Is Illegal

Burning CDs of copyrighted works for others without permission is illegal, no matter how easy it is to do or how many people seem to be doing it. Burning backup CDs of copyrighted works for yourself may be legal—but it's seldom entirely clear. For example, you'll see notices on many software CDs that say things like "Do not make illegal copies of this disc," suggesting that making *legal* copies (for backup) is acceptable. By contrast, many audio CDs bear notices such as "Unauthorized copying, reproduction, hiring, lending, public performance, and broadcasting prohibited."

> **NOTE** *At this writing, the iTunes Music Store agreement specifically permits you to burn files you buy from the iTunes Music Store to CD.*

Sharing MP3 Files of Copyrighted Material Is Illegal

Sharing files containing other people's copyrighted material without permission is illegal. For example, many of the MP3 files shared on peer-to-peer file-sharing services (such as the pioneering but now-defunct Napster and successors including Gnutella, Kazaa, and Aimster) are shared illegally.

That said, some artists encourage you to distribute their works freely. For example, artists who choose to make tracks available on web music sites such as www.iuma.com generally allow those tracks to be downloaded for free to generate publicity. Most of those artists encourage those who download the tracks to pass them on to other people to spread their music farther, in the hopes of increasing their audience or selling CDs of their other music.

Even some artists encourage you to distribute the copyrighted works that their CDs contain. For example, if you're one of the (apparently few) people who has an original copy (so to speak) of the album *Igneous Rock* by the Tempe, Arizona, band Sledville, you'll find that the CD insert card states "Unauthorized duplication is encouraged. Distribute freely."

Circumventing Copy Protection May Be Illegal

Copying CDs for others and sharing MP3 files with others are clearly illegal. But now we come to a strange item: as a result of Title I of the Digital Millennium Copyright Act (DMCA), which was passed in 1998, it's illegal to circumvent "effective technological measures" protecting a copyrighted work. There are various ifs and buts (for example, you can circumvent such measures to make another program interoperate with a copyrighted work), but essentially Title I says if someone has protected a copyrighted work with a technological measure that could be argued to be "effective" (whatever that means), it's illegal to crack that measure. There are heavy penalties if you do so deliberately and for "commercial advantage" or private gain: fines of up to $500,000 and five years' imprisonment for a first offense, and double those for a second offense.

How the DMCA will pan out in the real world is still very much open to question. Here are some examples for you to chew on:

- In December 2002, the Russian software company Elcomsoft was acquitted of breaking the law by creating a program that enabled people to read Adobe eBook files that used technological protection. As the judge saw it, the crux of the question was whether Elcomsoft had *intended* the software to be used to violate copyright, not whether the software *could* be used to violate copyright.

- In January 2003, a Norwegian hacker was acquitted of breaking the law by creating a software decoder to play back DVDs on Linux. No Linux DVD decoder was available, so the hacker took advantage of some unprotected code in a commercial DVD player to create his own DVD decoder. In a decision that was widely seen as sensible, the Norwegian judges ruled that because the hacker owned the DVDs in question, he hadn't broken into them. The Oslo City Court ruling said, "The court finds that someone who buys a DVD film that has been legally produced has legal access to the film"—a finding most consumers can easily understand.

- A major retailer has used the DMCA to claim that its price lists constitute trade secrets. (Most people have a hard time accepting this one.)

- Chamberlain Group, a manufacturer of garage-door openers, filed suit against Skylink Technologies, a competitor, under the DMCA because Skylink was offering garage-door transmitters that worked with Chamberlain openers. Chamberlain claimed that Skylink had circumvented its access controls, contravening the DMCA. Fortunately, again, a judge took a sane stance, declaring that "the homeowner has a legitimate expectation that he or she will be able to access the garage even if his transmitter is misplaced or malfunctions."

Understand Current Copy-Protection Techniques on the CDs You Buy

To prevent customers from ripping or burning copies of the CDs they buy, record companies have turned to a variety of copy-protection solutions. High-profile copy-protection solutions include Cactus-200 Data Shield (developed by the Israel-based company Midbar Tech Ltd.; www.midbartech. com) and key2audio (from Sony DADC; www.key2audio.com). Macrovision Corporation acquired Midbar Tech in 2002; you'll probably recognize the name Macrovision from their video-protection products.

Midbar Tech claims that Cactus-200 Data Shield is the leading copy-protection solution; as of January 2003, more than 30 million discs using key2audio protection have been sold, so altogether there are plenty of these discs out there in the wild. Anecdotal evidence suggests that most of these protected audio discs have been sold in Europe, with smaller numbers having been sold in the U.S.

This section outlines how these two copy-protection solutions work, the effects you'll see when you encounter such protected discs, ways some users have found of using protected discs on computers, and why it may be illegal to do so. But first, I'd like to make sure you're aware of why the CD has been such a success, and why the record companies are so worried about piracy.

Understand the Wonders of the Audio CD

You've probably never bothered to contemplate the wonders of the audio CD. But if you have, you may have realized that the CD is pretty wonderful. It's not wonderful for the sound quality (although that was a great improvement on the cassette tapes and the vinyl LPs that preceded it) nor for its capacity (because other storage technologies, such as DVDs and magneto-optical disks, have far exceeded that), but for its standards-based universality.

You can buy a CD in just about any country on the planet, buy a CD player or CD drive in just about any other country, insert the CD, and play it. Depending on the quality of the CD player and the playback system, the audio should sound more or less as the artist and producer intended. As a result of this universality, CDs became widespread in the 1980s and remain the most popular medium for music distribution.

At first, record companies loved CDs more than consumers did, because CDs allowed them to sell to consumers the same music for a second or even a third time: the consumers had bought the music on LP; some of them had bought it on cassette tapes to play in their Walkmans; and now they could buy it once again on CD to play in their CD players. Better yet, because the CD was a newer, more faithful, and ostensibly more expensive-to-produce medium, the record companies could charge around twice as much for CDs as for LPs or cassette tapes. Since then, CD prices have come down a bit, but they remain far more profitable for the record companies than LPs or cassette tapes.

But soon, despite the prices, consumers began to love CDs as well, because CDs began to deliver on their promise of combining portability and acceptable durability with high-quality sound. And as you'll know, by 2003 CDs had almost entirely replaced vinyl and cassettes as the medium on which people buy their music.

As mentioned in the previous section, starting in late 1999 and taking effect in 2000, Napster put a severe crimp in the dominance of the CD as the primary means of distributing music. Other file-sharing services followed. Around the same time, CD recording became easier, and recordable (and rewritable) CD media became very affordable. So consumers could easily share compressed digital audio files with friends and strangers alike on file-sharing services, or burn perfect copies of CDs to give to people they knew.

CD sales fell by 5 percent in 2001, by 7 percent in the first half of 2002, and by 9.3 percent in the whole of 2002. The Recording Industry Association of America (RIAA), which represents the record companies, has claimed that "illegal music downloading was the main culprit in the drop in sales" and has also put part of the blame on recordable CDs, even though it acknowledges that "the decline in consumer spending [has] played a role."

Other commentators argue that other factors have almost certainly reduced CD sales as well. For example, the record industry released approximately 27,000 CDs in 2001 compared to nearly 39,000 CDs in 1999. Less choice, less appealing music: it makes sense that consumers would buy fewer CDs, especially if they have substantially less disposable income to spend on music thanks to the economic downturn.

In August 2002, the analysts at Forrester Research argued that the decline in CD sales was mostly attributable to the economic downturn. Forrester also argued MP3 had been *good* for the music business, because people who download MP3 files still tend to buy CDs. In effect, MP3 lets people preview music they might not otherwise have heard. If they like the music, they may well buy the CDs.

How CD-Protection Solutions Work (in Brief)

In brief, and at the risk of generalizing wildly, CD-protection solutions work by corrupting the data on audio discs so the data can still be read by audio CD players but can't be read by computer CD drives. Some high-end audio players, such as car CD players and DVD players, also have trouble reading some copy-protected audio discs.

key2audio uses a hidden signature on the disc to prevent playback on computers. Sony DADC claims the "audio part" of discs protected with key2audio fully complies with the Red Book standard because "no uncorrectable errors are used to protect the audio data." However, because by design key2audio discs don't work with Red Book–compliant CD drives and DVD drives, the discs themselves clearly aren't Red Book–compliant. This might seem like a fine point, but it's not—if the disc won't play back on a CD drive, it's not a CD.

According to Midbar Technologies, Cactus-200 Data Shield is an "engineering solution" (rather than a software solution) that "slightly alters the information on the CD [*sic*] in several ways while maintaining perfect audio quality."

Consumer advocates put it differently: Cactus introduces errors in the data on the audio disc that require the error-correction mechanisms on the player to compensate. Using the error-correction mechanism on the player like this makes the disc less resistant to damage (for example, scratches), because the player will be unable to correct many damage-related errors on top of the deliberate copy-protection errors. The discs may also degrade more quickly than unprotected CDs. Some consumer advocates claim copy-protection solutions may also lead older or more delicate CD players to fail sooner than they would otherwise have done because they make the players work harder than unprotected CDs do, much as driving at full speed over rough roads will wear out your car's suspension much more quickly than driving at the same speed on freeways will.

If You Can't Play It on *Any* CD Player, It's Not a CD

As you learned in "Understand Ripping, Encoding, and 'Copying'," earlier in this chapter, most audio CDs use the Red Book format, while others use the CD Extra format (a subset of Red Book) to put non-audio data on the CD as well.

Philips and Sony defined Red Book in 1980. (The standard was published in a red binder—hence the name. Subsequent standards include Orange Book and Yellow Book—three guesses why.) Red Book ensures the disc will work with all drives that bear the Compact Disc logo and entitles the disc to bear the Compact Disc Digital Audio logo.

How to Recognize Copy-Protected Discs

Copy-protected discs won't play on all CD drives and, so, technically and legally are *not* CDs. You should be able to recognize them as follows:

- The discs shouldn't bear the Compact Disc Digital Audio logo (because they're not CDs), but some do. And in any case, many Red Book CDs don't bear this logo, usually for reasons of label design or laziness.

- The disc may carry a disclaimer, warning, or notice such as "Will *not* play on PC or Mac," "This CD [*sic*] cannot be played on a PC/Mac," "Copy Control," or "Copy Protected."

- The disc won't play on your computer, or it will play but won't rip.

How to ... Eject Stuck Audio Discs

If you insert a non-CD audio disc into your CD drive and your PC or Mac can't handle it, you may be unable to eject the disc. The PC or Mac may hang. If your computer is a Mac, and you restart it with the disc in the CD drive, your Mac may start up to a gray screen.

On PCs and some Macs, you can use the manual eject hole on the CD drive to eject the disc. Straighten one end of a sturdy paper clip and push it into the hole to eject the disc.

If your Mac doesn't have a manual eject hole, don't go prodding the wrong hole. Instead, follow as many of these steps as necessary to fix the problem:

1. Restart your Mac. If it's too hung to restart by conventional means, press the Reset button (if it has one), or hold down COMMAND, CTRL, and the power button. At the system startup sound, hold down the mouse button until your Mac finishes booting. This action may eject the disc.

2. If you're using System 9 and have Mac OS X installed, restart your Mac and boot Mac OS X. Again, if your Mac is too hung to restart by conventional means, press the Reset button, or hold down COMMAND, CTRL, and the power button. At the system startup sound, hold down X to boot Mac OS X. Open iTunes from the dock or the Applications folder, and then click the Eject button.

3. Restart your Mac. Once again, if it's too hung to restart by conventional means, press the Reset button, or hold down COMMAND, CTRL, and the power button. At the system startup sound, hold down COMMAND-OPTION-O-F to boot to the Open Firmware mode. You'll see a prompt screen that contains something like the text shown here (the exact text varies depending on the model of Mac):

```
Apple PowerBook3, 5 4.5.3f2 BootROM built on 10/25/02 at 10:31:30
Copyright 1994-2002 Apple Computer, Inc.
All Rights Reserved

Welcome to Open Firmware, the system time and date is:  10:27:06 02/03/2003

To continue booting, type "mac-boot" and press return.
To shut down, type "shut-down" and press return.

 ok
0> _
```

Type **eject cd** and press RETURN. If all is well, the CD drive will open. If not, you may see the message "read of block0 failed. can't OPEN the EJECT device." Either way, type **mac-boot** and press RETURN to reboot your Mac.

If Open Firmware mode won't fix the problem, you'll need to take your Mac to a service shop.

3

What Happens when You Try to Use a Copy-Protected Disc on a Computer

When you try to use a copy-protected disc on a computer, any of the following may happen:

- The disc may play back without problems. You may even be able to rip it by using a conventional audio program (such as iTunes) or a specialized, heavy-duty ripper (such as Exact Audio Copy). If you can rip the disc, the copy protection has failed (or your drive has defeated it). You may be liable for five years' imprisonment and a half-million-dollar fine.

- The disc may not play at all.

- The disc may cause your computer's operating system to hang.

- You may be unable to eject the disc on some PCs and many Macs. (See the sidebar "How to Eject Stuck Audio Discs.")

TIP
If your Mac has a SuperDrive, download the Apple SuperDrive Update from www.apple. com/hardware/superdrive/ before attempting to use any copy-protected audio discs in the drive. Once you've installed this update, you'll be able to eject copy-protected audio discs.

Learn Ways to Get Around Copy Protection

Customers annoyed by copy-protected audio discs quickly found ways to circumvent the copy protection. In many cases, the most effective solution is to experiment with different drives. Some drives can play audio discs protected with some technologies; others can't.

TIP
Many DVD drives are better at playing copy-protected discs than many plain CD-ROM drives. This is because the DVD drives are designed to work with multiple types of discs— DVDs, CDs, recordable CDs (CD-Rs), rewritable CD (CD-RWs), and even various types of recordable DVDs, depending on the capabilities of the drive.

If you don't have multiple CD or DVD drives to experiment with, you might be interested to hear of two crude solutions that have proved successful with some copy-protected audio discs:

- Stick a strip of tape on the disc to mask the outermost track. This track contains extra information intended to confuse computer CD drives. By masking the track, people have managed to obviate the confusion.

- Use a marker to color the outermost track on the disc dark so the laser of the drive won't read it.

Both of these techniques require a steady hand—and both constitute willful circumvention of the copy protection, possibly exposing those performing them to retribution under the DMCA.

A subtler means of bypassing copy protection made headlines in August 2003, when a Princeton PhD student published a paper that revealed that SunnComm's MediaMax CD3 copy-protection mechanism could be bypassed by holding down SHIFT when loading the CD on a Windows PC for the first time. Holding down SHIFT prevents the CD from automatically loading a driver used to protect the music. Holding down SHIFT might be interpreted as an active attempt to bypass the copy-protection mechanism. But you can also turn off the Autoplay feature for a CD drive permanently in the CD drive's Properties dialog box (shown here). Once you've done that, the CD3 copy-protection mechanism simply does nothing.

Chapter 4

Load Music onto Your iPod or iPod mini Using a Mac

How to...

- ■ Configure iTunes to suit your preferences
- ■ Identify the main elements in the iTunes interface
- ■ Choose suitable settings for ripping and encoding AAC, MP3, AIFF, and WAV files
- ■ Create, build, and manage your music library
- ■ Play back music with iTunes
- ■ Use the graphical equalizer to improve the sound of music
- ■ Synchronize your music library with your iPod automatically or manually
- ■ Listen to Audible.com spoken-word files on your iPod
- ■ Create custom playlists containing only the tracks you like
- ■ Use the Smart Playlist feature to create playlists based on your preferences
- ■ Share music and access shared music
- ■ Add artwork to songs
- ■ Listen to Internet radio

This chapter discusses how to use iTunes to enjoy digital audio on the Mac and manage your iPod or iPod mini. iTunes provides a graphical interface for ripping and encoding songs on CDs to digital audio files you can store and manipulate on your Mac, together with fast and easy synchronization with your iPod.

This chapter assumes you're using iTunes 4 or a later version on Mac OS X. iTunes 4 runs on Mac OS X 10.1.5 or a later version, but you need Mac OS X 10.2.4 or a later version if you want to use iTunes' features for sharing music with other users (or accessing the music they're sharing) and burning DVDs. For best results, upgrade to Panther (Mac OS X 10.3) or the latest version available.

iTunes contains a fair number of configuration options. Rather than lumping all the configuration options together into a heavy-going section you'll refuse to read, this chapter presents the configuration options as needed to accomplish particular tasks you're likely to want to undertake.

NOTE *iTunes for Windows (discussed in Chapter 5) works in much the same way as iTunes for the Mac—which shouldn't be a surprise, as Apple built iTunes for Windows on the basis of the very successful iTunes for the Mac. But because there are a fair number of differences between running iTunes on Windows and running iTunes on Mac OS X, this book covers the two operating systems in separate chapters rather than cramming them into a single chapter stuffed with ifs, buts, and digressions.*

One iTunes topic this chapter doesn't discuss is burning CDs and DVDs. You'll find a complete discussion of burning with iTunes (on both Mac OS X and Windows) in Chapter 9.

Configure iTunes on Your Mac

Launch iTunes by clicking the iTunes icon on the Dock or (if you've removed that icon) by choosing Go | Applications (or pressing COMMAND-SHIFT-A) and double-clicking the iTunes icon in your Applications folder.

If you've never used iTunes before on this Mac, iTunes launches the iTunes Setup Assistant. The Setup Assistant walks you through the setup process, in which you make the following decisions:

■ Whether to let iTunes connect to the Internet automatically to download information about CDs you insert in your CD drive or information about streaming broadcasts. In most cases, letting iTunes connect automatically is convenient, but not if you share a dial-up phone line that's often busy with voice calls.

■ Whether to have iTunes scan your hard disk for any music files so that it can add them to your music library. Scanning now is usually a good idea, but you may prefer to add files manually later (see "Add Songs to iTunes to Expand Your Music Library," later in this chapter).

This chapter shows screens from iTunes 4. If your Mac still has iTunes 3, run Software Update and upgrade to iTunes 4 to get the extra features it offers: Advanced Audio Coding (AAC), music sharing with other computers on the local network, DVD burning, using the iTunes Music Store, and more. Alternatively, download the latest version from www.apple.com/itunes/download.

Meet the iTunes Interface

After you launch iTunes, or after you finish the iTunes Setup Assistant, you see the iTunes interface (Figure 4-1):

If iTunes displays a dialog box telling you that you can't open iTunes because another user currently has it open, see "iTunes Won't Start on the Mac," in Chapter 17, for help on what to do.

These are the main parts of the iTunes interface. You'll use them later in this chapter and in subsequent chapters.

Source Pane

The Source pane contains the music sources available to you at any given time. They may include the following:

■ **Library**   This is your music library, which is typically stored on your local hard disk. You can rename it by double-clicking its title, typing the new name, and pressing RETURN or clicking elsewhere.

■ **Radio**   This entry lists Internet radio stations that you can access via your Internet connection.

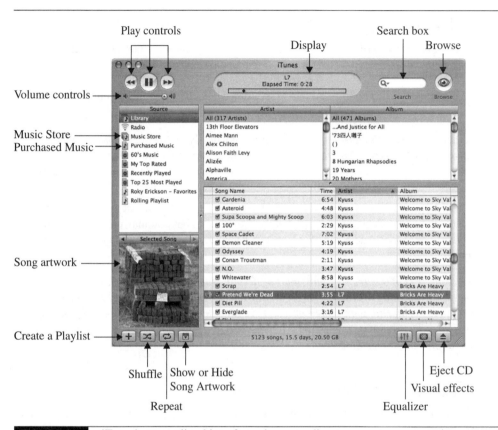

Play controls

Display

Search box

Browse

Volume controls

Music Store
Purchased Music

Song artwork

Create a Playlist

Shuffle | Show or Hide
Song Artwork

Repeat

Eject CD

Visual effects

Equalizer

FIGURE 4-1   iTunes's streamlined interface gives you direct access to your music.

- **Music Store**   Clicking this entry in the Source pane connects you to the iTunes Music Store via your Internet connection.

- **Purchased Music**   This special playlist contains all the songs you buy from the iTunes Music Store. This playlist doesn't appear until you buy your first song from the iTunes Music Store.

- **Audio CD**   If your Mac has an audio CD loaded in a CD drive, the CD appears in the Source pane. If iTunes can connect to the Internet to look up the title of the CD, the CD appears by name. Otherwise, it appears as "Audio CD."

- **iPods**   Any iPods connected to your Mac appear in the Source pane.

- ■ **Shared Music Libraries**   If your Mac is connected to a local network, and if other iTunes users are sharing music on the network, the shared music libraries appear here. If there's just one shared library, it appears under its name. If there are two or more shared libraries, they appear under a collapsible Shared Music entry.

- ■ **Smart Playlists**   iTunes starts you off with several *smart playlists*—playlists that automatically update themselves according to criteria programmed into them. The 60's Music smart playlist contains all songs whose Year tag is in the range 1960–1969. The My Top Rated smart playlist contains all songs you've assigned a rating of three stars or more. The Recently Played smart playlist contains all songs you've played in the last two weeks. The Top 25 Most Played smart playlist contains the 25 songs you've played most overall. You can customize these smart playlists, or create additional smart playlists of your own. See "Automatically Create Smart Playlists Based on Your Ratings and Preferences," later in this chapter.

- ■ **Playlists**   These are conventional (or "dumb") playlists—ones that don't automatically update themselves. You can create as many playlists as you want so that you can arrange songs in the order you want them and burn them to CD. You can change or delete a playlist at any time.

Browser Panes

The Browser panes let you quickly navigate by artist and album to the songs you want to play. You can toggle the display of the Browser panes by clicking the Browse button, pressing COMMAND-B, or choosing Edit | Show Browser or Edit | Hide Browser.

Songs List

The Songs list lets you select the song to play. Double-click a song to start playing it, and clear a song's check box to tell iTunes not to play it.

Choose Where to Store Your Music Library

Because your music library can contain dozens—or even hundreds—of gigabytes of music files, you must store it in a suitable location if you choose to keep all your music files in it. The alternative to keeping all your music files *in* your music library is to store in it references to where the files are located in other folders. Doing so enables you to minimize the size of your music library. But for maximum flexibility and to make sure you can access all the tracks in your music library all the time, keeping all your music files in your music library folder is best—if you can do so.

To change the location of your music library, follow these steps:

1. Press COMMAND-COMMA (or COMMAND-Y) or choose iTunes | Preferences to display the Preferences dialog box.

2. Click the Advanced button to display the Advanced sheet:

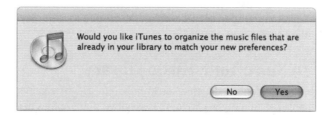

3. Click the Change button to display the Change Music Folder Location dialog box.

4. Navigate to the folder that will contain your music library, select the folder, and then click the Open button. iTunes closes the Change Music Folder Location and returns you to the Advanced sheet of the Preferences dialog box.

5. Click the OK button to close the Preferences dialog box.

   ■ iTunes displays the following dialog box, asking if you want iTunes to move your existing music library files to the folder you specified:

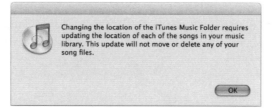

   ■ If you've told iTunes not to copy each song file you add to your music library to the music library's folder, iTunes displays the following dialog box when you change the location of the music library folder:

Click the OK button (there's no other choice). iTunes then displays the Updating Song Locations dialog box, showing its progress as it updates its records of the songs' locations.

6. To keep all of your music library files together in the new location, click the Yes button. You'll see the Organizing Files dialog box as iTunes organizes the files into the new location. To keep your existing music library files in their current locations but put any new files in the new location, click the No button.

NOTE   *To reset your music library folder to its default location (the iTunes/iTunes Music folder), click the Reset button on the Advanced sheet of the Preferences dialog box. Again, iTunes asks if you want to move your existing files to the new location. Click the Yes button or the No button, as appropriate.*

Choose Whether to Store All Song Files in Your Music Library

As mentioned in the previous section, iTunes can store references to where song files are located in other folders than your music library folder instead of creating a copy of each file in the music library folder. To make iTunes store references, clear the Copy Files To iTunes Music Folder When Adding To Library check box on the Advanced sheet of the Preferences dialog box.

Storing references is great when you have too little space free on your hard disk to accommodate your colossal music library. For example, if you have an iBook whose hard disk is bulging at the seams, you might choose to store in your music library references to music located on an external hard disk rather than trying to import a copy of each song. But you won't be able to play any song stored on the external hard disk when your iBook isn't connected to it.

CAUTION   *Before allowing iTunes to copy each song file to your music library, make sure you have plenty of hard-disk space. iTunes doesn't check that there's enough extra space to hold the copies of the song files, so using this option could run you out of hard-disk space and leave you with only some song files copied to your music library.*

Choose Whether iTunes Automatically Connects to the Internet

iTunes can automatically download CD information from the CD Database site on the Web (CDDB; www.cddb.com). This saves you a large amount of typing and is great if you have a permanent Internet connection or an Internet connection you can establish at any time. But if you'll need to rip and encode CDs when you have no Internet connection available, or if you prefer to enter the CD information manually (for example, to make sure it's letter-perfect), you can turn off this feature.

TIP   *You can also rip and encode songs when offline from CDDB, then go online, select the songs, and choose Advanced | Get CD Track Names to download the CD data and apply it to the songs.*

To choose whether iTunes automatically connects to the Internet to download CD data (artist, album, and track information), choose iTunes | Preferences or press COMMAND-COMMA or COMMAND-Y. On the General sheet of the Preferences dialog box, select or clear the Connect To Internet When Needed check box.

Change the Importing Settings in iTunes to Specify Audio Quality

Before you rip any CDs using iTunes, check that the settings are suitable for your needs. iTunes' default settings—to encode to AAC files at 128 Kbps in stereo—are a fair choice for defaults, but you may well want to change them. It's worth investing a little time in choosing the right settings for ripping and encoding, because ripping tracks more than once quickly becomes a severe waste of time.

NOTE *See Chapter 3 for a discussion of how audio compression works and why you need to use it; the differences between the AAC, MP3, AIFF, and WAV formats; how to choose a suitable bitrate and (for MP3) stereo settings for the files you encode; and more.*

To recap quickly, creating a high-quality compressed audio file involves several variables:

■ If the audio source is a CD, reading the CD accurately.

■ If the audio source is analog rather than digital, converting the analog signal to digital with minimal loss of quality.

■ Using an encoder capable of creating high-quality encodings. iTunes' encoders produce high quality results, so this shouldn't be a problem.

■ Choosing a suitable compression rate to save the right amount of data.

■ Making sure the data saved is as accurate as possible.

To check or change the importing settings, follow these steps:

1. Choose iTunes | Preferences or press COMMAND-COMMA to display the Preferences dialog box.

2. Click the Importing tab:

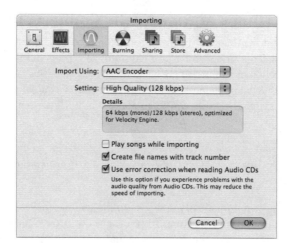

3. In the Import Using drop-down list, specify the file format you want to use by choosing the appropriate encoder:

   ■ The default setting is AAC Encoder, which creates compressed files in AAC format. AAC files combine high audio quality with compact size, making AAC the format you're most likely to want to try first.

   ■ The other setting you're likely to want to try is MP3 Encoder, which creates compressed files in the MP3 format. MP3 files have slightly lower audio quality than AAC files for the same file size, but you can use them with a wider variety of software applications and hardware players than AAC files.

   ■ AIFF files and WAV files are uncompressed audio files, so they take up a huge amount of space but have audio quality as high as the source. AIFF files are mostly used on Macs, while WAV files are mostly used on Windows. Sometimes you may want to use one or other of these settings when quality is paramount. To create AIFF files, choose AIFF Encoder. To create WAV files, choose WAV Encoder.

4. In the Setting drop-down list, choose the setting you want to use:

   ■ For the AAC Encoder, the Setting drop-down list offers the settings High Quality (128 Kbps) and Custom. When you select Custom, iTunes displays the AAC Encoder dialog box so you can specify custom settings. See "Choose Custom AAC Encoding Settings," next, for a discussion of these options.

   ■ For the MP3 Encoder, the Configuration drop-down list offers the settings Good Quality (128 Kbps), High Quality (160 Kbps), Higher Quality (192 Kbps), and Custom. When you select Custom, iTunes displays the MP3 Encoder dialog box so you can specify custom settings. See "Choose Custom MP3 Encoding Settings," later in this chapter, for a discussion of these options.

   ■ For the AIFF Encoder and the WAV Encoder, the Configuration drop-down list offers the settings Automatic and Custom. When you select Custom, iTunes displays the AIFF Encoder dialog box or the WAV Encoder dialog box (as appropriate) so you can specify custom settings. See "Choose Custom AIFF and WAV Encoding Settings," later in this chapter, for a discussion of these options.

5. If you want iTunes to play each CD as you import it, leave the Play Songs While Importing check box selected (it's selected by default). Listening to the CD may slow down the rate of ripping and encoding, so you may prefer not to use this option.

6. If you want iTunes to include track numbers in song names (creating names such as *01 Cortez the Killer* instead of *Cortez the Killer*), leave the Create File Names With Track Number check box selected (it's selected by default).

   ■ Including the track numbers in the filenames isn't necessary for iTunes itself to keep the tracks in order, as iTunes can use the track-number information in a track's tag. (Some utilities for downloading songs from an iPod can sort songs by tag information, too.) But you may want to include the numbers so that you can sort the songs easily into album order in the Finder.

   ■ Including the track number is useful for keeping tracks in order when you create MP3 CDs.

FIGURE 4-2 On the General sheet of the Preferences dialog box, specify what iTunes should do when you insert a CD.

Those are all the options on the Importing sheet. But a couple of options on the General sheet of the Preferences dialog box (see Figure 4-2) are also relevant to importing:

- In the On CD Insert drop-down list, choose the action you want iTunes to perform when you insert a CD: Show Songs, Begin Playing, Import Songs, or Import Songs And Eject. These settings are easy to understand, but bear in mind that Show Songs, Import Songs, and Import Songs And Eject all involve looking up the song names in CDDB (unless you've already played the CD and so caused iTunes to look them up), so iTunes will need to use your Internet connection.

- If you have a dial-up Internet connection, select the Connect To Internet When Needed check box if you want iTunes to be able to establish an Internet connection when it needs to look up data in CDDB.

Choose Custom AAC Encoding Settings

To choose custom AAC encoding settings, follow these steps:

1. On the Importing sheet of the Preferences dialog box, choose AAC Encoder in the Import Using drop-down list.

2. In the Setting drop-down list, choose the Custom item to display the AAC Encoder dialog box:

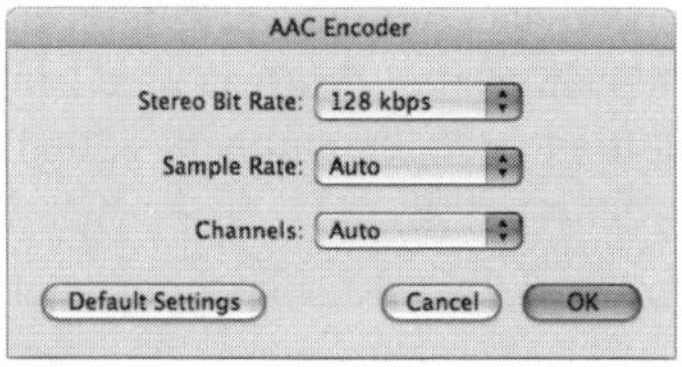

3. In the Stereo Bit Rate drop-down list, specify the bit rate. You can use from 16 Kbps to 320 Kbps. The default is 128 Kbps.

   ■ 128 Kbps provides high-quality audio suitable for general music listening. You may want to experiment with higher bitrates to see if you can detect a difference. If not, stick with 128 Kbps so as to get the largest possible amount of quality music on your iPod.

   ■ If you listen to spoken-word audio, experiment with the bitrates below 64 Kbps to see which bitrate delivers suitable quality for the material you listen to.

4. In the Sample Rate drop-down list, specify the sample rate by choosing Auto, 44.100 KHz, or 48.000 KHz. 44.100 KHz is the sample rate used by CD audio; unless you have a data source that uses a 48.000 KHz sampling rate, there's no point in choosing this option. For most purposes, you'll get best results by using the Auto setting (the default setting), which makes iTunes use a sampling rate that matches the input quality. For example, for CD-quality audio, iTunes uses the 44.100 KHz sampling rate.

5. In the Channels drop-down list, select Auto, Stereo, or Mono, as appropriate. In most cases, Auto (the default setting) is the best bet, as it makes iTunes choose stereo or mono as appropriate to the sound source. However, you may occasionally need to produce mono files from stereo sources.

6. Click the OK button to close the AAC Encoder dialog box.

Choose Custom MP3 Encoding Settings

To choose custom MP3 encoding settings, follow these steps:

1. On the Importing sheet of the Preferences dialog box, choose MP3 Encoder in the Import Using drop-down list.

2. In the Setting drop-down list, choose the Custom item to display the MP3 Encoder dialog box:

3. In the Stereo Bit Rate drop-down list, select the bitrate you want to use.

- The choices range from 16 Kbps to 320 Kbps. 16 Kbps produces shoddy-sounding audio even for the spoken word, but it may be useful when you need to get long passages of low-quality audio into a small file. At the other extreme, 320 Kbps produces audio high enough in quality that most people can't distinguish it from CD-quality audio.

- iTunes uses the bitrate you select as the exact bitrate for CBR encoding and as the minimum bitrate for VBR encoding.

- See the section "What Does CD-Quality Audio Mean?," in Chapter 3, for a discussion of CD-quality audio. See the section "Choose an Appropriate Compression Rate, Bitrate, and Stereo Settings," also in Chapter 3, for advice on choosing a compression rate that matches your needs.)

4. Select the Use Variable Bit Rate Recording check box if you want to create VBR-encoded files instead of CBR-encoded files.

- See the section "Choose Between CBR and VBR for MP3," in Chapter 3, for a discussion of CBR and VBR.

- If you select this check box, choose a suitable setting in the Quality drop-down list. The choices are Lowest, Low, Medium Low, Medium, Medium High, High, and Highest. iTunes uses the bitrates specified in the Stereo Bit Rate drop-down list as the guaranteed minimum bitrates. The Quality setting controls the amount of processing iTunes applies to making the file sound as close to the original as possible. More processing requires more processor cycles, which will make your Mac work harder. If your Mac is already working at full throttle, encoding will take longer.

5. In the Sample Rate drop-down list, set a sample rate manually only if you're convinced you need to do so.

- You might want to use a lower sample rate if you're encoding spoken-word audio rather than music and don't need such high fidelity.

- Choices range from 8 KHz to 48 KHz (higher than CD-quality audio, which uses 44.1 KHz).

- The default setting is Auto, which uses the same sample rate as does the music you're encoding. Using the same sample rate usually delivers optimal results.

6. In the Channels drop-down list, select Auto, Mono, or Stereo. The default setting is Auto, which uses mono for encoding mono sources and stereo for stereo sources.

7. In the Stereo Mode drop-down list, choose Normal Stereo or Joint Stereo. See the section "Choose Between Normal Stereo and Joint Stereo for MP3," in Chapter 3, for a discussion of the difference between normal stereo and joint stereo. If you select Mono in the Channels drop-down list, the Stereo Mode drop-down list becomes unavailable because its options don't apply to mono.

8. Select or clear the Smart Encoding Adjustments check box and the Filter Frequencies Below 10 Hz check box, as appropriate. These check boxes are selected by default. In most cases, you'll do best to leave them selected.

    ■ Smart Encoding Adjustments allows iTunes to tweak your custom settings to improve them if you've chosen an inappropriate combination.

    ■ As discussed in Chapter 3, frequencies below 10 Hz are infrasound and are of interest only to animals such as elephants, so filtering them out makes sense for humans.

NOTE *To restore iTunes to using its default settings for encoding MP3 files, click the Use Default Settings button in the MP3 Encoder dialog box.*

9. Click the OK button to close the MP3 Encoder dialog box.

10. Click the OK button to close the Importing sheet of the Preferences dialog box.

Choose Custom AIFF and WAV Encoding Settings

Other than creating different file formats, the AIFF Encoder dialog box (shown on the left in Figure 4-3) and the WAV Encoder dialog box (shown on the right in Figure 4-3) offer the same settings. This isn't surprising, because AIFFs and WAVs are essentially the same apart from the file header, which distinguishes the file formats from each other.

In either of these dialog boxes, you can choose the following settings:

■ **Sample Rate**   Choose Auto (the default setting) to encode at the same sample rate as the original you're ripping. Otherwise, choose a value from the range available (8 KHz to 48 KHz).

■ **Sample Size**   Select Auto to have iTunes automatically match the sample size to that of the source. Otherwise, select 8 Bit or 16 Bit, as appropriate. PCM audio uses 16 bits, so if you're encoding files from CDs, iTunes automatically uses a 16-bit sample size.

■ **Channels**   Select Auto (the default setting) to encode mono files from mono sources and stereo files from stereo sources. Otherwise, select Mono or Stereo, as appropriate.

AIFF Encoder	WAV Encoder
Sample Rate: Auto	Sample Rate: Auto
Sample Size: Auto	Sample Size: Auto
Channels: Auto	Channels: Auto
Default Settings Cancel OK	Default Settings Cancel OK

FIGURE 4-3   If you choose to encode to AIFF or WAV files, you can set encoding options in the AIFF Encoder dialog box (left) or the WAV Encoder dialog box (right).

Change the Columns Displayed to Show the Information You Need

By default, iTunes displays the following columns: Song Name, Time, Artist, Album, Genre, My Rating, Play Count, and Last Played. (The Play Count item stores the number of times you've played the song in iTunes. iTunes uses this information to determine your favorite tracks—for example, to decide which tracks Smart Playlist should add to a playlist. You can also use this information yourself if you so choose. The other items are self-explanatory.)

You can change the columns displayed for the current item (for example, your music library or a playlist) by using either of two techniques.

To change the display of multiple columns in the same operation, press COMMAND-J or choose Edit | View Options to display the View Options dialog box (Figure 4-4). The icon and label in the upper-left corner of the dialog box indicate which item's view you're customizing—for example, Library or Music Store. Select the check boxes for the columns you want to display, and then click the OK button to close the dialog box and apply your choices.

To change the display of a single column in the current item, right-click or CTRL-click the heading of one of the columns currently displayed. iTunes displays a menu of the available columns, showing a check mark next to those currently displayed. Select an unchecked column to display it. Select a checked column to remove it from the display.

From the context menu, you can also select the Auto Size Column command to automatically resize the column whose heading you clicked so the column's width best fits its contents. Select the Auto Size All Columns command to automatically resize all columns like this.

> **TIP**
>
> *You can change the column width by dragging a column heading to the left or right.*

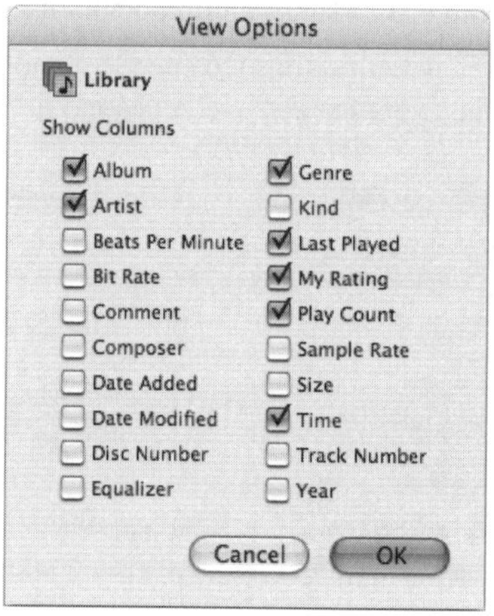

View Options

🎵 Library

Show Columns

☑ Album   ☑ Genre
☑ Artist   ☐ Kind
☐ Beats Per Minute   ☑ Last Played
☐ Bit Rate   ☑ My Rating
☐ Comment   ☑ Play Count
☐ Composer   ☐ Sample Rate
☐ Date Added   ☐ Size
☐ Date Modified ☑ Time
☐ Disc Number   ☐ Track Number
☐ Equalizer   ☐ Year

[Cancel]   [OK]

FIGURE 4-4   Use the View Options dialog box to choose which columns iTunes displays for the current item.

Create, Build, and Manage Your iTunes Music Library

Before you can load music onto your iPod, you need to create your music library in iTunes. Most likely, you'll start by ripping some of your CDs and encoding them to AAC files or MP3 files. You may also need to add to your music library those songs you already have on your Mac, consolidate your music library (putting the whole library in one folder), and change the tags on some AAC files or MP3 files so iTunes and your iPod list them correctly.

Rip and Encode Songs from CDs

As discussed in Chapter 2, there are two steps to getting the audio off a CD and into a digital audio file your computer can use: ripping the audio from the CD, and encoding it to the file (for example, an MP3 file). But because most people speak simply of "ripping" a CD rather than ripping and encoding it, this book also uses the phrase "rip a CD" rather than "rip and encode a CD." To make things even more complicated, iTunes uses the term "import a CD," so this book uses that term when referring to iTunes-specific features.

TIP   *To rip a stack of CDs as quickly as possible, select the Import Songs And Eject option in the On CD Insert drop-down list on the General sheet of the Preferences dialog box (COMMAND-COMMA or iTunes | Preferences), and clear the Play Songs While Importing check box on the Importing sheet.*

To rip and encode a CD to MP3 files, follow these steps:

1. Start iTunes from the Dock or from any convenient shortcut.

2. Insert in your Mac's CD drive the CD whose contents you want to rip and encode.

3. Enter the CD details—the CD title, artist name, song titles, and genre.

   ■ The easiest way to enter the details is to let iTunes connect automatically to the Internet, download the CD details automatically, and enter them in the appropriate fields. (See "Choose Whether iTunes Automatically Connects to the Internet," earlier in this chapter, for details on how to control whether iTunes connects automatically.)

   ■ Alternatively, choose Advanced | Get CD Track Names to force iTunes to search CDDB for the information.

   ■ If you don't have an Internet connection, enter the data manually. See the sidebar "Tag Your Song Files Most Efficiently by Hand," a little later in this chapter, for suggestions on how to proceed.

4. By default, iTunes selects the check box for each song on the CD. Clear the check boxes for any songs you don't want to rip and encode. To select or clear all the check boxes, COMMAND-click any check box.

5. Click the Import button to start the importing process. iTunes displays its progress, as shown here. If you need to stop the import process, click the Import button again.

Join Tracks Together Without Gaps

iTunes' default settings are to create a separate file (AAC, MP3, AIFF, or WAV, depending on your preferences) from each song on CDs you rip. For most CDs, this works well. But sometimes you'll want to rip multiple tracks from a CD into a single file so they play back without a break. For example, some CDs are produced so one song runs into the next.

To rip two or more tracks from a CD into a single file, select the tracks, and then choose Advanced | Join CD Tracks. iTunes brackets the tracks, as shown in Figure 4-5. These tracks then rip to a single file.

 Use the Join CD Tracks command to rip two or more tracks to a single file.

How to ... Submit CD Information to CDDB Using iTunes

If a CD you want to rip turns out not to have an entry in CDDB, you can submit an entry yourself. Users submitting entries like this have added many of the entries in CDDB for older or less widely known CDs. Mainstream entries are submitted by the record companies themselves: they submit a listing to CDDB (and other online CD-information services, such as WindowsMedia.com) as a matter of course when they release a new CD.

At this writing, CDDB contains entries for an enormous number of CDs—so unless you have an unusual CD, chances are any CD you want to rip already has an entry in CDDB. You may find that your CD is listed under a slightly different title or artist name than you're expecting—for example, the artist might be listed as *Sixpack, Joe* rather than *Joe Sixpack*. Check carefully for any close matches before submitting an entry so you don't waste your time.

You may also find CDDB contains two or more entries for the same CD. This can happen when two or more people simultaneously submit information for a CD that doesn't have an entry, or someone submits information for a previously existing selection. The people who run CDDB discard duplicate entries routinely when they find them, but given how many CD entries CDDB contains, it's not surprising that they're unable to catch all duplicates. When you run into a duplicate, you need to guess from the names shown which entry matches your CD.

When submitting an entry to CDDB, type the CD title, artist name, and song titles carefully using standard capitalization, and double-check all of the information before you submit it. Otherwise, if your entry is accepted and entered in CDDB, anyone who looks up that CD will get the misspellings or wrong information you entered.

To submit an entry to CDDB, follow these steps:

1. Insert the CD in your CD drive and check that CDDB doesn't already have an entry for it.

2. Enter the song names in the Song Name column.

3. Choose Advanced | Submit CD Track Names to display the CD Info dialog box:

4. Enter as much information as possible in the Artist, Composer, Album, Disc Number, Genre, and Year fields. Select the Compilation CD check box if the CD is a compilation rather than a work by an individual artist.

5. Establish an Internet connection if you need to do so manually.

6. Click the OK button. iTunes connects to CDDB and submits the information. iTunes also enters the information in the appropriate columns for the CD.

NOTE   *If you made a mistake with the tracks you joined, select one or more of the joined tracks, and then choose Advanced | Unjoin CD Tracks to separate the tracks again.*

Add Songs to iTunes to Expand Your Music Library

You can add songs to iTunes in any of the following ways:

- Import the songs from CD as described in the section "Rip and Encode Songs from CDs," earlier in this chapter. Alternatively, import the songs from another sound source.

- Drag one or more song files, folders, or volumes and drop them in the iTunes main window.

NOTE   *If you left the Copy Files To iTunes Music Folder When Adding To Library check box (on the Advanced sheet of the Preferences dialog box) selected, iTunes copies the song files to your music library. If you cleared this check box, iTunes simply adds to the library references to the song files.*

- Choose File | Add To Library and use the Add To Library dialog box to specify the file or the folder or volume of songs you want to add. Select the item, and then click the Choose button.

- Drag one or more files, folders, or volumes to the iTunes icon in the Dock. Once you've dropped the files, folders, or volumes on a representation of iTunes, Mac OS X opens or activates iTunes, which adds the song files to the music library and starts playing the first of them.

Delete Songs from Your Music Library

To delete songs from your music library, select them, and then either press DELETE or issue a Clear command from the Edit menu or the context menu. By default, iTunes displays a confirmation dialog box to check that you want to remove the songs. Click the Yes button to delete the tracks. To turn off the confirmation, select the Do Not Ask Me Again check box before dismissing the dialog box.

How to ... Tag Your Song Files Most Efficiently by Hand

Downloading CD information from CDDB is usually the fastest way of entering tag information in your song files. But you may sometimes need to enter tag information manually or tweak the CDDB information. You may also want to specify an equalizer preset, volume adjustment, or rating when ripping the songs so that you don't have to specify this information later.

Here's the best way to proceed:

- If you need to change only the artist, composer, album, genre, disc number, or year, or if you need to specify whether the CD is a compilation CD, right-click the entry for the CD in the Source pane and use the CD Info dialog box. Change the appropriate information, and then click the OK button to close the dialog box and apply the change.

- To change any of this information and other information for all the songs, select all the songs (press COMMAND-A or choose Edit | Select All) and display the Multiple Song Information dialog box (shown in Figure 4-7, later in this chapter) by pressing COMMAND-I, or by issuing a Get Info command from the File menu or the shortcut menu. Enter the appropriate information, and then click the OK button to close the dialog box and apply the changes.

- To enter the song names or other song-specific information, select the song and issue a Get Info command from the File menu or the shortcut menu to display the Song Information dialog box. Change the appropriate fields on the Info tab (shown in Figure 4-6, later in this chapter) or set the volume, equalizer preset, rating, start time, or stop time on the Options tab. Then click the Previous button to move on to the previous song, the Next button to move on to the next song, or the OK button to close the dialog box.

If any of the songs are located in your iTunes music folder, iTunes displays the following dialog box to tell you so and ask if you want to move these files to the Trash. Select the Yes button, the No button, or the Cancel button as appropriate.

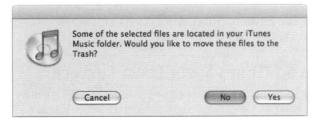

Consolidate Your Music Library So You Can Always Access All Its Songs

As you saw in "Choose Whether to Store All Song Files in Your Music Library," earlier in this chapter, if you clear the Copy Files To iTunes Music Folder When Adding To Library check box on the Advanced sheet of the iTunes Preferences dialog box, iTunes places in the music library only a pointer to the file. When your external drives, network drives, or removable media aren't available (for example, when you grab your iBook and head over to a friend's house for a night of gaming), the songs stored on those drives or media won't be available.

To make sure you can play the music you want wherever you want, you can *consolidate* your music library, making iTunes copy all the files currently outside your iTunes music folder to the music folder. Consolidation is new in iTunes 3.

Don't rush into consolidating your music library without understanding its implications:

- Consolidation can take a long time, depending on the number of files to be copied and the speed of the network connection you're using. Don't consolidate your library just as the airport shuttle is about to arrive.

- The drive that holds your music library must have enough space free to hold all your songs. If lack of space was the reason you didn't copy the songs to your music library in the first place, you probably don't want to consolidate your library.

- Songs on removable media such as CDs or Zip disks won't be copied unless the medium is in the drive at the time.

To consolidate your music library, follow these steps:

1. Choose Advanced | Consolidate Library. iTunes displays the following dialog box:

2. Click the Consolidate button. iTunes displays the Copying Files dialog box as it copies the files to your music library.

Tag Your Songs So iTunes Sorts Them Correctly

Each AAC file and MP3 file (and most other compressed audio files, such as Windows Media Audio files and Ogg Vorbis files) contains a *tag*—a container with a number of slots for different types of information, from the song name, artist name, and album name to the year and the genre.

iTunes displays some of this information by default in its Artist, Album, and Genre columns, but it can handle files without tag information. Your iPod, on the other hand, requires the artist, song, and album information to be supplied so it can add a song to its database and allow you to access it.

The easiest way to add tag information to an AAC file or MP3 file is by downloading the information from CDDB when you rip the CD. But sometimes you'll need to enter (or change) tag information manually to make iTunes sort the files correctly.

NOTE   *Often, MP3 files distributed illegally on the Internet lack tag information or include incorrect tags.*

To edit the tag information for a single song, select it and issue a Get Info command (press COMMAND-I or choose Get Info from the File menu or the shortcut menu), and then work on the Info tab of the Song Information dialog box (see Figure 4-6; this dialog box's title bar shows the name of the song).

TIP   *If your music library contains many untagged or mistagged files, you may need heavier-duty tagging features than iTunes provides. Chapter 6 discusses the best options available for retagging files.*

To edit the tag information for multiple songs at once, select the songs by SHIFT-clicking (to select contiguous songs) or COMMAND-clicking (to select noncontiguous songs), and then press COMMAND-I or choose File | Get Info. In the Multiple Song Information dialog box (Figure 4-7), enter the information common to the songs you selected.

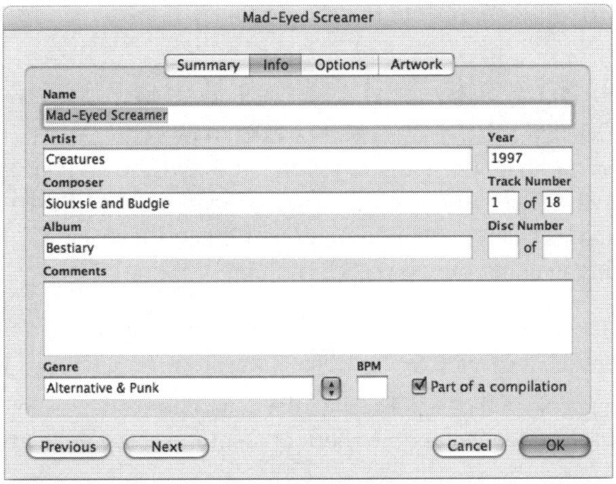

FIGURE 4-6   Use the Info tab of the Song Information dialog box to edit the tag information for a single song.

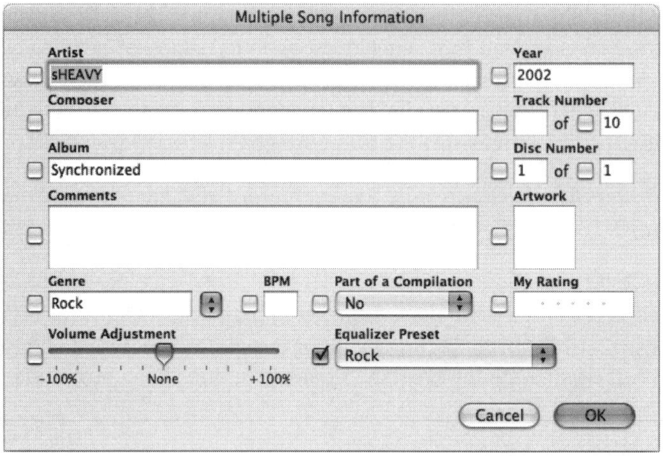

FIGURE 4-7 Instead of editing tag information one song at a time, you can edit tag information for multiple songs at once by using the Multiple Song Information dialog box.

NOTE   *By default, when you issue a Get Info command with multiple songs selected, iTunes displays a dialog box to check that you want to edit the information for multiple songs. Click the Yes button to proceed; click the Cancel button to cancel. If you're less adept with the Mac interface, this double-check may help prevent you from entering the wrong tag information for multiple songs. But if you frequently want to edit tag information for multiple songs, select the Do Not Ask Me Again check box in the confirmation dialog box to turn off confirmations in the future.*

Apply Ratings to Songs to Tell iTunes Which Music You Like

iTunes' My Rating feature lets you assign a rating of one star to five stars to each song in your music library. You can then sort the songs by rating or tell Smart Playlist to add only songs of a certain ranking or better to a playlist. (See "Automatically Create Smart Playlists Based on Your Ratings and Preferences," later in this chapter, for a discussion of Smart Playlist.)

You can apply a rating in either of two ways:

■ Right-click (or CTRL-click) a song, choose My Rating from the shortcut menu, and select the appropriate number of stars from the submenu.

■ Use the My Rating box on the Options tab of the Song Information dialog box (COMMAND-I or Get Info from the File menu or the shortcut menu) to specify the number of stars.

You can also rate a song on third-generation and later iPods. See "Rate Songs on Your iPod," in Chapter 2, for instructions.

Enjoy Music with iTunes

This section discusses what you need to know to enjoy music on your Mac with iTunes: how to play music back, how to use the graphical equalizer to improve the sound of the music, how to fade one song into another, and how to skip the boring start or end of a song.

Browse Quickly by Using the Browser Panes

Use the Browser panes (shown in Figure 4-1, earlier in this chapter) to browse quickly by artist or album. You can toggle the display of the Browser panes by clicking the Browse button, pressing COMMAND-B, or choosing Edit | Show Browser or Edit | Hide Browser. Once the Browser panes are displayed, click an item in the Artist column to display the albums by that artist in the Album column, and then click an item in the Albums column to display that album in the lower pane.

As well as browsing by artist and album, you can browse by genre (Figure 4-8). This capability can be useful when you want to find particular types of songs, because it makes iTunes display only the artists and albums whose songs are tagged with the genre you choose. When you don't want to restrict the view by genre, select the All item at the top of the Genre pane so that you see all genres at once.

FIGURE 4-8   Select the Show Genre When Browsing check box on the General sheet of the Preferences dialog box to enable yourself to browse your songs by genre as well as artist and album.

To turn browsing by genre on or off, press COMMAND-COMMA (or COMMAND-Y) or choose iTunes | Preferences to display the Preferences dialog box, select or clear the Show Genre When Browsing check box on the General sheet, and then click the OK button.

NOTE *The line of text at the bottom of the full iTunes window shows you how many songs are in the current selection and how long they last. This readout has two formats:* 5738 songs, 17.4 days, 22.98 GB *and* 5738 songs, 17:10:06:58 total time, 22.98 GB. *To toggle between the two formats, click the songs-and-time display.*

Play Back Music with iTunes

Playing back music with iTunes is straightforward:

- Navigate to the album, playlist, or song you want to play, select it, and then click the Play button.

- Drag the diamond on the progress bar in the display to scroll forward or backward through the current track.

- Use the Shuffle button to shuffle the order of the tracks in the current album or playlist. (To change whether iTunes shuffles by song or by album, select the Song option button or the Album option button on the Advanced sheet of the Preferences dialog box.) To reshuffle the current playlist, OPTION-click the Shuffle button.

- Use the Repeat button to repeat the current song or the current playlist.

- If you've scrolled the Song list so that the current song isn't visible, press COMMAND-L to quickly scroll back to where the current song is.

- To open a Finder window to the folder that contains the selected song file, press COMMAND-R.

- To toggle the display of the artwork, click the Show Or Hide Song Artwork button, press COMMAND-G, or choose Edit | Show Artwork or Edit | Hide Artwork.

- You can also control iTunes by right-clicking or CTRL-clicking its Dock icon and making the appropriate choice from the shortcut menu:

Search for Particular Songs

Browsing for songs works well, but sometimes you may need to search for particular songs. You can also turn up interesting collections of unrelated songs by searching on a word that appears somewhere in the artist name, song name, or album name.

To search all categories of information, type the search text in the Search box and press RETURN. To constrain the search to Artists, Albums, Composers, or Songs, click the drop-down button and make the appropriate choice from the menu:

Then type the search text and press RETURN to search.

To clear the Search box after searching, click the X button:

Control iTunes via Keyboard Shortcuts

As you've seen so far in this book, iTunes has a straightforward graphical interface that gives you easy access to almost all of iTunes' features via the mouse. But you can also control most of iTunes' features by using the keyboard. This can be useful both when your mouse is temporarily out of reach and when you've reduced the iTunes window to its small size or minute size, and thus hidden some of the controls.

Table 4-1 lists the keyboard shortcuts you can use to control iTunes. Most of these shortcuts work in any of iTunes' three display modes (maximized, small, and minute), but the table notes the shortcuts that work only in some modes.

Keystroke	Action
RETURN	Plays the selected song.
UP ARROW	Increases the volume.
DOWN ARROW	Decreases the volume.
COMMAND-1	Toggles the display of the iTunes main window.
COMMAND-2	Toggles the display of the Equalizer window.
SPACEBAR	Plays/pauses the song.
RIGHT ARROW	Skips to the next song.
LEFT ARROW	Skips to the previous song.
COMMAND–RIGHT ARROW	Skips to the next song.
COMMAND–LEFT ARROW	Skips to the previous song.
COMMAND-OPTION–LEFT ARROW	Rewinds the song.
COMMAND-OPTION–RIGHT ARROW	Fast-forwards the song.
OPTION–RIGHT ARROW	Skips to the next album in the list.
OPTION–LEFT ARROW	Skips to the previous album in the list.
SHIFT–UP ARROW	Turns the iTunes volume to maximum. This keyboard shortcut doesn't work when iTunes is maximized; instead, it extends the selection to the next track in the current list (or reduces the existing selection by one song downward).
SHIFT–DOWN ARROW	Mutes iTunes. This keyboard shortcut doesn't work when iTunes is maximized; instead, it reduces the existing selection by one song upward in the current list (or extends the existing selection by one song downward).
COMMAND-OPTION–UP ARROW	Toggles muting (even with iTunes maximized).
COMMAND-M	Minimizes iTunes.
COMMAND-U	Displays the Open Stream dialog box.
COMMAND-T	Toggles the Visualizer on and off.
COMMAND-F	Toggles full-screen mode on the Visualizer.

TABLE 4-1   Keyboard Shortcuts for iTunes on the Mac

Accompany Your Music with Visualizations

Like many music applications, iTunes can produce stunning visualizations to accompany your music. You can display visualizations at any of three sizes within the iTunes window (which can provide visual distraction while you work or play) or display them full-screen to make your Mac the life of the party.

Here's how to use visualizations:

- Set the size to use by choosing Visualizer | Small, Visualizer | Medium, or Visualizer | Large. If you want the visualizations to start in full-screen mode, choose Visualizer | Full Screen.
- To start a visualization of the size you specified, press COMMAND-T or choose Visualizer | Turn Visualizer On.
- To turn a windowed visualization off, press COMMAND-T or choose Visualizer | Turn Visualizer Off.
- To launch full-screen visualizations, press COMMAND-F or choose Visualizer | Full Screen.
- To stop full-screen visualizations, click your mouse button anywhere or press ESC or COMMAND-T.

Configure Visualizations to Get the Best Results

iTunes even lets you configure visualizations to make them look as good as possible on your Mac. To configure visualizations, follow these steps:

1. If iTunes is in small mode or minute mode, click the green button on the window frame to switch iTunes to maximized mode.

2. Start a song playing if you're currently running in silent mode.

3. Press COMMAND-T or choose Visualizer | Turn Visualizer On to start a visualization running (unless you have one running already).

4. Click the Options button in the upper-right corner of the maximized iTunes window to display the Visualizer Options dialog box:

5. Select and clear the check boxes to specify the options you want:
   - **Display Frame Rate**   Controls whether iTunes displays the frame rate (the number of frames being generated each second) superimposed on the upper-left corner of the visualization. This check box is cleared by default. The frame rate is useless information that adds nothing to the visualization, but it can be useful as a point of reference. For example, you may want to compare the visualization frame rates generated by different Macs, or you might want to try the Faster But Rougher Display option (discussed in a moment) to see how much difference it produces. Bear in mind that the frame rate will vary depending on the size of the visualization window, the complexity of the visualization, and what other tasks your Mac is working on at the time.

- **Cap Frame Rate At 30 Fps**   Controls whether iTunes stops the frame from exceeding 30 frames per second. This check box is selected by default. iTunes is configured to cap the frame rate to reduce the demands on the visualization on your Mac's graphics card and processor. The cap is at 30 fps because most people find 30 fps provides smooth and wonderful visualizations—so there's no point in trying to crank out extra frames.

- **Always Display Song Info**   Controls whether iTunes displays the song information overlaid on the visualization all the time or just at the beginning of a song and when you change the visualizer size while playing a song. This check box is cleared by default.

- **Use OpenGL**   Controls whether iTunes uses OpenGL, a graphics-rendering system, to create the visualizations. This check box is selected by default; leave it selected for best results.

- **Faster But Rougher Display**   Lets you tell iTunes to lower the quality of the visualizations to increase the frame rate. This check box is cleared by default. You may want to try selecting this check box on a less powerful Mac if you find the visualizations are too slow.

TIP   *You can also trigger most of these options from the keyboard while a visualization is playing, without displaying the Visualizer Options dialog box. Press F to toggle the frame rate display, press T to toggle frame-rate capping, press I to toggle the display of song information, and press D to restore the default settings.*

6. Click the OK button to close the Visualizer Options dialog box.

TIP   *You can change the information shown in the display window by clicking the items in it. Click the top line to move among the song title, the artist's name, and the album title; click the Play icon at the left of the display window to toggle between the track information and the equalization graph; and click the time readout to move among Elapsed Time, Remaining Time, and Total Time.*

Choose Crossfading and Sound Enhancer Settings

The Effects sheet of the Preferences dialog box (Figure 4-9) offers options for crossfading playback and changing the Sound Enhancer.

- **Crossfade Playback**   Makes iTunes fade in the start of the next track as the current track is about to end. This option lets you eliminate gaps between songs the way most DJs do. Drag the slider to increase or decrease the length of time that's crossfaded. This check box is selected by default; turn off crossfading if you don't like it.

- **Sound Enhancer**   Applies iTunes' sound enhancement to the music being played back. Experiment with different settings on the Low–High scale by dragging the slider to see which setting sounds best to you—or turn off sound enhancement if you don't like it (this check box is selected by default). Sound enhancement can make treble sounds appear brighter and can add to the effect of stereo separation, but the results don't suit everybody. You may prefer to adjust the sound manually by using the graphical equalizer, as described in the next section.

| **FIGURE 4-9** | Choose playback options on the Effects sheet of the Preferences dialog box. |

Use the Graphical Equalizer to Make Music Sound Great

iTunes includes a graphical equalizer that you can use to change the sound of the music (or other audio) you're playing. You can apply an equalization directly to the playlist you're currently playing, much as you would apply an equalization manually to a physical amplifier or receiver. But you can also apply a specific equalization to each song in your iTunes music library. Once you've done this, iTunes always uses that equalization when playing that song, no matter which equalization is currently applied to iTunes itself. After playing a song that has an equalization specified, iTunes switches back to the previous equalization for the next song that doesn't have an equalization specified.

Apply an Equalization to the Current Playlist

To apply an equalization to the current playlist, display the Equalizer window by choosing Window | Equalizer or pressing COMMAND-2:

Select the equalization from the drop-down list. If you're playing music, you'll hear the effect of the new equalization in a second or two.

Specify an Equalization for an Individual Song

To specify the equalization iTunes should use for a particular song, follow these steps:

1. Select the song in your music library or in a playlist.

NOTE *It doesn't matter whether you apply the equalization to the song in the music library or in a playlist, because applying the equalization even in a playlist affects the song in the music library. So if you can access a song more easily through a playlist than through your music library, start from the playlist.*

2. Press COMMAND-I, or choose Get Info from the File menu or the shortcut menu, to display the Song Information dialog box.

3. Click the Options tab to display the Options tab:

Wayward Bob

Summary Info **Options** Artwork

Volume Adjustment: ———●———
-100%   None   +100%

Equalizer Preset: Electronic

My Rating: ★★★ · ·

☐ Start Time: 0:00
☐ Stop Time: 4:39.127

Previous Next   Cancel OK

4. Select the equalization for the song in the Equalizer Preset drop-down list.

5. Choose other options as necessary, and then click the OK button to close the Song Information dialog box. Alternatively, click the Prev Song button or the Next Song button to display the information for the previous song or next song in the Song Information dialog box.

NOTE *If the equalization you apply to a song is one of the equalizations built into your iPod, your iPod also automatically uses the equalization for playing back the track. But if the equalization is a custom one your iPod doesn't have, your iPod can't use it. Your iPod doesn't pick up custom equalizations you create in iTunes.*

Create a Custom Equalization That Sounds Good to You

The preset equalizations in iTunes span a wide range of musical types—but even if there's one named after the type of music you're currently listening to, you may not like the effects it produces. When this happens, try all the other equalizations—however unsuitable their names may make them seem—to see if any of them just happens to sound great with this type of music. (For example, some people swear the Classical equalization is perfect for many Grateful Dead tracks.) If none of them suits you, create a custom equalization that delivers the goods.

To create a new custom equalization, follow these steps:

1. Drag the frequency sliders to the appropriate positions for the sound you want the equalization to deliver. When you change the first slider in the current preset, the drop-down list displays Manual.

2. If appropriate, drag the Preamp slider to a different level. For example, you might want to boost the preamp level on all the songs to which you apply a certain equalization.

3. Choose Make Preset from the drop-down list. iTunes displays the Make Preset dialog box:

Make Preset
New Preset Name:
Neolithic
Cancel   OK

4. Enter the name for the equalization and click the OK button.

You can then apply your equalization from the drop-down list as you would any other preset equalization.

Delete and Rename Preset Equalizations

If you don't like a preset equalization, you can delete it. If you find an equalization's name unsuitable, you can rename it.

To delete or rename an equalization, follow these steps:

1. Select the Edit List item from the drop-down list in the Equalizer window. iTunes displays the Edit Presets dialog box:

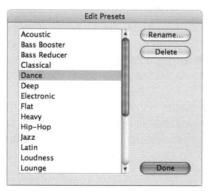

2. Select the preset equalization you want to affect.

3. To rename the equalization, follow these steps:

   A. Click the Rename button to display the Rename dialog box.

   B. Type the new name in the New Preset Name text box.

   C. Click the OK button. iTunes displays a dialog box like this, asking whether you want to change all songs currently set to use this equalization under its current name to use the equalization under the new name you've just specified:

   D. Click the Yes button or the No, button as appropriate.

4. To delete a preset equalization, click the Delete button. iTunes displays a dialog box like this, asking you to confirm the deletion:

   Click Yes or No, as appropriate. To stop iTunes from confirming the deletion of preset equalizations, select the Do Not Warn Me Again check box before clicking Yes or No.

Skip a Song's Boring Intro or Outro

If you disagree with the producer of a song about when the song should begin or end, use the Start Time and Stop Time controls on the Options page of the Song Information dialog box to specify how much of the track to lop off. This trimming works both in iTunes and on your iPod.

To trim the intro, in the Start Time text box, enter the point at which you want the song to start. For example, enter **1:15** to skip the first minute and a quarter of a song. When you start typing in the Start Time text box, iTunes selects the Start Time check box for you, so you don't need to select it manually.

Similarly, you can change the value in the Stop Time text box to stop the song playing before its end. By default, the Stop Time text box contains a time showing when the song ends, down to thousandths of a second—for example, 4:56:769. When you reduce this time, iTunes automatically selects the Stop Time check box.

TIP *When skipping an intro or outro isn't enough, you can edit a song file down to only that part you want. See Chapter 6 for details.*

Synchronize Your Music Library with Your iPod

By default, iTunes synchronizes all the changes you make to your music library with your iPod. When you buy a couple of CDs and rip them to compressed files in your music library, iTunes adds them to your iPod the next time you synchronize. If you build a new playlist, iTunes adds it to your iPod. And if you delete your playlists in iTunes in a fit of pique, they'll disappear from your iPod at its next synchronization.

These default settings work well provided your iPod has enough free disk space to contain your entire music library. If not, you'll probably prefer to control synchronization manually, as described in this section.

To synchronize, connect your iPod to your Mac as described in "Connect Your iPod to Your Mac," in Chapter 2, either directly via a FireWire cable or via the iPod Dock. When iTunes detects your iPod, it displays an entry for it in the Source pane. When this entry is selected, as in Figure 4-10, the lower-right corner of iTunes displays a Display Options For Player button and an Eject iPod button. Your desktop also displays an icon for your iPod. You can eject your iPod by dragging this icon to the trash.

4

TIP *If you make changes to your music library after iTunes has automatically updated your iPod but before you've unplugged your iPod, you can force an update by choosing File | Update Songs on iPod, where iPod is the name assigned to your iPod.*

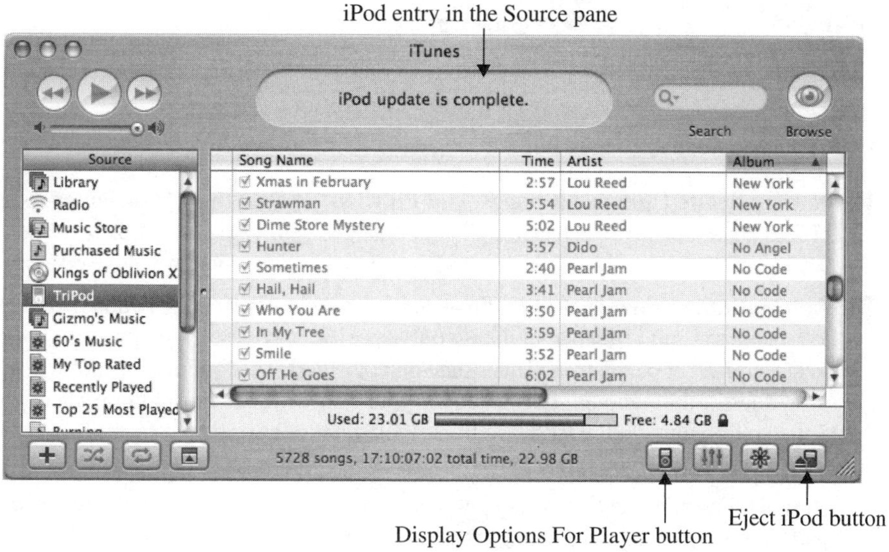

FIGURE 4-10   iTunes displays your iPod in the Source pane, together with buttons for manipulating it.

Control Synchronization to Get the Music You Want on Your iPod

If your iPod's default synchronization settings don't agree with you, change them. To do so, follow these steps:

1. Connect your iPod to your Mac as usual.

2. Select the iPod icon in the Source pane.

3. Click the Display Options For Player button in the lower-right corner of the iTunes window to display the iPod Preferences dialog box:

> **iPod Preferences**
>
> ● Automatically update all songs and playlists
> ○ Automatically update selected playlists only:
>
> ☐ Purchased Music
> ☐ 60's Music
> ☐ My Top Rated
> ☐ Recently Played
> ☐ Top 25 Most Played
>
> ○ Manually manage songs and playlists
>
> ☑ Open iTunes when attached
> ☐ Enable disk use
> ☐ Only update checked songs
>
> (Cancel) (OK)

4. Choose the appropriate option button:

   ■ **Automatically Update All Songs And Playlists**   Select this option button to have iTunes automatically synchronize all your changes with your iPod. This is the default setting and works well—provided that your music library fits on your iPod.

   ■ **Automatically Update Selected Playlists Only**   Select this option button if you want to be able to limit iTunes to updating only specific playlists. This option allows you to keep different playlists in iTunes than on your iPod. This option is useful when your iPod doesn't have enough free space for your entire iTunes music library, and you've gotten onto your iPod most of the tracks you want to have on it.

   ■ **Manually Manage Songs And Playlists**   Select this option button to take manual control of synchronization. This option is useful both when you need to choose which parts of your colossal music library to pack onto your iPod's comparatively puny amount of storage space, and when you want to add more music to your iPod than will fit onto your Mac. (See the section "Load More Music on Your iPod Than Will Fit on Your Mac," later in this chapter, for a discussion of how to do this.) When you click to select this option button, iTunes displays this warning dialog box to make sure you understand that you'll need to unmount your iPod manually before disconnecting it:

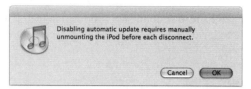

Click the OK button if you're happy with this, and iTunes will select the Manually Manage Songs And Playlists option button. (iTunes also selects the Enable Disk Use check box if it wasn't already selected and makes it unavailable, so that you can't clear it manually.) Otherwise, click the Cancel button, and iTunes will leave the current option button selected.

5. Click the OK button to close the iPod Preferences dialog box.

Even if you leave automatic updating enabled, you can override it if necessary. To do so, hold down COMMAND-OPTION as you connect your iPod to your Mac. Release the keys when the Source pane displays an entry for your iPod.

Control Synchronization Manually

If you chose the Manually Manage Songs And Playlists option button in the iPod Preferences dialog box, iTunes displays your iPod as an expandable list of playlists in the Source pane:

Now you can manage synchronization manually by using the steps in the following sections. As a bonus, you can play songs back directly from the iPod by navigating to them, selecting them, and clicking the Play button or pressing SPACEBAR.

Add Songs to Your iPod Manually

To add songs to your iPod manually, follow these steps:

1. Select your iPod's icon in the Source pane to display your iPod's contents.

2. Select the songs you want to copy to your iPod, either in your iTunes music library or in a Finder window.

3. Drag the songs to the iPod's icon or to the appropriate playlist. If you're dragging from a Finder window and you have the iPod's contents displayed in the main iTunes pane, you can drop the tracks there.

Remove Songs from Your iPod

The other half of the battle is removing songs from your iPod so you can put other songs on it. To remove songs, follow these steps:

1. Select your iPod's icon in the Source pane to display your iPod's contents.

2. Select the songs you want to remove.

3. Drag the songs to the Trash. (Alternatively, press DELETE.) iTunes displays a confirmation dialog box.

4. Click the Yes button. Select the Do Not Ask Me Again check box first if you don't want iTunes to confirm each deletion with you in the future.

NOTE   *This technique removes the songs only from your iPod, not from your Mac.*

CAUTION   *Use only iTunes—not the Finder—to remove songs from your iPod. This is because iTunes updates the iPod's database when removing songs, while the Finder doesn't. So if you remove songs using the Finder, the iPod thinks they're still there, even though they're not.*

Synchronize Only Part of Your Music Library with Your iPod

If your music library is too big to all fit on your iPod (or that portion of your iPod capacity you're using for music), you can specify which songs and playlists to synchronize with your iPod in two ways:

- Select the Automatically Update Selected Playlists Only option button in the iPod Preferences dialog box. Then, in the list box in the iPod Preferences dialog box, select the check boxes for the playlists you want to synchronize. This technique works only for songs included in playlists.

- Control all synchronization manually, as described in "Control Synchronization Manually," earlier in this chapter.

Load More Music on Your iPod Than Will Fit on Your Mac

If you have a newish iPod and an older Mac, the boot may be on the other foot: your Mac may not have enough free disk space to hold all the songs you want to load on your iPod. To get around this problem, follow these steps:

1. Turn on manual synchronization in the iPod Preferences dialog box. (See "Control Synchronization to Get the Music You Want on Your iPod," earlier in this chapter.)

2. Synchronize your iPod manually, as described in "Control Synchronization Manually," earlier in this chapter.

If your Mac is connected to a network on which it can access drives, you can get around the lack of disk space on your Mac in two other ways:

- Keep a significant part of your music library on a network drive to supplement that part you can fit on your hard drive. To prevent iTunes from copying files to your hard drive, clear the Copy Files To iTunes Music Folder When Adding To Library check box on the Advanced sheet of the Preferences dialog box.

- Keep your entire music library on a network drive. Use the procedure described in "Choose Where to Store Your Music Library," earlier in this chapter, to change the music library's folder from its default location on your startup disk to the appropriate folder on the network drive. In this case, you don't need to clear the Copy Files To iTunes Music Folder When Adding To Library check box.

In either case, if you use automatic updating, you'll need to make sure the network drive is available whenever you synchronize your iPod. If it's not, you'll be unable to synchronize any of the tracks on that drive.

Return to Automatic Updating from Manual Updating

If you've read the preceding sections, you'll probably suspect that returning your iPod to automatic updating is as simple as selecting one of the automatic-updating options in the iPod Preferences dialog box, lighting the blue touch paper, and retiring smartly to a prudent distance. But there's a complication: automatic updating will overwrite your manually managed iPod library with either the complete iTunes music library (if you select the Automatically Update All Songs And Playlists option button) or with the playlists you specify (if you select the Automatically Update Selected Playlists Only option button).

So before you return to automatic updating, make sure your library will fit on your iPod, and that you won't lose any tracks stored only on your iPod and not in your music library.

When you select either of the automatic-updating options in the iPod Preferences dialog box, iTunes displays the following dialog box to warn you of what will happen:

Click the OK button if you're comfortable with this.

Listen to Audible.com Spoken-Word Files on Your iPod

Even if your iPod is laden nearly to the gunwales with songs, you may be able to cram on a good amount of spoken-word audio. This is because spoken-word audio can sound great at much lower bitrates than music.

Audible.com provides a wide variety of content—such as audio books, magazines, and plays—in a selection of different subscription types and accounts. To get started, go to the Audible.com web site (www.audible.com) and set up an account.

CAUTION *Audible is an interesting service, but read the terms and conditions carefully for the account type you choose. Otherwise, Audible policies such as canceling any unused book credits at the end of each subscription month may give you an unpleasant surprise.*

After setting up an account, you can download files to up to three different computers for that account. The first time you download Audible.com content to a particular computer, you need to enter your Audible.com account information on it, as shown here. After that, you can simply drag an Audible file to the iTunes window to add it to your music library.

When playing an Audible file, you can press COMMAND-SHIFT–RIGHT ARROW to go to the next chapter or COMMAND-SHIFT–LEFT ARROW to go to the previous chapter.

If you need to transfer one of the three manifestations of your Audible.com account from one Mac to another, follow these steps:

1. Establish an Internet connection if you need to do so manually.

2. In iTunes, choose Advanced | Deauthorize Computer to display the Deauthorize Computer dialog box:

3. Select the Deauthorize Computer For Audible Account option button.

4. Click the OK button to display the Remove Audible Account dialog box:

5. Enter your Audible user account and password.

6. Click the OK button.

Create Custom Playlists to Enjoy in iTunes or on Your iPod

Typically, a CD presents its songs in the order the artist or the producer thought best, but often you'll want to rearrange the songs into a different order—or mix the songs from different CDs in a way that suits only you. To do so, you create playlists in iTunes, and iTunes automatically shares them with your iPod so that you can use them there as well.

To create a playlist, follow these steps:

1. Click the + button in the Source pane, choose File | New Playlist, or press COMMAND-N. iTunes adds a new playlist to the Source pane, names it *untitled playlist* (or the next available name, such as *untitled playlist 2*), and displays an edit box around it.

2. Type the name for the playlist, and then press RETURN or click elsewhere to apply the name.

3. Select the Library item in the Source pane to display your songs. If you want to work by artist and album, press COMMAND-B or choose Edit | Show Browser to display the Browser pane.

4. Select the songs you want to add to the playlist, and then drag them to the playlist's name. You can drag one song at a time or multiple songs—whatever you find easiest.

5. Click the playlist's name in the Source pane to display the playlist.

6. Drag the tracks into the order in which you want them to play.

NOTE   *For you to be able to drag the tracks around in the playlist, the playlist must be sorted by the track-number column. If any other column heading is selected, you won't be able to rearrange the order of the tracks in the playlist.*

You can also create a playlist by selecting the tracks you want to include and then pressing COMMAND-SHIFT-N or choosing File | New Playlist From Selection. iTunes organizes the songs into a new playlist provisionally named *untitled playlist* and displays an edit box around the title so that you can change it immediately. Type the new name and press RETURN, or click elsewhere to apply the name.

To delete a playlist, select it in the Source pane and press DELETE or right-click it (or CTRL-click it) and choose Clear from the shortcut menu. iTunes displays a confirmation dialog box:

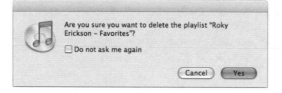

Click the Yes button to delete the playlist. If you want to turn off the confirmation for playlists you delete from now on, select the Do Not Ask Me Again check box before clicking Yes.

iTunes also offers more complex ways of deleting playlists and their contents:

- If you choose not to turn off confirmation of deleting playlists, you can override confirmation by pressing COMMAND-DELETE when deleting a playlist.

- To delete a playlist *and the songs it contains* from your library, select the playlist and press OPTION-DELETE. iTunes displays a confirmation dialog box for the deletion. Click the Yes button. As before, you can select the Do Not Ask Me Again check box to suppress this confirmation dialog box in future, but because you're removing song files from your library, it's best not to do so.

- To delete a playlist and the songs it contains from your library, *and* to temporarily suppress the confirmation dialog box while doing so, select the playlist and press COMMAND-OPTION-DELETE.

Automatically Create Smart Playlists Based on Your Ratings and Preferences

The Smart Playlist feature lets you instruct iTunes about how to build a list of songs automatically for you. You can tell Smart Playlist to build playlists by artist, composer, or genre; to select up to a specific number of songs at random, by artist, by most played, by last player, or by song name; and to automatically update a playlist as you add tracks to or remove tracks from your music library. For example, if you tell Smart Playlist to make you a playlist of songs by Shakira, Smart Playlist can update the list with new Shakira tracks after you import them into your music library.

By using Smart Playlist's advanced features, you can even specify multiple conditions. For example, you might choose to include songs tagged with the genre Gothic Rock but exclude certain artists by name, such as The Fields of the Nephilim.

NOTE   *Smart Playlist maintains playlists such as the My Top Rated playlist, the Recently Played playlist, and the Top 25 Most Played playlist, that iTunes creates by default.*

1. Press COMMAND-ALT-N, choose File | New Smart Playlist, or OPTION-click the Add button to display the Smart Playlist dialog box:

4

Smart Playlist
☑ Match the following condition:
[Artist ‡] [contains ‡] [   ] ⊖ ⊕
☐ Limit to [25] [songs ‡] selected by [random ‡]
☐ Match only checked songs
☑ Live updating
(Cancel) (OK)

2. Make sure the Match The Following Condition check box is selected so that you can specify criteria. (The other option is to create a random Smart Playlist, which can sometimes be entertaining.) If you create multiple conditions, this check box offers the choices Match All Of The Following Conditions and Match Any Of The Following Conditions. Choose the appropriate one.

3. Use the controls in the first line to specify the first condition. The first drop-down list offers an extensive range of choices: Album, Artist, Bit Rate, Comment, Compilation, Composer, Date Added, Date Modified, Genre, Kind, Last Played, My Rating, Play Count, Sample Rate, Size, Song Name, Time, Track Number, and Year. The second drop-down list offers options suitable to the item you chose in the first drop-down list—for example, Contains, Does Not Contain, Is, Is Not, Starts With, or Ends With for a text field, or Is, Is Not, Is Greater Than, Is Less Than, or Is In The Range for the bit rate.

4. To create multiple conditions, click the + button at the end of the line. iTunes adds another line of condition controls, which you can then set as described in step 3. To remove a condition, click the – button at the end of the line.

5. To limit the playlist to a maximum number of tracks, time, or disk space, select the Limit To check box, and specify the limit and how iTunes should select the songs. For example, you could specify Limit To 30 Songs Selected By Least Often Played or Limit To 8 Hours Selected By Random.

6. To make iTunes omit songs whose check boxes you've cleared, select the Match Only Checked Songs check box.

7. Select or clear the Live Updating check box to specify whether iTunes should update the playlist periodically according to your listening patterns.

8. Click the OK button to close the Smart Playlist dialog box. iTunes creates the playlist, assigns a name to it (for example, *untitled playlist*), and displays an edit box around the name so you can change it.

9. Type the new name for the playlist, and then press RETURN.

Share Music and Access Shared Music

No Mac is an island, entire of itself; every Mac is a piece of the Internet, a part of the digital main. With iTunes, no music library need stand alone either. iTunes provides features for sharing your music with other iTunes users on your network and for playing the music they're sharing.

You may also want to share music with other users of your Mac—which, interestingly, requires a little more effort. See Special Project 3 (on the colored pages) for details on how to do this.

Share Your Music with Other Local iTunes Users

Running on Mac OS X 10.2.4 or a later version, iTunes 4 lets you share either your entire music library or selected playlists with other users on your network (or, more technically, on the same TCP/IP subnet as your computer). You can share MP3 files, AAC files, AIFF files, WAV files, and links to radio stations. You can't share Audible files or QuickTime sound files.

You can share your music with up to five other users at a time, and you can be one of up to five users accessing the shared music on another computer. Each Mac must be running Mac OS X 10.2.4 (or a later version), and each Windows PC must be running Windows 2000, Windows XP, or a later version.

Shared music remains on the computer that's sharing it, and when a participating computer goes to play a song, the song is streamed across the network. (In other words, the song isn't copied from the computer that's sharing it to the computer that's playing it in a way that leaves a usable file on the computer that's playing the music.) When a computer goes offline or is shut down, any music it has been sharing stops being available to other users. Participating computers can play the shared music but can't do anything else with it: they can't burn the shared music to CD or DVD, download it to an iPod, or copy it to their own libraries.

To share some or all of your music, follow these steps:

1. Choose Edit | Preferences or press COMMAND-COMMA (or COMMAND-Y) to display the Preferences dialog box.

2. Click the Sharing button to display the Sharing sheet:

3. Select the Share My Music check box. (This check box is cleared by default.) By default, iTunes then selects the Share Entire Library option button; if you want to share only some playlists, select the Share Selected Playlists option button and select the appropriate check boxes in the list box.

4. The Shared Name text box controls the name that other users trying to access your music will see. The default name is *username*'s music, where *username* is your username—for example, Anna Connor's Music. You can probably improve on this description.

5. By default, your music is available to any other user on the network. To restrict access to people with whom you share a password, select the Require Password check box and enter a strong (unguessable) password in the text box.

6. Click the OK button to apply your choices and close the Preferences dialog box.

NOTE *When you set iTunes to share your music, iTunes displays a message reminding you that "Sharing music is for personal use only"—in other words, remember not to violate copyright law. Select the Do Not Show This Message Again check box if you want to prevent this message from appearing again.*

Disconnect Other Users from Your Shared Music

To disconnect other users from your shared music library, follow these steps:

1. Press COMMAND-COMMA (or COMMAND-Y) or choose iTunes | Preferences to display the Preferences dialog box.

2. Click the Sharing button to display the Sharing sheet.

3. Clear the Share My Music check box.

4. Click the OK button. If any other user is connected to your shared music library, iTunes displays this message box to warn you:

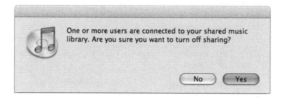

Click Yes or No, as appropriate. If you choose to stop sharing your music library, anyone playing music from it will be cut off abruptly without notice.

Access and Play Another Local iTunes User's Shared Music

To access another person's shared music, your computer must have iTunes 4 running on Mac OS X 10.2.4 or a later version. You can then access shared music by following the instructions in the next three sections.

Set Your Computer to Look for Shared Music

First, set your computer to look for shared music. Follow these steps:

1. Choose Edit | Preferences or press COMMAND-COMMA to display the Preferences dialog box.

2. Click the Sharing button to display the Sharing sheet.

3. Select the Look For Shared Music check box.

4. Click the OK button to close the Preferences dialog box.

Access Shared Music on the Same TCP/IP Subnet

Once you've selected the Look For Shared Music check box on the Sharing sheet of the Preferences dialog box, iTunes automatically detects shared music when you launch it while your Mac is connected to a network. If iTunes finds shared music libraries or playlists, it displays them in the Source pane. Figure 4-11 shows an example of browsing the music shared by another computer.

If a shared music source has a password, iTunes displays the Music Library Password dialog box:

Enter the password and click the OK button to access the library.

FIGURE 4-11 Computers sharing music appear in the iTunes Source pane, allowing you to quickly browse the music that's being shared.

Disconnect a Shared Music Library

To disconnect shared music you've connected to, follow these steps:

1. In the Source pane, select the shared music source.

2. Press COMMAND-E or choose Controls | Disconnect "*Source.*"

Alternatively, CTRL-click or right-click the shared music source and choose Disconnect "*Library*" from the shortcut menu (where *Library* is the name of the shared music library).

Add Artwork to Songs

iTunes 4 lets you add artwork to songs and then display the artwork while the song is playing or while the song is selected. Most songs you buy from the iTunes Music Store include the appropriate artwork—for example, the cover of the single, EP, album, or CD that includes the song. For other songs, you can add your own artwork manually. For example, you might download album art or other pictures from an artist's web site, and then apply those to the song files you ripped from the artist's CDs. You can use JPG, GIF, TIFF, or PNG files, PhotoShop images, or even PDFs for artwork, although iTunes can display only the first page of a multipage PDF.

iTunes provides three different ways to add artwork to songs. To add artwork to a song directly from the iTunes window, follow these steps:

1. Open a Finder window to the folder that contains the picture you want to use for the artwork. (If the picture is on your desktop, you're ready to go, but your desktop is likely to get cluttered fast.)

2. Press COMMAND-G or click the Show Or Hide Song Artwork button below the Source pane to display the artwork pane below the Source pane.

3. Drag the picture file from the Finder window to the artwork pane and drop it there. iTunes displays the picture there and associates it with the song file.

4. Drag other picture files from the Finder window to the artwork pane and drop them there as appropriate.

You can also add one or more images to a single song by working in the Song Information dialog box. Follow these steps:

1. Right-click the song you want to affect and choose Get Info from the shortcut menu to display the Song Information dialog box for the song.

2. Click the Artwork tab to display its contents.

3. To add an image, click the Add button, use the Choose A File dialog box to navigate to the file and select it, and then click the Choose button.

> **TIP** *You can also drag a picture from iPhoto and drop it in the picture box on the Artwork tab of the Song Information dialog box.*

4. To delete an existing image, select it in the artwork box and click the Delete button.

5. To resize the picture to the size you want, drag the slider to the left or right.

6. To work with the previous or next song in the playlist, album, or library, click the Previous button or the Next button.

7. Click the OK button to close the Song Information dialog box.

To add artwork to multiple songs at the same time, follow these steps:

1. Open a Finder window to the folder that contains the picture you want to use for the artwork.

2. Select the songs you want to affect. SHIFT-click to select multiple contiguous songs. COMMAND-click to select multiple noncontiguous songs after clicking the first song.

3. Issue a Get Info command (for example, press COMMAND-I) to display the Multiple Song Information dialog box.

4. Drag the picture file from the Finder window to the Artwork box and drop it there. iTunes selects the Artwork check box, displays the picture, and associates it with the song file.

5. Click the OK button to close the Multiple Song Information dialog box. iTunes displays a confirmation dialog box.

6. Click the Yes button.

When you've added two or more pictures to the same song, the artwork pane displays Previous and Next buttons for browsing from picture to picture.

You can display the current picture at full size by clicking it in the artwork pane. Click the Close button to close the artwork window.

CAUTION   *If you associate a graphics file that's bigger than your desktop with a song, you may not be able to reach the Close button on the artwork window to close it. Press COMMAND-W to close the window.*

Listen to Internet Radio

You can use iTunes to listen to radio streamed over the Internet. You'll find a wide range of radio stations available—everything from giant commercial stations or public broadcasters that you can catch on the airwaves to people broadcasting their own opinions or personal playlists.

Streaming radio stations can use any of several different formats, including MP3 streams, Windows Media Audio streams, and RealAudio streams. iTunes can receive only MP3 streams.

TIP   *QuickTime Player can receive other stream types as well, as can the RealOne player from RealNetworks (www.real.com). RealOne requires Internet Explorer or Netscape; you can't use it with other browsers such as Safari, Opera, or Mozilla.*

Aside from using different formats, Internet radio stations also broadcast at different bitrates— typically 16 Kbps, 32 Kbps, 56 Kbps, 64 Kbps, 96 Kbps, and 128 Kbps. As with MP3 and AAC fidelity, the higher the bitrate, the better the radio will sound—provided that your Internet connection is fast enough to deliver it. For example, if you have a 64 Kbps ISDN connection, you won't be able to listen to a 128 Kbps stream, because your connection simply isn't fast enough, but you should be able to listen to a 64 Kbps stream. Because 56K modems typically connect at speeds lower than 56 Kbps, you can't usually listen to a 56 Kbps stream satisfactorily on a modem connection—it'll keep breaking up.

To connect to an Internet radio station, follow these steps:

1. Click the Radio item in the Source pane to display the list of genres available. You can force iTunes to refresh the list of genres by clicking the Refresh button in the upper-right corner of the iTunes window.

2. Double-click the genre you're interested in to make iTunes display the list of stations for that genre. Depending on the number of stations available, iTunes may need several seconds to download the details.

3. Check the station speeds in the Bit Rate column to see which of them are broadcasting at suitable bit rates for your Internet connection and listening requirements:

- By default, iTunes sorts the radio stations alphabetically by name, but you may prefer to sort them in ascending order or descending order by bitrate so that you can easily see which stations are broadcasting at rates you want to hear.

- To sort the stations by bit rate, click the Bit Rate column heading once (for an ascending sort) or twice (for a descending sort).

4. Double-click a station to start playing it. iTunes connects, buffers the stream (see the next note), and then starts playing back the audio. iTunes displays the station details in the display area, together with the time you've spend listening to the station:

NOTE   *When you connect to an Internet radio station, it usually takes a few seconds for the playback to start. Part of this time is required to establish the connection to the streaming server; most of this time is required for buffering enough of the stream to deliver smooth playback even if minor interruptions in Internet traffic occur. If major interruptions occur, the buffer will run out, and the audio will stop. If you see the error message "Network Stalled: Rebuffering Stream" frequently, you may need to increase the buffer size. Choose iTunes | Preferences or press COMMAND-COMMA to display the Preferences dialog box, click the Advanced button, adjust the Streaming Buffer Size setting to Medium or Large, and click the OK button.*

5. Click the Stop button to stop listening to the stream.

How to ... Create Your Own Internet Radio Station

Just as other people can broadcast their own Internet radio stations, so can you—with relatively little effort.

You can start broadcasting yourself in either of two ways: by downloading the QuickTime Streaming Server from Apple (www.apple.com/quicktime/products/qtss) and using it to stream music directly from your computer, or by using a radio hosting service such as Live365.com (www.live365.com). In either case, you're liable for paying broadcast royalties to artists whose works you broadcast.

Streaming music directly from your computer gives you more control over your radio station but requires an Internet connection with a fast enough upstream speed to deliver enough audio data to all the listeners you want to support. (Most Internet connections are far faster downstream—delivering data to you—than upstream.)

A radio hosting service removes the heavy lifting from your computer and Internet connection. Some radio hosting services also take care of royalty payments for you.

4

TIP   *The easiest way to give yourself quick access to your preferred radio stations is to create a playlist for them. Once you've located a radio station you like, drag it to the playlist. You can then quickly access a station by displaying the playlist and double-clicking the station's entry in it.*

NOTE   *If you enjoy Internet radio, you may sometimes want to record a stream so that you can play it back later. See "Save Audio Streams to Disk So You Can Listen to Them Later," in Chapter 6, for details on how to do so.*

Chapter 5

Load Music onto Your iPod or iPod mini Using Windows

How to...

- Configure iTunes to suit your preferences
- Identify the main elements in the iTunes interface
- Choose suitable settings for ripping and encoding AAC, MP3, AIFF, and WAV files
- Create, build, and manage your music library
- Play back music with iTunes
- Use the graphical equalizer to improve the sound of music
- Synchronize your music library with your iPod automatically or manually
- Listen to Audible.com spoken-word files on your iPod
- Create custom playlists containing only the tracks you like
- Use the Smart Playlist feature to create playlists based on your preferences
- Share music and access shared music
- Add artwork to songs
- Listen to Internet radio

This chapter discusses how to use iTunes to enjoy digital audio and manage your iPod on Windows. iTunes provides a graphical interface for ripping and encoding songs on CDs to digital audio files you can store and manipulate on your PC, together with fast and easy synchronization with your iPod.

This chapter assumes you're using iTunes 4 or a later version on Windows XP (Home Edition or Professional) or Windows 2000 (Professional or Server). All other things being equal (for example, if your hardware is capable of running Windows XP), you'll get better results from Windows XP than from Windows 2000. The screens shown in this chapter are from Windows XP only.

iTunes contains many configuration options. Rather than covering all these options in a single section that you'll skip, this chapter discusses them individually or in groups as needed to accomplish particular tasks you're likely to want to undertake.

NOTE *This chapter covers much the same ground as does Chapter 4, but for Windows instead of for the Mac. If you have both a Mac and a PC and have already read Chapter 4, or if you've already doggedly read Chapter 4 even though you don't have a PC, you'll probably find this chapter slow going. But because there are a fair number of differences between iTunes on Windows and iTunes on Mac OS X, it seemed better to cover the two operating systems in separate chapters rather than cramming them into a single chapter stuffed with ifs, buts, and digressions. (And if this note seems repetitive—yes, there was a similar note at the beginning of Chapter 4.)*

One iTunes topic this chapter doesn't discuss is burning CDs and DVDs. You'll find a complete discussion of burning with iTunes (on both Windows and Mac OS X) in Chapter 9.

How to ...   **Run iTunes Frequently—or Always on Startup**

Running iTunes from the iTunes icon on your desktop or your Start menu works well enough, but if you intend to run iTunes frequently, or always, you can do better. Read on.

If you plan to run iTunes frequently, navigate to the iTunes icon on the Start menu in Windows XP, right-click it, and choose Pin To Start Menu from the shortcut menu to force Windows XP to display an iTunes icon on the Pinned Items section of the Start menu. You'll then be able to get at it quickly by displaying the Start menu.

To run iTunes even more quickly, configure a CTRL-ALT keyboard shortcut for it. Follow these steps:

1. Right-click the iTunes icon (if you have one) on your desktop or on your Start menu and choose Properties from the shortcut menu to display the iTunes Properties dialog box.

2. If the Shortcut tab isn't already displayed, click it.

3. Click in the Shortcut Key text box.

4. Press the letter you want to use in the CTRL-ALT shortcut. For example, press I to create the shortcut CTRL-ALT-I.

5. Click the OK button to close the Properties dialog box.

Now you'll be able to start iTunes by pressing the keyboard shortcut either from the desktop or from within an application.

But if you use iTunes whenever you're using your computer, the best solution is to make Windows start iTunes automatically whenever you log on. To do so, follow these steps:

1. Right-click the iTunes icon (if you have one) on your desktop or on your Start menu and choose Copy from the shortcut menu to copy the shortcut to the Clipboard.

2. Choose Start | Run to display the Run dialog box.

3. Type **%userprofile%\Start Menu\Programs\Startup.** (%userprofile% is a system variable that returns the path to your user profile folder—the folder that contains your My Documents folder and the folders in which your settings are stored.) As you type the path, Windows will try to help you complete it. Press DOWN ARROW to accept a suggestion, and then press ENTER to enter it in the text box.

4. Click the OK button. Windows opens the Startup folder, which contains shortcuts to applications that run when you log on to Windows. (This folder may be empty when you open it.)

5. Right-click in the Startup folder and choose Paste from the shortcut menu to paste a copy of the iTunes shortcut into the folder.

6. Click the Close button (the X button), press ALT-F4, or choose File | Close to close the Windows Explorer window.

Configure iTunes on Your PC

Launch iTunes by double-clicking the iTunes icon on your desktop (if you allowed the setup routine to create one) or by choosing Start | All Programs | iTunes | iTunes.

NOTE
If you've never used iTunes before on this PC, iTunes launches the iTunes Setup Assistant. Turn back to "Install iTunes and the iPod Software," in Chapter 2, for coverage of setting up iTunes and performing basic configuration.

Meet the iTunes Interface

After you launch iTunes, or after you finish the iTunes Setup Assistant, you see the iTunes interface (shown in Figure 5-1).

NOTE
If iTunes displays a dialog box telling you that you can't open iTunes because another user currently has it open, see "iTunes Won't Start on Windows," in Chapter 17, for help on what to do.

These are the main parts of the iTunes interface. You'll use them later in this chapter and in subsequent chapters.

Source Pane

The Source pane contains the music sources available to you at any given time. They may include the following:

- **Library** This is your music library, which typically is stored on your local hard disk. You can rename it by double-clicking its title, typing the new name, and pressing ENTER or clicking elsewhere.

- **Radio** This entry lists Internet radio stations that you can access via your Internet connection.

- **Music Store** Clicking this entry in the Source pane connects you to the iTunes Music Store via your Internet connection.

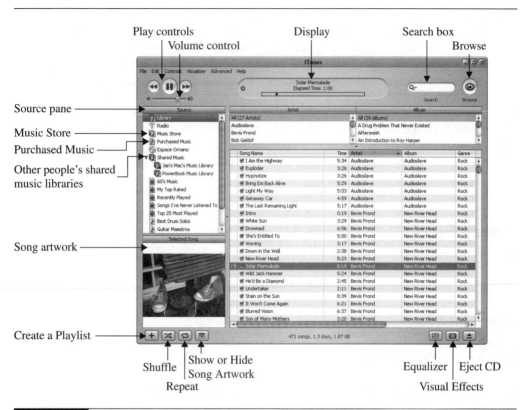

Play controls — Volume control

Display

Search box — Browse

Source pane —

Music Store —

Purchased Music —

Other people's shared music libraries

Song artwork —

Create a Playlist —

Shuffle — Repeat — Show or Hide Song Artwork

Equalizer — Eject CD — Visual Effects

FIGURE 5-1   iTunes' streamlined interface gives you direct access to your music.

- **Purchased Music**   This special playlist contains all the songs you buy from the iTunes Music Store. This playlist doesn't appear until you buy your first song from the iTunes Music Store.

- **Audio CD**   If your CD drive has an audio CD loaded, the CD appears in the Source pane. If iTunes can connect to the Internet to look up the title of the CD, the CD appears by name. Otherwise, it appears as "Audio CD."

- **iPods**   Any iPods connected to your PC appear in the Source pane.

- **Shared Music Libraries**   If your PC is connected to a local network, and if other iTunes users are sharing music on the network, the shared music libraries appear here. If there's just one shared library, it appears under its name. If there are two or more shared libraries, they appear under a collapsible Shared Music entry.

- **Smart Playlists**   iTunes starts you off with several *smart playlists*—playlists that update themselves automatically according to criteria programmed into them. The 60's Music smart playlist contains all songs whose Year tag is in the range 1960–69. The My Top Rated smart playlist contains all songs you've assigned a rating of three stars or more. The Recently Played smart playlist contains all songs you've played in the last two weeks. The Top 25 Most Played smart playlist contains the 25 songs you've played most overall. You can customize these smart playlists, or create further smart playlists of your own. See "Automatically Create Smart Playlists Based on Your Ratings and Preferences," later in this chapter.

- **Playlists**   These are conventional (or "dumb") playlists—ones that don't update themselves automatically. You can create as many playlists as you want so that you can arrange songs in the order you want them and burn them to CD. You can change or delete a playlist at any time.

Browser Panes

The Browser panes let you navigate quickly by artist and album to the songs you want to play. You can toggle the display of the Browser panes by clicking the Browse button, pressing CTRL-B, or choosing Edit | Show Browser or Edit | Hide Browser.

Songs List

The Songs list lets you select the song to play. Double-click a song to start playing it. Clear a song's check box to tell iTunes not to play it.

Choose Whether to Let iTunes Organize Your Music Library

Before you make any other choices—including the crucial choice of where to store your music library—you should decide whether to let iTunes organize your music library for you. "Organize" means that iTunes does the following:

- Renames each file to a two-digit number and the song title, plus the appropriate extension—for example, 05 Cry Me a River.mp3. If you've cleared the Create Filenames With Track Number check box on the Importing tab of the iTunes dialog box, iTunes uses only the song title (for example, Cry Me a River.mp3).

- Stores the files in folders using the format *Artist\Album*, where *Artist* is the artist's name (for example, Justin Timberlake) and *Album* is the name of the album or CD (for example, Justified): Justin Timberlake\Justified\05 Cry Me a River.mp3.

This arrangement can be convenient, but many other applications and music enthusiasts use other conventions for naming digital audio files. For instance, many people and some applications use the convention Artist – Song Name (for example, Sheryl Crow – Steve McQueen.mp3), while others use Artist – Album – Song Name (for example, Sheryl Crow – Very Best – Steve McQueen.mp3), and others yet use Artist – Album – Song Number – Song Name (for example, Sheryl Crow – Very Best – 12 - Steve McQueen.mp3).

If you're using a different naming convention, iTunes' "organization" can mean a lot of renaming and extra folders. For example, if you import the file Kings of Oblivion – So Turned On.mp3 (which is track 2 from the album "Real Cool Ravers"), iTunes does the following:

■ Creates a folder named Kings of Oblivion in your iTunes Music folder (unless that folder already exists).

■ Creates a folder named Real Cool Ravers in the Kings of Oblivion folder (unless that folder already exists, too).

■ Renames the file to 02 So Turned On.mp3 to follow its standard naming conventions. (If you've cleared the Create Filenames With Track Number check box on the Importing tab of the iTunes dialog box, iTunes renames the file to So Turned On.mp3 instead.)

iTunes' default setting is *not* to organize your music library for you. Think carefully before deciding to let iTunes organize your music library: having files and folders stored in an orderly fashion can be helpful if you're committed to using iTunes, but if you use other digital audio players, it could be a menace.

To control whether iTunes organizes your music library for you, follow these steps:

1. Press CTRL-COMMA (or CTRL-Y) or choose Edit | Preferences to display the iTunes dialog box.

2. Click the Advanced tab:

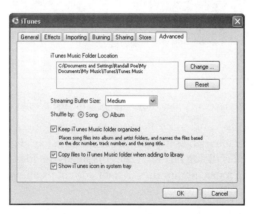

3. Select the Keep iTunes Music Folder Organized check box if you want iTunes to organize your music folder. Otherwise, make sure this check box is cleared.

4. Click the OK button to close the iTunes dialog box.

Choose Where to Store Your Music Library

Because your music library can contain dozens—or even hundreds—of gigabytes of music files, you must store it in a suitable location if you choose to keep all your music files in it. The alternative to keeping all your music files *in* your music library is to store references to where the files are located in other folders. Doing so enables you to minimize the size of your music library. But for maximum flexibility and to make sure you can access all the tracks in your music library all the time, keeping all your music files in your music library folder is best—if you can do so.

To change the location of your music library, follow these steps:

1. Press CTRL-COMMA (or CTRL-Y) or choose Edit | Preferences to display the iTunes dialog box.

2. Click the Advanced tab.

3. Click the Change button to display the Browse For Folder dialog box.

4. Navigate to the folder that will contain your music library, select the folder, and then click the OK button. iTunes closes the Browse For Folder dialog box and returns you to the Advanced tab of the iTunes dialog box.

5. Click the OK button to close the iTunes dialog box:

   ■ iTunes then displays the Updating Song Locations dialog box, showing its progress as it updates its records of the songs' locations.

   ■ If you have the Keep iTunes Music Folder Organized check box selected, iTunes displays the following dialog box, asking if you want iTunes to move and rename the files in your new iTunes Music folder

   Click the Yes button to let iTunes move and rename the files as discussed in the previous section.

6. To keep all your music library files together in the new location, click the Yes button. You'll see the Organizing Files dialog box as iTunes organizes the files into the new location. To keep your existing music library files in their current locations but put any new files in the new location, click the No button.

NOTE   *To reset your music library folder to its default location (your My Documents\My Music\ iTunes\iTunes Music folder), click the Reset button on the Advanced tab of the iTunes dialog box. Again, iTunes asks if you want to move your existing files to the new location. Click the Yes button or the No button, as appropriate.*

Choose Whether to Store All Song Files in Your Music Library

As mentioned in the previous section, iTunes can store references to where song files are located in folders other than your music library folder instead of creating a copy of each file in the music library folder. To make iTunes store references, clear the Copy Files To iTunes Music Folder When Adding To Library check box on the Advanced tab of the iTunes dialog box.

Storing references is great when you have too little space free on your hard disk to accommodate your colossal music library. For example, if you have a laptop whose hard disk is already stuffed to the gills, you'll probably prefer to store in your music library references to music located on an external hard disk rather than trying to import a copy of each song. But you won't be able to play any song stored on the external hard disk when your laptop isn't connected to it.

CAUTION *Before allowing iTunes to copy each song file to your music library, make sure you have plenty of hard-disk space. iTunes doesn't check that there's enough extra space to hold the copies of the song files, so using this option could run you out of hard-disk space and leave you with only some song files copied to your music library.*

Choose Whether iTunes Automatically Connects to the Internet

iTunes can download CD information automatically from the CD Database web site (CDDB; www.cddb.com). This saves you a large amount of typing and is great if you have a permanent Internet connection or an Internet connection you can establish at any time. But if you'll need to rip and encode CDs when you have no Internet connection available, or if you prefer to enter the CD information manually (for example, to make sure it's letter-perfect), you can turn off this feature.

TIP *You can also rip and encode songs when offline from CDDB, then go online, select the songs, and choose Advanced | Get CD Track Names to download the CD data and apply it to the songs.*

To choose whether iTunes connects to the Internet automatically to download CD data (artist, album, and track information), choose iTunes | Preferences or press CTRL-COMMA or CTRL-Y. On the General tab of the iTunes dialog box, select or clear the Connect To Internet When Needed check box.

Change the Importing Settings in iTunes to Specify Audio Quality

Before you rip any CDs using iTunes, check that the settings are suitable for your needs. iTunes' default settings—to encode to AAC files at 128 Kbps in stereo—are a fair choice for defaults, but you may well want to change them. It's worth investing a little time in choosing the right settings for ripping and encoding, because ripping tracks more than once quickly becomes a severe waste of time.

NOTE *See Chapter 3 for a discussion of how audio compression works and why you need to use it; the differences between the AAC, MP3, AIFF, and WAV formats; how to choose a suitable bitrate and (for MP3) stereo settings for the files you encode; and more.*

To recap quickly, creating a high-quality compressed audio file involves several variables:

■ If the audio source is a CD, reading the CD accurately.

■ If the audio source is analog rather than digital, converting the analog signal to digital with minimal loss of quality.

■ Using an encoder capable of creating high-quality encodings. iTunes' encoders produce high-quality results, so this shouldn't be a problem.

■ Choosing a suitable compression rate to save the right amount of data.

■ Making sure the data saved is as accurate as possible.

To check or change the importing settings, follow these steps:

1. Choose Edit | Preferences or press CTRL-COMMA or CTRL-Y to display the iTunes dialog box.

2. Click the Importing tab:

3. In the Import Using drop-down list, specify the file format you want to use by choosing the appropriate encoder:

■ The default setting is AAC Encoder, which creates compressed files in the Advanced Audio Coding (AAC) format. AAC files combine high audio quality with compact size, making AAC the format you're most likely to want to try first.

■ The other setting you're likely to want to try is MP3 Encoder, which creates compressed files in the MP3 format. MP3 files have slightly lower audio quality than AAC files for the same file size, but you can use them with a wider variety of software applications and hardware players than AAC files.

■ AIFF files and WAV files are uncompressed audio files, so they take up a huge amount of space but have audio quality as high as the source. AIFF files are used mostly on Macs, while WAV files are used mostly on Windows, but iTunes can handle AIFF files just fine on Windows as well as on Mac OS. Sometimes you may want to use one or other of these settings when quality is paramount. To create AIFF files, choose AIFF Encoder. To create WAV files, choose WAV Encoder.

4. In the Setting drop-down list, choose the setting you want to use:

- For the AAC Encoder, the Setting drop-down list offers the settings High Quality (128 Kbps) and Custom. When you select Custom, iTunes displays an iTunes dialog box for configuring the AAC encoder. See "Choose Custom AAC Encoding Settings," next, for a discussion of these options.

- For the MP3 Encoder, the Configuration drop-down list offers the settings Good Quality (128 Kbps), High Quality (160 Kbps), Higher Quality (192 Kbps), and Custom. When you select the Custom item, iTunes displays the MP3 Encoder dialog box so you can specify custom settings. See "Choose Custom MP3 Encoding Settings," later in this chapter, for a discussion of these options.

- For the AIFF Encoder and the WAV Encoder, the Configuration drop-down list offers the settings Automatic and Custom. When you select Custom, iTunes displays the AIFF Encoder dialog box or the WAV Encoder dialog box (as appropriate) so you can specify custom settings. See "Choose Custom AIFF and WAV Encoding Settings," later in this chapter, for a discussion of these options.

5. If you want iTunes to play each CD as you import it, leave the Play Songs While Importing check box selected (as it is by default). Listening to the CD may slow down the rate of ripping and encoding a little, so you may prefer not to use this option.

6. If you want iTunes to include track numbers in song names (creating names such as *01 All I Wanna Do* instead of *All I Wanna Do*), leave the Create File Names With Track Number check box selected (this check box is selected by default).

- Including the track numbers in the filenames isn't necessary for iTunes itself to keep the tracks in order, as iTunes can use the track-number information in a track's tag. (Some utilities for downloading songs from an iPod can sort songs by tag information too.) But you may want to include the numbers so that you can sort the songs easily into album order in Windows Explorer.

- Including the track number is useful for keeping tracks in order when you create MP3 CDs.

Those are all the options on the Importing tab of the iTunes dialog box. But a couple of options on the General tab (Figure 5-2) of the iTunes dialog box are also relevant to importing:

- In the On CD Insert drop-down list, choose the action you want iTunes to perform when you insert a CD: Show Songs, Begin Playing, Import Songs, or Import Songs And Eject. These settings are easy to understand, but bear in mind that Show Songs, Import Songs, and Import Songs And Eject all involve looking up the song names in CDDB (unless you've played the CD already and so caused iTunes to look them up). So iTunes will need to use your Internet connection.

- If you have a dial-up Internet connection, select the Connect To Internet When Needed check box if you want iTunes to be able to establish an Internet connection when it needs to look up data in CDDB.

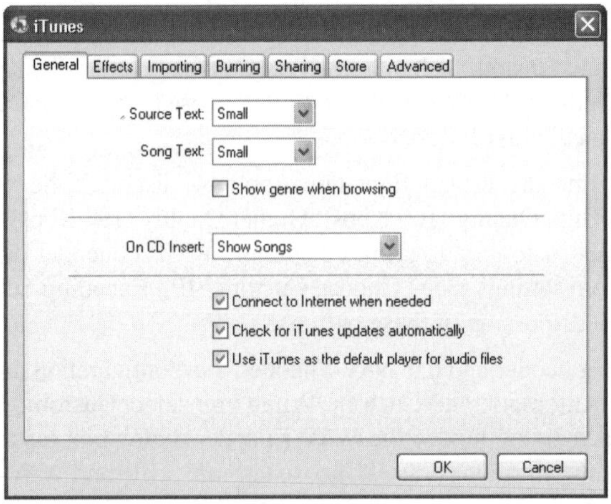

FIGURE 5-2 On the General tab of the iTunes dialog box, specify what iTunes should do when you insert a CD.

Choose Custom AAC Encoding Settings

To choose custom AAC encoding settings, follow these steps:

1. On the Importing tab of the iTunes dialog box, choose AAC Encoder in the Import Using drop-down list.

2. In the Setting drop-down list, choose the Custom item to display the iTunes dialog box for changing AAC settings:

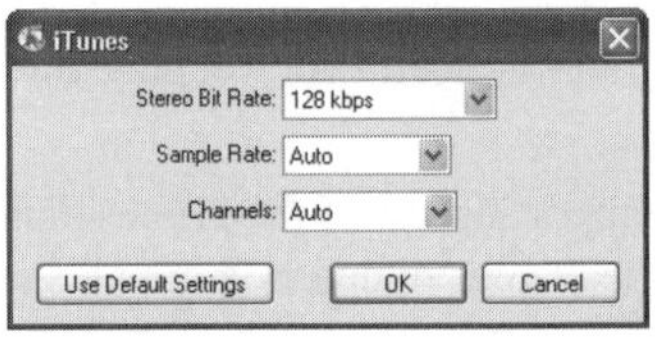

3. In the Stereo Bit Rate drop-down list, specify the bitrate. You can use from 16 Kbps to 320 Kbps. The default is 128 Kbps.

   ■ 128 Kbps provides high-quality audio suitable for general music listening. You may want to experiment with higher bitrates to see if you can detect a difference. If not, stick with 128 Kbps so as to get the largest possible amount of quality music on your iPod.

   ■ If you listen to spoken-word audio, experiment with the bitrates below 64 Kbps to see which bitrate delivers suitable quality for the material you listen to.

4. In the Sample Rate drop-down list, specify the sample rate by choosing Auto, 44.100 kHz or 48.000 kHz. CD audio uses the 44.100 kHz sample rate, so if you need to choose a manual setting, usually this will be the best choice. But if you have a data source that uses a 48.000 kHz sampling rate, choose this setting instead. For most purposes, you'll get best results by using the Auto setting (the default setting), which makes iTunes use a sampling rate that matches the input quality. For example, for CD-quality audio, iTunes uses the 44.100 kHz sampling rate.

5. In the Channels drop-down list, select Auto, Stereo, or Mono, as appropriate. In most cases, Auto (the default setting) is the best bet, as it makes iTunes choose Stereo or Mono, as appropriate to the sound source. However, you may occasionally need to produce mono files from stereo sources.

6. Click the OK button to close the iTunes dialog box for AAC encoding.

Choose Custom MP3 Encoding Settings

To choose custom MP3 encoding settings, follow these steps:

1. On the Importing tab of the iTunes dialog box, choose MP3 Encoder in the Import Using drop-down list.

2. In the Setting drop-down list, choose the Custom item to display the MP3 Encoder dialog box:

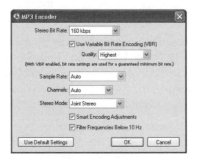

3. In the Stereo Bit Rate drop-down list, select the bitrate you want to use.

   ■ The choices range from 16 Kbps to 320 Kbps. 16 Kbps produces shoddy-sounding audio even for the spoken word, but it may be useful when you need to get long passages of low-quality audio into a small file. At the other extreme, 320 Kbps produces audio high enough in quality that most people can't distinguish them from CD-quality audio.

   ■ iTunes uses the bitrate you select as the exact bitrate for CBR encoding and as the minimum bitrate for VBR encoding.

   ■ See the section "What Does CD-Quality Audio Mean?," in Chapter 3, for a discussion of CD-quality audio. See the section "Choose an Appropriate Compression Rate, Bitrate, and Stereo Settings," also in Chapter 3, for advice on choosing a compression rate that matches your needs.

4. Select the Use Variable Bit Rate Encoding (VBR) check box if you want to create VBR-encoded files instead of CBR-encoded files:

- See the section "Choose Between CBR and VBR for MP3," in Chapter 3, for a discussion of CBR and VBR.

- If you select this check box, choose a suitable setting in the Quality drop-down list. The choices are Lowest, Low, Medium Low, Medium, Medium High, High, and Highest. iTunes uses the bitrates specified in the Stereo Bit Rate drop-down list as the guaranteed minimum bitrates. The Quality setting controls the amount of processing iTunes applies to making the file sound as close to the original as possible. More processing requires more processor cycles, which will make your PC work harder. If your PC is already working at full throttle, encoding will take longer.

5. In the Sample Rate drop-down list, set a sample rate manually only if you're convinced you need to do so:

- You might want to use a lower sample rate if you're encoding spoken-word audio rather than music and don't need such high fidelity.

- Choices range from 8 kHz to 48 kHz (higher than CD-quality audio, which uses 44.1 kHz).

- The default setting is Auto, which uses the same sample rate as does the music you're encoding. Using the same sample rate usually delivers optimal results.

6. In the Channels drop-down list, select Auto, Mono, or Stereo. The default setting is Auto, which uses mono for encoding mono sources and stereo for stereo sources.

7. In the Stereo Mode drop-down list, choose between normal stereo and joint stereo. See the section "Choose Between Normal Stereo and Joint Stereo for MP3," in Chapter 3, for a discussion of the difference between normal stereo and joint stereo. If you select Mono in the Channels drop-down list, the Stereo Mode drop-down list becomes unavailable because its options don't apply to mono.

8. Select or clear the Smart Encoding Adjustments check box and the Filter Frequencies Below 10 Hz check box, as appropriate. These check boxes are selected by default. In most cases, you'll do best to leave them selected:

- Smart Encoding Adjustments allows iTunes to tweak your custom settings to improve them if you've chosen an inappropriate combination.

- As discussed in "What Does CD-Quality Audio Mean?" in Chapter 3, frequencies below 10 Hz are infrasound and are of interest only to animals such as elephants, so filtering them out makes sense for humans.

NOTE *To restore iTunes to using its default settings for encoding MP3 files, click the Use Default Settings button in the MP3 Encoder dialog box.*

9. Click the OK button to close the MP3 Encoder dialog box.

10. Click the OK button to close the iTunes dialog box.

Choose Custom AIFF and WAV Encoding Settings

Other than creating different file formats, the AIFF Encoder dialog box (shown on the left in Figure 5-3) and the WAV Encoder dialog box (shown on the right in Figure 5-3) offer the same settings. This isn't surprising, because AIFFs and WAVs are essentially the same apart from the file header, which distinguishes the file formats from each other.

In either of these dialog boxes, you can choose the following settings:

- **Sample Rate** Choose Auto (the default setting) to encode at the same sample rate as the original you're ripping. Otherwise, choose a value from the range available (8 kHz to 48 kHz).

- **Sample Size** Select Auto to have iTunes automatically match the sample size to that of the source. Otherwise, select 8-Bit or 16-Bit, as appropriate. PCM audio uses 16 bits, so if you're encoding files from CDs, iTunes uses a 16-bit sample size automatically. Sometimes, you may want to use 8 bits to reduce the size of the audio file at the expense of quality.

- **Channels** Select Auto (the default setting) to encode mono files from mono sources and stereo files from stereo sources. Otherwise, select Mono or Stereo as appropriate.

Change the Columns Displayed to Show the Information You Need

By default, iTunes displays the following columns for your music library and for playlists: Song Name, Time, Artist, Album, Genre, My Rating, Play Count, and Last Played. (The Play Count item stores the number of times you've played the song in iTunes. iTunes uses this information to determine your favorite tracks—for example, to decide which tracks Smart Playlist should add to a playlist. You can also use this information yourself if you so choose. The other items are self-explanatory.)

You can change the columns displayed for the current item (for example, your music library or a playlist) by using either of two techniques.

To change the display of multiple columns in the same operation, press CTRL-J or choose Edit | View Options to display the View Options dialog box (Figure 5-4). The icon and label in the upper-left corner of the dialog box indicate which item's view you're customizing—for example,

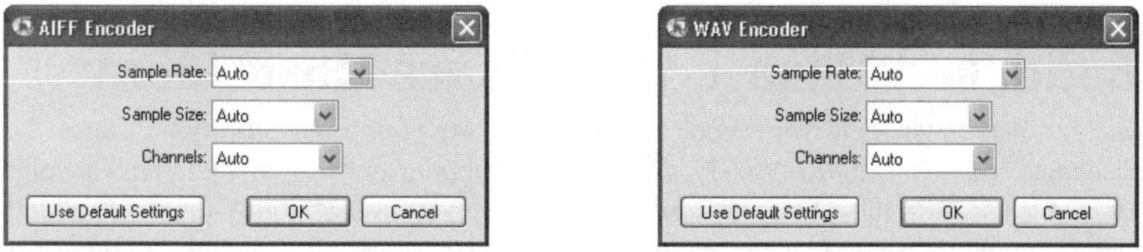

FIGURE 5-3   If you choose to encode to AIFF or WAV files, you can set encoding options in the AIFF Encoder dialog box (left) or the WAV Encoder dialog box (right).

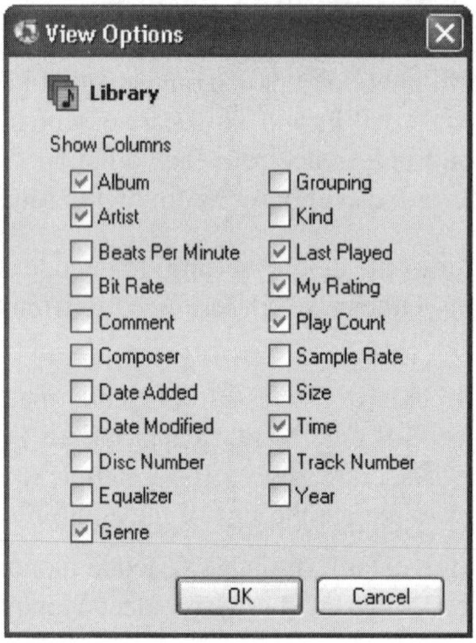

FIGURE 5-4 Use the View Options dialog box to choose which columns iTunes displays for the current item.

Library or Music Store. Select the check boxes for the columns you want to display, and then click the OK button to close the dialog box and apply your choices.

To change the display of a single column in the current item, right-click the heading of one of the columns currently displayed. iTunes displays a menu of the available columns, showing a check mark next to those currently displayed. Select an unchecked column to display it. Select a checked column to remove it from the display.

From the context menu, you can also select the Auto Size Column command to automatically resize the column whose heading you clicked so the column's width best fits its contents. Select the Auto Size All Columns command to automatically resize all columns like this.

TIP *You can also change the column width by dragging the right border of a column heading to the left or right. To move a column, drag its column heading left or right until iTunes displays shading where you want the column to appear, and then drop the column.*

Create, Build, and Manage Your iTunes Music Library

Before you can load music onto your iPod, you need to create your music library in iTunes. This section discusses how to do so. Most likely, you'll start by ripping some of your CDs and encoding them to AAC files or MP3 files. You may also need to add to your music library tunes you already have on your computer. You may also need to consolidate your music library (putting the whole library in one folder) and change the tags on some AAC files or MP3 files so iTunes and your iPod list them correctly.

Rip and Encode Your CDs

As discussed in Chapter 2, there are two steps to getting the audio off a CD and into a digital audio file your computer can use: extracting the audio from the CD in a process called *ripping,* and encoding it to the file (for example, an AAC file or an MP3 file). iTunes makes the process as straightforward as possible, and Windows' Autoplay feature can help move things along even faster.

Configure Autoplay to Rip and Encode CDs Using iTunes

When you insert an audio CD into a PC running Windows XP with default settings, Windows XP displays the Audio CD dialog box, identifying the drive the CD is in (in case your computer has multiple optical drives) and offering you a series of actions you can take with it: Play Audio CD Using Windows Media Player, Show Songs Using iTunes, Play Audio CD Using iTunes, Import Songs Using iTunes, Open Folder To View Files Using Windows Explorer, or Take No Action. (If you've turned off Autoplay, you won't see this dialog box.)

Select the action you want to take. If you'll always want to take the same action, select the Always Do The Selected Action check box. For example, when you're ripping your entire CD collection to AAC or MP3 files, you might select the Import Songs Using iTunes item and select the Always Do The Selected Action check box. Then click the OK button to close the Audio CD dialog box.

TIP   *To rip a stack of CDs as quickly as possible, select the Import Songs And Eject option in the On CD Insert drop-down list on the General tab of the iTunes dialog box (press CTRL-COMMA or choose iTunes | Preferences), and clear the Play Songs While Importing check box on the Importing tab.*

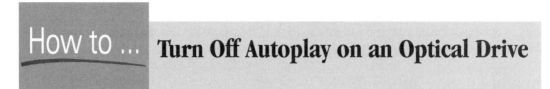

Windows XP's default settings are to use Autoplay for all CD drives and DVD drives in your computer. (Windows XP also uses Autoplay for removable drives.) To turn off Autoplay, follow these steps:

1. Choose Start | My Computer to display a My Computer window listing all your drives.

2. Right-click the entry for the CD drive or DVD drive and choose Properties from the shortcut menu to display the Properties dialog box for the drive.

3. Click the Autoplay tab:

4. In the drop-down list, select the Music CD item.

5. In the Actions group box, select the Select An Action To Perform option button.

6. Select the Take No Action item.

7. Click the OK button to close the Properties dialog box.

8. Click the Close button (the X button) to close the My Computer window.

Rip and Encode Automatically or Manually

To rip and encode a CD to compressed files, insert the CD in your PC's CD drive. If you configured Autoplay with the Import Songs Using iTunes setting, that's all you need to do; Windows launches iTunes (if it's not already running) or activates it (if it is running). iTunes looks up the CD's information in CDDB if necessary, and then starts ripping and encoding with the settings that you specified on the Importing tab of the iTunes dialog box:

If you prefer to start ripping manually, follow these steps:

1. Insert the CD you want to rip and encode in your PC's CD drive.

2. Enter the CD details—the CD title, artist name, song titles, and genre:

   ■ The easiest way to enter the details is to let iTunes connect automatically to the Internet to download the CD details automatically and enter them in the appropriate fields. (See "Choose Whether iTunes Automatically Connects to the Internet," earlier in this chapter, for details on how to control whether iTunes connects automatically.)

   ■ Alternatively, choose Advanced | Get CD Track Names to force iTunes to search CDDB for the information.

   ■ If you don't have an Internet connection, enter the data manually. See the sidebar "Tag Your Song Files Most Efficiently by Hand," a little later in this chapter, for suggestions on how to proceed.

3. By default, iTunes selects the check box for each song on the CD. Clear the check boxes for any songs you don't want to rip and encode. To select or clear all the check boxes, CTRL-click any check box.

4. Click the Import button to start the importing process. iTunes displays its progress. If you need to stop the import process, click the Import button again.

How to ... Tag Your Song Files Most Efficiently by Hand

Downloading CD information from CDDB is usually the fastest way of entering tag information in your song files. But sometimes you may need to enter tag information manually (for example, for a CD that doesn't have an entry in CDDB) or tweak the CDDB information. You may also want to specify an equalizer preset, volume adjustment, or rating when ripping the songs so that you don't have to specify this information later.

Here's the best way to proceed:

■ If you need to change only the artist, composer, album, genre, disc number, or year, or specify whether the CD is a compilation CD, right-click the entry for the CD in the Source pane, choose Get Info from the shortcut menu, and use the CD Info dialog box. Change the appropriate information, and then click the OK button to close the dialog box and apply the change.

■ To change any of this information and other information for all the songs, select all the songs (click one track, then press CTRL-A or choose Edit | Select All) and display the Multiple Song Information dialog box by pressing CTRL-I or issuing a Get Info command from the File menu or the shortcut menu. Enter the appropriate information, and then click the OK button to close the dialog box and apply the changes.

■ To enter the song names or other song-specific information, select the song and issue a Get Info command from the File menu or the shortcut menu to display the Song Information dialog box. Change the appropriate fields on the Info tab or set the volume, equalizer preset, rating, start time, or stop time on the Options tab. Then click the Previous button to move on to the previous song, the Next button to move on to the next song, or the OK button to close the dialog box.

How to ... Submit CD Information to CDDB Using iTunes

If a CD you want to rip turns out not to have an entry in CDDB (as indicated by the dialog box shown below), you can submit an entry yourself. Users submitting entries like this have added many of the entries in CDDB for older or less widely known CDs. Mainstream entries are submitted by the record companies themselves: they submit a listing to CDDB (and other online CD-information services, such as WindowsMedia.com) as a matter of course when they release a new CD.

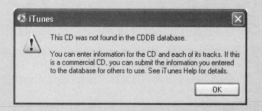

At this writing, CDDB contains entries for an enormous number of CDs—so unless you have an unusual CD, chances are any CD you want to rip already has an entry in CDDB. You may find that your CD is listed under a slightly different title or artist name than you're expecting— for example, the artist might be listed as *Sixpack, Joe* rather than *Joe Sixpack.* Check carefully for any close matches before submitting an entry so you don't waste your time.

You may also find CDDB contains two or more entries for the same CD. This can happen when two or more people submit information simultaneously for a CD that doesn't have an entry, or someone submits information for a previously existing selection. The people who run CDDB discard duplicate entries routinely when they find them, but given how many CDs CDDB contains entries for, it's not surprising that they're unable to catch all duplicates. When you run into a duplicate, you need to guess from the names shown which entry matches your CD.

When submitting an entry to CDDB, type the CD title, artist name, and song titles carefully using standard capitalization, and double-check all the information before you submit it. Otherwise, if your entry is accepted and entered in CDDB, anyone who looks up that CD will get the misspellings or wrong information you entered.

To submit an entry to CDDB, follow these steps:

1. Insert the CD in your CD drive and check that CDDB doesn't already have an entry for it.

2. Use the techniques described in "Tag Your Song Files Most Efficiently by Hand" to enter all the information for the CD into the available tags.

3. Choose Advanced | Submit CD Track Names to display the CD Info dialog box.

5

4. Check the information in the Artist, Composer, Album, Disc Number, Genre, and Year fields. Select the Compilation CD check box if the CD is a compilation rather than a work by an individual artist.

5. Establish an Internet connection if you need to do so manually.

6. Click the OK button. iTunes connects to CDDB and submits the information.

Join Tracks Together Without Gaps

iTunes' default settings are to create a separate file (AAC, MP3, AIFF, or WAV, depending on your preferences) from each song on CDs you rip. For most CDs, this works well. But sometimes you'll want to rip multiple tracks from a CD into a single file so they play back without a break. For example, some CDs are produced so one song runs into the next.

To rip two or more tracks from a CD into a single file, select the tracks, and then choose Advanced | Join CD Tracks. iTunes brackets the tracks, as shown here, so that they rip to a single file:

NOTE *If you made a mistake with the tracks you joined, select one or more of the joined tracks, and then choose Advanced | Unjoin CD Tracks to separate the tracks again.*

Add Songs to iTunes to Expand Your Music Library

You can add songs to iTunes in any of the following ways:

- Import the songs from CD as described earlier in this chapter. Alternatively, import the songs from another sound source.

- Drag one or more song files, or folders containing song files, and drop them in the iTunes main window. (If the iTunes window isn't visible, drag the selection to the iTunes button on the taskbar and hover it there to display the iTunes window, then drag the selection to the window and drop it there.)

NOTE   *If you left the Copy Files To iTunes Music Folder When Adding To Library check box (on the Advanced tab of the iTunes dialog box) selected, iTunes copies the song files to your music library. If you cleared this check box, iTunes simply adds to the library references to the song files.*

- Press CTRL-O or choose File | Add File To Library to display the Add To Library dialog box. Select the file or files you want to add, and then click the Open button.

- Choose File | Add Folder To Library to display the Browse For Folder dialog box. Navigate to the folder you want to add, select it, and then click the OK button.

- Drag one or more files or folders to the iTunes icon on your desktop or on the Start menu. When you use this technique, iTunes starts playing the song (or first song) automatically after copying it or storing the reference to it.

Delete Songs from Your Music Library

To delete songs from your music library, select them, and then either press DELETE or issue a Clear command from the Edit menu or the context menu. By default, iTunes displays a confirmation dialog box to check that you want to remove the songs. Click the Yes button to delete the tracks. To turn off the confirmation, select the Do Not Ask Me Again check box before dismissing the dialog box.

If any of the songs are located in your iTunes music folder, iTunes displays the following dialog box to tell you so and ask if you want to move these files to the Recycle Bin. Select the Yes button, the No button, or the Cancel button as appropriate.

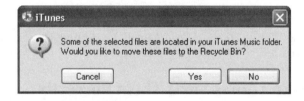

Consolidate Your Music Library So You Can Always Access All Its Songs

As you saw in "Choose Whether to Store All Song Files in Your Music Library," earlier in this chapter, if you clear the Copy Files To iTunes Music Folder When Adding To Library check box on the Advanced tab of the iTunes dialog box, iTunes places in the music library only a reference to the file. When your external drives, network drives, or removable media aren't available (for example, when you grab your notebook and head over to a friend's house for an evening of music and visualizations), the songs stored on those drives or media won't be available.

To make sure you can play the music you want wherever you want, you can *consolidate* your music library, making iTunes copy all the files currently outside your iTunes music folder to the music folder.

Don't rush into consolidating your music library without understanding its implications:

■ Consolidation can take a long time, depending on the number of files to be copied and the speed of the network connection you're using. Don't consolidate your library just as the airport shuttle is about to arrive.

■ The drive that holds your music library must have enough space free to hold all your songs. If lack of space was the reason you didn't copy the songs to your music library in the first place, you probably don't want to consolidate your library.

■ Songs on removable media such as CDs or Zip disks won't be copied unless the medium is in the drive at the time.

To consolidate your music library, follow these steps:

1. Choose Advanced | Consolidate Library. iTunes displays the following dialog box:

2. Click the Consolidate button. iTunes displays the Copying Files dialog box as it copies the files to your music library.

TIP *iTunes claims consolidation can't be undone, but in fact you* can *undo it—if you put in some effort. See "Letting iTunes Copy All Song Files to Your Music Library Runs You Out of Hard-Disk Space," in Chapter 17, for instructions.*

Tag Your Songs So iTunes Sorts Them Correctly

Each AAC file and MP3 file (and most other compressed audio files, such as Windows Media Audio files and Ogg Vorbis files) contains a *tag*—a container with a number of slots for different types of information, from the song name, artist name, and album name to the year and the genre. iTunes displays some of this information by default in its Artist, Album, and Genre columns, but it can handle files without tag information. Your iPod, on the other hand, requires the artist, song, and album information to be supplied so it can add a song to its database and allow you to access it.

The easiest way to add tag information to an AAC file or MP3 file is by downloading the information from CDDB when you rip the CD. But sometimes you'll need to enter (or change) tag information manually to make iTunes sort the files correctly.

NOTE *MP3 files distributed illegally on the Internet often lack tag information or include incorrect tags.*

To edit the tag information for a single song, select it and issue a Get Info command (press CTRL-I or choose Get Info from the File menu or the shortcut menu), and then work on the Info tab of the Song Information dialog box (see Figure 5-5). This dialog box's title bar shows the name of the song.

TIP *If your music library contains many untagged or mistagged files, you may need heavier-duty tagging features than iTunes provides. Chapter 6 discusses the best options available for retagging files.*

To edit the tag information for multiple songs at once, select the songs by SHIFT-clicking (to select multiple contiguous songs) or CTRL-clicking (to add noncontiguous songs to those currently selected), and then press CTRL-I or choose Get Info from the File menu or the shortcut menu. In the Multiple Song Information dialog box (see Figure 5-6), enter the information common to the songs you selected.

NOTE *By default, when you issue a Get Info command with multiple songs selected, iTunes displays a dialog box to check that you want to edit the information for multiple songs. Click the Yes button to proceed; click the Cancel button to cancel. Select the Do Not Ask Me Again check box in the confirmation dialog box if you want to turn off this safeguard.*

Apply Ratings to Songs to Tell iTunes Which Music You Like

iTunes' My Rating feature lets you assign a rating of zero to five stars to each song in your music library. Then you can sort the songs by rating or tell Smart Playlist to add only songs of a certain ranking or better to a playlist. (See the section "Automatically Create Smart Playlists Based on Your Ratings and Preferences," later in this chapter, for a discussion of the Smart Playlist feature.)

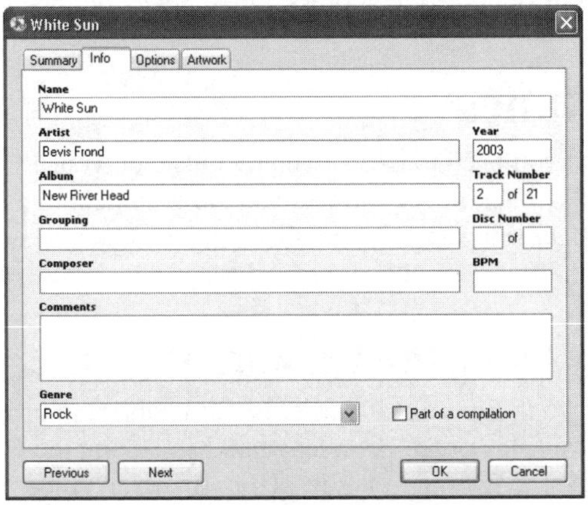

FIGURE 5-5 Use the Info tab of the Song Information dialog box to edit the tag information for a single song.

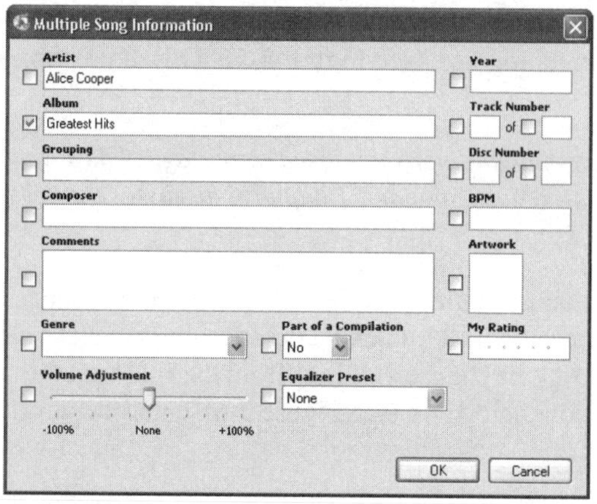

FIGURE 5-6   Instead of editing tag information one song at a time, you can edit tag information for multiple songs at once by using the Multiple Song Information dialog box.

You can apply a rating in any of three ways:

■ Right-click a song, choose My Rating from the shortcut menu, and select the appropriate number of stars from the submenu.

■ Use the My Rating box on the Options tab of the Song Information dialog box (CTRL-I or Get Info from the File menu or the shortcut menu) to specify the number (or absence) of stars.

■ On a third-generation iPod or iPod mini, you can rate the currently playing song by pressing the Select button twice in quick succession, scrolling to the left or right to select the appropriate number of stars, and then pressing the Select button again.

Enjoy Music with iTunes

This section shows you what you need to know to enjoy music on your PC with iTunes: how to browse for songs, how to play back music, how to use the graphical equalizer to improve the sound of the music, how to fade one song into another song, and how to skip the boring start or end of a song.

Browse Quickly by Using the Browser Panes

Use the Browser panes (shown in Figure 5-1, earlier in this chapter) to browse quickly by artist or album. You can toggle the display of the Browser panes by clicking the Browse button, pressing CTRL-B, or choosing Edit | Show Browser or Edit | Hide Browser. Once the Browser panes are displayed, click an item in the Artist column to display the albums by that artist in the Album column, and then click an item in the Albums column to display that album in the lower pane.

As well as browsing by artist and album, you can browse by genre (see Figure 5-7). This capability can be useful when you want to find particular types of songs, because it makes iTunes

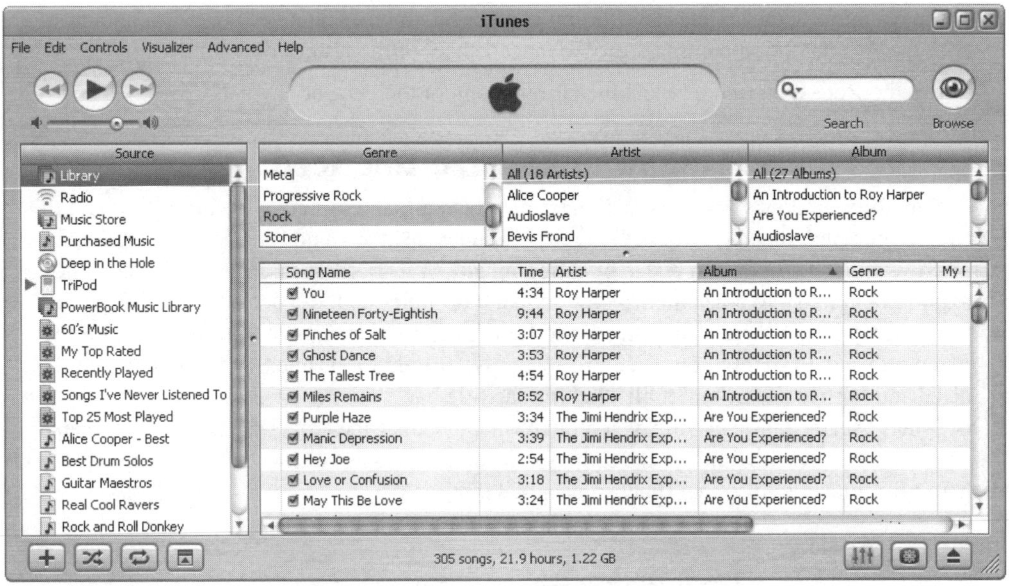

FIGURE 5-7   Select the Show Genre When Browsing check box on the General tab of the iTunes dialog box to enable yourself to browse your songs by genre as well as artist and album.

display only the artists and albums whose songs are tagged with the genre you choose. When you don't want to restrict the view by genre, select the All item at the top of the Genre pane so that you see all genres at once.

To turn browsing by genre on or off, press CTRL-COMMA (or CTRL-Y) or choose iTunes | Preferences to display the iTunes dialog box, select or clear the Show Genre When Browsing check box on the General tab, and then click the OK button.

> **NOTE**   *The readout at the bottom of the full iTunes window shows you how many songs are in the current selection and how long they last. This readout has two formats: 5738 songs, 17.4 days, 22.98 GB and 5738 songs, 17:10:06:58 total time, 22.98 GB. To toggle between the two formats, click the readout.*

Play Back Music with iTunes

Playing back music with iTunes is straightforward:

■   Navigate to the album, playlist, or song you want to play, select it, and then click the Play button.

■   Drag the diamond on the progress bar in the display to scroll forward or backward through the current track.

■ Use the Shuffle button to shuffle the order of the tracks in the current album or playlist. (To change whether iTunes shuffles by song or by album, select the Song option button or the Album option button on the Advanced sheet of the iTunes dialog box.)

■ Use the Repeat button to repeat the current song or the current playlist.

Resize the iTunes Window to the Size You Need

iTunes offers four window sizes—normal, maximized, small, and minute—to suit the amount of space you're prepared to dedicate to it. By default, iTunes opens in a normal (in other words, not maximized) window that you can resize by dragging any of its borders or corners. You can click the Maximize button to maximize the window so that it occupies all the space on your screen (apart from the taskbar, if you have it displayed), and click the Restore Down button to restore the maximized window to its previous size. You can also toggle the iTunes window between its maximized and normal states by double-clicking the title bar.

Once you've set the music playing, you'll often want to reduce the iTunes window to its essentials so that you can get on with your work (or play). To do so, press CTRL-M or choose Advanced | Switch To Mini Player to display iTunes in its small size:

From here, you can drag the sizing handle in the lower-right corner to shrink iTunes down even further to its minute size. This can be handy when you're pushed for space, but it isn't very informative:

To restore iTunes to its normal size from the small size or the minute size, press CTRL-M or click the Restore button.

Control iTunes via Keyboard Shortcuts

Like most Windows applications (and Mac applications), iTunes has a graphical interface that you can easily manipulate using the mouse. But you can also control most of iTunes' features by using the keyboard. This can be useful both when your mouse is temporarily out of reach and when you've reduced the iTunes window to its small size or minute size and thus hidden some of the controls.

Table 5-1 lists the keyboard shortcuts you can use to control iTunes. Most of these shortcuts work in any of iTunes' display modes (discussed in the previous section), but the table notes the shortcuts that work only in some modes.

Keystroke	Action
UP ARROW	Increases the volume (in the small and minute sizes only).
DOWN ARROW	Decreases the volume (in the small and minute sizes only).
CTRL-UP ARROW	Increases the volume.
CTRL-DOWN ARROW	Decreases the volume.
SPACEBAR	Plays/pauses the song.
RIGHT ARROW	Plays the next song.
LEFT ARROW	Plays the previous song.
CTRL-ALT-LEFT ARROW	Rewinds the song.
CTRL-ALT-RIGHT ARROW	Fast-forwards the song.
SHIFT-UP ARROW	Turns the iTunes volume to maximum. This keyboard shortcut works only in the small and minute sizes. In the normal and maximized sizes, it extends the selection to the next track in the current list (or reduces the existing selection by one song downward).
SHIFT-DOWN ARROW	Mutes iTunes. This keyboard shortcut works only in the small and minute sizes. In the normal and maximized sizes, it reduces the existing selection by one song upward in the current list (or extends the existing selection by one song downward).
CTRL-ALT-UP ARROW, CTRL-ALT-DOWN ARROW	Toggles muting (even with iTunes maximized).
CTRL-M	Toggles iTunes to and from its small size.
CTRL-U	Displays the Open Stream dialog box.
CTRL-T	Toggles the Visualizer on and off.
CTRL-F	Toggles full-screen mode on the Visualizer.

TABLE 5-1

Accompany Your Music with Visualizations

Like many music applications, iTunes can produce stunning visualizations to accompany your music. You can display visualizations at any of three sizes within the iTunes window (which can provide visual distraction while you work or play) or display them full-screen to make your PC the life of the party.

Here's how to use visualizations:

- Set the size to use by choosing Visualizer | Small, Visualizer | Medium, or Visualizer | Large. If you want the visualizations to start in full-screen mode, choose Visualizer | Full Screen.

- To start a visualization of the size you specified, press CTRL-T or choose Visualizer | Turn Visualizer On.

■ To turn a windowed visualization off, press CTRL-T or choose Visualizer | Turn Visualizer Off.

■ To launch full-screen visualizations, press CTRL-F or choose Visualizer | Full Screen.

■ To stop full-screen visualizations, click your mouse button anywhere or press ESC or CTRL-T.

Configure Visualizations to Get the Best Results

iTunes even lets you configure visualizations to make them look as good as possible on your computer. To configure visualizations, follow these steps:

1. If iTunes is displayed at its small or minute size, click the Restore button to return iTunes to a normal window.

2. Start a song playing.

3. Press CTRL-T or choose Visualizer | Turn Visualizer On to start a visualization running (unless you have one running already).

4. Click the Options button in the upper-right corner of the maximized iTunes window to display the Visualizer Options dialog box:

5. Select and clear the check boxes to specify the options you want:

■ **Display Frame Rate**   Controls whether iTunes displays the frame rate (the number of frames being generated each second) superimposed on the upper-left corner of the visualization. This check box is cleared by default. The frame rate is useless information that adds nothing to the visualization, but it can be useful as a point of reference. For example, you may want to compare the visualization frame rates generated by different computers, or you might want to try the Faster But Rougher Display option (discussed in a moment) to see how much difference it produces. Bear in mind that the frame rate will vary depending on the size of the visualization window, the complexity of the visualization, and what other tasks your computer is working on at the time.

■ **Cap Frame Rate At 30 fps**   Controls whether iTunes stops the frame from exceeding 30 frames per second. This check box is selected by default. iTunes is configured to cap the frame rate to reduce the demands on the visualization on your computer's graphics card and processor. The cap is at 30 fps because most people find 30 fps provides smooth and wonderful visualizations—so there's no point in trying to crank out extra frames.

- **Always Display Song Info**   Controls whether iTunes displays the song information overlaid on the visualization all the time or just at the beginning of a song and when you change the visualizer size while playing a song. This check box is cleared by default.
- **Faster But Rougher Display**   Lets you tell iTunes to lower the quality of the visualizations to increase the frame rate. This check box is cleared by default. You may want to try selecting this check box on a less powerful computer if you find the visualizations are too slow.

TIP   *You can also trigger most of these options from the keyboard while a visualization is playing, without displaying the Visualizer Options dialog box. Press F to toggle the frame rate display, T to toggle frame rate capping, I to toggle the display of song information, and D to restore the default settings.*

6. Click the OK button to close the Visualizer Options dialog box.

TIP   *You can change the information shown in the display window by clicking the items in it. Click the top line to move among the song title, the artist's name, and the album title. Click the Play icon at the left of the display window to toggle between the track information and the equalization graph. Click the time readout to move among Elapsed Time, Remaining Time, and Total Time.*

Choose Crossfading and Sound Enhancer Settings

The Effects tab of the iTunes dialog box (see Figure 5-8) offers options for crossfading playback, configuring the Sound Enhancer, and toggling the Sound Check feature on and off:

- **Crossfade Playback**   Makes iTunes fade in the start of the next track as the current track is about to end. This option lets you eliminate gaps between songs the way most DJs do. Drag the slider to increase or decrease the length of time that's crossfaded. This check box is selected by default; turn off crossfading if you don't like it.
- **Sound Enhancer**   Applies iTunes' sound enhancement to the music being played back. Experiment with different settings on the Low–High scale by dragging the slider to see which setting sounds best to you—or turn off sound enhancement if you don't like it (this check box is selected by default). Sound enhancement can make treble sounds appear brighter and can add to the effect of stereo separation, but the results don't suit everybody. You may prefer to adjust the sound manually by using the graphical equalizer, as described in the next section.
- **Sound Check**   Controls whether iTunes automatically adjusts the playback level of each song to the same level. (Some players call this "normalization.") Sound Check can help you avoid getting your ears blasted by playing a loud song after a quiet song. Clear the check box, which is selected by default, if you don't like the results.

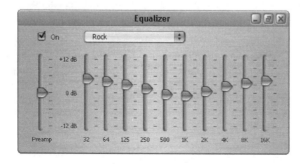

FIGURE 5-8   Choose playback options on the Effects tab of the iTunes dialog box.

Use the Graphical Equalizer to Make the Music Sound Great

iTunes includes a graphical equalizer that you can use to change the sound of the music (or other audio) you're playing. You can apply an equalization directly to the playlist you're currently playing, much as you would apply an equalization manually to a physical amplifier or receiver. But you can also apply a specific equalization to each song in your iTunes music library. Once you've done this, iTunes always uses that equalization when playing that song, no matter which equalization is applied currently to iTunes itself. After playing a song that has an equalization specified, iTunes switches back to the previous equalization for the next song that doesn't have an equalization specified.

Apply an Equalization to the Current Playlist

To apply an equalization to the current playlist, display the Equalizer window by clicking the Equalizer button at the lower-right corner of the iTunes window. Select the equalization from the drop-down list. If you're playing music, you'll hear the effect of the new equalization in a second or two.

Specify an Equalization for an Individual Song

You can specify the equalization iTunes should use for a particular song by working either from the main iTunes window or the Song Information dialog box:

■ Make the main iTunes window wide enough to display the Equalizer column, or rearrange the columns so that the Equalizer column is visible in the window. Then use the drop-down list in the Equalizer column to set the equalization to apply to the song in the same row.

NOTE *It doesn't matter whether you apply the equalization to the song in the music library or in a playlist, because applying the equalization even in a playlist affects the song in the music library. So if you can access a song more easily through a playlist than through your music library, start from the playlist.*

5

■ Select a song and press CTRL-I (or choose Get Info from the File menu or the shortcut menu) to display the Song Information dialog box. On the Options tab, select the equalization in the Equalizer Preset drop-down list, and then click the OK button.

NOTE *If the equalization you apply to a song is one of the equalizations built into your iPod, your iPod also uses the equalization automatically for playing back the track. But if the equalization is a custom one your iPod doesn't have, your iPod can't use it. Your iPod doesn't pick up custom equalizations you create in iTunes.*

Create a Custom Equalization That Sounds Good to You

The preset equalizations in iTunes span a wide range of musical types—but even if there's one named after the type of music you're currently listening to, you may not like the effects it produces. When this happens, try all the other equalizations—however unsuitable their names may make them seem—to see if any of them just happens to sound great with this type of music. (For example, some people swear the Classical equalization is perfect for many Grateful Dead tracks.) If none of them suits you, create a custom equalization that delivers the goods.

To create a new custom equalization, follow these steps:

1. If the Equalizer window isn't displayed, click the Equalizer button in the main iTunes window to display it.

2. Drag the frequency sliders to the appropriate positions for the sound you want the equalization to deliver. When you change the first slider in the current preset, the drop-down list displays Manual.

3. If appropriate, drag the Preamp slider to a different level. For example, you might want to boost the preamp level on all the songs to which you apply a certain equalization.

4. Choose Make Preset from the drop-down list. iTunes displays the Make Preset dialog box:

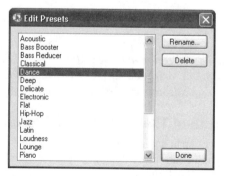

5. Enter the name for the equalization and click the OK button.

Then you can apply your equalization from the drop-down list as you would any other preset equalization.

Delete and Rename Preset Equalizations

If you don't like a preset equalization, you can delete it. If you find an equalization's name unsuitable, you can rename it. To delete or rename an equalization, follow these steps:

1. Select the Edit List item from the drop-down list in the Equalizer window. iTunes displays the Edit Presets dialog box:

2. Select the preset equalization you want to affect.

3. To rename the equalization, follow these steps:

   A. Click the Rename button to display the Rename dialog box.

   B. Type the new name in the New Preset Name text box.

   C. Click the OK button. iTunes displays a dialog box like this one, asking whether you want to change all songs currently set to use this equalization under its current name to use the equalization under the new name you've just specified:

   D. Choose the Yes button or the No button, as appropriate.

4. To delete a preset equalization, follow these steps:

   A. Click the Delete button. iTunes displays a dialog box like this, asking you to confirm the deletion:

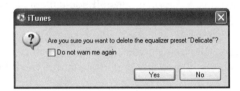

   B. Click the Yes button or the No button, as appropriate. To stop iTunes from confirming the deletion of preset equalizations, select the Do Not Warn Me Again check box before clicking Yes or No.

   C. If you click Yes, iTunes displays a dialog box asking if you want to remove the preset from all songs that are set to use it:

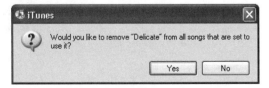

5. Click the Yes button or the No button, as appropriate.

5

Skip the Boring Intro or Outro on a Song

If you disagree with the producer of a song about when the song should begin or end, use the Start Time and Stop Time controls on the Options tab of the Song Information dialog box to specify how much of the track to lop off. This trimming works both in iTunes and on your iPod.

To trim the intro, enter in the Start Time text box the point at which you want the song to start. For example, enter **1:15** to skip the first minute and a quarter of a song. When you start typing in the Start Time text box, iTunes selects the Start Time check box for you, so you don't need to select it manually.

Similarly, you can change the value in the Stop Time text box to stop the song playing before its end. By default, the Stop Time text box contains a time showing when the song ends, down to thousandths of a second—for example, 4:56:769. When you reduce this time, iTunes selects the Stop Time check box automatically.

 When skipping an intro or outro isn't enough, you can edit a song file down to only that part you want. See Chapter 6 for details.

Synchronize Your Music Library with Your iPod

By default, iTunes synchronizes all the changes you make to your music library with your iPod. When you buy a couple of CDs and rip them to compressed files in your music library, iTunes adds them to your iPod the next time you synchronize. If you build a new playlist, iTunes adds it to your iPod. And if you delete your playlists in iTunes in a fit of pique, they'll disappear from your iPod at its next synchronization.

These default settings work well provided your iPod has enough free disk space to contain your entire music library. If not, you'll probably prefer to control synchronization manually, as described in this section.

To synchronize, connect your iPod to your PC as described in "Connect Your iPod to Your PC," in Chapter 2, either directly via a FireWire cable or via the iPod Dock, or via a USB cable. When iTunes detects your iPod, it displays an entry for it in the Source pane. When this entry is selected, as in Figure 5-9, the lower-right corner of iTunes displays a Display Options For Player button and an Eject iPod button. Your iPod also appears as a drive on your computer. You can eject your iPod by choosing Start | My Computer, right-clicking the drive, and choosing Eject from the shortcut menu.

If you make changes to your music library after iTunes has automatically updated your iPod but before you've unplugged your iPod, you can force an update by choosing File | Update Songs on iPod, where iPod *is the name assigned to your iPod.*

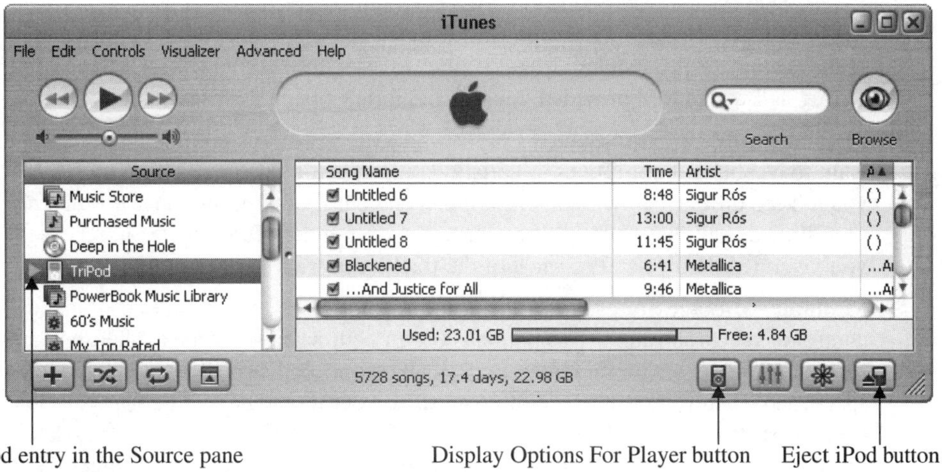

iPod entry in the Source pane   Display Options For Player button   Eject iPod button

FIGURE 5-9   iTunes displays your iPod in the Source pane, together with buttons for manipulating it.

Control Synchronization to Get the Music You Want on Your iPod

If your iPod's default synchronization settings don't agree with you, change them. To do so, follow these steps:

1. Connect your iPod to your PC as usual.

2. Select the iPod icon in the Source pane.

3. Click the Display Options For Player button in the lower-right corner of the iTunes window to display the iPod Preferences dialog box:

4. Choose the appropriate option button:

- **Automatically Update All Songs And Playlists**   Select this option button to have iTunes automatically synchronize all your changes with your iPod. This is the default setting and works well provided your music library fits on your iPod.

- **Automatically Update Selected Playlists Only**   Select this option button if you want to be able to limit iTunes to updating only specific playlists. This option allows you to keep different playlists in iTunes than on your iPod. This option is useful when your iPod doesn't have enough free space for your entire iTunes music library, and you've gotten onto your iPod most of the tracks you want to have on it.

- **Manually Manage Songs And Playlists**   Select this option button to take manual control of synchronization. This option is useful both when you need to choose which parts of your massive music library to pack onto your iPod's smaller amount of storage space, and when you want to add more music to your iPod than will fit onto your PC. (See the section "Load More Music on Your iPod Than Will Fit on Your PC," later in this chapter, for a discussion of how to do this.) When you click to select this option button, iTunes displays this warning dialog box to make sure you understand that you'll need to unmount your iPod manually before disconnecting it:

Click the OK button if you're happy with this, and iTunes will select the Manually Manage Songs And Playlists option button. (iTunes also selects the Enable Disk Use check box if it wasn't already selected and makes it unavailable, so that you can't clear it manually.) Otherwise, click the Cancel button, and iTunes will leave the current option button selected.

5. Click the OK button to close the iPod Preferences dialog box.

Control Synchronization Manually

If you chose the Manually Manage Songs And Playlists option button in the iPod Preferences dialog box, iTunes displays your iPod as an expandable list of playlists in the Source pane:

Now you can manage synchronization manually by using the steps in the following sections. You can also play back songs directly from the iPod by navigating to them, selecting them, and clicking the Play button or pressing SPACEBAR.

Add Songs to Your iPod Manually

To add songs to your iPod manually, follow these steps:

1. Select your iPod's icon in the Source pane to display your iPod's contents.

2. Select the songs you want to copy to your iPod, either in your iTunes music library or in a Windows Explorer window.

3. Drag the songs to the iPod's icon or to the appropriate playlist. If you're dragging from a Windows Explorer window and you have the iPod's contents displayed in the main iTunes pane, you can drop the tracks there.

Remove Songs from Your iPod

To remove songs from your iPod manually, follow these steps:

1. Select your iPod's icon in the Source pane to display your iPod's contents.

2. Select the songs you want to remove.

3. Drag the songs to the Trash. (Alternatively, press DELETE.) iTunes displays a confirmation dialog box.

4. Click the Yes button. Select the Do Not Ask Me Again check box first if you don't want iTunes to confirm each deletion with you in the future.

This technique removes the songs only from your iPod, not from your music library.

CAUTION *Use only iTunes to remove songs from your iPod—don't use Windows Explorer or another file-management application. This is because iTunes updates the iPod's database when removing songs, while Windows Explorer doesn't. So if you remove songs using Windows Explorer, the iPod thinks they're still there, even though they're not.*

Synchronize Only Part of Your Music Library with Your iPod

If your music library is too big to all fit on your iPod (or that portion of your iPod capacity you're using for music), you can specify which songs and playlists to synchronize with your iPod in either of two ways:

- Select the Automatically Update Selected Playlists Only option button in the iPod iTunes dialog box. Then, in the list box in the iPod iTunes dialog box, select the check boxes for the playlists you want to synchronize. This technique works only for songs included in playlists.

- Control all synchronization manually, as described in "Control Synchronization Manually," earlier in this chapter.

Load More Music on Your iPod Than Will Fit on Your PC

If you have a newish iPod and an older PC, your PC may not have enough free disk space to hold all the songs you want to load on your iPod. To get around this problem, follow these steps:

1. Turn on manual synchronization in the iPod iTunes dialog box. (See "Control Synchronization to Get the Music You Want on Your iPod," earlier in this chapter.)

2. Synchronize your iPod manually, as described in "Control Synchronization Manually," earlier in this chapter.

If your PC is connected to a network on which it can access drives, you can get around the lack of disk space on your PC in two other ways:

- Keep a significant part of your music library on a network drive to supplement that part you can fit on your hard drive. To prevent iTunes from copying files to your hard drive, clear the Copy Files To iTunes Music Folder When Adding To Library check box on the Advanced tab of the iTunes dialog box.

- Keep your entire music library on a network drive. Use the procedure described in "Choose Where to Store Your Music Library," earlier in this chapter, to change the music library's folder from its default location on your startup disk to the appropriate folder on the network drive. In this case, you don't need to clear the Copy Files To iTunes Music Folder When Adding To Library check box.

In either case, if you use automatic updating, you'll need to make sure the network drive is available whenever you synchronize your iPod. If it's not, you'll be unable to synchronize any of the tracks on that drive.

Return to Automatic Updating from Manual Updating

To return to automatic updating from manual updating, follow these steps:

1. Make sure that your iPod doesn't contain any songs that your music library doesn't contain—or that, if your iPod does contain other songs, they're expendable. Returning your iPod to automatic updating will overwrite all the iPod's current contents.

2. Make sure your music library will fit on your iPod (if you're planning to synchronize the entire library) or that the selected playlists will fit (if you're planning to synchronize only some playlists).

3. Connect your iPod to your PC and let iTunes discover your iPod.

4. Click the Display Options For Player button to display the iPod Preferences dialog box.

5. Select the Automatically Update All Songs And Playlists option button or the Automatically Update Selected Playlists Only option button. iTunes displays this warning dialog box:

6. Click the OK button to return to the iPod Preferences dialog box.

7. Click the OK button to close the iPod Preferences dialog box. iTunes updates your iPod with your music library or the selected playlists.

Listen to Audible.com Spoken-Word Files on Your iPod

Even if your iPod is stuffed nearly full with songs, you may still have plenty of space to pack on plenty of spoken-word audio. This is because spoken-word audio can sound great at much lower bitrates than music.

Audible.com provides a wide variety of content, such as audio books, magazines, and plays, in a selection of different subscription types and accounts. To get started, go to the Audible.com website (www.audible.com) and set up an account.

CAUTION   *Audible is an interesting service, but read the terms and conditions carefully for the account type you choose. Otherwise, Audible policies such as canceling any unused book credits at the end of each subscription month may give you an unpleasant surprise.*

After setting up an account, you can download files to up to three different computers for that account. The first time you download Audible.com content to a particular computer, you need to enter your Audible.com account information in the Audible Account dialog box while connected to the Internet. After that, you can simply drag an Audible file to the iTunes window to add it to your music library.

If you need to transfer one of the three manifestations of your Audible.com account from one computer to another, follow these steps:

1. If you need to establish your Internet connection manually, do so.

2. In iTunes, choose Advanced | Deauthorize Computer to display the Deauthorize Computer dialog box:

3. Select the Deauthorize Computer For Audible Account option button.

4. Click the Finish button.

Create Custom Playlists to Enjoy in iTunes or on Your iPod

Typically, a CD presents its songs in the order the artist or the producer thought best, but you'll often want to rearrange the songs into a different order—or mix the songs from different CDs in a way that suits only you. To do so, you create playlists in iTunes, and iTunes automatically shares them with your iPod so that you can use them there as well.

To create a playlist, follow these steps:

1. Click the + button in the Source pane, choose File | New Playlist, or press CTRL-N. iTunes adds a new playlist to the source pane, names it *untitled playlist* (or the next available name, such as *untitled playlist 2*), and displays an edit box around it.

2. Type the name for the playlist, and then press ENTER or click elsewhere to apply the name.

3. Select the Library item in the Source pane to display your songs. If you want to work by artist and album, press CTRL-B or choose Edit | Show Browser to display the Browser pane.

4. Select the songs you want to add to the playlist, and then drag them to the playlist's name. You can drag one song at a time or multiple songs—whatever you find easiest.

5. Click the playlist's name in the source pane to display the playlist in the main window.

6. Drag the tracks into the order in which you want them to play.

NOTE *For you to be able to drag the tracks around in the playlist, the playlist must be sorted by the track-number column. If you select any other column heading, you won't be able to rearrange the order of the tracks in the playlist.*

You can also create a playlist by selecting the tracks you want to include and then pressing CTRL-SHIFT-N or choosing File | New Playlist From Selection. iTunes organizes the songs into a new playlist provisionally named *untitled playlist* and displays an edit box around the title so that you can change it immediately. Type the new name, and press ENTER or click elsewhere to apply the name.

Automatically Create Smart Playlists Based on Your Ratings and Preferences

The Smart Playlist feature lets you instruct iTunes about how to build a list of songs automatically for you. You can tell Smart Playlist to build playlists by artist, composer, or genre; to select up to a specific number of songs at random, by artist, by most played, by last player, or by song name; and to automatically update a playlist as you add tracks to your music library or remove tracks from it. For example, if you tell Smart Playlist to make you a playlist of songs by Christina Aguilera, Smart Playlist can update the list with new songs after you buy them from the iTunes Music Store or import them into your music library.

Smart Playlist lets you specify multiple conditions to describe which songs you want it to select. For example, you might specify a range of years (say, the '70s) but exclude certain artists by name to keep the music up to a certain standard.

NOTE *Smart Playlist maintains playlists such as the My Top Rated playlist, the Recently Played playlist, and the Top 25 Most Played playlist, which iTunes creates by default.*

5

To create a new smart playlist, follow these steps:

1. Press CTRL-ALT-N, choose File | New Smart Playlist, or SHIFT-click the Create A Playlist button to display the Smart Playlist dialog box (shown here with a playlist under construction):

2. Make sure the Match The Following Condition check box is selected so that you can specify criteria. (The other option is to create a random Smart Playlist, which can sometimes be entertaining.) If you create multiple conditions, this check box offers the choices Match All Of The Following Conditions and Match Any Of The Following Conditions. Choose the appropriate one.

3. Use the controls in the first line to specify the first condition. The first drop-down list offers an extensive range of choices: Album, Artist, BPM (beats per minute), Bit Rate, Comment, Compilation, Composer, Date Added, Date Modified, Genre, Grouping, Kind, Last Played, My Rating, Play Count, Sample Rate, Size, Song Name, Time, Track Number, and Year. The second drop-down list offers options suitable to the item you chose in the first drop-down list—for example, Contains, Does Not Contain, Is, Is Not, Starts With, or Ends With for a text field, or Is, Is Not, Is Greater Than, Is Less Than, or Is In The Range for the bitrate.

4. To create multiple conditions, click the + button at the end of the line. iTunes adds another line of condition controls, which you can then set as described in step 3. To remove a condition, click the – button at the end of a line.

5. To limit the playlist to a maximum number of tracks, time, or disk space, select the Limit To check box and specify the limit and how iTunes should select the songs. For example, you could specify Limit To 30 Songs Selected By Least Often Played or Limit To 8 Hours Selected By Random.

6. To make iTunes omit songs whose check boxes you've cleared in your music library, select the Match Only Checked Songs check box.

7. Select or clear the Live Updating check box to specify whether iTunes should periodically update the playlist according to your listening patterns.

8. Click the OK button to close the Smart Playlist dialog box. iTunes creates the playlist, assigns a name to it (for example, *untitled playlist*), and displays an edit box around the name so you can change it.

9. Type the new name for the playlist, and then press ENTER.

Share Your Music with Other Local iTunes Users

Running on Windows 2000, Windows XP, or a later version of Windows, iTunes 4 lets you share either your entire music library or selected playlists with other users on your network (or, more technically, on the same TCP/IP subnet as your computer). You can share MP3 files, AAC files, AIFF files, WAV files, and links to radio stations. You can't share Audible files or QuickTime sound files.

You can share your music with up to five other users at a time, and you can be one of up to five users accessing the shared music on another computer. Each Mac must be running Mac OS X 10.2.4 (or a later version), and each Windows PC must be running Windows 2000, Windows XP, or a later version.

Shared music remains on the computer that's sharing it, and when a participating computer goes to play a song, the song is streamed across the network. (In other words, the song isn't copied from the computer that's sharing it to the computer that's playing it in a way that leaves a usable file on the computer that's playing the music.) When a computer goes offline or is shut down, any music it has been sharing stops being available to other users. Participating computers can play the shared music but can't do anything else with it; they can't burn the shared music to CD or DVD, download it to an iPod, or copy it to their own libraries.

To share some or all of your music, follow these steps:

1. Choose Edit | Preferences or press CTRL-COMMA (or CTRL-Y) to display the iTunes dialog box.

2. Click the Sharing tab:

3. Select the Share My Music check box. (This check box is cleared by default.) By default, iTunes then selects the Share Entire Library option button; if you want to share only some playlists, select the Share Selected Playlists option button and select the appropriate check boxes in the list box.

4. The Shared Name text box controls the name that other users trying to access your music will see. The default name is *username*'s music, where *username* is your username—for example, Anna Connor's Music. You might choose to enter a more descriptive name, especially if your computer is part of a well-populated network (for example, in a dorm).

5. By default, your music is available to any other user on the network. To restrict access to people with whom you share a password, select the Require Password check box and enter a strong (unguessable) password in the text box.

6. Click the OK button to apply your choices and close the iTunes dialog box.

NOTE   *When you set iTunes to share your music, iTunes displays a message reminding you that "Sharing music is for personal use only"—in other words, remember not to violate copyright law. Select the Do Not Show This Message Again check box if you want to prevent this message from appearing again.*

Access and Play Another Local iTunes User's Shared Music

To access another person's shared music, your computer must have iTunes 4 running on Windows 2000, Windows XP, or a later version of Windows. You can then access shared music by following the instructions in the next three sections.

Set Your Computer to Look for Shared Music

First, set your computer to look for shared music. Follow these steps:

1. Choose Edit | Preferences or press CTRL-COMMA (or CTRL-Y) to display the iTunes dialog box.

2. Click the Sharing tab.

3. Select the Look For Shared Music check box.

4. Click the OK button to close the iTunes dialog box.

Access Shared Music on the Same TCP/IP Subnet

Once you've selected the Look For Shared Music check box on the Sharing tab of the iTunes dialog box, iTunes automatically detects shared music when you launch it while your PC is connected to a network. If iTunes finds shared music libraries or playlists, it displays them in the Source pane.

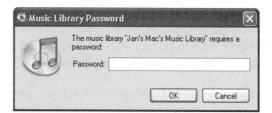

FIGURE 5-10 Computers sharing music appear in the iTunes Source pane, allowing you to quickly browse the music that's being shared.

Click a shared library to display its contents in the main iTunes window, or double-click a shared library to open it in a different window. Figure 5-10 shows an example of browsing the music shared by another computer.

If a shared music source has a password, iTunes displays the Music Library Password dialog box. Enter the password and click the OK button to access the library.

Disconnect a Shared Music Library

To disconnect shared music you've connected to, follow these steps:

1. In the Source pane, select the shared music source.

2. Press CTRL-E or choose Controls | Disconnect "*Library*" (where *Library* is the name assigned to the shared music library).

Alternatively, right-click the shared music source and choose Disconnect "*Library*" from the shortcut menu (where *Library* is the name assigned to the shared music library).

Disconnect Other Users from Your Shared Music

To disconnect other users from your shared music library, follow these steps:

1. Press CTRL-COMMA (or CTRL-Y) or choose Edit | Preferences to display the iTunes dialog box.

2. Click the Sharing tab to display its contents.

3. Clear the Share My Music check box.

4. Click the OK button. If any other user is connected to your shared music library, iTunes displays the following dialog box to warn you. Click the Yes button or the No button, as appropriate.

If you choose to stop sharing your music library, anyone playing music from it will be cut off abruptly without notice.

Add Artwork to Songs

iTunes 4 lets you add artwork to songs and then display the artwork while the song is playing or while the song is selected.

Most songs you buy from the iTunes Music Store include the appropriate artwork—for example, the cover of the single, EP, album, or CD that includes the song. For other songs, you can add your own artwork manually. For example, you might download album art or other pictures from an artist's web site, and then apply those to the song files you ripped from the artist's CDs. You can use any image file format that QuickTime supports. This includes JPG, GIF, TIFF, PNG, BMP, and PhotoShop images.

iTunes provides three different ways to add artwork to songs. To add artwork to a song directly from the iTunes window, follow these steps:

1. Open a Windows Explorer window to the folder that contains the picture you want to use for the artwork.

2. If the artwork pane isn't displayed (below the Source pane), press CTRL-G or click the Show Or Hide Song Artwork button to display it.

3. Select the song to which you want to apply the picture.

4. Drag the picture file from the Windows Explorer window to the artwork pane and drop it there. iTunes displays the picture there and associates it with the song file.

5. Drag other picture files from the Windows Explorer window to the artwork pane and drop them there as appropriate.

You can also add one or more images to a single song by working in the Song Information dialog box. Follow these steps:

1. Right-click the song you want to affect and choose Get Info from the shortcut menu to display the Song Information dialog box for the song.

2. Click the Artwork tab.

3. To add an image, click the Add button, use the resulting iTunes dialog box to navigate to the file and select it, and then click the Open button.

4. To delete an existing image, select it in the artwork box and click the Delete button.

5. To resize the picture or pictures to the size you want it or them, drag the slider to the left or right.

6. To work with the previous or next song in the playlist, album, or library, click the Previous button or the Next button.

7. Click the OK button to close the Song Information dialog box.

To add artwork to multiple songs at the same time, follow these steps:

1. Open a Windows Explorer window to the folder that contains the picture you want to use for the artwork.

2. Select the songs you want to affect. SHIFT-click to select multiple contiguous songs. CTRL-click to select multiple noncontiguous songs after clicking the first song.

3. Issue a Get Info command (for example, press CTRL-I) to display the Multiple Song Information dialog box.

4. Drag the picture file from the Windows Explorer window to the Artwork box and drop it there. iTunes selects the Artwork check box, displays the picture, and associates it with the song file.

5. Click the OK button to close the Multiple Song Information dialog box.

When you've added two or more pictures to the same song, the artwork pane displays a Previous button and a Next button for browsing from picture to picture.

You can display the current picture at full size by clicking it in the artwork pane. Click the Close button (the X button) to close the artwork window.

Listen to Internet Radio

You can use iTunes to listen to radio streamed over the Internet. You'll find a wide range of radio stations available—everything from giant commercial stations or public broadcasters that you can catch on the airwaves to people broadcasting their own opinions or personal playlists.

Streaming radio stations can use any of several different formats, including MP3 streams, Windows Media Audio streams, and RealAudio streams. iTunes can receive only MP3 streams.

Aside from using different formats, Internet radio stations also broadcast at different bitrates—typically 16 Kbps, 32 Kbps, 56 Kbps, 64 Kbps, 96 Kbps, and 128 Kbps. As with MP3 and AAC fidelity, the higher the bitrate, the better the radio will sound—provided that your Internet connection is fast enough to deliver it. For example, if you have a 64 Kbps ISDN connection, you won't be able to listen to a 128 Kbps stream, because your connection simply isn't fast enough, but you should be able to listen to a 64 Kbps stream. Because 56K modems typically connect at speeds lower than 56 Kbps, you can't usually listen to a 56 Kbps stream satisfactorily on a modem connection—it'll keep breaking up.

To connect to an Internet radio station, follow these steps:

1. Click the Radio item in the Source pane to display the list of genres available. You can force iTunes to refresh the list of genres by clicking the Refresh button in the upper-right corner of the iTunes window.

2. Double-click the genre you're interested in to make iTunes display the list of stations for that genre. Depending on the number of stations available, iTunes may need several seconds to download the details.

3. Check the station speeds in the Bit Rate column to see which of them are broadcasting at suitable bitrates for your Internet connection and listening requirements:

   ■ By default, iTunes sorts the radio stations alphabetically by name, but you may prefer to sort them in ascending order or descending order by bitrate so that you can easily see which stations are broadcasting at rates you want to hear.

   ■ To sort the stations by bit rate, click the Bit Rate column heading once (for an ascending sort) or twice (for a descending sort).

4. Double-click a station to start playing it. iTunes connects, buffers the stream (see the next Note), and then starts playing back the audio. iTunes displays the station details in the display area, together with the time you've spent listening to the station:

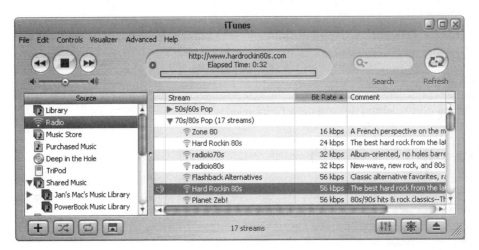

How to ...   Create Your Own Internet Radio Station

Just as other people can broadcast as their own Internet radio stations, so can you—with relatively little effort.

You can start broadcasting yourself in either of two ways: by downloading a Windows-based server product such as SHOUTcast (from www.shoutcast.com) and using it to stream music directly from your computer, or by using a radio hosting service such as Live365.com (www.live365.com). In either case, you're liable for paying broadcast royalties to artists whose works you broadcast.

Streaming music directly from your computer gives you more control over your radio station but requires an Internet connection with a fast enough upstream speed to deliver enough audio data to all the listeners you want to support. (Most Internet connections are far faster downstream—delivering data to you—than upstream.)

A radio hosting service removes the heavy lifting from your computer and Internet connection. Some radio hosting services also take care of royalty payments for you.

5

NOTE   *When you connect to an Internet radio station, it usually takes a few seconds for the playback to start. Part of this time is required to establish the connection to the streaming server; most of this time is required for buffering enough of the stream to deliver smooth playback even if minor interruptions in Internet traffic occur. If major interruptions occur, the buffer will run out, and the audio will stop. If you see the error message "Network Stalled: Rebuffering Stream" frequently, you may need to increase the buffer size. Choose Edit \ Preferences or press CTRL-COMMA (or CTRL-Y) to display the iTunes dialog box, click the Advanced tab, adjust the Streaming Buffer Size setting to Medium or Large, and click the OK button.*

5.   Click the Stop button to stop listening to the stream.

TIP   *The easiest way to give yourself quick access to your preferred radio stations is to create a playlist for them. Once you've located a radio station you like, drag it to the playlist. Then you can access a station quickly by displaying the playlist and double-clicking the station's entry in it.*

NOTE   *If you enjoy Internet radio, you may sometimes want to record a stream so that you can play it back later. See "Save Audio Streams to Disk So You Can Listen to Them Later," in Chapter 6, for details on how to do so.*

Part II

Create and Buy Music Files, and Burn CDs and DVDs

Chapter 6

Create, Edit, and Tag Your Audio Files

How to…

- Convert audio files from other audio formats to AAC or MP3
- Create AAC files or MP3 files from cassettes, vinyl, or other sources
- Remove scratches, hiss, and hum from audio files
- Trim, sever, and otherwise abbreviate MP3 files
- Rename MP3 files efficiently
- Save audio streams to disk

As you saw in Chapters 3 and 4, iTunes offers great features for creating AAC files and MP3 files from CDs, organizing them into playlists, playing them back, synchronizing with your iPod, and more. But sometimes you'll want to do things with AAC files and MP3 files that iTunes doesn't support. For example, you may receive (or acquire) files in formats your iPod can't handle, so you'll need to convert the files before you can use them on your iPod. You may want to create AAC files or MP3 files from cassettes, LPs, or other media you own, and you may need to remove clicks, pops, and other extraneous noises from such recordings you make. You may want to trim intros or outros off audio files, split files into smaller files, or retag batches of files in ways iTunes can't handle. Last, you may want to record streaming audio to your hard disk.

While iTunes now prefers AAC to MP3, most of the world is still using MP3. For this reason, at this writing there are many more—and more capable—MP3 applications than AAC applications. You'll find that the coverage in this chapter reflects this situation. But unless you've been creating AAC files with an application other than iTunes, you'll probably need to edit and tag MP3 files rather than AAC files, so the slight bias toward MP3 shouldn't be a problem.

NOTE   *Where many applications offer similar functionality, this chapter discusses freeware applications and applications that offer functional evaluation versions rather than applications that insist you buy them outright without giving you a chance to try them.*

Convert Other File Types to MP3, AIFF, or WAV So You Can Play Them on Your iPod

Your iPod can play AAC files, MP3 files (including Audible files), AIFF files, and WAV files—four of the most common digital-audio formats. But if you receive files from others, or download audio from the Internet (as described in Chapter 7), you'll encounter many other digital-audio formats. This section describes a couple of utilities for converting files from one format to another—preferably to a format your iPod can use, or to a format from which you can encode an AAC file or MP3 file.

Did you know?

What Happens when You Convert a File from One Compressed Format to Another

Before we get started, here's a point that's essential to grasp: when you convert audio from one compressed format to another, audio quality is liable to suffer even further. So the results may not sound too great.

For example, say you have a WMA file. The audio is already compressed with lossy compression, so some parts of the audio have been lost. (Lossy compression discards some data; see "How Compressed Audio Works (in Brief)," in Chapter 3, for details.) When you convert this file to an MP3 file, the conversion utility has to expand the compressed WMA audio to uncompressed audio—essentially, to a PCM file (such as WAV or AIFF)—and then recompress it to the MP3 format, again using lossy compression.

The uncompressed audio contains a faithful rendering of all the defects in the WMA file. The MP3 file will contain as faithful a rendering of this defective audio as the MP3 encoder can provide at that compression rate, plus any defects the MP3 encoding introduces. But you'll be able to play the file on your iPod—which may be your main concern.

6

Convert a Song from AAC to MP3 (or Vice Versa)

Sometimes, you may need to convert a song from the format in which you imported it, or (more likely) in which you bought it, to a different format. For example, you may need to convert a song in AAC format to MP3 so that you can use it on an MP3 player other than your iPod. (If the AAC is a protected song you bought from the iTunes Music Store, you'll need to burn it to a CD before you can convert it.)

Don't convert a song from one compressed format to another compressed format unless you absolutely must, because such a conversion gives you the worst of both worlds. To convert a compressed file to another format, iTunes has to uncompress it first, and then compress it again. The compressed audio has already lost some information, which cannot be restored by uncompressing the audio; the uncompressed file simply contains the same audio in a less compact format. When this uncompressed file is then compressed using another compression format, further information is lost. (How much information is lost depends on the format used, the bitrate, the processing level, and so on). So when you convert, say, an AAC file to an MP3 file, the MP3 file contains not only such defects as were present in the AAC file, but also defects of its own.

So if you still have the CD from which you imported the song, import the song again using the other compressed format rather than converting the song from one compressed format to another. Doing so will give you significantly higher quality. But if you don't have the CD—for example, because you bought the song in the compressed format—converting to the other format will produce usable results.

To convert a song from one compressed format to another, follow these steps:

1. In iTunes, display the Advanced menu and see which format is listed in the Convert Selection To command (for example, Convert Selection To AAC or Convert Selection To MP3). If this is the format you want, you're all set, but you might want to double-check the settings used for the format.

2. Press COMMAND-COMMA (on the Mac) or CTRL-COMMA (on Windows), or choose iTunes | Preferences (on the Mac) or Edit | Preferences (on Windows), to display the Preferences dialog box (on the Mac) or the iTunes dialog box (on Windows).

3. Click the Importing button to display the Importing sheet (on the Mac) or the Importing tab (on Windows).

4. In the Import Using drop-down list, specify the encoder you want to use. For example, choose MP3 Encoder if you want to convert an existing file to an MP3 file, or choose AAC Encoder if you want to create an AAC file.

5. If necessary, use the Setting drop-down list to specify the details of the format. (See "Change the Importing Settings in iTunes to Specify Audio Quality" in Chapter 4 for instructions on changing the settings on the Mac, and "Change the Importing Settings in iTunes to Specify Audio Quality" in Chapter 5 for instructions on changing the settings on Windows.)

6. Click the OK button to close the Preferences dialog box.

7. In your music library, select the song or songs you want to convert.

8. Choose Advanced | Convert Selection To MP3 or Advanced | Convert Selection To AAC as appropriate. (The Convert Selection To item on the Advanced menu changes to reflect the encoder you chose in Step 4.) iTunes converts the file or files, saves it or them in the folder that contains the original file or files, and adds it or them to your music library.

NOTE *Because iTunes automatically applies tag information to converted files, you may find it hard to tell in iTunes which file is in AAC format and which is in MP3 format. The easiest way to find out is to issue a Get Info command for the song (for example, right-click the song and choose Get Info from the shortcut menu) and check the Kind readout on the Summary tab of the Song Information dialog box.*

After converting the song or songs to the other format, remember to restore your normal import setting on the Importing sheet or Importing tab of the Preferences dialog box before you import any more songs from CD.

Convert WMA Files to MP3 or AAC

If you buy music from any of the online music stores that focuses on Windows rather than on the Mac, chances are that the songs will be in WMA format. WMA is the stores' preferred format for selling online music because it offers digital rights management (DRM) features for protecting the music against being stolen.

If you buy WMA files protected with DRM, you'll be limited in what you can do with them. In most cases, you'll be restricted to playing the songs with Windows Media Player (which is one of the underpinnings of the WMA DRM scheme), which won't let you convert the songs directly to another format. But most online music stores allow you to burn the songs you buy to CD. In this case, you can convert the WMA files to MP3 files or AAC files by burning them to CD, and then using iTunes to rip and encode the CD as usual.

Windows: GoldWave

GoldWave, from GoldWave, Inc. (www.goldwave.com), is a powerful audio editor that lets you convert files from various audio formats to other formats. GoldWave's Batch Processing feature (File | Batch Processing) is great for converting a slew of files at once. Figure 6-1 shows the Batch Processing dialog box.

You can download a 15-day evaluation version of GoldWave from the GoldWave, Inc., web site or from various Internet locations, including CNET's www.download.com. The registered version of GoldWave costs $40.

Mac: SoundApp

You can get various audio-conversion utilities for the Mac. Most of them cost money, but one of the best is free. That utility is called SoundApp, and you can download it from www.spies.com/ ~franke/SoundApp (and many Internet archives). At this writing, the current version has a minimalist interface and runs in Classic, but it works fine.

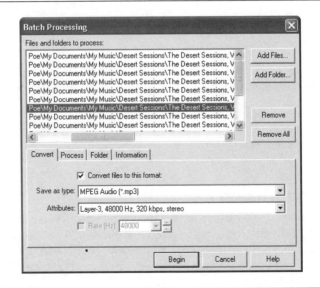

FIGURE 6-1   GoldWave's Batch Processing dialog box lets you quickly convert many files at once from one format to another.

6

Create AAC or MP3 Files from Cassettes or Vinyl Records

If you have audio on analog media such as cassette tapes, vinyl records, or other waning technologies, you may want to transfer that audio to your computer so you can listen to it on your iPod. Dust off your gramophone, cassette deck, or other audio source, and then work your way through the following sections.

Before you start, however, remember the legalities of creating audio files that contain copyrighted content. (See "Copyright Law for Digital Audiophiles," in Chapter 3, for a discussion of this topic.) If you hold the copyright to the audio, you can copy it as much as you want. If not, you need specific permission to copy it, unless it falls under a specific copyright exemption. For example, the Audio Home Recording Act (AHRA) personal use provision lets you copy a copyrighted work (for example, an LP) onto a different medium so you can listen to it—provided that you use a "digital audio recording device," a term that doesn't cover computers.

Connect the Audio Source to Your Computer

Start by connecting the audio source to your computer with a cable that has the right kinds of connectors for the audio source and your sound card. For example, to connect a typical cassette player to a typical sound card, you'll need a cable with two RCA plugs at the cassette player's end (or at the receiver's end) and a male-end stereo miniplug at the other end to plug into your sound card. If the audio source has only a headphone socket or line out socket for output, you'll need a miniplug at the source end, too.

NOTE   *Because record players produce a low volume of sound, you'll almost always need to put a record player's output through the Phono input of an amplifier before you can record it on your computer.*

If your sound card has a Line In port and a Mic port, use the Line In port. If your sound card has only a Mic port, turn the source volume down to a minimum for the initial connection, because Mic ports tend to be sensitive.

TIP   *If you have a Mac that doesn't have an audio input, consider a solution such as the Griffin iMic (www.griffintech.com), which lets you record via USB.*

Record Audio on Windows

To record audio on Windows, you can use the minimalist sound-recording application, Sound Recorder, or add (and usually pay for) a more powerful application. This section discusses how to use Sound Recorder and how to use two other applications, MUSICMATCH Jukebox Plus and GoldWave. But first, whichever application you choose, you'll need to specify the audio source.

TIP

If you have a lot of records and tapes that you want to copy to digital audio files, consider buying an audio-cleanup application that includes recording capabilities instead of an application whose strengths lie mainly in recording. For example, applications such as Magix's Audio Cleaning Lab and Steinberg's Clean Plus focus mainly on audio cleanup (removing crackle, pops, hiss, and other defects) but include more-than-adequate recording capabilities.

Specify the Audio Source for Recording

To set Windows to accept input from the source so you can record from it, follow these steps:

1. If the notification area includes a Volume icon, double-click this icon to display the Volume Control window. Otherwise, choose Start | Control Panel to display the Control Panel, and open the Volume Control window from there. For example, in Windows XP, click the Advanced button in the Device Volume group box on the Volume tab of the Sounds And Audio Devices Properties dialog box.

NOTE

Depending on your audio hardware and its drivers, the Volume Control window may have a different name (for example, Play Control).

2. Choose Options | Properties to display the Properties dialog box, then select the Recording option button to display the list of devices for recording (as opposed to the devices for playback). The left screen in Figure 6-2 shows this list.

3. Select the check box for the input device you want to use—for example, select the Line-In check box or the Microphone check box, depending on which you're using.

4. Click the OK button to close the Properties dialog box. Windows displays the Record Control window, an example of which is shown on the right in Figure 6-2. (Like the Volume Control window, this window may have a different name—for example, Recording Control.)

5. Select the Select check box for the source you want to use.

Leave the Record Control window open for the time being so you can adjust the input volume on the device if necessary.

Record with Sound Recorder

Sound Recorder is one of the applets that comes built into Windows. To run Sound Recorder, choose Start | All Programs | Accessories | Entertainment | Sound Recorder.

Sound Recorder works fine except that it can't record files longer than 60 seconds, which makes it next to useless for recording music. But you can sidestep around this limitation by creating a blank file longer than the longest item you want to record, and then recording over this blank file. Like many of the free things in life, this process is a little tortuous, but if you don't have another sound-recording application, you'll probably find it worth the effort.

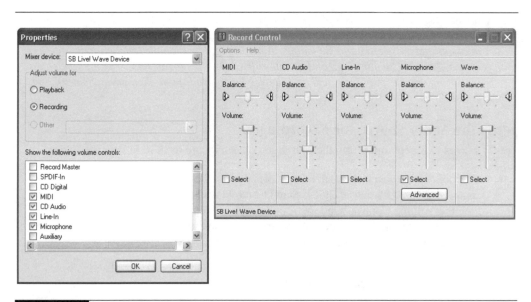

FIGURE 6-2   Select the Recording option button in the Properties dialog box (left) to display the Record Control window (right) instead of the Volume Control.

There are two parts to making Sound Recorder record files longer than 60 seconds. The first part, which is compulsory, is to create a blank dummy file long enough to contain whatever you want to record. The second part, which is optional, is to make Sound Recorder open this file automatically when you start it so that you don't have to open it manually.

Create the Dummy File   To create the blank dummy file, follow these steps:

1. Choose Start | All Programs | Accessories | Entertainment | Sound Recorder to launch Sound Recorder:

2. Mute your sound source.

3. Click the Record button (the button with the red dot) to start recording a blank file. Sound Recorder makes the file 60 seconds long, its default maximum:

4. Let the recording run until it stops automatically at 60 seconds.

5. Choose File | Save to display the Save As dialog box.

6. Save the file under a descriptive name such as dummy.wav.

7. Choose Edit | Insert File to display the Insert File dialog box.

8. Select the file you saved and click the Open button to insert it in the open version of the file. This adds another 60 seconds to the file's length, doubling it.

9. Repeat the procedure of inserting the saved file in the open file until the open file reaches the length you need.

TIP   *To increase the file's size more quickly, save the open file after inserting another one or two minutes in it. You can then insert the saved file, adding two or three minutes at a time to the open file.*

10. When the file reaches the length you need, choose File | Save to save it.

11. Press ALT-F4 or choose File | Exit to close Sound Recorder.

Make Sound Recorder Open the Dummy File Automatically   To make Sound Recorder open the dummy file automatically, follow these steps:

1. Right-click the Sound Recorder entry on your Start menu and choose Properties from the shortcut menu to display its Properties dialog box:

2. In the Target text box, enter the path and filename to the file you recorded, inside double quotation marks, after the path and filename of the executable, so that it looks something like this:

    %SystemRoot%\System32\sndrec32.exe "C:\Documents and Settings\Your Name\ My Documents\Dummy.wav"

3. Click the OK button to close the Properties dialog box.

Now, when you start Sound Recorder, it automatically opens the dummy file. You can then record audio of up to the length of the dummy file.

Record a Sound File   To record a file with Sound Recorder, follow these steps:

1. Choose Start | All Programs | Accessories | Entertainment | Sound Recorder to launch Sound Recorder and make it open the dummy file.

NOTE   *If you didn't change the Sound Recorder shortcut, open your dummy file manually.*

2. Get the audio source ready to play.

3. Click the Record button to start recording.

4. Start the audio playing.

5. To stop recording, click the Stop button.

6. Choose File | Save As to display the Save As dialog box:

7. Specify the location and name for the file. (Don't overwrite your dummy file.)

8. Make sure the Format field, at the bottom of the Save As dialog box, is displaying the format in which you want to save the file. This field gives brief details of the format—for example, "PCM 22 050 kHz, 8 Bit, Mono" or "Windows Media Audio V2, 160 Kbps, 48 kHz, Stereo." To set a different format, click the Change button and work in the Sound Selection dialog box:

   ■ To select a predefined set of attributes, select CD Quality, Radio Quality, or Telephone Quality in the Name drop-down list. If you're recording music you want to turn into an AAC file or MP3 file, choose the CD Quality item.

TIP

You can define your own named formats by choosing appropriate settings in the Format drop-down list and Attributes drop-down list, and then clicking the Save As button. You can then reuse these formats more quickly the next time you need the same settings.

   ■ Otherwise, choose the format in the Format drop-down list, and then select the appropriate attributes in the Attributes drop-down list. For example, you might choose PCM in the Format drop-down list and the 48 000 kHz, 16 Bit, Stereo setting in the Attributes drop-down list to record pulse code modulation audio at the highest quality that Sound Recorder supports.

   ■ Click the OK button to close the Sound Selection dialog box.

9. Click the Save button in the Save As dialog box to save the file.

TIP

If you examine the Format drop-down list, you'll notice an MPEG Layer-3 item. As you read in Chapter 3, MPEG-1 Layer 3 is MP3, so you might hope to use this setting to encode directly to MP3 files. You can *do this, but the encoder included with Windows can encode only up to 56 Kbps at 24 KHz, which makes it useless for high-quality audio. (This restriction is due to a licensing issue.) So you'll get much better results from creating WAV files with Sound Recorder, and then using iTunes to encode them to MP3 files or AAC files.*

6

Record with MUSICMATCH Jukebox Plus

One of the best solutions for recording audio files on Windows is MUSICMATCH Jukebox Plus, which you can download from the MUSICMATCH web site (www.musicmatch.com) and activate for $19.99. MUSICMATCH Jukebox Plus includes ripping and encoding to MP3, mp3PRO, and other formats; music library management; CD burning; and legitimate music downloads from its online music service. When recording audio input, MUSICMATCH Jukebox Plus can automatically detect the end of songs, which can make recording from cassettes or records much simpler.

> **NOTE** *Apple included MUSICMATCH Jukebox Plus as the Windows application for managing second- and third-generation iPods until Apple released iTunes for Windows. You can still use MUSICMATCH Jukebox Plus to manage your iPod on Windows if you choose.*

To record audio on Windows using MUSICMATCH Jukebox Plus, work through the steps in the following sections.

Set MUSICMATCH Jukebox Plus to Record from the Source   First, set MUSICMATCH Jukebox Plus to accept input from the same device. To do so, choose Options | Recorder | Source | Line In or Options | Recorder | Source | Mic In as appropriate. Alternatively, choose Options | Recorder | Settings to display the Recorder tab of the Settings dialog box, and then select Line In or Mic in the Recording Source drop-down list.

> **TIP** *If you're recording several tracks' worth of material from an external source, consider using the Auto Song Detect feature. To use it, select the Active check box in the Advanced Recorder Options dialog box, and then use the Gap Length and Gap Level text boxes to specify the amount and level, respectively, of silence that represent a break between tracks. The default is 2000 ms (two seconds) at 10 percent volume. These settings work well for many CDs, but if you're recording music that includes dramatic pauses, you may need to increase the gap length to avoid truncating songs just before the music starts up again.*

Start Recording   To start recording in MUSICMATCH Jukebox Plus, follow these steps:

1. Get the sound source ready to play.

2. In the Recorder window, enter the artist name, album name, and track name. (Otherwise, MUSICMATCH Jukebox Plus uses the default data: Artist, Album, and "line in track *NN*"—so if you're using the default naming convention, you'll find the tracks in the Artist\Album folder.

3. Click the Record button in the Recorder window in MUSICMATCH Jukebox Plus to start recording from the source.

4. Click the Stop button to stop recording the current track. MUSICMATCH Jukebox Plus adds the track to your music library and sets you up to record another track.

Record Audio with GoldWave

To record audio with GoldWave (mentioned earlier in this chapter), follow these steps:

1. Click the New button to display the New Sound dialog box:

2. Specify the quality settings you want to use:

- You can choose a preset in the Preset Quality Settings drop-down list. For example, to record audio at CD quality, select the CD Audio item.

- Alternatively, use the Manual Quality Settings controls to specify exactly what you want. Select the number of channels (1 or 2) in the Channels drop-down list, and then select the sampling rate in the Sampling Rate drop-down list.

3. In the Initial File Length drop-down list, select an initial file length longer than the audio you want to record. The default length is one minute, which is too short for most songs.

4. Click the OK button to close the New Sound dialog box. GoldWave creates a new sound file named Untitled*N,* where *N* is the next unused number (for example, Untitled1), and displays the Control window.

5. Click the Record button in the Control window to start recording the sound:

6. Click the Stop Recording button in the Control window to stop the recording.

Import the Sound into iTunes and Convert It

After saving the sound file in an audio format that iTunes can handle (preferably the WAV format), import the sound file into iTunes, and then use the Advanced | Convert Selection To command to convert the sound file to an AAC file or an MP3 file. Once you've done that, tag the compressed file with the appropriate information so that you can access it easily in iTunes and copy it to your iPod.

Record Audio on the Mac

To record audio on the Mac, specify the audio source, and then choose which of the following two subsections to work through.

Specify the Source

To specify the source on the Mac, follow these steps:

1. Choose Apple | System Preferences to display the System Preferences window.

2. Click the Sound item to display the Sound preferences sheet.

3. Click the Input tab to display it:

4. In the Choose A Device For Sound Input list box, select the device to use (for example, Line In).

5. Start some audio playing on the sound source. Make sure that it's representative of the loudest part of the audio you will record.

6. Watch the Input Level readout as you drag the Input Volume slider to a suitable level.

Record Audio with iMovie

If you don't have a custom audio-recording application (we'll examine a couple in a moment), you can record audio into a blank iMovie movie and export it as a sound file. Follow these steps:

1. Click the iMovie icon in the Dock to launch iMovie. (Alternatively, choose Go | Applications and double-click the iMovie icon.)

2. Press COMMAND-N (or choose File | New Project) to start a new project.

3. In the resulting dialog box, enter the filename, choose where to save it, and then click the Save button.

4. In iMovie, click the Audio button to display the audio controls.

5. Click the Record Audio button to start recording the audio. iMovie displays the progress on the timeline.

6. Click the Stop button (which replaces the Record Voice button) to stop recording the audio.

7. Manipulate the audio if necessary.

8. Choose File | Share (or press COMMAND-SHIFT-E) to display the Share sheet.

9. Click the QuickTime button to display the QuickTime sheet:

10. In the Compress Movie For drop-down list, select the Export Settings item.

11. Click the Share button to display the Save Exported File As dialog box:

12. Specify the name and location for the exported file.

13. In the Export drop-down list, select the Sound To AIFF item or the Sound To Wave item, as appropriate. (If you have other QuickTime plug-ins installed, other choices may be available, such as Sound To Ogg Vorbis.) If appropriate, click the Options button to display a dialog box for setting any options available in the format.

14. In the Use drop-down list, select the quality setting—for example, 44.1 kHz 16 Bit Stereo.

15. Click the Save button to save the audio file.

From here, you can import the AIFF file or WAV file into iTunes and convert it to another format (such as AAC or MP3) if necessary, as described in the next section.

Two Other Options for Recording Audio

iMovie is a workable tool for recording audio, and it comes free with every Mac. But if you're prepared to spend a few fistfuls of dollars, you can have sound-recording and -editing software that's much easier to use and that offers far greater capabilities. Better yet, if you choose the right application, you'll get audio-cleanup features into the bargain.

Two such applications you may want to try are Amadeus II and Sound Studio for OS X.

Amadeus II   Amadeus II from HairerSoft (www.hairersoft.com/Amadeus.html) is a powerful application for recording and editing audio. You can download a 15-day trial version of Amadeus II. The full version costs $25 for a single-user license.

> TIP   *Amadeus II includes repair functions you can use to eliminate hiss and crackles from recordings.*

Sound Studio for OS X   Sound Studio for OS X from Felt Tip Software (www.felttip.com) is a digital audio editor with a wide range of features. You can download an evaluation version of the software from the Felt Tip Software web site. The full version costs $49.99. Figure 6-3 shows Sound Studio for OS X recording audio.

> TIP   *Sound Studio for OS X also includes repair features for eliminating noise from recordings.*

Remove Scratches and Hiss from Audio Files

If you record tracks from vinyl records, audio cassettes, or other analog sources, you may well get some clicks or pops, hiss, or background hum in the file. Scratches on a record can cause clicks and pops, audio cassettes tend to hiss (even with noise-reduction such as Dolby), and record players or other machinery can add hum.

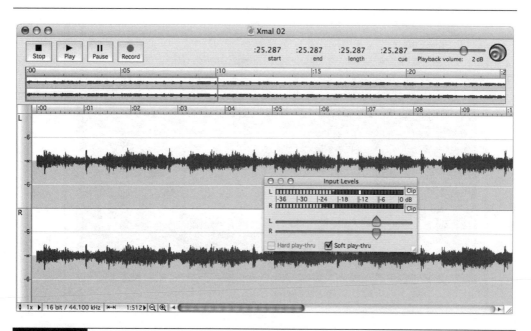

FIGURE 6-3   Recording audio with Sound Studio for OS X

All these noises—very much part of the analog audio experience, and actually appreciated as such by some enthusiasts—tend to annoy people accustomed to digital audio. The good news is that you can remove many such noises by using the right software.

Windows: GoldWave

Earlier in this chapter you met GoldWave, an audio editor you can use to convert audio files from one format to another. GoldWave also includes features for filtering audio and eliminating unwanted sounds. Figure 6-4 shows GoldWave working on eliminating the pops and clicks from a WAV file.

Windows: Audio Cleaning Lab

Audio Cleaning Lab from Magix (www.magix.com) provides strong features for cleaning up audio, together with features for recording audio into several formats, including WAV, MP3, and Ogg Vorbis.

Depending on where you shop, you can find various different versions of Audio Cleaning Lab, starting at around $29.99. Figure 6-5 shows Audio Cleaning Lab Deluxe, which features an idiosyncratic and loud interface (I find shades help) but is relatively easy to use.

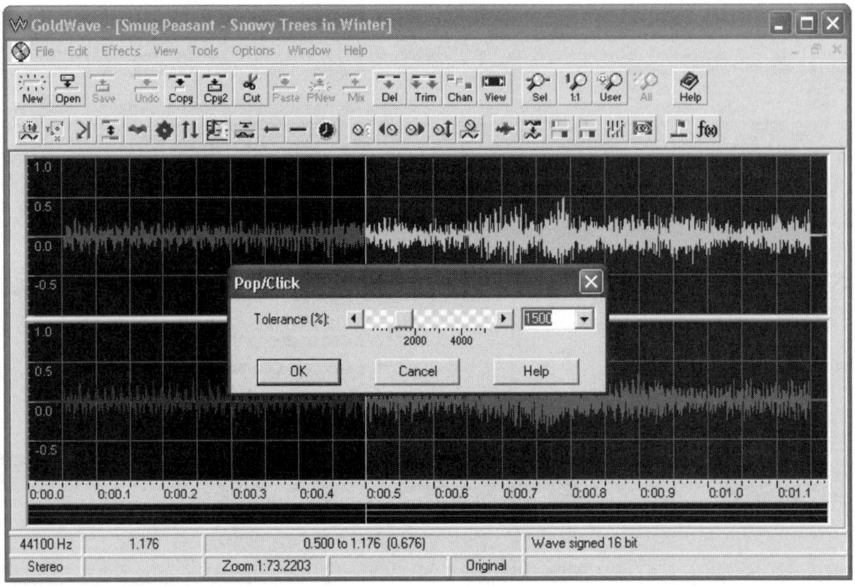

FIGURE 6-5   GoldWave can also remove pops and clicks from an audio file.

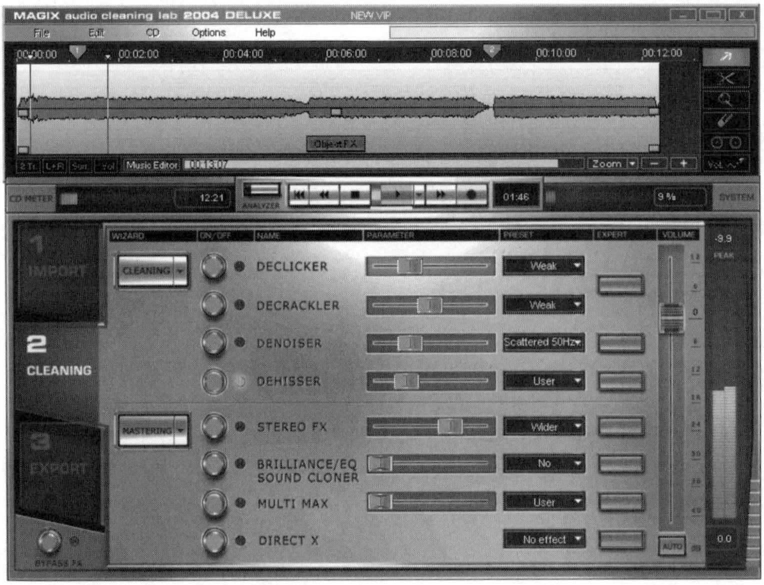

FIGURE 6-4   Audio Cleaning Lab comes in a variety of versions, including Deluxe.

Mac: Amadeus II

Amadeus II, introduced a bit earlier in this chapter, offers the following strong features for cleaning up audio files:

■ Use the Repair Centre (Effects | Sound Repair | Open Repair Centre) to hunt down and eliminate clicks and pops in a sound.

■ The Effects | Denoising submenu contains options for suppressing various types of noise (for example, white noise).

■ The Filter window (Effects | Filter) lets you apply specific filtering to a channel.

Trim MP3 Files to Get Rid of Intros and Outros You Don't Like

As you saw in Chapters 4 and 5, the Start Time and Stop Time features in iTunes let you suppress the beginning and end of a file if you don't want to hear them: the file remains unchanged, but you tell iTunes to omit the parts you don't want to hear. But you may want to go further and actually remove the introduction or the end of the file—or you may want to split a file into two or more separate files. This section presents a Windows utility and a Mac utility for doing that with MP3 files.

Windows: MP3 TrackMaker

MP3 TrackMaker, from Heathco Software (www.heathcosoft.com), is a small utility for dividing MP3 files into smaller files and for joining two or more MP3 files into a single MP3 file. You can download an almost fully functional demo version (it's limited to joining three tracks or splitting a file into three tracks) for free, or you can pay $13 for the full version.

MP3 TrackMaker needs little explanation. Use the controls on its Split tab (shown on the left in Figure 6-6) to divide an MP3 file into smaller files. Use the controls on its Join tab (shown on the right in Figure 6-6) to join two or more MP3 files into a single MP3 file.

Mac: mEdit

mEdit is a freeware tool for cropping MP3 files on the Mac. You can download it from various software archives on the Internet. It runs in Classic mode but still functions well.

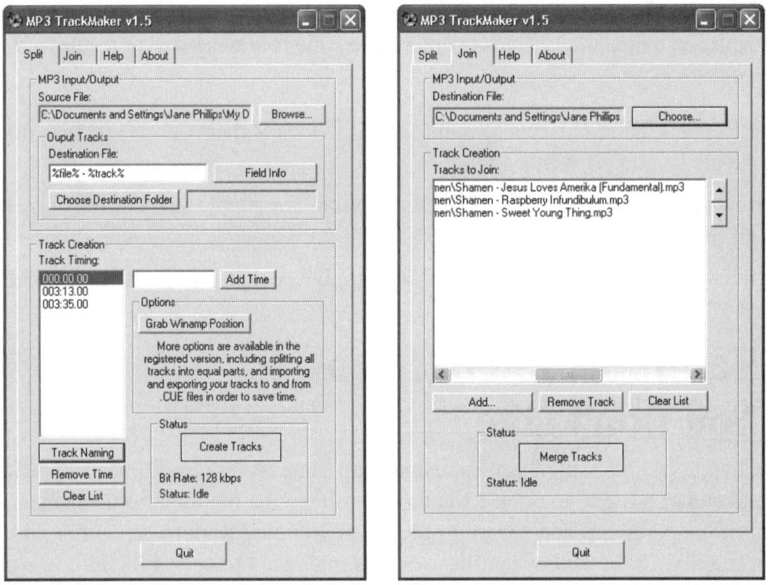

FIGURE 6-6   Use MP3 TrackMaker to divide MP3 files into smaller MP3 files or to join multiple MP3 files into a single MP3 file.

mEdit is straightforward to use. You open the file you want to crop, specify cropping options, execute the crop, and then save the file. You can also use mEdit to cut a section out of the middle of a file. By cropping the same source file twice (or more times) to different destination files, you can effectively use mEdit to split MP3 tracks into multiple files as well.

Tag Your MP3 Files with the Correct Information for Sorting

As you saw in Chapters 4 and 5, your iPod needs correct artist, album, and track name information in tags to be able to organize your AAC files and MP3 files correctly. iTunes provides solid if basic features for tagging one or more files at once manually.

But if your music library contains many untagged or mistagged files, you may need a heavier-duty application. This section presents two such applications—Tag&Rename for Windows, and MP3 Rage for the Mac.

Windows: Tag&Rename

Tag&Rename, from SOFTPOINTER, Ltd., is a terrific tag-editing application for various types of files, including AAC and MP3. You can download a free 30-day evaluation version from www.softpointer.com/tr.htm and from various other sites on the Internet.

Tag&Rename can derive tag information by breaking down a file's name into its constituents. For example, if you set Tag&Rename on the file Aimee Mann - Lost in Space - 06 - Pavlov's Bell.mp3, Tag&Rename can derive the artist name (Aimee Mann), the album name (*Lost in Space*), the track number (06), and the song name ("Pavlov's Bell") from the file, and apply that information to the tag fields.

It can also derive tag information from the folder structure that contains an MP3 file that needs tagging. For example, if you have the file 06 - Pavlov's Bell.mp3 stored in the folder Aimee Mann\Lost in Space, Tag&Rename will be able to tag the file with the artist name, album name, track name, and track number.

Figure 6-7 shows Tag&Rename in action, working on the ID3 tags of some AAC files.

Mac: MP3 Rage

MP3 Rage, from Chaotic Software (www.chaoticsoftware.com), is an impressive bundle of utilities for tagging, organizing, and improving your MP3 files. The tagging features in MP3 Rage include deriving tag information from filenames and folder paths (see the left screen in Figure 6-8) and changing the tags on multiple files at once (see the right screen in Figure 6-8).

You can download a fully functional evaluation version of MP3 Rage from the Chaotic Software web site. The registered version of MP3 Rage costs $24.95.

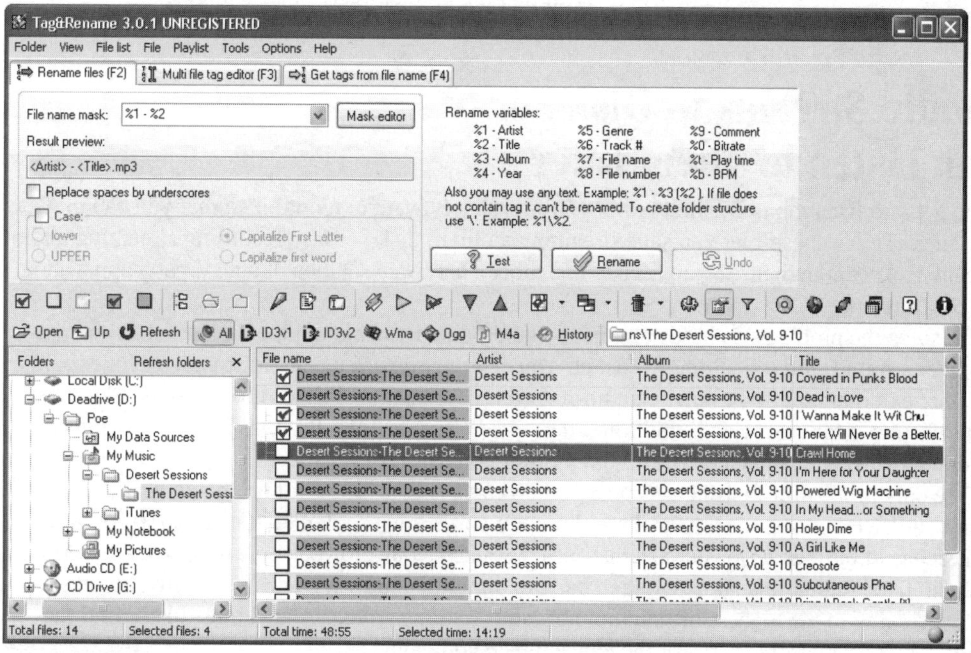

FIGURE 6-7   Tag&Rename can edit multiple ID3 tags at once.

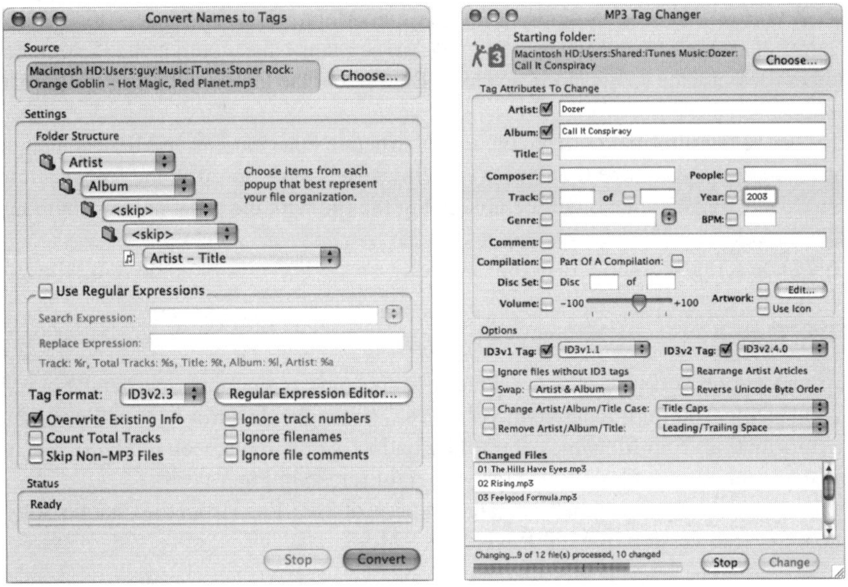

FIGURE 6-8   MP3 Rage includes powerful tagging among many other features.

Save Audio Streams to Disk So You Can Listen to Them Later

If you get into listening to Internet radio, you'll probably want to record it so that you can play it back later. iTunes doesn't let you save streaming audio to disk because recording streaming audio typically violates copyright. So you need to use either a hardware solution or a third-party application to record streams.

To solve the problem via hardware, use a standard audio cable to pipe the output from your computer's sound card to its Line In socket. You can then record the audio stream as you would any other external input by using an audio-recording application such as those discussed earlier in this chapter—for example, Sound Recorder, GoldWave, or MUSICMATCH Jukebox Plus on Windows, or iMovie, Amadeus II, or Sound Studio on Mac OS X.

The only problem with using a standard audio cable is that you won't be able to hear the audio stream you're recording via external speakers. To solve this problem, get a stereo Y-connector. Connect one of the outputs to your external speakers and the other to your Line In socket. Converting the audio from digital to analog and then back to digital like this degrades its quality, but unless you're listening to the highest-bitrate Internet radio stations around, you'll most likely find the quality you lose a fair trade-off for the convenience you gain.

To solve the problem via software, get an application that can record the audio stream directly. This section discusses some possibilities for Windows and Mac OS X.

Windows: FreeAmp (If You Can Get It)

For Windows, the easiest option for recording MP3 streams is FreeAmp, a freeware open-source MP3 player. The FreeAmp web site (www.freeamp.org) appears to have been taken over by commercial interests, but you can still find FreeAmp in various freeware software archives.

To record MP3 streams with FreeAmp, follow these steps:

1. Click the Options button to display the FreeAmp Preferences dialog box (shown on the right here):

2. Click the Streaming tab to display it.

3. Select the Save SHOUTcast/icecast Streams Locally check box.

4. Use the Browse button and the resulting Browse For Folder dialog box to specify the folder in which to save the streamed files. Make sure the drive on which the folder is located contains plenty of free space.

5. Click the OK button to close the FreeAmp Preferences dialog box.

6. Tune into the audio stream. FreeAmp records the stream automatically under an autonamed file.

Windows: TotalRecorder

If you can't get FreeAmp, or if you want to record stream types other than MP3 streams, you may want to try TotalRecorder, from High Criteria, Inc. (www.highcriteria.com):

TotalRecorder comes in a Standard Edition ($11.95 for a license), a Professional Edition ($35.95), and a Developer Edition ($64, but you probably won't want this unless you're developing software). Both Standard and Professional can save MP3 streams. High Criteria provides trial versions of TotalRecorder, but they're so thoroughly crippled you'll need to open your wallet to actually get anything done.

Mac: RadioLover

For the Mac, perhaps the most promising option at the time of writing for recording streams from iTunes or other sources is RadioLover (shown in Figure 6-9), which you can download from VersionTracker.com (www.versiontracker.com). RadioLover, formerly known as StreamRipperX, is $15 shareware that can tap into and record iTunes' Internet radio streams.

Mac: Audio Hijack

Audio Hijack, from Rogue Amoeba Software (www.rogueamoeba.com/audiohijack/), is a full-featured application for recording the audio output of programs and manipulating their output. Audio Hijack includes timers that you can set ahead of time to record the shows you're interested in. It can also apply equalization to applications that don't have equalizers themselves. For example, you can use Audio Hijack to equalize the output of Apple's DVD player.

FIGURE 6-9   RadioLover can record Internet radio streams from iTunes.

Chapter 7

Buy Music from the iTunes Music Store

How to…

- Understand what the iTunes Music Store is
- Understand digital rights management (DRM)
- Set up an account with the iTunes Music Store
- Configure iTunes Music Store settings
- Access the iTunes Music Store
- Buy songs from the iTunes Music Store
- Listen to songs you've purchased
- Authorize and deauthorize computers for the iTunes Music Store

If you use your iPod or iPod mini with iTunes 4 on Mac OS X or Windows, you can buy music from the iTunes Music Store, Apple's online music service. This chapter discusses what the iTunes Music Store is, how it works, and how to use it. Because the iTunes Music Store works in almost exactly the same way on Mac OS X and Windows, this chapter discusses both operating systems and, for balance, shows some screens from each.

The early part of this chapter also discusses digital rights management (DRM), because you should understand a little about it before using the store.

Understand What the iTunes Music Store Is

So far, the iTunes Music Store is one of the largest and most successful attempts to sell music online. (The next chapter discusses other online music services, including Wal-Mart and Napster 2.0.) The iTunes Music Store is far from perfect, and its selection is still very limited compared to what many users would like to be able to buy, but it's an extremely promising start. At the time of this writing, the iTunes Music Store is available to users of iTunes users on the Mac and Windows (but not to users of other music applications).

These are the basic parameters of the iTunes Music Store:

- Songs cost $0.99 each. The cost of albums varies, but many cost $9.99 or so—around what you'd pay for a discounted CD in many stores. Some CDs are available only as "partial CDs," which typically means that you can't buy the songs you're most likely to want. Extra-long songs (for example, those 13-minute jam sessions used to max out a CD) are sometimes available for purchase only with an entire CD.

- You can listen to a 30-second preview of any song to make sure it's what you want. After you buy a song, you download it to your music library.

- You can burn songs to CD an unlimited number of times, although you can burn any given playlist only 10 times without changing it or re-creating it under another name.

- The songs you buy are encoded in the AAC format (discussed in "What Is AAC? Should You Use It?," in Chapter 3) and are protected with DRM (discussed in the following section).

Turn Your iPod into Your Digital Camera's Inseparable Companion

This Special Project describes how you can use your iPod as a traveling companion for your digital camera. To work through this project, you'll need a Belkin Media Reader for iPod ($109.99 from all the best retailers), a third-generation or later iPod, and a digital camera that stores its photos on a removable card. You can perform this project on both Mac OS X and Windows.

Why Use a Media Reader?

If you have a third-generation or later iPod, you can use your iPod as a traveling companion to your digital camera by using Belkin's Media Reader for iPod. Instead of having to download the pictures you've taken from your digital camera to your PC or Mac once you've filled your camera's memory, you can use the Media Reader to download them to your iPod and store them there—and then continue shooting freely.

These days, digital cameras are increasing rapidly in resolution, which means that they're creating ever-larger picture files. Given the modest amount of storage in many digital cameras, and given the expense of buying a larger memory card, using your iPod for temporary storage for your pictures makes a lot of sense. An iPod can hold thousands of pictures comfortably as well as thousands of song files (provided that you haven't packed it full of music or other files, of course) .

Requirements for Using the Media Reader

The Media Reader for iPod works with six types of removable storage: Type 1 and Type 2 CompactFlash cards, SmartMedia cards, Secure Digital (SD) cards, Memory Stick cards, and MultiMedia Card (MMC) cards. If you've got a camera with removable storage, chances are good that it's one of these types.

To use the Media Reader for iPod, you need a regular iPod of the third generation or later—not an iPod mini. (Working with the Media Reader and the Voice Recorder are two features that the iPod mini's software doesn't have.) Your iPod must be running iPod Software 2.1 or a later version. (If you're not sure which version of iPod Software your iPod is running, choose Settings | About to display the About screen, and then check the Version readout.)

The Media Reader for iPod runs off of four AAA batteries. You can use either alkalines or rechargeables. Depending on the media you're using, Belkin reckons you should be able to transfer around 3GB or more of data on a single but sturdy set of batteries. If your average picture size is 1MB (including compression), 3GB is 3000 pictures—enough for a good-length road trip.

Set Up the Media Reader

Connecting the Media Reader to your iPod could hardly be simpler. You insert the media card you want to read in the appropriate slot on the Media Reader, and then plug the Dock connector on the Media Reader into the iPod.

The Media Reader's user interface consists of a single LED on the top of the unit:

- A solid green light indicates that the Media Reader is on and the battery has plenty of power.

- A flashing green light indicates that the Media Reader is transferring data.

- A solid amber light indicates that the battery is low.

When you connect the Media Reader, your iPod displays the Import screen, which identifies the type of media card found, the number of photos it contains, and the amount of free space on it. Here's an example:

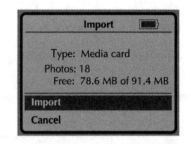

NOTE

If your iPod doesn't display the Import screen, choose Extras | Photos | Import | Photos to display the Import screen manually.

Make sure the Import item is selected (scroll if necessary), and then press the Select button to start the import process. Your iPod displays the Importing screen to show you the progress:

When the import is finished, your iPod displays the Import Done screen:

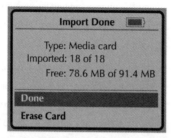

NOTE

Most digital cameras save their images as JPG files by default, but many can also create RAW (uncompressed) image files. Many digital cameras also have a movie mode that takes a series of lower-resolution images in sequence and saves them in a format such as Audio Video Interleave (AVI). You can transfer both RAW files and movie files to your iPod using the Media Reader.

Delete the Photos from the Memory Card or a Roll

To leave the photos on the memory card (for example, if you want to erase them using your camera's commands), leave the Done item selected and press the Select button. To delete the pictures from the memory card, scroll down to the Erase Card item and press the Select button. Your iPod displays the Erase Card screen:

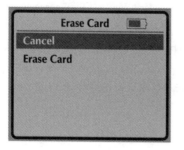

Scroll down to the Erase Card item, and then press the Select button to erase the contents of the memory card.

After erasing the card, or after you select the Done item, your iPod displays the Photos screen, from which you can check the details of the rolls you've imported.

Because you can't view the photos on the iPod, it's best to leave any deleting until after you've downloaded the photos to your computer and had a chance to assess which ones make the grade. But if you're pushed for space on your iPod when on the road, sometimes you may need to delete a roll from the iPod. To do so, follow these steps:

1. From the Photos screen, scroll down to select the roll, and then press the Select button to display its screen. Here's an example:

2. Check the roll's date and the number of photos on it to make sure you're deleting the right roll.

3. Scroll up to the Delete Roll item, and then press the Select button. Your iPod displays the Delete Roll screen:

4. Scroll down to the Delete item and press the Select button. Your iPod displays the Deleting Roll screen while it deletes the photos, and then displays the Photos screen. If the roll you deleted was the last roll on your iPod, it displays the Extras menu instead.

Transfer Photos from Your iPod to Your Computer

When you return to your computer, transfer the photos from your iPod to your computer so that you can work with them. You'll find the photos in your iPod's DCIM folder. (DCIM is the industry standard abbreviation for digital camera images.)

Inside the DCIM folder, you'll find a folder for each roll of photos you stored on the iPod. The folders are numbered sequentially with a three-digit number and APPLE, starting with 100APPLE, 101APPLE, and so on.

Transfer Photos from Your iPod to Your Mac

To transfer photos from your iPod to your Mac, follow these steps:

1. Connect your iPod to your Mac. If your iPod is set to synchronize with iTunes, allow it to do so.

2. Enable disk mode on your iPod (see "Enable Disk Mode," in Chapter 14, for details).

3. Double-click your iPod's icon on the desktop to open a Finder window to its contents.

4. Double-click the DCIM folder to open it. You'll see a folder for each roll of photos.

5. To load your photos into iPhoto, drag each folder in turn into the iPhoto window and drop it there:

   ■ To add the photos to your Photo Library, select your Photo Library in the Source

pane, and then drop the photos in the viewing area.

   ■ To add the photos to an existing album, select the album in the Source pane, and then drop the photos in the viewing area.

   ■ To create a new album and put the pictures of a folder into it, drag the folder to the Source pane in iPhoto and drop it in open space. iPhoto creates a new album with the name of the folder.

6. To copy the photos to a folder on your hard disk, use normal Finder techniques.

7. After importing or copying all the photos to your Mac, delete the photos from your iPod if appropriate. (You might also choose to keep the photos on your iPod as a backup.)

Transfer Photos from Your iPod to Your PC

To transfer photos from your iPod to your PC, follow these steps:

1. Connect your iPod to your PC. If your iPod is set to synchronize with iTunes, allow it to do so.

2. Choose Start | My Computer to open a My Computer window.

3. Double-click the drive allocated to your iPod to display its contents in a window.

4. Double-click the DCIM folder to open it. You'll see a folder for each roll of photos.

5. Copy or move the folders to your hard disk by using standard Windows Explorer techniques.

6. After importing or copying all the photos to your PC, delete the photos from your iPod if appropriate. (You might also choose to keep the photos on your iPod as a backup.)

Start Up Your Mac from Your iPod

You can start up (or *boot*) your Mac from your iPod by turning your iPod into a bootable FireWire disk. This capability can be useful for backup—you can start your Mac from your iPod even when your Mac hard disk has gone south—but you may also want to use it for security: by making your iPod the only bootable disk for your Mac, you can prevent other people from booting your Mac when your iPod isn't present. If you carry your iPod with you, you can extend that restriction to any time you're not using your Mac.

CAUTION

Two warnings here before we get started. First: Apple doesn't support using your iPod as a bootable FireWire disk. So if you can't make this work, you don't get to complain to Apple. Second: even though FireWire is a fast bus, booting from your iPod will take much longer than booting from your hard disk, and your Mac will run more slowly than usual. Be prepared for this before you make grand plans for your iPod.

You can make your iPod bootable in either of two ways:

- By installing Mac OS X (or System 9) on it directly
- By cloning an existing installation of Mac OS X (or System 9)

At the time of writing, booting a Mac works only with a regular, full-size iPod, not with the iPod mini. You can install Mac OS X or System 9 on an iPod mini and then designate the iPod mini as your Mac's startup disk, but your Mac doesn't notice the iPod mini when it boots, so it boots from its hard disk instead.

This restriction is perhaps a pity, but the iPod mini's smaller capacity (4 marketing gigabytes, 3.7 real gigabytes) makes it less useful for booting a Mac in any case. Even if you strip Mac OS X down to its leanest possible state, it takes more than 1GB, which leaves you little room for the music you presumably want to carry on your iPod mini.

This Special Project covers both installing and cloning Mac OS X, with brief mentions of how to proceed in System 9.

NOTE

You can't start up your PC from your iPod. And for this capability to work with the Mac, the Mac needs to have a built-in FireWire port. As you've read earlier in this book, most recent Macs do. But if you have (for example) a PowerBook G3 without a FireWire port, you won't be able to boot it from a bootable FireWire disk via a PC Card FireWire card.

Install Mac OS X (or System 9) Directly on Your iPod

The most straightforward way to make your iPod bootable is to install Mac OS X (or System 9) on it directly. To do so, you run the installation routine from your Mac OS X (or System 9) installation CD exactly as you would do to install the operating system on your Mac, except that you specify your iPod, rather than your Mac's hard disk, as the destination disk for the install.

Installing the operating system directly works fine if you have a version of the operating system that fits on a single disc—either a single CD or a single DVD. In practice, this means that you can install Mac OS X versions before 10.2 (for example, 10.1.x) or System 9 from a CD, because those operating systems fit on a single CD. But to install Mac OS X 10.2 or later, you need to have a DVD (and a DVD drive), because 10.2 takes up two CDs. The problem with having two CDs is that installing to the iPod tends to fail when you switch to the second CD.

To install a Mac operating system on your iPod, follow these steps:

1. Make sure your iPod has plenty of free space. You'll need between 1GB and 2GB for Jaguar, and between 2GB and 3GB for Panther, depending on which files you choose to install. For System 9, you'll need a more modest amount of space—from 250MB to 500MB, depending on the options you choose.

2. Connect your iPod to your Mac.

3. Enable disk mode on your iPod if it isn't already enabled.

4. Insert the Mac OS CD in your CD drive or the DVD in your DVD drive.

5. Double-click the Install Mac OS X application icon to display the Install Mac OS X window, and then click the Restart button.

NOTE

If you're installing System 9, skip step 5. Restart your Mac, and when you hear the system sound, hold down C to boot from the CD drive or DVD drive.

6. Follow through the installation procedure until you reach the Select A Destination screen.

7. Specify your iPod as the destination for the installation, and then click the Continue button.

CAUTION

The Mac OS X installation routine offers you the option of erasing your hard drive and formatting it using either Mac OS Extended (HFS Plus) or Unix File System. Don't use this option. Erasing the disk will do more harm than good.

8. When installing Mac OS X, it's a good idea to customize the installation to reduce the amount of space it takes up. On the Installation Type screen, click the Customize button instead of accepting the default Easy Install option. On the resulting Custom Install screen, clear the check boxes for the items you don't want to install.

- You must install the Essential System Software item, so the Installer doesn't let you clear its check boxes.

- You'll know if you need the BSD Subsystem files (225MB on Panther), the Additional Printer Drivers files (more than 700MB in all on Panther), the Fonts For Additional Languages (3MB), the Additional Asian Fonts (167MB on Panther), the Language Translations (695MB altogether on Panther), and X11 (100MB on Panther).

- You might choose to include only some of the printer drivers and only some of the language translations to keep down the amount of space needed.

9. Click the Install button to start the installation.

10. When the installation routine for Mac OS X displays the message that your system will restart in 30 seconds, unplug your iPod. Otherwise, your Mac will try to boot from it, even though it isn't configured for booting. Go to the section "Designate Your iPod As the Startup Disk," later in this chapter, and tell your Mac you want it to boot from your iPod.

NOTE

BSD is the acronym for the Berkeley Software Distribution, a family of Unix versions. You need the BSD Subsystem files to use features such as sharing files via File Transfer Protocol (FTP), to share your Internet connection, or to use Telnet or Secure Shell (SSH). You'll probably need these features on your Mac, but you may not want them on your iPod.

Clone an Existing Operating System onto Your iPod

The second way to make your iPod bootable is to clone an existing operating system onto it. This operating system can be either Mac OS X or System 9, provided that the cloning tool you use supports cloning that operating system.

Reasons to Clone an Existing Operating System

If you can't install your version of Mac OS X for the technical reasons discussed in the previous section, cloning may be your only option. But if you want to create a bootable backup of parts or all of your current configuration, cloning may also be a better option than installing a fresh copy of Mac OS X.

Prepare for Cloning

Before using the cloning utility, set up the operating system as you want it to be cloned. That might mean stripping it down to include only the items you want on your iPod so as not to waste its precious disk space with unnecessary files. Or it might mean including a full set of troubleshooting tools and applications so you can use your iPod to troubleshoot any problems you run into.

Choose a Cloning Utility

At the time of writing, perhaps the best cloning tool for Mac OS X is Mike Bombich's Carbon Copy Cloner (CCC), which you can download from www.bombich .com/software/ccc.html. Carbon Copy Cloner is donationware—if you like it, you can make a donation to the author.

Another cloning tool is SuperDuper (www.shirtpocket .com/SuperDuper/SuperDuperDescription.html), which offers more power than CCC and costs $19.95, but there's a trial edition for you to see if you like it.

Clone Your Mac OS X Installation with Carbon Copy Cloner

This section discusses how to use Carbon Copy Cloner to clone an existing installation of Mac OS X from your Mac onto your iPod.

> **NOTE**
>
> If your Mac is running Mac OS X, you may need to install the BSD Tools for CCC before you can install Carbon Copy Cloner. (Again, BSD is the abbreviation for the Berkeley Software Distribution, a family of Unix versions.) The CCC installation routine warns you if you need to install the BSD Tools for CCC and helps you to download them, so you won't have any difficulty with that step.

To clone your installation of Mac OS X, follow these steps:

1. Prepare your installation of Mac OS X for cloning, as discussed a little earlier in this Special Project.

2. Download the appropriate version of CCC for your version of Mac OS X from www.bombich.com/software/ccc.html and install it on your Mac.

3. Connect your iPod and enable disk mode. Make sure your iPod has enough free space for the installation of Mac OS X that you want to clone.

4. Run Carbon Copy Cloner. It displays the Cloning Console (shown on the next page with the source disk and target disk selected).

5. In the Source Disk drop-down list, choose the disk that contains the installation of Mac OS X that you want to clone. CCC displays a list of the disk's contents in the Items To Be Copied list box.

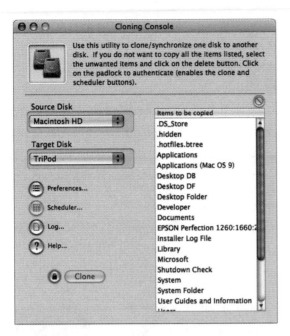

6. By default, CCC clones everything on your disk. To remove an item, select it in the Items To Be Copied list box, and then click the Delete button (the button bearing a red circle with a line through it). For example, you might choose not to clone your Applications (Mac OS 9) folder if you don't need to have it on your iPod.

7. In the Target Disk drop-down list, select your iPod.

8. Click the lock button in the lower-left corner of the CCC window to display the Enter Your Administrative Password pane.

9. Type your password and click the OK button. CCC closes the pane and activates the Clone button.

10. Click the Clone button to start the cloning operation. CCC displays a progress readout (in the bottom-left corner of the Cloning Console, shown above in the right-hand screen) as it works.

11. CCC displays a message box to tell you when it has finished cloning your Mac OS X installation:

The clone operation has completed.

Donate   OK

12. Click the OK button to close the message box, and then press COMMAND-Q or choose Carbon Copy Cloner | Quit Carbon Copy Cloner to quit CCC.

Designate Your iPod As the Startup Disk

 fter installing or cloning the operating system onto your iPod, you need to designate your iPod as the startup disk to make your Mac boot from it.

To designate your iPod as the startup disk, follow these steps:

1. Choose Apple | System Preferences to display the System Preferences window.

2. Click the Startup Disk icon in the System area to display the Startup Disk sheet:

![Startup Disk sheet with Mac OS X options on Macintosh HD and TriPod]

3. Select the item that represents your iPod.

4. To restart immediately and check that your bootable iPod works, click the Restart button. Mac OS X displays this confirmation dialog box:

![Startup Disk confirmation dialog asking Are you sure you want to restart the computer?]

5. Click the Restart button. Your Mac restarts and boots the operating system from your iPod.

If you don't want to restart your Mac immediately, press COMMAND-Q or choose System Preferences | Quit System Preferences to quit System Preferences. Then restart your Mac as normal whenever you want to.

To stop your Mac from booting from your iPod, use the Startup Disk sheet of System Preferences to designate the appropriate operating system on your hard disk as the startup disk.

Display All Available Startup Disks

If your Mac fails to boot from your iPod, you may have a nasty moment—or your Mac may give up on looking for your iPod and decide to boot from its hard disk anyway. If it *doesn't* boot at all, and you find yourself looking forlornly at a blank screen, take the following steps:

1. Press CONTROL-COMMAND-POWER to force a restart.

2. When your Mac plays the system sound, hold down OPTION to display a graphical screen of the available startup disks. Here's an example:

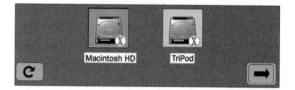

3. Click the disk from which you want to start the computer.

4. Click the arrow button on the screen to start your Mac using that startup disk.

SHARE Your Music More Effectively with Other Local Users

As you saw in Chapters 4 and 5, iTunes makes it easy for you to share either your music library or specific playlists with other iTunes users on your local area network (LAN): in the Preferences dialog box (on the Mac) or in the iTunes dialog box (on Windows), select the Share My Music check box and either the Share Entire Library option button or the Share Selected Playlists option button, and iTunes makes your music available to others. Similarly, you can play music that others are sharing by selecting the Look For Shared Music check box in the Preferences dialog box or the iTunes dialog box.

Problems with Sharing iTunes

 haring via iTunes could hardly be simpler, but with such simplicity comes a couple of problems:

- Music sharing works only with other computers—not with other users of your computer. If you share your computer with other people, you probably trust them at least well enough to share your music with them. But the security features of Windows and Mac OS X prevent you from doing so.

- The Mac or PC that is sharing a music library must be attached to the network and powered up for other computers to be able to access its music. If John puts his iMac to sleep, it drops off the network, and Mary can't play any of the music it was sharing. If Mary packs up her iBook and drags it off to school, neither John nor anyone else can access her music library. Stated simply like this, this problem seems too obvious to mention, but it can greatly reduce the amount of music available on your LAN.

This Special Project shows you how to share your music with other users of your computer, and then it discusses how to create a music server for your household so that you can keep your music available all the time.

Share Your Music Library with Other Users of Your Mac

Mac OS X's security system prevents other users from accessing your Home folder or its contents—which, by default, include your music library. So if you want to share your music library with other users of your Mac, you need to change permissions to allow others to access your Home folder (or parts of it), or you must move your music library to a folder they can access.

The easiest way to give other users access to your music is to put your music library in the Users/Shared folder and tell iTunes where to find it. To do so, follow these steps:

1. Use the Finder to move the iTunes Music folder from your ~/Music/iTunes folder to the /Users/Shared folder.

2. Press COMMAND-COMMA (or COMMAND-Y) or choose iTunes | Preferences to display the Preferences dialog box.

3. Click the Advanced button to display the Advanced sheet.

4. Click the Change button and use the resulting Change Music Folder Location dialog box to navigate to and select the /Users/Shared/iTunes Music folder.

5. Click the Choose button to close the Change Music Folder Location dialog box, and enter the new path in the iTunes Music Folder Location text box on the Advanced sheet.

6. Make sure the Keep iTunes Music Folder Organized check box is selected.

7. Click the OK button to close the Advanced sheet. iTunes displays the Changing The Location Of The iTunes Music Folder dialog box.

8. Click the OK button. iTunes displays the Updating Song Locations dialog box as it updates the locations in its database, and then it displays a dialog box asking whether you want to let it organize your music preferences.

9. Click the Yes button to move the music files in your library to the new, shared music library.

10. If you want other users to be able to put song files in the shared music library (for example, if they import

them from CD), you need to give them Write permission for it. To do so, follow these steps:

A. Open a Finder window to the /Users/Shared folder.

B. CTRL-click or right-click the iTunes Music folder, and choose Get Info from the shortcut menu to display the iTunes Music Info window, shown below.

C. In the Ownership & Permissions area, click the Details arrow to expand its display, if necessary.

D. In the Others drop-down list, select the Read & Write item.

![iTunes Music Info window]

iTunes Music Info

▼ General:

iTunes Music

Kind: Folder
Size: 477.7 MB on disk (500,882,819 bytes)
Where: Macintosh HD:Users:Shared:
Created: Friday, May 16, 2003 6:48 PM
Modified: Friday, January 2, 2004 12:50 PM

☐ Locked

▶ Name & Extension:
▶ Content index:
▶ Preview:
▼ Ownership & Permissions:
  You can [Read & Write]
  ▼ Details:
    Owner: [guy] 🔒
    Access: [Read & Write]

    Group: [staff]
    Access: [Read only]

    Others: [Read & Write]
    [Apply to enclosed items...]
▶ Comments:

E. Click the Apply To Enclosed Items button. Mac OS X displays this dialog box:

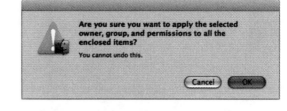

Are you sure you want to apply the selected owner, group, and permissions to all the enclosed items?
You cannot undo this.

[Cancel] [OK]

F. Click the OK button.

G. Click the Close button (the X button) to close the Info window.

After you move your music library to the /Users/Shared folder, the other users of your Mac can do one of two things:

■ Move their music library to the /Users/Shared folder, using the technique described here, so that all music is stored centrally. Users can then add songs they import to the shared music library, and all users can access them.

■ Keep their music library separate but add the contents of the shared music library folder to it:

  1. Press COMMAND-Q or choose File | Add To Library to display the Add To Library dialog box.

  2. Navigate to the /Users/Shared/iTunes Music folder.

  3. Click the Open button. iTunes adds all the latest songs to your music library.

In either case, there's a small complication: songs that other users have added to the shared music library don't appear automatically in your music library. To add all the latest tracks, use the Add To Library dialog box, as just described.

Share Your Music Library with Other Users of Your PC

Like Mac OS X, Windows XP (and Windows 2000, but we'll focus on Windows XP here) automatically prevents other users from accessing your personal files, assigning each user a user account, and keeping them out of other users' accounts. The result of this is that your iTunes music library, which is stored in your My Music\iTunes\iTunes Music folder by default, is securely protected from other users of your computer—which is great if you want to keep your music to yourself, but not so great if you want to share it with your friends, family, or coworkers.

NOTE

Windows Media Player, the audio and video player that Microsoft includes with Windows at the time of this writing, gets around this restriction by making the music and video files that any user adds to their music library available to all users. This is great if you want to share all your files, but it's less appealing if you want to keep some of them private.

The easiest way to give other users access to your music library is to move it to the Shared Music folder, which Windows XP automatically shares with other users of your computer but not with other computers on the network. The Shared Music folder is located in the \Documents and Settings\All Users\Documents\My Music folder. Alternatively, you can put the music

library in another shared folder. This example uses the Shared Music folder; if you're using another folder, substitute it where appropriate.

Moving your music library to the Shared Music folder involves two steps: moving the files and telling iTunes where you've moved them.

To move your music library files to the Shared Music folder, follow these steps:

1. Close iTunes if it's running. (For example, press ALT-F4.)

2. Choose Start | My Music to open a Windows Explorer window showing My Music.

3. Double-click the iTunes folder to open it. You'll see an iTunes Music Library.xml file, an iTunes 4 Music Library.itl file, and an iTunes Music folder. The first two files must stay in your My Music folder. If you remove them, iTunes won't be able to find your music, and it will create these files again from scratch.

4. Right-click the iTunes Music folder and choose Cut from the shortcut menu to cut it to the Clipboard.

5. In the Other Places task pane, click the Shared Music link to display the Shared Music folder. (If the Shared Music folder doesn't appear in the Other Places task pane, click the My Computer link, click the Shared Documents link, and then double-click the Shared Music folder.)

6. Right-click in open space and choose Paste from the shortcut menu to paste the iTunes Music folder into the Shared Music folder.

7. Close the Windows Explorer window.

Next, you need to tell iTunes where the song files are. Follow these steps:

1. Start iTunes (for example, double-click the iTunes icon on your desktop.)

2. Press CTRL-COMMA or choose Edit | Preferences to display the iTunes dialog box.

3. Click the Advanced tab.

4. Click the Change button to display the Browse For Folder dialog box.

5. Navigate to the Shared Music folder (for example, click the My Computer item, click the Shared Documents item, click the Shared Music item, click the iTunes Music item, and then click the iTunes Music item) and then click the OK button.

6. Click the OK button to close the iTunes dialog box.

After you've done this, iTunes knows where the song files are, and you can play them back as usual. When you rip more song files from CD or import files, iTunes will store them in the Shared Music folder.

You're all set. The other users of your PC can do either of two things:

- Move their music library to the Shared Music folder, using the techniques described here, so that all music is stored centrally. Instead of moving the iTunes Music folder itself, move the folders it contains. Users can then add songs they import to the shared music library, and all users can access them.

- Keep their music library separate, but add the contents of the shared music library folder to it:

  1. Choose File | Add Folder To Library to display the Browse For Folder dialog box.

2. Navigate to the Shared Music folder.

3. Select the iTunes Music folder.

4. Click the Open button. iTunes adds all the latest songs to your music library.

In either case, there's a small complication: songs that other users have added to the shared music library don't appear automatically in your music library. To add all the latest tracks, use the Add To Library dialog box, as just described.

Build a Music Server for Your Household

If you find that trying to play songs stored in music libraries that keep disappearing off the network is too tedious, another option is to build a music server for your household. You can either build a server from scratch on a new computer or change the role of one of your existing computers—even a pensioned-off computer that's too old to run Mac OS X or Windows XP at a decent speed.

Whether you buy (or build) a new computer or repurpose an existing computer will color your choices for your server. Here are notes on the key components for the server:

- **Operating system** The server can run Windows or Mac OS X if you have a copy that you can spare; if not, you might consider using a less expensive (or even free) operating system, such as one of the many distributions of Linux.

- **Processor** The server can run on a modest processor—even an antiquated one by today's standards, such as a 500 MHz or faster processor for a Windows or Linux server or a slower G3 processor for a Mac server.

- **RAM** The server needs only enough RAM to run the operating system unless you'll need to run applications on it. For example, 256MB RAM is adequate for a server running Windows XP or Mac OS X.

- **Disk space** The server must have enough disk space to store all the songs you want to have available—and perhaps store video files, too, in the near future. A desktop computer is likely to be a better bet than a notebook computer, because you can add internal drives to it. Alternatively, you might use one or more external USB or FireWire drives to provide plenty of space.

- **Network connection** The server must be connected to your network, either via network cable or via wireless. A wireless connection is adequate for serving a few computers, but in most cases, a wired connection (Fast Ethernet or Gigabit Ethernet) is a much better choice.

- **Monitor** If the server will be running somewhere convenient (rather than being used for other computing tasks, such as running applications), all you need is an old monitor capable of displaying the bootup and login screens for the operating system. After that, you can turn off the monitor until you need to restart or configure the server.

- **Keyboard and mouse** Like the monitor, the keyboard and mouse can be basic devices, because you'll need to use them only for booting and configuring the server.

- **CD-ROM drive** Your server needs a CD-ROM drive only if you'll use it for ripping. If you'll rip on the clients, the server can get by without one.

- **Sound card** Your server needs a sound card only if you'll use it for playing music.

- **Reliability** Modest your server may be, but it must be reliable—otherwise the music won't be available when you want to play it. Make sure also that the server has plenty of cooling, and configure its power settings so that it doesn't go to sleep.

- **Location** If you choose to leave your server running all the time, locate it somewhere safe from being switched off accidentally. Because the running server will probably make some noise, you may be tempted to hide it away in a closet. If you do, make sure there's enough ventilation so that it doesn't overheat.

After setting up the server and sharing a folder that will contain the songs, configure iTunes on the client computers to use that folder for the music library.

■ You can play the songs you buy on any number of iPods that you synchronize with your Mac or PC. (You may have trouble playing the songs on other music players.)

■ You can play the songs you buy on up to three computers at once. These computers are said to be "authorized." You can change which computers are authorized for the songs bought on a particular iTunes Music Store account.

■ You can download each song you buy only once (assuming the download is successful). After that, the song is your responsibility. If you lose the song, you have to buy it again.

Understand DRM

Currently, the music industry and consumers are engaged in a vigorous tussle over how music is sold (or stolen) and distributed:

■ The record companies are aggressively rolling out copy-protection mechanisms on audio discs (see "Understand Current Copy-Protection Techniques on the CDs You Buy," in Chapter 3) to prevent their customers from making unauthorized pure-digital copies of music (for example, AAC files or MP3 files).

■ Some consumers are trying to protect their freedom to enjoy the music they buy in the variety of ways that law and case law have established to be either definitely legal or sort-of legal. For example, time-shifting, place-shifting, and personal use (see Chapter 3) suggest that it's probably legal to create AAC files or MP3 files from a CD, as long as they're for your personal use.

■ Other people—"consumers" in a sense other than the usual, perhaps—are deliberately infringing the record companies' copyrights by copying, distributing, and stealing music via P2P networks, recordable CDs and DVDs, and other means. Chapter 8 discusses this topic in some detail.

Behind this struggle rears the specter of DRM—technologies for defining which actions a user may take with a particular work and restricting the user to those actions, preferably without preventing them from using or enjoying the work in the ways they expect to. (Yes, that's deliberately vague. Understanding and satisfying the user's expectations is a vital component of an effective implementation of DRM.)

DRM is often portrayed by consumer activists as being the quintessence of the Recording Industry Association of America's and Motion Picture Association of America's dreams and of consumers' nightmares. The publisher of a work can use DRM to impose a wide variety of restrictions on the ways in which a consumer can use the work.

For example, some digital books are delivered in an encrypted format that requires a special certificate to decrypt, which effectively means that the consumer can read them only on one authorized computer. DRM also prevents the consumer from printing any of the book or copying any of it directly from the reader application. As you'd imagine, these restrictions are unpopular with most consumers, and such books haven't exactly made a splash in the marketplace: consumers prefer traditional physical books that they can read wherever they want to, lend to a friend, photocopy, rip pages out of, drop in the bath, and so on.

But how good or bad DRM is in practice depends on the implementation. When both publishers and consumers stand to gain from DRM being implemented effectively, compromise of the kind that Apple has achieved with the iTunes Music Store makes sense.

Music is almost ideal for digital distribution, and the record companies are sitting on colossal archives of songs that are out of print but still well within copyright. It's not economically viable for the record companies to sell pressed CDs of these songs, because demand for any given CD is likely to be relatively low. But demand is there, as has been demonstrated by the millions of illegal copies of such songs that have been downloaded from P2P services. If the record companies can make these songs available online with acceptable DRM, they'll almost certainly find buyers.

NOTE *In passing, it's worth mentioning that some enterprising smaller operators* have *managed to make an economic proposition out of selling pressed CDs or recorded CDs of out-of-print music to which they've acquired the rights. By cutting out middlemen and selling directly via web sites and mail order, and in some cases by charging a premium price for a hard-to-get product, such operators have proved that making such music available isn't impossible. But doing so certainly requires a different business model than the lowest-common-denominator, pack-'em-high-and-hope-they-fly model that the major record companies so doggedly pursue.*

What the iTunes Music Store DRM Means to You

At this writing, the iTunes Music Store provides a nicely weighted implementation of DRM, known as FairPlay, that's designed to be acceptable both to customers and to the record companies that are providing the songs. The iTunes Music Store started with more than 200,000 songs—an impressive number for the record companies to agree to provide, although only a few drops in the bucket compared to the many millions of songs that music enthusiasts would like to be able to purchase online. By December 2003, the iTunes Music Store had more than 500,000 songs available.

For customers, the attraction is being able to find songs easily, acquire them almost instantly for reasonable prices, and be able to use them in enough of the ways they're used to (play the songs on their computer, play them on their iPod, or burn them to CD). For the record companies, the appeal is a largely untapped market that can provide a revenue stream at minimal cost (no physical media are involved) and with an acceptably small potential for abuse. (For example, most people who buy songs won't burn them to CD, rip the CD to MP3, and then distribute the MP3 files.) To the surprise of many analysts, Steve Jobs revealed in late 2003 that Apple makes hardly any money from the iTunes Music Store, which seems to mean that most of the revenue (apart from the overheads of administering the service, running the servers, and providing bandwidth) goes to the record companies.

Being able to download music like this is pretty wonderful: you can get the songs you want, when you want them, and at a price that's more reasonable than buying a whole CD. But it's important to be aware of the following points, even if they don't bother you in the least:

■ When you buy a CD, you own it. As you've seen earlier in this book, you can't necessarily do what you want with the music—not legally, anyway. But you can play it as often as you want on whichever player, lend it to a friend, and so on.

- When you buy a song from the Apple Music Store, you don't own it. Instead, you have a very limited license. If your Mac's hard disk crashes so that you lose your music library, you can't download the songs again from the Apple Music Store without paying for them again.

- The record labels that provide the music reserve the right to change the terms under which they provide the music in the future. If history tells us anything, it's that the record labels won't grant users more generous terms—instead, they'll tighten the restrictions when users have become used to the relatively loose restrictions imposed at first.

What the iTunes Music Store Means for DRM

At the time of writing, DRM is having a hard time gaining acceptance in the consumer market, particularly in music. For example, the copy-protection mechanisms that the record companies have been putting on audio discs have caused considerable resentment among consumers, because they're perceived as (and are) a disabling technology: they prevent many CD players from playing the audio and prevent many computers from ripping it.

By contrast, the iTunes Music Store has been greeted mostly with enthusiasm, probably for the following reasons:

- Many people want to be able to buy music online and enjoy it without undue hassle.

- Apple has implemented the DRM in a slick and effective technology package: iTunes, the iTunes Music Store, and the iPod.

- Apple has positioned itself very carefully, using public relations and advertising, as the hardware and software company for people who don't conform blindly to fashion and who want to think for themselves (remember "Think Different"?), are especially creative, or are rebels. This positioning is somewhat at odds with the extremely tight control that Apple exercises over its market (consider briefly that Apple made your Mac, its operating system, your iPod, its operating system, iTunes, and QuickTime, and runs the iTunes Music Store), but it has become widely accepted by dint of repetition.

Since the successful launch of the iTunes Music Store, several other companies (including RealNetworks and MUSICMATCH) have launched online music stores that feature DRM with similar terms to those of the iTunes Music Store. See the next chapter for details.

NOTE   *In an interesting counterpoint, Apple Corporation (the Beatles' record label) is suing Apple Computer for entering the music market, which Apple Computer had twice earlier agreed not to do.*

Set Up an Account with the iTunes Music Store

To use the iTunes Music Store, you need a Mac or PC running iTunes 4 as well as a .Mac account, an Apple ID, or an AOL screen name. (An Apple ID is essentially an account with the iTunes Music Store and takes the form of an e-mail address.)

FIGURE 7-1 The iTunes Music Store home page

To get started with the iTunes Music Store, click the Music Store item in the Source pane in iTunes. (Alternatively, double-click the Music Store item to display a separate Music Store window.) iTunes accesses the iTunes Music Store and displays its home page, of which Figure 7-1 shows an example on the Mac.

To sign in or to create an account, click the Sign In button. iTunes displays the Sign In To Buy Music On The iTunes Music Store dialog box:

If you have a .Mac account or an Apple ID, enter it in the Apple ID text box, enter your password in the Password text box, and click the Sign In button. Likewise, if you have an AOL screen name, select the AOL option button, enter your screen name and password, and click the Sign In button.

NOTE   *Remember that your Apple ID is the full e-mail address, including the domain—not just the first part of the address. For example, if your Apple ID is a .Mac address, enter* **yourname@mac.com** *rather than just* **yourname.**

The first time you sign on to the iTunes Music Store, iTunes displays a dialog box pointing out that your Apple ID or AOL screen name hasn't been used with the iTunes Music Store and suggesting you review your account information:

This AOL screen name has not yet been used with the iTunes Music Store.

Please review your account information.

Cancel   Review

Click the Review button to review it. (This is a compulsory step. Clicking the Cancel button doesn't skip the review process, as you might hope—instead, it cancels the creation of your account.)

To create a new account, click the Create New Account button, then click the Continue button on the Welcome To The iTunes Music Store page. The subsequent screens then walk you through the process of creating an account. As you'd imagine, you have to provide your credit card details and (at this writing) a U.S. billing address. Beyond this, you get a little homily on what you may and may not legally do with the music you download, and you have to agree to the terms of service of the iTunes Music Store.

Understand the Terms of Service

Almost no one ever reads the details of software licenses, which is why the software companies have been able to establish as normal the sales model in which you buy not software itself but a limited license to use it, and you have no recourse if it corrupts your data or reduces your computer to a puddle of silicon and steel. But you'd do well to read the terms and conditions of the iTunes Music Store before you buy music from it, because you should understand what you're getting into.

TIP   *The iTunes window doesn't give you the greatest view of the terms of service. To get a better view, direct your browser to www.info.apple.com/usen/musicstore/terms.html.*

The following are the key points of the terms of service:

- You can use songs that you download on three computers at any time. You can authorize and deauthorize computers, so you can (for example) transfer your songs from your old computer to a new computer you buy.

- You can use, export, copy, and burn songs for "personal, noncommercial use." Burning and exporting are an "accommodation" to you and don't "constitute a grant or waiver (or other limitation or implication) of any rights of the copyright owners." If you think that your being allowed to burn what would otherwise be illegal copies must limit the copyright owners' rights, I'd say you're right logically but wrong legally.

- After you buy and download songs, they're your responsibility. If you lose them or destroy them, Apple won't replace them. (You have to buy new copies of the songs.)

- You agree not to violate the Usage Rules imposed by the agreement.

- You agree that Apple may disclose your registration data and account information to "law enforcement authorities, government officials, and/or a third party, as Apple believes is reasonably necessary or appropriate to enforce and/or verify compliance with any part of this Agreement." The implication is that if a copyright holder claims that you're infringing their copyright, Apple may disclose your details without your knowledge, let alone your agreement. In these days of the Patriot Act and Patriot II, you can safely assume that the government and the law enforcement authorities can easily find out anything they decide they want to know about you. But few will like the idea of (say) Sony Music or the RIAA being able to learn the details of their e-mail address, physical address, credit card, and listening habits by claiming a suspicion of copyright violation.

- Apple and its licensors can remove or prevent you from accessing "products, content, or other materials."

- Apple reserves the right to modify the Agreement at any time. If you continue using the iTunes Music Store, you're deemed to have accepted whatever additional terms Apple imposes.

- Apple can terminate your account for failing to "comply with any of the provisions" in the Agreement—or for being suspected of such failure. Terminating your account prevents you from buying any more music immediately, but you might be able to set up another account. More seriously, termination might prevent you from playing music you've already bought—for example, if you need to authorize a computer to play it.

As you can see, there's a lot to dislike here. You might take the view that many of the provisions are merely Apple ensuring that its rear is well covered. But it's hard to see the terms of service as being pro-consumer or pro-freedom in the way that Apple's ads suggest the company is.

Configure iTunes Music Store Settings

By default, iTunes 4 is configured to display the iTunes Music Store icon in the Source pane and to use 1-Click buying and downloading. You may want to remove the iTunes Music Store icon or to use the shopping basket. To change your preferences, follow these steps:

1. Press COMMAND-COMMA (or COMMAND-Y) or choose iTunes | Preferences on the Mac to display the Preferences dialog box. Press CTRL-COMMA (or CTRL-Y) or choose Edit | Preferences on Windows to display the iTunes dialog box.

2. Click the Store tab to display the Store sheet (on the Mac; shown here) or Store tab (on Windows):

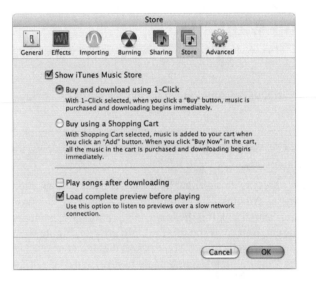

3. To prevent the iTunes Music Store item from appearing in the Source pane, clear the Show iTunes Music Store check box. Doing this disables all the other controls on the Store sheet or tab, so you've nothing left to do but click the OK button to close the dialog box.

4. If you choose to use the iTunes Music Store, select the Buy And Download Using 1-Click option button or the Buy Using A Shopping Cart option button, as appropriate. 1-Click is great for impulse shopping and instant gratification, whereas the shopping cart enables you to round up a collection of songs, weigh their merits against each other, and decide which ones you feel you must have. (In other words, using the shopping cart is the more sensible approach. So Apple has made 1-Click the default setting.)

TIP   *If you have a slow connection, consider using the Buy Using A Shopping Cart option to queue up a stack of tracks to download overnight when the download won't compete with you for your meager bandwidth.*

5. Select or clear the Play Songs After Downloading check box. This setting lets you hear a song the instant you've downloaded it; if you usually listen to music while downloading, you may prefer to keep this check box cleared, as it is by default.

6. If you're using a slow Internet connection (for example, dial-up or ISDN) to download songs, you may want to select the Load Complete Preview Before Playing check box. Otherwise, the download stream may be too slow to sustain play through the preview without interruptions. (Faster Internet connections should be able to stream the previews without breaking a sweat.)

7. Click the OK button to apply your choices and close the Preferences dialog box or iTunes dialog box.

Find the Songs You Want

You can find songs in the iTunes Music Store in several ways that will seem familiar if you've used other online stores:

- You can meander through the interface looking for songs by clicking links from the home page.

- You can browse by genre, artist, and album. Click the Browse button, choose Edit | Show Browser, or press COMMAND-B (on the Mac) or CTRL-B (on Windows) to display the Browse interface (see Figure 7-2).

- You can search for specific music either by using the Search Music Store box (which you can restrict to Artists, Albums, Composers, or Songs by using the drop-down list), or by clicking the Power Search link (on the home page or on the Search drop-down list) and using the Power Search page to specify multiple criteria. Figure 7-3 shows the Power Search page with some results found. You can sort the search results by a column heading by clicking it. Click the column heading again to reverse the sort order.

Preview Songs

One of the most attractive features of the iTunes Music Store is that it lets you listen to a preview of a song before you buy it. This feature helps you ensure both that the song you're buying is the song you think you're buying and that you like it.

For some songs, the previews are of the first 30 seconds. For most songs, the previews feature one of the most distinctive parts of the song (for example, the chorus or a catchy line).

A typical download of a 30-second clip involves around 600K of data. If you have a slow Internet connection, downloading the previews will take a while. It's best to select the Load Complete Preview Before Playing check box on the Store sheet of the Preferences dialog box (on the Mac) or the Store tab of the iTunes dialog box (on Windows).

Double-click a song's listing to start the preview playing (or downloading, if you choose to load complete previews before playing).

FIGURE 7-2 Use the Browse feature to browse through the iTunes Music Store's offerings.

FIGURE 7-3 Use the Power Search feature to search for songs by song title, artist, album, genre, and composer.

7

Understand A******s and "Explicit"

The iTunes Music Store is oddly censorial in a way that most people associate with Tipper Gore rather than the Apple culture:

■ Songs deemed to have potentially offensive lyrics are marked EXPLICIT in the Song Name column. Where a sanitized version of the same song is available, it's marked CLEAN in the Song Name column. Some of the supposedly explicit songs contain words no more offensive than "love." Others are instrumentals.

■ Strangely, other songs that contain words that are offensive to most people (such as George Carlin's "Seven Words You Can't Say on Television") aren't flagged as being explicit. So if you worry about what you and yours hear, don't trust the iTunes Music Store ratings too far.

■ Any word deemed offensive is censored with asterisks (**), at least in theory. (In practice, some words sneak through.) When searching, use the real word rather than censoring it yourself.

Request Music You Can't Find

Half a million songs sounds like an impressive number, but it's a mere teacup in the bucket of all the songs that have ever been recorded (and that music enthusiasts would like to buy). As a result, the iTunes Music Store's selection of music pleases some users more than others. Not surprisingly, Apple and the record companies seem to be concentrating first on the songs that are most likely to please (and be bought by) the most people. If you want the biggest hits—either the latest ones or longtime favorites—chances are that the iTunes Music Store has you covered. But if your tastes run to the esoteric, you may not find the songs you're looking for on the iTunes Music Store.

If you can't find a song you're looking for in the iTunes Music Store, you can submit a request for it. If a search produces no results, the iTunes Music Store offers you a Request link that you can click to display the Make A Request form for requesting music by song name, artist name, album, composer, or genre. You can also display this form by clicking the Requests & Feedback link on the home page.

Beyond the immediate thank-you-for-your-input screen that the iTunes Music Store displays, requesting songs feels unrewarding at present. Apple doesn't respond directly to song requests, so unless you keep checking for the songs you've requested, you won't know that they've been posted. Nor will you learn if the songs will never be made available. Besides, given the complexities involved in licensing songs, it seems highly unlikely that Apple will make special efforts to license any particular song unless a truly phenomenal number of people request it. Instead, Apple seems likely to continue doing what makes much more sense—licensing as many songs as possible that are as certain as possible to appeal to plenty of people.

Navigate the iTunes Music Store

To navigate from page to page in the iTunes Music Store, click the buttons in the toolbar. Alternatively, use these keyboard shortcuts:

- On the Mac, press COMMAND-[to return to the previous page and COMMAND-] to go to the next page.
- On Windows, press CTRL-[to return to the previous page and CTRL-] to go to the next page.

Buy a Song from the iTunes Music Store

To buy a song from the iTunes Music Store, simply click the Buy Song button.

If you're not currently signed in, iTunes displays the Sign In To Buy Music On The iTunes Music Store dialog box:

Enter your ID and password, and then click the Buy button. (If you want iTunes to handle the password for you automatically in the future, select the Remember Password For Purchasing check box before clicking the Buy button.)

iTunes then displays a confirmation message box like this:

Click the Buy button to make the purchase. Select the Don't Warn Me About Buying Songs Again check box if appropriate. Some people prefer to have this double-check in place to slow down the pace at which they assault their credit cards. For others, even having to confirm the purchase is an annoyance.

iTunes then downloads the song to your music library and adds an entry for it to your Purchased Music playlist.

Listen to Songs You've Purchased

When you download a song from the iTunes Music Store, iTunes adds it to the playlist named Purchased Music in the Source pane. When you display the Purchased Music playlist, iTunes automatically displays this message box to explain what the playlist is:

Select the Do Not Show This Message Again check box before dismissing this message box, because otherwise it will soon endanger your sanity.

Purchased Music is there to provide a quick and easy way to get to all the music you buy. Otherwise, if you purchase songs on impulse without keeping a list, the songs might vanish in the maelstrom of music that your music library contains.

To delete the entry for a song in the Purchased Music playlist, right-click it, choose Clear from the shortcut menu, and click the Yes button in the confirmation message box. However, unlike for regular song files, iTunes doesn't offer you the opportunity to delete the song file itself—the file remains in your music library on the basis that, having paid for it, you don't actually want to delete it.

You can drag songs that you haven't purchased to the Purchased Music playlist as well.

Restart a Failed Download

If the download of a song fails, you may see an error message that invites you to try again later. If this happens, iTunes terminates the download but doesn't roll back the purchase of the song.

To restart a failed download, choose Advanced | Check For Purchased Music. Enter your password in the Enter Account Name And Password dialog box and click the Check button. iTunes attempts to restart the failed download.

Review What You've Purchased from the iTunes Music Store

To see what you've purchased from the iTunes Music Store, follow these steps:

1. Click the Account button (the button that displays your account name) to display the Account Information window. (If you're not currently signed in, you'll need to enter your password.)

2. Click the Purchase History button to display details of the songs you've purchased.

3. Click the arrow to the left or an order date to display details of the purchases on that date.

4. Click the Done button when you've finished examining your purchases. iTunes returns you to your Apple Account Information page.

TIP   *From the Apple Account Information page, you can also access the iTunes Music Store's features for setting up allowances for users to buy music and for buying gift certificates.*

5.   Click the Done button to return to the iTunes Music Store home page.

(Try to) Fix Problems with Your iTunes Music Store Bill

If something seems to have gone wrong with your iTunes Music Store bill—for example, you seem to have been billed for songs you didn't buy—choose Help | Music Store Customer Service and use the resulting form to try to get redress.

Authorize and Deauthorize Computers for the iTunes Music Store

As mentioned earlier in this chapter, when you buy a song from the iTunes Music Store, you're allowed to play it on up to three different computers at a time. iTunes implements this limitation through a form of license that Apple calls *authorization*. Essentially, iTunes tracks which computers are authorized to play songs you've purchased and stops you from playing the songs when you're out of authorizations.

If you want to play songs you've purchased on a fourth computer, you need to *deauthorize* one of the first three computers so as to free up an authorization for use on the fourth computer. You may also need to specifically deauthorize a computer to prevent it from listening to the songs you've bought. For example, if you sell or give away your Mac, you'd probably want to deauthorize it. You might also need to deauthorize a computer if you're planning to rebuild it.

NOTE   *Your computer must be connected to the Internet in order to authorize and deauthorize computers.*

Authorize a Computer to Use iTunes Music Store

To authorize a computer, simply try to play a song purchased from the iTunes Music Store. For example, access a shared computer's Purchased Music playlist and double-click one of the songs. iTunes displays the Authorize Computer dialog box:

Enter your Apple ID and password, and click the Authorize button. iTunes accesses the iTunes Music Store and (all being well) authorizes the computer. iTunes displays no notification message box, but simply starts playing the song.

Deauthorize a Computer from Using iTunes Music Store

To deauthorize a computer, follow these steps:

1. Choose Advanced | Deauthorize Computer to display the Deauthorize Computer dialog box:

2. Select the Deauthorize Computer For Apple Account option button if it's not already selected.

3. Click the OK button. iTunes displays the next Deauthorize Computer dialog box:

4. Enter the appropriate Apple ID and password, and then click the OK button. iTunes accesses the iTunes Music Store, performs the deauthorization, and then tells you the deed is done:

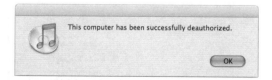

Chapter 8

Download Audio Files from the Internet

How to…

- Understand the conflict between consumers and the music industry
- Guess which files are legitimate and which are illegal
- Know what's happening on the darknet—and what the dangers are
- Understand the basics of P2P networks
- Find legal audio online

Ripping your own CDs, tapes, and LPs can produce an impressive library of song files, but in the process it's likely to make you wonder if you couldn't just get the song files directly without needing to mess with the physical media. And of course you can, by downloading them via the Internet in an entertaining variety of ways—some legal and some not.

How you actually download a file from the Internet depends on the technologies used, but most of those currently in circulation make downloading very simple—in most cases, as easy as clicking a button or a link. So this chapter concentrates not on the process of downloading but on the more difficult issues involved, such as the legalities surrounding downloading audio, and how to tell which audio files are aboveboard and which are stolen.

Quick Reality Check on the Music Market

In pretty much every marketplace, there's a tension between the supply side and the demand side, between the suppliers (the sellers or producers) and the consumers. Usually, the tension is straightforward: the consumers want only products that appeal to them, and are prepared to pay only a certain amount for them; the suppliers want consumers to buy various products and, in general, pay as much as possible for them.

Generally, this tension between supply and demand creates a balance between the suppliers and the consumers. For example, if your nearest clothing store tried to charge $100 for a basic pair of jeans, you'd probably go elsewhere. So the clothing store will offer the jeans for a good price but hope to "upsell" you to a shirt, belt, or complete outfit when you come in for the jeans.

The tension in the music market between the music industry and the consumers is extreme at present. This is partly because of the way people regard music and partly because music is almost ideal for digital distribution. But it's mostly because digital distribution of music has endangered the market for traditional media—records (singles, EPs, and LPs), cassettes, and CDs—and the music industry hasn't yet worked out how to cope. Also, many artists have entered the fray instead of allowing the music industry to represent them. For example, many artists make some of their music available on the Internet in the hope of enlarging their fan base and their sales.

What Most Consumers Want

Most consumers want high-quality music that they can acquire easily and inexpensively and then do what they please with. These wishes explain why MP3 has been such a resounding success in many areas of the world, and why Microsoft has expended huge amounts of effort into trying to make Windows Media Audio (WMA), its proprietary audio format that also offers DRM, supplant MP3.

For example, as a consumer, you may well want to do the following:

- Download music from the Internet—either for free or at an acceptable cost.
- Rip and encode digital files of your music so you can listen to it on any of your computers, on your iPod, or on another portable player.
- Put the music on that computer or portable player and play the music on it.
- Send music to friends so they can listen to it.
- Have friends send you music so that you can listen to it.
- Burn custom CDs containing the tracks you want to listen to.

Computers and the Internet enable you to do all of the above. The law lets you do some of it. And the music industry wants something quite different.

What the Music Industry Wants

The music industry has been based on selling music on physical media—records, cassettes, and CDs—and is struggling to come to terms with digital distribution. The problem is that digital media enables consumers to copy music and distribute it worldwide with minimal effort and cost. For example, in theory, only one person needs to buy the next Christina Aguilera CD. They can then copy it and distribute it instantly on the Internet or on physical media (such as recordable CDs).

From a consumer's point of view, looking at the various unsatisfactory copyright-protection schemes that have so far appeared, the music industry appears to want an unreasonable degree of control over its products. For example, some copyright-protection schemes for digital audio files permanently lock a file to a particular computer. If you upgrade your computer, or if your operating system gets so confused that you need to reinstall it, you lose the files permanently. Similarly, for CDs protected with anticopy technologies, record companies have offered to sell consumers digital audio files separately from the CDs. So you'd need to buy a CD to use on your CD player and then buy MP3 files to use on your MP3 player.

For the music industry, the ultimate sales goal would be pay-per-use, so not only would they know how often any consumer had played a particular track, but they'd also receive a micropayment for each use. Consumers are likely to give the music industry a hard time on pay-per-use.

What's Happening Between Consumers and the Music Industry

The tension between consumers and the music industry has been playing out for several years now and most likely will continue to play out as you read this. Here's a summary of what's happened so far:

- Many consumers have taken to ripping their music collections to formats such as MP3, WMA, and Ogg Vorbis so they can place-shift the music more easily (and enjoy them in a variety of places), manage the music using their computers, and share the music with their friends. Many Mac users now use AAC because it's built into iTunes (or, more accurately, into QuickTime) and the iPod, and because it offers better audio quality than MP3. Now that iTunes is available in a Windows version, increasing numbers of Windows-based iPod users are preferring AAC as well.

■ Many consumers—some in ignorance of the law but many in open defiance of it—have embraced the unauthorized distribution of copyrighted content. Popular distribution mechanisms have included physical media (such as recordable CDs), e-mail, newsgroups, instant messaging, and custom P2P file-sharing technologies such as the original Napster, Aimster/Madster, Kazaa, and Freenet.

■ To prevent people from ripping the audio discs they buy, the music industry has started introducing assorted copyright-protection mechanisms, such as the copy-protection on some recent audio discs (see the section "Understand Current Copy-Protection Techniques on the CDs You Buy," in Chapter 3).

■ To prevent people from sharing music, the music industry (led by the RIAA—the Recording Industry Association of America) has pushed for restrictive legislation. (Other interested parties, such as the Motion Picture Association of America and the movie studios, are also pushing for legislation to protect their copyrighted content and their interests, but we'll concentrate on the music side here.) As a result, some ill-thought-out and strongly anti-consumer legislation has been passed, and more is being put forward at this writing. For example, as you saw in Chapter 3, the DMCA (Digital Millennium Copyright Act) makes it illegal to circumvent anti-copying measures on works.

■ Computer hardware and software manufacturers are exploring the possibility of including digital rights management (DRM) hardware and software in computer components and operating systems. For example, some Creative Labs sound cards already won't output digital audio from audio discs marked with copyright-protection systems; they'll output only analog audio, preventing you from making perfect digital copies via the sound card. Further out, Microsoft is working on an operating-system component, codenamed Palladium, that will work with hardware developed by the Trusted Computing Platform Alliance (TCPA) to secure transactions. In this sense, a "transaction" can be anything from playing back a protected song or movie to something that actually involves money changing hands.

■ On a more positive note, some music is finally being sold legally via download. Chapter 7 showed you how to use the iTunes Music Store, which is the most successful online music store to date. You'll meet several other online music stores later in this chapter.

Understand the Darknet and the Light

(So to speak. The light is relative here—as it is always. Only darkness can be absolute.)

As you read in Chapter 7, the iTunes Music Store offers more than half a million songs at this writing, and Apple is working to add more songs week by week. So far, so good—but most people find the iTunes Music Store's selection has only some, or only a few, of the songs they want. The same goes for the other legitimate online music services you'll meet later in this chapter.

But if you look elsewhere on the Internet, you can find just about any song you can name (and millions more that you can't). Depending on where you go for the files and the tools you use, the files may be entirely aboveboard and legitimate, or wholly illegal.

As discussed in Chapter 3, sharing digital files of other people's copyrighted content without permission is illegal. So is receiving such illegal files. The No Electronic Theft Act (NET Act) of 1997 and the Digital Millennium Copyright Act (DMCA) of 1998 provide savage penalties for people caught distributing copyrighted materials illegally. So before you start searching for and downloading music from the Internet, it's a good idea to know whom you're dealing with and whether the files are legal or illegal.

What Is the Darknet?

The *darknet* is an umbrella term some observers use for the unauthorized distribution of copyrighted digital content via computers. At present, the darknet uses the Internet extensively, because the Internet provides an easy and efficient distribution mechanism. But the darknet can also use many other types of networks, some of which are networks only in the loosest sense of the word. For example, Sneakernet (a pun on the networking technology called Ethernet) can also be part of the darknet. Using Sneakernet involves transferring files by physically carrying a disk from one computer to another.

How the Darknet Works

So far, the darknet has used various forms of distribution, including e-mail attachments, newsgroup attachments, web sites, FTP sites, custom P2P software (more on this in a moment), direct connections, and Sneakernet with physical media.

Like most aspects of any underground economy, the darknet mutates to circumvent any restrictions placed upon it. For example, if the music industry (or any other body) is successful in preventing the distribution of music or other copyrighted content across the Internet, the darknet will turn to non-Internet methods of distributing the content, such as direct connections, local networks, or Sneakernet.

The darknet has been around since the early days of the Internet, but it assumed significant proportions only in the late 1990s. The darknet's growth in the late '90s was spurred largely by the widespread adoption of the Internet (including broadband connections such as cable and DSL) and the incorporation of multimedia features in computers, which meant that even relatively modest computers could be used for enjoying high-quality audio and acceptable video.

At the same time, hardware and software for creating digital content became widely available and affordable. With rippers and audio-compression technologies (notably MP3 encoders), users could add music from CDs or other sources to the darknet. With scanners, they could add pictures and text from books and magazines. With video-capture boards, they could capture video from a variety of sources. With an Internet connection, they could share those files with others and download the files others were sharing. With a broadband Internet connection, they could share even large files quickly.

How P2P Networks Enlarged the Darknet

The key to the explosion of the darknet was the rapid development of peer-to-peer (P2P) networks in 1999 and 2000. This development was spearheaded by Napster—the company, eponymous service, and eponymous application that made music-swapping a household pursuit. Napster was followed by a slew of similar services that exploited the power, flexibility, and legal uncertainty of P2P networks.

In a P2P network, instead of the shared files being stored on centralized file servers and controlled by the network's host, the files are stored on the computers of the individual users who connect to the network. When connecting to the network, each user supplies a list of the files they're sharing, together with other relevant information such as their IP address and the speed of their Internet connection. (When a user logs out of the P2P network, their files become unavailable.) The list of files and their associated information is added to the central database, which all users of the network can then search by various criteria. For example, a user could search for MP3 files by a certain artist that include a particular word in their titles, or that have a specific bitrate or higher bitrate.

When a user has found a file he or she wants to download, the P2P service puts the user in direct communication with the host offering the file. The user then downloads the file from the host (as opposed to downloading it from the P2P service).

That's a very basic description of how P2P networks work. Most have further features—for example, some P2P services let users search the files a host is offering, resume a download that was broken off, or switch a download in progress to a different host when the current host goes offline.

Since Napster was closed down by legal attack in 2001, P2P network developers have taken measures to protect their networks. These measures include the following:

- **Expand the categories of files shared on the network.** While Napster was written to share MP3 files, other P2P networks have been developed to share specific other types of files (such as pictures, video, and other music formats) or any files at all. (Many other types of files, from application software files to pornographic movies, were shared via Napster by being disguised as MP3 files.)

- **Locate the servers in countries where the RIAA and similar U.S.-based bodies have less direct leverage than in the United States.** For example, Sharman Networks Ltd., the parent company of the Kazaa P2P network, is based in Australia and incorporated in Vanuatu, a South Pacific nation.

- **Build a true peer network rather than a peer network coordinated by a server.** For example, in P2P networks based on the Gnutella protocol, users join the network by attaching to a participating peer rather than to a central server.

- **Distribute the database across clients rather than storing it on central servers.** Again, Gnutella is an example of this. Each computer in a Gnutella network routes search requests to and from the peers to which it's connected. Passing the search from one client to another greatly increases the traffic across any given node in the network, but it makes the network far less vulnerable to attack, because the network can easily survive the loss of any node. True P2P networks are also less vulnerable to legal attack, because there's no central server acting as a conduit for file transfers. The central server represents the focus of legal attack and also a single point of failure for the network.

NOTE   *Gnutella searches are inefficient, flooding the network with data that chokes performance. Applications such as Grokster and Kazaa route searches through users with fast connections for better performance. Developers are working on creating a Content-Addressable Network (CAN) with better search mechanisms. Add CAN to your P2P buzzword list, together with Chord (a scalable lookup service for P2P networks) and Tapestry (a decentralized, fault-tolerant, scalable location and routing infrastructure).*

■ **Encrypt the files placed on the hosts or redistribute the shared files so a host doesn't know which files it's sharing.**   This arrangement, which is used by P2P networks such as Freenet and Mnemosyne, works only when each network user commits some space to the P2P network that the network can then use for its own purposes. (By contrast, under Napster and similar models, hosts choose exactly which folders to share and control which files are placed in those folders.)

■ **Hide the identity of the endpoints of the network by routing traffic through intermediate hosts.**   This technique, used by Freenet among other networks, is intended to help P2P network users avoid identification and the possible consequences.

Darknet Users: Super-Peers and Free Riders

As P2P networks developed, their users swiftly and effortlessly gravitated into two classes, which researchers have termed super-peers and free riders. A *super-peer* is a user who offers a large number of files for download, whereas a *free rider* is a user who offers few files (or even none) but actively downloads the files others are sharing.

Both classes of user make perfect sense. Free riders (also called *leechers*) use the P2P network as a method of free consumption. Perhaps many feel that because they're not offering materials for download, they either are not breaking the law, could claim ignorance of it, or will simply remain under the radar while more visible users take any heat that comes down. By contrast, super-peers tend to take a higher-profile, often political position, sometimes claiming that the record companies are profiteers or "pigopolists," that music (or other content) "wants to be free," or that they believe in the redistribution of resources (for example, their college's or company's fast Internet connection). Some super-peers look down on free riders as freeloaders willing to benefit from others' generosity but not reciprocate; some super-peers even block downloads to users they've decided are free riders.

Efforts to Close Down the Darknet

To date, efforts to close down the darknet have concentrated, naturally enough, on those parts of it that use the Internet for transmission. (These parts represent the easiest target—imagine trying to track down the people who had purchased recordable CDs and trying to determine exactly what, if anything, they had done with them.) The following subsections briefly discuss some of the efforts made so far.

Targeting the Services

The first targets have been the high-profile P2P services. Napster, Inc., was closed down in 2001 after an entertaining series of high-profile court battles with enough back-and-forth to give lay minds a nasty case of whiplash. Madster (formerly named Aimster until AOL forced it to change its name) was closed in 2002.

Looking at Napster and the mind-boggling number of files being shared illegally on it, many people wondered why it wasn't shut down immediately. Certainly the RIAA and the music industry *wanted* Napster shut down as soon as possible. But because some of the files were being shared legally, the case against Napster wasn't open-and-shut. Just because the service *could* be (and was being) used to share material illegally didn't make the service itself illegal.

Besides, Napster itself (so Napster claimed) wasn't doing anything illegal, even if some of its users were. Napster was merely providing a service, enabling people to find files: it wasn't hosting illegal files or allowing people to download them. This may seem like a sophism, but in the real world, it's an important point legally. If you doubt that, consider that the United States Postal Service doesn't have to open your parcels to make sure they don't contain anything wicked before conveying them to their destination, even though some of the parcels undoubtedly contain illegal materials. And your local friendly telephone company doesn't have to eavesdrop on your phone calls to see if you say anything illegal, even though some phone calls are definitely of questionable legality. In fact, the Postal Service and your phone company are expressly forbidden from examining transmissions under most circumstances. And your ISP would campaign vigorously against having to chaperone your online sessions.

Sophism or not, the law ultimately didn't buy Napster's arguments and closed down the service. Briefly, Napster was found to be acting as a conduit for file transfers, which made it complicit in copyright infringements perpetrated by its users.

After closing down Napster, the RIAA has targeted other P2P networks, including Madster, MusicCity, and Grokster. However, at this writing, many P2P networks are still running, and huge numbers of files are still being shared—most of them apparently without permission.

In April 2003, the U.S. District Court ruled that, because Grokster and Morpheus have legitimate uses that don't infringe copyright, these services can't be held responsible for copyright infringements perpetrated by their users. This ruling follows the precedent set by the Supreme Court in its Betamax Decision in 1984 (see "Time-Shifting and Place-Shifting," in Chapter 3, for an explanation of the Betamax Decision).

Targeting the Super-Peers

After the services themselves, the next most obvious target is the super-peers—the users who, together, provide the bulk of the files available on particular aspects of the darknet and who provide some of the darknet's broadest connections.

Super-peers can be targeted either directly by legal action (or threats) or indirectly by convincing the users' ISPs to close their accounts. Anecdotal evidence abounds of ISPs closing users' accounts when presented with even halfway convincing evidence that the users had been sharing files illegally.

Many super-peer sites have been hosted on computers that universities own. This is for largely obvious reasons: universities tend to have fast Internet connections and internal networks, which are great for sharing large amounts of data quickly; universities usually provide Internet access for their students; many students like music and don't have huge amounts of money to spend on it; some students either don't know the details of copyright law or choose to disregard those parts of it they don't like; and so on.

In early 2003, the RIAA targeted some universities, with mixed results. Some universities (such as Loyola University Chicago) surrendered the names of students who had been using P2P services with little or no resistance. But other schools (including MIT and Boston College) struck back, claiming the subpoenas weren't issued from the appropriate court and didn't give the universities reasonable time to provide the students with prior notice as required under the Family Educational Rights and Privacy Act.

Targeting the Users

After targeting the super-peers, the RIAA escalated the war of musical attrition to the next stage by targeting selected users with subpoenas. The idea appears to have been to spread FUD (fear, uncertainty, and doubt) among P2P users to discourage them from sharing files themselves and downloading files that others share. U.S. copyright law provides for damages of between $750 and $150,000 per song shared, so the financial threat is severe.

At this writing, the RIAA is proceeding on several fronts. The first is to capture details of the files that particular users are sharing (for example, on Kazaa) and to derive the users' names from their IP addresses. To get the names, the RIAA filed suit against several ISPs to force them to disclose the names under the terms of the DMCA.

The DMCA makes it ridiculously simple for a copyright owner to get a subpoena. Whereas before the DMCA, the copyright owner needed to apply to a judge to get a subpoena, under the DMCA, the copyright owner can simply get a subpoena from a district court clerk by filling in a form.

In January 2003, the RIAA won a court order against the ISP Verizon, which had argued that a court order approved by a judge, rather than a subpoena, was necessary to meet the constitutional guarantee of due process of law. Such a court order would be based on real evidence of criminal activity, not on the unsupported claim of the copyright owner. However, the Department of Justice asserted that, because the Fourth Amendment doesn't expressly state that a judge must authorize a "reasonable" search or seizure, a do-it-yourself subpoena was adequate. While the Fourth Amendment *can* be interpreted in this way, more than two hundred years of case law supports the argument that a "reasonable" search or seizure must be backed by solid evidence rather than unsupported claims.

In June 2003, the RIAA started filing subpoenas against individual users, supposedly prolific sharers of illegal files. After a brief setback in which the Massachusetts court ruled that the RIAA couldn't target violators by issuing all its subpoenas from Washington D.C., but must issue each subpoena in the appropriate local jurisdiction, the subpoenas started to hit home.

In August 2003, a survey by NPD showed a drop of 23 percent in the number of songs being shared by a sample group of 40,000 P2P users. In the same month, the RIAA announced that it would target only large-scale copyright infringers, not those sharing only a few files.

In September 2003, the RIAA made international headlines by filing a lawsuit against a 12-year-old New York girl, Brianna LaHara, who had supposedly assumed that her mother's paying a fee to Kazaa entitled her to download and share files freely. The RIAA speedily negotiated a settlement of $2,000 with LaHara's mother—a far cry from the $150,000-per-song maximum penalty.

Did you know?

How Individual MP3 Files Can Be Distinguished from Each Other

At this point, you may be asking this: How can the RIAA tell that you've downloaded a particular MP3 file rather than, say, ripped it from an LP that you own?

The first danger comes from the ID3 tag information. If the tags on a file contain unique information that matches the information on a file that's known to have been shared, and the file size is the same, the file is probably the same. Some MP3 encoders automatically add unique information, as do some users. (One person used "sinned" persistently in both song names and tags, sometimes including "-sinned-ego" in the filename and other times including comments such as "ripped by sinned soul [EGO]" in tags. Other people include anti-RIAA sentiments.)

Beyond the ID3 tag information contained in each MP3 file (which you can edit by using iTunes, another MP3 player, or a dedicated ID3 tag editor), each MP3 file contains a *hash value,* a sort of digital fingerprint that uniquely identifies a file. So if the RIAA can match the hash value of a MP3 file you possess with the hash value of a file that's known to have been shared on a P2P network, they can prove you downloaded the file.

You may be interested to know that editing the ID3 tag on an MP3 file changes the hash value of the file.

In September 2003, the RIAA also floated the idea of a file-sharing amnesty under which offenders would declare their guilt and promise never to share files illegally again. The RIAA would agree not to proceed against the offenders, but other copyright holders would be free to proceed, making the amnesty unattractive to many people.

In December 2003, the RIAA made further headlines by having employees in paramilitary-style uniforms confiscate suspected bootleg discs from street vendors. Also in December 2003, the Court of Appeals in the District of Columbia ruled that the RIAA can no longer subpoena ISPs to disclose customers' names but must instead file individual "John Doe" lawsuits against people suspected of trading files.

Dangers of Using the Darknet

By now, enough people have probably told you the Internet is a dangerous place for the claim to have stopped having any effect. But before you start exploring the darknet and downloading files of other people's copyrighted content from it, be clear on the dangers you might face. The following subsections detail the most obvious dangers.

Legal Retribution

The first danger is that you may expose yourself to legal retribution. Distributing other people's copyrighted content is illegal, even if you're not charging money for it. In the eyes of the law, receiving anything in return for material you've shared illegally constitutes benefiting from that sharing. For example, if you offered a handful of MP3 files for download, and if you yourself downloaded a video file from someone else, the law would see you as having benefited from offering those files for download.

As you saw a couple of pages ago, the ease with which copyright holders or their proxies can extract customers' names from ISPs is still being wrangled over in the courts. Some ISPs are more protective of their customers than others; some ISPs can easily be persuaded to close the account of any user who appears to be, or is accused of, sharing material illegally. But the key point is that, while P2P networks offer the illusion of anonymity, your computer almost always exposes its Internet Protocol (IP) address (not to mention the address of the network interface your computer is using to access the Internet) when you use a P2P network, so your actions can be tracked.

If your Internet connection has a static IP address (an IP address that doesn't change from one connection to the next), your computer can be identified with minimal effort. But even if your connection receives a different IP address from your ISP each time you connect, your ISP can easily look you up in the records they're obliged to keep for billing and security purposes. So any agency that can persuade or compel your ISP to divulge information can determine exactly what your computer has been doing.

Unwanted Fellow Travelers

Developing complex software applications costs money—plenty of it. To finance their development, cover their other expenses, or make money, companies that produce P2P software have taken to including other applications with their products. Some of these applications are shareware and can be tolerably useful; others are adware that are useless and an irritant; still others are spyware that report users' sharing and downloading habits.

> **TIP** *To detect and remove spyware from your computer, use an application such as the free Ad-aware from LavaSoft (www.lavasoft.de).*

Attacks, Viruses, and Social Engineering

Apart from adware and spyware lurking amidst the program files, P2P networks can also expose your computer to attacks and viruses. A file offered for download may not contain what its name or tag suggests. For example, a tempting picture file might prove to be a virus or other malware.

> **TIP** *Use virus-checking software to scan all incoming files to your computer, whether they come from friends, family, coworkers, or the Internet.*

Even if a file contains what it's supposed to, it may also harbor a virus, worm, or Trojan horse. Even apparently harmless files can have a sting in the tail. For example, the tags in music files can contain URLs to which your player's browser component automatically connects. The site can then run a script on your computer, doing anything from opening some irritating advertisement windows, to harvesting any sensitive information it can locate, to deleting vital files or destroying the firmware on your computer.

P2P networks also expose users to social-engineering attacks through the chat features that most P2P tools include. However friendly other users are, and however juicy the files they provide, it can be a severe mistake to divulge personal information.

Current P2P Networks

At this writing, there is a large number of P2P networks, some of which interoperate with each other. The following examples illustrate three of the longer-lasting networks:

- **Gnutella** (www.gnutella.com) is a P2P protocol used by a wide variety of clients. At this writing, the leading Gnutella clients include BearShare (Windows only), Morpheus (Windows only), LimeWire (Windows, Mac, and Linux), Phex (Windows, Mac, and Linux), Gnucleus (Windows only), and Acquisition (Mac OS X only).

- **Kazaa** (www.kazaa.com) is a P2P network based on the FastTrack engine and organized by Sharman Networks, Ltd. Kazaa provides the Windows-only Kazaa Media Desktop application, which puts a slick graphical interface on searching the Kazaa network. Kazaa routes searches through *supernodes* (users with fast connections) to get around the inefficiency of Gnutella-like peer searching. Kazaa uses a metric called *participation level* that measures two items: the amount of data a user downloads against the amount of data they let others download from them, and the percentage of the files the user is offering that are "integrity rated" (have accurate information about them). When multiple users try to download a file from another user, Kazaa prioritizes the users with high participation levels over those with low levels.

- **Freenet** (freenetproject.org) is a P2P network designed to allow "anybody to publish and read information with complete anonymity" and to prevent the network from being shut down. Freenet requires users to make space available to the network, automatically distributes files so no computer knows which files it's hosting, and encrypts the files placed on each computer for security. You can get Freenet clients for Windows, Mac OS X, and Linux. At this writing, Freenet is at its 0.5 release and, while growing in power and functionality, lags far behind the leading P2P networks for ease of use. (The Freenet interface is more user-friendly than it used to be: the Freenet Node Properties dialog box now offers tabs named Normal Settings, Advanced Settings, and Serious Geeks Only.) However, should other P2P networks be suppressed, Freenet may be able to pick up the slack.

Download Music Files from Online Music Services

In contrast to the darknet, where you can find just about any song if you search hard enough, the range of songs available on legitimate online music services has been disappointing to date. But now that the success of the iTunes Music Store has persuaded the record companies to license music, Apple and its competitors are rushing to make available as many songs as they can license. So the situation is improving—but there's a long way to go before music enthusiasts can hope to find most of the songs they want to buy on legitimate online music services.

To complicate things further for Mac users, most of the online music services work only with Windows at the time of writing. To complicate things still more for anyone using an iPod, most of the online music services use WMA files protected with DRM for their songs (see the following note). Some services are also tied to specific hardware players, some to their own software players, and some to Windows Media Player.

> **NOTE** *To use protected WMA files with an iPod, you would need to burn them to CD, and then rip and encode the CD to AAC files or MP3 files. Most of the online music services permit you to burn songs to CD, but creating further copies of the songs could be interpreted to be against the terms and conditions of some services.*

This section briefly discusses the online music stores that have been launched or announced at this writing. It also mentions a legitimate source for free music from new artists.

> **NOTE** *It looks like 2004 is the year of online music promotion via can and bottle. Apple has a song-giveaway going with Pepsi, as do RealNetworks with Heineken, and Roxio (Napster) with Miller Brewing products. So be careful to watch your drinks for free music content. You may also need to scrutinize your burgers for more than gristle and BSE, as McDonald's reportedly has a music promotion in its horoscope. More creatively, Sony will be promoting its Connect service by allowing United Airlines passengers to trade their frequent flier miles for songs.*

Walmart.com

Wal-Mart's web site (www.walmart.com) includes a Music Downloads section that offers songs for $0.88 and albums from $8.80 and up. Songs from Walmart.com come as protected WMA files and work only with Windows Media Player and hardware players that Windows Media Player supports. With an easy-to-use interface, "hundreds of thousands of songs" available, and low prices, Walmart.com is an attractive option for anyone using Windows Media Player.

BuyMusic.com

BuyMusic.com (www.buymusic.com) claims to be the "world's largest download music store." It is a Windows-only service that supplies files in the protected WMA format for its custom music player. Most songs cost $0.99, and most albums $9.99, but some songs are less expensive. Different songs have different licensing terms setting out the number of computers you can play them on, the number of transfers to SDMI-compliant digital audio players, and the number of times you can burn them to CD.

Sony Connect

Sony has announced that it will launch a service named Connect in spring 2004 that will offer 500,000 songs at $0.99 each. At first, Connect will work only with Sony music players, which will greatly limit its appeal, even to people with United frequent flier miles. Later, Connect will offer downloads that will work with other devices.

MusicMatch Downloads

MusicMatch, Inc., has been one of the leading names for Internet music on Windows-based PCs with its MUSICMATCH Jukebox Basic and MUSICMATCH Jukebox Plus applications. The latest versions of MUSICMATCH Jukebox integrate with the MusicMatch Downloads service (www.musicmatch.com) and deliver similar features to iTunes, except they work only on Windows. (In the past, MusicMatch has released Mac versions of MUSICMATCH Jukebox, but these don't support MusicMatch Downloads.)

At the time of writing, MusicMatch Downloads offers more than 360,000 songs at $0.99 each and albums starting at $9.99. MusicMatch Downloads provides songs in WMA format with DRM that allows you to burn them to CD and transfer them to some portable devices, but not to an iPod.

Listen.com RHAPSODY

Listen.com's RHAPSODY application and service (www.listen.com) offers more than 450,000 songs from more than 33,000 albums, which Listen.com claims is the "deepest catalog of legal online music in the world." (Pop quiz: define "deep" in this context.) Listen.com provides subscription plans for RHAPSODY Radio PLUS ($4.95 a month) and RHAPSODY All Access ($9.95 a month, plus $0.79 for each song you want to burn to CD).

RHAPSODY runs on Windows only and is a streaming service rather than a download service, so you need a broadband Internet connection to use it. Listen.com is a subsidiary of Real Networks (www.realnetworks.com), which also offers the RealPlayer Music Store (discussed next).

RealPlayer Music Store

The RealPlayer Music Store (www.real.com/musicstore/) uses the AAC format and the 192 Kbps bitrate, which provides very high audio quality. To access the RealPlayer Music Store, you must use RealPlayer 10, which is free but runs only on Windows.

Songs cost $0.99 each, and most albums cost $9.99 each. You can burn songs to CD and download them to some Creative players and some Palm devices.

Napster 2.0

Napster 2.0 (www.napster.com) claims to have "the world's largest collection of digital music," with more than 500,000 songs at this writing. Napster 2.0 is run by Roxio, Inc., and has nothing to do with the pioneering file-sharing application Napster except the name and logo, which Roxio acquired via a tortuous path of other companies. Napster 2.0 sells songs for $0.99 each and albums for $9.95. The Napster 2.0 Premium service costs $9.95 a month and lets you stream full-length songs (instead of 30-second clips) and tune into 45 "fully-interactive, commercial-free stations" of Internet radio.

Napster 2.0 integrates with the Samsung Napster digital audio player, which competes more or less directly with the iPod except that it works only with Windows and supports WMA. Napster 2.0 uses the WMA format protected with DRM.

Other Sources of Legitimate Files

Beyond the big-name services discussed in the previous sections, various independent record companies have started selling music online. Some, such as the British electronic label Warp Records (www.warprecords.com/bleep/), sell songs without DRM restrictions—so once you've bought a song, you can do what you want with it, pretty much.

Wippit (www.wippit.com) provides a variety of tracks for download in a mixture of unprotected MP3 and protected WMA formats. Unlike the music services mentioned earlier, Wippit uses a subscription model for access to its music: for around $50 per year, you get all-you-can-eat access to Wippit's catalog. At this point, Wippit offers more than 60,000 songs from 96 record labels—most of them independents, but EMI also provides songs.

Also, the Internet still contains some sources of songs that are distributed for free by the artists who created them. Although one of the largest sites, MP3.com, has sadly been sold and its archives commercialized, one of the Internet's longest-running audio sites, the Internet Underground Musical Archive (IUMA; www.iuma.com) is still going strong.

IUMA's banner—"discover unsigned artists, independent bands, local talent"—neatly summarizes what IUMA is about. Artists who use IUMA are typically looking to distribute their music as widely as possible in the hope of increasing their audience, so IUMA offers MP3 downloads as well as MP3 and RealAudio streams. That means you can download music and listen to it as often as you want, burn it to CDs, share it with friends, and so on. This approach makes IUMA a great place for exploring new artists and different kinds of music. If you're looking for established artists, however, look elsewhere.

8

Chapter 9

Burn CDs and DVDs from iTunes

How to...

- Understand why to burn your music to CD or DVD
- Understand the basics of burning CDs and DVDs
- Configure iTunes for burning CDs and DVDs
- Burn CDs and DVDs
- Troubleshoot the problems you run into when burning CDs

iTunes makes it as easy as possible to burn playlists to CD, enabling you to create either regular audio CDs that will work in any CD player or MP3 CDs that will work only in MP3-capable CD players. You can also burn a playlist to a data CD or data DVD for backup or portability—for example, to back up your music library. Such data DVDs work in computer DVD drives but not in commercial DVD players—but since each DVD can store around 150 CDs' worth of audio compressed at 128 Kbps, they're great for backup.

Burning with iTunes works in the same way on both Windows and the Mac, so this chapter discusses both operating systems together, showing some screens from each. The chapter starts by quickly running through the basics of burning. You'll then learn how to choose suitable settings for burning, and how to burn CDs and DVDs. You'll also learn how to minimize avoidable problems and how to troubleshoot common problems you may run into.

Why Burn Song Files to CD or DVD?

Typically, you'll want to burn song files to CD or DVD for one of three reasons:

- You want to create an audio CD that you (or someone else) can play either on a regular CD player or on a computer. An *audio CD* is a CD that conforms to the Red Book standard (see "Understand Ripping, Encoding, and 'Copying'," in Chapter 3). Audio CDs contain uncompressed audio: up to 74 minutes for a 650MB CD, 80 minutes for a 700MB CD, and 90 minutes for an 800MB CD. You can play audio CDs on CD players (for example, a boom box or a hi-fi component) as well as on CD drives. Audio CDs created on recordable CDs are compatible with all CD players and with most (but not all) DVD players.

- You want to create an MP3 CD that you (or someone else) can play on a computer or on a CD player than can handle MP3 CDs. MP3 CDs have the advantage of being able to store far more music than audio CDs. For example, if you encode your MP3 files at 128 Kbps, you can fit about 12 hours of music on a CD. The disadvantages are that most CD players can't play MP3 CDs, and you can't burn protected AAC files to an MP3 CD—at least, not without burning them to an audio CD, ripping the CD to MP3 files, and then burning those files to the CD.

NOTE

As the name suggests, an MP3 CD can contain only MP3 files—not AAC, WAV, or AIFF files. If you've encoded your entire CD collection to AAC files, you won't be able to burn them to MP3 CDs without reeencoding them. Because iTunes doesn't distinguish visibly among file types in your music library and in playlists, it's easy to trip up on this limitation: you gaily queue a hundred or so files for burning to an MP3 CD, but iTunes burns only 20 or so files to the CD, because the rest are in AAC or other non-MP3 formats.

■ You want to back up part of your music library to CD or DVD to protect it against loss. For example, you'll probably want to back up your Purchased Music playlist to CD or DVD, because if you lose that music, you'll need to buy it again. A backup disc is called a *data CD* or *data DVD*. Data discs won't play on most audio CD players, regular DVD players, or even most MP3-capable CD players; essentially, data discs are for computers only, but the occasional sophisticated CD player or DVD player may surprise you by being able to handle them.

Understand the Basics of Burning CDs and DVDs

Burning CDs has progressed from being very tricky and unreliable in the mid 1990s to being a capability built into mainstream operating systems such as Mac OS X and Windows XP. At the time of writing, most new PCs and all new Macs sold include CD burners; many also include DVD burners or drives that burn both DVDs and CDs.

To burn CDs with iTunes, your computer must have a CD burner or DVD burner. If your computer has a CD burner, it can be either a CD recorder (CD-R) drive or a CD rewriter (CD-RW) drive.

NOTE

A CD-R burner can burn only CD-recordable discs—discs that can be burned only one time. A CD-RW burner can burn both CD-recordable discs and CD-rewritable discs; the latter can be burned, erased, and burned again multiple times. Similarly, DVD-R discs can be burned only once, but DVD-RW discs can be rewritten multiple times.

If your computer doesn't have a burner, you can add a compatible internal CD-R or CD-RW drive (to a PowerMac or most desktop PCs) or a compatible external FireWire or USB CD-R or CD-RW drive (to a PC notebook, PC desktop, PowerBook, iBook, iMac, eMac, or PowerMac).

TIP

Before buying a burner for a Mac, consult the Apple Support web site (www.apple.com/ support/) for the latest list of compatible drives.

To burn DVDs (either DVD-R discs or DVD-RW discs), your Mac must have either an internal SuperDrive or another compatible DVD burner, and must be running Mac OS X 10.2.4 or later. Your PC needs a DVD burner that's compatible with iTunes.

NOTE

You can burn a playlist to a DVD-R disc or a DVD-RW disc, but not to a DVD-Audio disc.

9

Burn CDs and DVDs

iTunes makes the process of burning CDs and DVDs straightforward. You can burn only a playlist to CD or DVD; you can't burn any other subdivision of your music library, such as an album or an artist's entire works, unless you add them to a custom playlist. So you need to arrange your music files into suitable playlists before attempting to burn them to CD or DVD.

Typically, you'll want to start by choosing burning options, as described first in this section. Then you'll be ready to burn a disc, as described second.

Choose Burning Options

To choose burning options for iTunes, display the Burning sheet or Burning tab as follows:

- On the Mac, press COMMAND-COMMA (or COMMAND-Y) or choose iTunes | Preferences to display the Preferences dialog box. Click the Burning tab to display the Burning sheet:

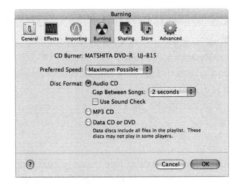

- On Windows, press CTRL- COMMA (or CTRL-Y) or choose Edit | Preferences to display the iTunes dialog box. Click the Burning tab to display its contents:

As you can see, the Burning tab of the iTunes dialog box offers the same options as the Burning sheet of the Preferences dialog box.

Next, choose options as follows:

- **CD Burner label or list**   If you have multiple CD or DVD burners, make sure iTunes has chosen the right burner. If you have only one burner, there's no decision to make here.

- **Preferred Speed drop-down list**   Choose the Maximum Possible setting to burn discs at the fastest speed iTunes and the drive can manage. If you don't get good results from the maximum possible speed, reduce the speed by choosing one of the other settings in the list. Test the setting and reduce the speed further if necessary.

- **Disc Format options**   To create an audio CD, select the Audio CD option button (the default). Use the Gap Between Songs drop-down list to specify whether to include a gap between the tracks on the CD (you can choose from one second to five seconds; the default is two seconds) or not (choose None). Select the Use Sound Check check box to make iTunes use Sound Check to normalize the volume on the tracks. Using Sound Check should produce CDs with much more consistent volume across their tracks than CDs created without Sound Check. To create an MP3 CD, select the MP3 CD option button. To create a data CD or DVD, select the Data CD Or DVD option button. (If you don't have a compatible DVD burner, this option button is named Data CD.)

Click the OK button to close the Preferences dialog box (on the Mac) or the iTunes dialog box (on Windows).

Burn a CD or DVD

To burn a CD or DVD with iTunes, follow these steps:

1. Decide which type of CD or DVD—an audio CD, an MP3 CD, a data CD, or a data DVD—you want to create. If necessary, change your iTunes preferences as discussed in the previous section.

2. Add to a playlist the songs that you want to have on the CD or DVD. Alternatively, open an existing playlist. For example, select your Purchased Music playlist so that you can burn the music you've purchased from the iTunes Music Store.

3. If necessary, change the name of the playlist to the name you want the CD to have. To do so, double-click the name, type the new name, and then press RETURN (on the Mac) or ENTER (on Windows).

4. Click the Burn Disc button in the upper-right corner of the iTunes window. (The Burn Disc button replaces the Browse button when you select a playlist in the Source pane.)

5. When iTunes prompts you to insert a blank CD, do so. (If you take too long inserting the disc, iTunes decides you don't really want to burn a disc, and stops flashing the message at you.)

NOTE   *If you insert a blank recordable CD in your CD-RW drive before clicking the Burn button in iTunes, Mac OS X may display a dialog box inviting you to choose what to do with the CD. Select the Open iTunes item in the Action drop-down list. Select the Make This Action The Default check box if you always want to launch iTunes when you insert a blank CD. Then click the OK button to close the dialog box.*

6. If the playlist you've chosen is too long to fit on the type of disc you've inserted in the format set in the Preferences dialog box or the iTunes dialog box, iTunes warns you and asks what you want to do:

   ■ If your Burning preferences are set to create an audio CD, and the playlist you've chosen is too long, iTunes lets you choose whether to split the playlist across multiple CDs. Click the Audio CDs button to split the playlist across as many CDs as necessary. Click the Cancel button if you want to fix the problem yourself. For example, you might slim down the playlist so that it will fit on a single CD, or you might change your burning preferences to burn a different type of CD.

   ■ If your Burning preferences are set to create an MP3 CD, and the playlist you've chosen is too long, iTunes warns you that some of the tracks won't fit, and lets you choose whether to proceed:

   ■ If your Burning preferences are set to create a data disc, and the playlist you've chosen is too long, iTunes lets you choose whether to split the playlist across multiple discs. Click the Data Discs button to have iTunes split the playlist automatically, or click the Cancel button if you want to change the playlist or the type of disc you're burning.

Note that when you cancel a burn like this, you'll need to eject the unburned disc manually. If your drive has an Eject button, press it to eject the disc. If not, in Windows, choose Start | My Computer to display a My Computer window. Right-click the drive letter that represents the burner, and choose Eject from the shortcut menu to eject the disc. On the Mac, quit iTunes to force Mac OS X to eject the disc.

7. Click the Burn Disc button to start burning the CD:

8. When iTunes has finished burning the disc, or the last disc, it plays a notification sound. Eject the disc by right-clicking its entry in the Source pane and choosing Eject Disc from the shortcut menu. Then label it carefully, test it to make sure it's playable, and store it safely.

9. If you're burning multiple CDs, iTunes ejects each completed CD in turn and prompts you to insert a blank disc. Insert the disc, and then click the Burn Disc button when iTunes prompts you to do so.

Troubleshoot Burning CDs and DVDs

Despite the advances in CD and DVD burning, many things can still go wrong, wasting your time, effort, and media. This section discusses how to avoid causing your burner problems and how to solve problems when they nonetheless occur.

Avoid Causing Your Burner Problems

First, avoid avoidable problems with burning CDs and DVDs. To do so, balance quality, speed, and cost sensibly; devote as many processor cycles as possible to the burning; make sure your computer has plenty of memory; and prevent your computer from going to sleep during a burn.

Balance Quality, Speed, and Cost

If you've worked for a demanding boss, you're probably familiar with this plaintive truism: "Here are your options for the product: quickly, cheaply, and high quality. Choose any two." (If you haven't needed to use this truism yet, file it away in your memory tickler file. Unless you have a trust fund, you'll probably need it before you're much older, given the way the economy is going—or not going, depending on how you view it.)

In the meantime, your burner and burning software are probably giving you the same message. So, here's what the message means in the context of burning:

- Buy only high-quality recordable media. (Low-quality media isn't worth using; there's no upside to losing your data—at least, unless the Department of Justice is on your case.) Expect to pay a market price for this media. If anyone offers you recordable media at bargain-basement prices, be duly suspicious. (Remember: once badly burnt, forever shy.)

- In burning, speed is worthless without accuracy. If your options are to record a CD at 48X with errors or 1X without errors, choose the 1X speed. Otherwise, your data will be useless.

- If you're buying a CD burner, get a good one. Rather than buying the latest, fastest, and sexiest drive, consider buying a somewhat older model—you may be able to get good speed and reliability at a bargain price.

- If you're buying a DVD burner for a Mac, your best bet is to buy an internal SuperDrive so that you can use it fully with the iLife applications. If you must buy an external drive, double-check beforehand that it'll work with the relevant iLife applications.

NOTE *Different brands of recordable discs use different colors of dye: some green, some blue, some a faint shade of yellowy-brown. In theory, the color doesn't matter—but in practice, it sometimes can make the difference between a burner being able to burn a disc or not, or between a player being able to play a disc back or not. So if you find your burner or player seems to prefer one color of recordable media to another, you're not necessarily imagining things. Stick with the brand and color that gives best results.*

Give the Burner As Many Processor Cycles As Possible

Windows XP and Mac OS X are multitasking operating systems on which you can have multiple applications working actively at the same time. But because burning CDs or DVDs is a processor-intensive activity, it's a good idea not to multitask actively while burning unless you've established that your PC or Mac can comfortably handle the demands of burning and of whatever other work you're doing.

To get the very best burning performance, quit any unnecessary applications, reduce other tasks to a minimum, leave the burner as the foreground application (in other words, don't move the focus to another application window), and take your hands off the keyboard and mouse until the burn is complete. (Because the mouse can do so much in a graphical user interface, mouse-enabled operating systems squander many processor cycles on tracking exactly what the mouse is doing at any given moment if it's moving.)

Get More Memory If You Don't Have Enough

Modern applications are memory hungry, modern operating systems doubly so. And burning CDs or DVDs is a demanding task.

Both Windows XP and Mac OS X will run with 128MB RAM, but that's a bare minimum—not a sensible choice in the real world. You'll get significantly better performance with 256MB, much better performance with 512MB, and great performance with around 1GB. Given that RAM prices are at historic low levels (at the time of writing), now is a good time to add RAM to your computer.

Prevent Your Mac from Starting a Screen Saver or Going to Sleep During a Burn

Your next preemptive strike is to prevent your computer from going to sleep or starting a screen saver during a burn. This section discusses the steps you need to take on Mac OS X; the next section talks about the steps to take on Windows XP.

Configure the sleep timing settings in the Energy Saver pane of System Preferences to ensure that neither your Mac nor its display goes to sleep during a burn. Even with modern burners, your Mac's going to sleep during a burn may cause errors on the disc. Having the display go to sleep during a burn shouldn't affect the burn in many cases, but in other cases it may—particularly if you press the wrong keys or buttons when reawakening the display. Unless you care to experiment with having your display go to sleep and checking the resulting discs, you may prefer to be safe than sorry.

To change your Mac's sleep timing settings, follow these steps:

1. Choose Apple | System Preferences to display the System Preferences window.

2. Click the Energy Saver item in the Hardware category to display the Energy Saver pane.

3. If the Energy Saver pane is in its small format, which hides the details, click the Show Details button to display the full pane (see Figure 9-1).

4. For a desktop Mac, or for a PowerBook or iBook running on the power adapter (rather than the battery), the easiest option is to choose the Automatic item in the Optimize Energy Settings drop-down list. This item puts the Mac to sleep after one hour of inactivity, which should be plenty long enough for burning any recordable CD—even at 2X speed. For burning a full DVD with one of the slower models of SuperDrive, however, you may need to allow a longer period of inactivity. Alternatively, you may prefer the Highest Performance item, which prevents the Mac from ever going to sleep without your putting it to sleep manually.

9

5. For a PowerBook or iBook running on battery power, you may find that the Automatic item in the Optimize Energy Settings drop-down list works okay for burning if your 'Book has a fast CD-RW drive or SuperDrive; the Automatic item puts the display to sleep after nine minutes and the computer to sleep after 25 minutes. On older 'Books, or with a slow SuperDrive, you may find these sleep settings too aggressive for comfort. In this case, you can choose the Highest Performance item if you don't care about exhausting your batteries quickly. Or you can choose the Custom item, and then choose custom settings as follows:

   ■ Drag the Put The Computer To Sleep When It Is Inactive For slider to a setting that will allow plenty of time for the burn to complete.

   ■ To configure a sleep setting for the display that is different from the setting for the computer, select the Put The Display To Sleep When The Computer Is Inactive For check box and drag the slider to a setting that will allow the burn to complete. For obvious reasons, you can't set a longer sleep delay for the display than for the computer.

   ■ Select the Put the Hard Disk(s) to Sleep When Possible check box if you want Mac OS X to shut down the hard disk whenever possible. Because the hard disk is used extensively (though not quite continuously) during a burn, Mac OS X shouldn't try to shut down the hard disk while the burn is happening.

TIP   *To prevent further changes to the Energy Saver configuration, click the lock icon at the lower-left corner of the Energy Saver pane. This will prevent anyone from shortening the sleep settings and throwing a monkey wrench into your burns. To unlock the Energy Saver pane, click the lock icon again, and enter your account name and password in the resulting Authenticate dialog box.*

6. Press COMMAND-Q or choose System Preferences | Quit System Preferences to quit System Preferences.

Prevent Your PC from Using Screen Savers or Powering Down During a Burn

Processor-intensive screen savers (in other words, most of the visually interesting screen savers) can cause problems with burns by diverting processor cycles from the burn at a critical moment. To avoid this, configure a long wait on your screen saver. Similarly, configure Windows so that it doesn't try to power down the computer during a burn. To do so, follow these steps:

1. Right-click the desktop and choose Properties from the shortcut menu to display the Display Properties dialog box.

2. On the Screen Saver tab (shown on the left in Figure 9-2), increase the time shown in the Wait text box so it's far longer than even the slowest burn your CD recorder will ever perform. (Better yet, choose None in the Screen Saver drop-down list to turn off your screen saver altogether.)

3. Click the Apply button to apply your choices.

4. Click the Screen Saver tab's Power button to prevent your computer from going to sleep during a burn. Windows displays the Power Options Properties dialog box.

5. On the Power Schemes tab (shown on the right in Figure 9-2), specify suitably lengthy times (or choose the Never item) in the Turn Off Monitor, Turn Off Hard Disks, System Standby, and System Hibernates drop-down lists to prevent these events from occurring during a burn.

6. Click the Apply button to apply your choices.

Troubleshoot Specific Problems

This section discusses how to troubleshoot problems in burning CDs and DVDs with iTunes. The section starts with the basics and then moves on to more challenging problems.

iTunes Doesn't List Your Burner on the Burning Sheet

If iTunes doesn't list your burner on the Burning sheet of the Preferences dialog box (on the Mac) or on the Burning tab of the iTunes dialog box (on Windows), the problem is most likely that iTunes doesn't support your burner.

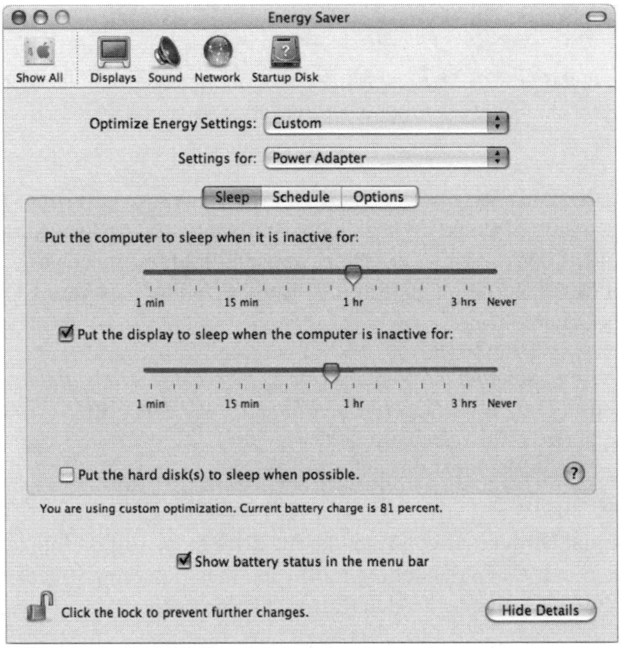

FIGURE 9-1 Configure the sleep timing settings in the Energy Saver pane of System Preferences to prevent your Mac from going to sleep during a burn.

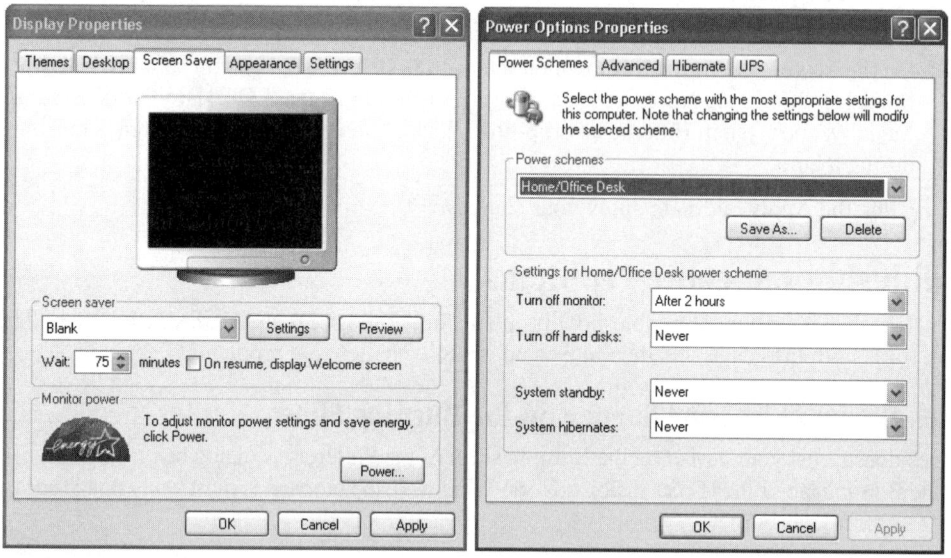

FIGURE 9-2   Configure your screen saver (left) and power schemes (right) to prevent interruptions to the burn.

TIP   *If you need to get a new drive for a Mac, check the list of FireWire, USB, and internal CD burners at www.apple.com/macosx/upgrade/storage.html first.*

On the Mac, press COMMAND- COMMA (or COMMAND-Y) or choose iTunes | Preferences to display the Preferences dialog box, and then click the Burning button to display the Burning sheet; on Windows, press CTRL- COMMA (or CTRL-Y) or choose Edit | Preferences to display the iTunes dialog box, and then click the Burning tab. If the CD Burner readout lists your CD or DVD burner by name, the drive works with iTunes.

NOTE   *The CD Burner readout identifies a SuperDrive by its formal name and model number—for example, Pioneer DVD-RW DVR-104 or Pioneer DVD-RW DVR-105—rather than by a description, such as SuperDrive.*

Reset an External Burner

If you're using an external burner and you find that the drive stops responding after a burn fails, reset the drive by powering it down (switching it off) and then powering it back up (switching it on again). If that doesn't work, you may need to restart your computer to regain control of the drive.

Give an External USB CD Burner a Better Chance

If you're having problems with an external CD burner connected via USB, try the following actions to reduce the problems:

- Disconnect all nonessential USB devices (in other words, don't disconnect a USB keyboard or mouse).

- If the CD burner is connected to the Mac through a USB hub, try removing the hub and plugging the burner directly into the Mac's USB port.

- Reduce the burn speed to 2X and see if that works. If so, increase the burn speed and test again.

Mac: Unable to Eject an Optical Disc

Sometimes Mac OS X doesn't eject a CD or DVD the first time you issue a command to eject it. For example, if you drag the CD's icon to the Trash, Mac OS X sometimes fails to eject it. In iTunes, click the Eject button to eject the CD. You may need to click the button more than once. Allow a few seconds after each click to allow iTunes to respond.

External CD-RW Drive Stutters or Skips During Playback

Some external CD-RW drives don't play back CDs correctly, and you may hear stutters or apparent skips. To check whether the CD or the drive is the problem, try playing the CD in a CD player or in an internal CD drive (if you have one). If you don't have another CD player or CD drive, try playing another CD in the external CD-RW drive and see if that works.

"None of the Items in This List Can Be Burned to CD" Error Message

iTunes displays the error message "None of these items in this list can be burned to CD" in three cases:

- You try to burn a CD containing a playlist, but you've cleared the check boxes for all the songs on the playlist. To solve the problem, select the check boxes for the songs you want to burn to the CD.

- You try to burn a CD, but iTunes discovers that it can't locate any of the songs on the playlist. This is most likely to happen if you move your music library to a different folder. You may need to change the iTunes Music Folder Location setting on the Advanced sheet of the Preferences dialog box (on the Mac) or the Advanced tab of the iTunes dialog box (on Windows) to show iTunes where your song files are.

- You try to burn a playlist that contains only protected AAC files that you've purchased from the iTunes Music Store, but iTunes is set to burn an MP3 CD rather than an audio CD or data CD. To solve the problem, choose a different CD type in the Preferences dialog box.

9

Long Gap Between Songs Prevents Playlist from Burning

Choosing a Gap Between Songs setting of five seconds may prevent iTunes from burning a playlist successfully. If this happens, choose a shorter setting for Gap Between Songs. Two or three seconds should be adequate for most purposes.

"Songs in the Playlist Are Not Authorized" Error Message

The error message "One or more of the songs in this playlist are not authorized for use on this machine" means just what it says—that you're trying to burn one or more songs that this computer isn't authorized to play. Click the OK button to close the message box.

The easiest way to fix this problem is to play each song on the playlist and go through the process of authorizing each song for which iTunes prompts you for authorization. (See Chapter 7 for details on authorization.) After doing this, start the burning process again.

"There Was a Problem with the Target Device" Error Message

The error message "There was a problem with the target device. Error code –7932" means that iTunes can't successfully write to the CD media you're using at the speed you're trying to use. Take one of the following actions to solve the problem:

- Reduce the burn speed to a lower setting on the Burning sheet of the iTunes Preferences dialog box.

- Use a different type of recordable CD—preferably a better-quality kind.

- If you're using CD-RW discs (rather than CD-R discs), don't use discs rated faster than 4X, because iTunes can't write to them successfully.

"You Have Inserted a Blank DVD" Error Message

The error message "You have inserted a blank DVD but originally selected a CD format. Are you sure you wish to create a data DVD instead?" occurs when your Burning preferences specify an audio CD but you insert a blank DVD instead. When you see this error message, you'll usually want to click the Cancel button, eject the DVD, and insert a blank CD-R or CD-RW disc instead. If you decide that you do want to burn a data DVD containing the discs instead of an audio CD, click the Data DVD button.

Remember that a data DVD has a huge capacity (typically more than 4.5GB) and that iTunes will store the songs on the DVD in their current format (for example, as AAC files or MP3 files)

How to ... Get the Highest Possible Audio Quality on the CDs You Burn

AAC and MP3 deliver high-quality compressed audio, especially when you use a high bitrate and other appropriate settings. But both AAC and MP3 use lossy compression, losing some of the data required to deliver a perfect audio signal.

If you need to burn CDs with the highest possible audio quality, make sure that your source files are uncompressed, high-quality audio. If you rip song files from CD, rip them to AIFF files (on the Mac) or WAV files (on Windows) rather than to either of the compressed formats (AAC or MP3). If you record audio from your own sources, record it to either AIFF or WAV instead of recording it to a compressed format.

Arrange the uncompressed audio files into a playlist, and then burn it to CD.

If the CD turns out satisfactorily (as it should), you'll probably want to delete the uncompressed source files from your hard disk to reclaim the space they take up.

rather than writing them out to uncompressed audio files, so the DVD will probably end up with most of its capacity unused.

On the Mac, if you click the Cancel button, you may need to quit iTunes (press COMMAND-Q) to force Mac OS X to eject the DVD.

iTunes Persistently Rejects a Blank Recordable Disc

If iTunes puzzles over a blank disc for a while and then ejects it without comment, chances are that the disc is either upside down or that it's not usable. Try the disc the other way up and see if iTunes accepts it. If not, try another disc.

Mac: SuperDrive Burns Very Slowly

Sadly, this problem falls into the "facts of life" category. SuperDrives are "super" in their ease of use with the iLife applications and other Mac applications, but they're less super in speed. The original SuperDrive burned DVDs at little better than real-time speeds; the next generation managed 2X burning; and the SuperDrives in the G5 PowerMacs manage 4X burning. The SuperDrives burn CDs faster than DVDs, but they're still considerably slower than the fastest burners available from other hardware manufacturers.

Part III

Put Your Contacts, Calendar, Notes, and Other Text on Your iPod or iPod mini

Chapter 10

Put Your Contacts on Your iPod or iPod mini

How to…

- Understand what vCards are and what they contain
- Create vCards from your contacts
- Use iSync to put your contacts on your iPod automatically from the Mac
- Put your contacts on your iPod manually from the Mac
- Put your contacts on your iPod manually from Windows
- View your contacts on your iPod

As you'll know from its interface, your iPod includes a Contacts category that lets you carry around your contact information and view records as necessary. You can't enter contact information directly on your iPod (because there's no means of entering it), but at least you don't have to carry around your Pocket PC or Palm handheld just to keep contact information with you. Nor do you need to type long addresses into the address book on your cell phone. (Nor do you have to do what some early adopters of the iPod did—create momentary MP3 files and insert the contact data in the tag fields. Yes, they actually did this.)

NOTE   *Apple added contacts to the iPod in the iPod Software 1.1 Updater. If your iPod can't display contacts, get the latest Updater right away from www.apple.com/ipod/download/.*

This chapter shows you how to create contacts from Mac OS X and Windows XP address applications, put them on your iPod, and view them on it. The chapter also shows you how to put contacts from other sources onto your iPod. To do so, you may need to export your contact records from their existing format into a common format (such as a comma-separated values, or CSV, file). This isn't hard, but you may have to do a little work.

If you're using Mac OS X and you keep your contacts in Address Book, you can use iSync to put your contacts and calendar on your iPod almost effortlessly. This chapter shows you how to do that, too.

This chapter covers both the regular (full-size) iPod models and the iPod mini. Where either the regular iPod or the iPod mini behaves differently, I'll point out the differences. Otherwise, I'll use the term *iPod* to cover both.

Understand the Wonders of vCards

vCard is a format for storing the information that constitutes a virtual business card: a name that consists of various parts, including first, last, middle initial, title, nickname, and suffix; a company or organization; a title; one or more addresses; e-mail addresses; phone numbers; notes; and other relevant information.

As that list suggests, vCard information is mostly text, and indeed many vCards are only text. This helps keep the vCard files, which use the .vcf extension, to a tiny size, so they can be transmitted quickly across even slow dial-up connections. But vCards can also include a picture (for example, a photo of the card's subject or a company logo) and an audio clip (which can be used for anything from a conventional greeting to something musical, exotic, or obscene).

A Brief History of vCard

vCard was the fruit of the versit Consortium, a group set up by Apple, IBM, AT&T, and Siemens to streamline what's grandly called *personal data interchange (PDI)*. PDI simply means one person communicating with someone else. For example, if you tell someone your name over the phone, or give someone your business card in person, that's PDI.

vCard lets you transfer an impressive set of standardized information to someone else electronically in a format they can easily accept. So they don't have to retype your business card into their address book or contact manager, introducing errors along the way, or struggle with one of those business-card scanners that decides your company name is your name and its logo is your picture.

versit got as far as defining version 2.1 of the Electronic Business Card Specification before handing over the reins to the Internet Mail Consortium (IMC) in December 1996. Along with vCard, the IMC also took over responsibility for developing and promoting vCalendar, a format for exchanging electronic calendaring and scheduling information. Subsequently, the IMC released version 3.0 of the Electronic Business Card Specification, but many otherwise up-to-date applications (for example, Address Book in Windows XP) still use version 2.1.

vCards haven't generated any great excitement in non-tech circles, but most e-mail programs and address books incorporate support for vCards. So if someone using a Linux e-mail application sends you a message with a vCard attached, you can import the vCard into your address book easily, whether you're using Windows, Mac OS, Linux, or another operating system.

> **NOTE** *There are substantial differences in formatting between version 2.1 and version 3.0 of the Electronic Business Card Specification, and many applications that use version 2.1 can't handle incoming vCards formatted with version 3.0. Your iPod can handle both versions, but it prefers version 3.0.*

10

For Curious Eyes Only: A Quick Look Inside a vCard

If you open a vCard that uses version 3.0 formatting in a text editor, you'll typically see text apparently formatted by someone who likes the spacebar. For example:

```
begin:vcard
version:3.0
fn:Philippa Jones
n:Jones;Philippa;;Mrs.;
title:Marketing Assistant
org:New Age Pharmaceutical Design;
Marketing
end:vcard
```

> **NOTE** *Not all version 3.0 vCards use spaces between every character, but most do.*

If you open a vCard that uses version 2.1 formatting in a text editor, you'll see relatively compact text, apparently tagged by someone who likes capital letters:

```
BEGIN:VCARD
VERSION:2.1
N:Jones;Philippa;;Mrs.
FN:Philippa Jones
ORG:New Age Pharmaceutical Design;Marketing
TITLE:Marketing Assistant
END:VCARD
```

Each of these data-bursts contains the same information, as you can probably see if you squint a little. Each is made up of a number of fields: fn (formatted name), n (name—the various components used to constitute it), org (organization), and title (job title), in this short example. The rest of the information that vCards can contain is similarly divided into fields—for example, EMAIL;PREF;INTERNET for the preferred e-mail address (in version 2.1 vCards) and "a d r ; t y p e = h o m e ; t y p e = p r e f" for a home address that's the default address (in version 3.0 vCards).

To keep itself as brief as possible, a vCard contains only those fields for which it has entries—it omits all blank fields. As long as each field included has the correct name, any combination of fields can be used in any order. The application that reads the vCard parses the data into the appropriate categories. (That's the theory, anyway. If you find your Polish contacts showing up under names such as Abstrakcja Konkretna 3. Warszawa in your address book, you'll know you've got a parsing problem.)

How Your iPod Handles vCards

Designed by Apple to be stylishly conscious of its own limitations, your iPod handles vCards in an idiosyncratic way: it knows it can't use all the information from a vCard, so it uses only a certain number of fields. Table 10-1 explains the data that your iPod displays in the order it displays them, together with examples of typical contents as you might see them and notes on other items. The bold rows in the table indicate the bold headings that your iPod uses to break up the vCard information. To help you retain your sanity (and I, mine), the column showing the vCard 3.0 fields omits the maddening spaces that version 3.0 vCards usually use.

NOTE   *You can put up to 1000 contacts on your iPod.*

Looking at the information in Table 10-1, you've no doubt realized there's nothing magical about the data stored in the vCard fields, so the vCard won't object if you enter the wrong type of text in a field. So, you can create vCards that contain memos, shopping lists, recipes, poems, and so on, if you use the fields in the right order. For example, you could use a vCard with a BEGIN:VCARD statement, a VERSION statement, an N field, an ORG field, and an END VCARD statement

Field	vCard 2.1 Field	vCard 3.0 Field (Spaces Omitted)	Example or Notes
Contact's Name	**FN**	**fn**	**Gerald Dixon**
Nickname	NICKNAME	nickname	"Jerry"
Job Title	TITLE	title	Family Doctor
Company	ORG (first part)	org (first part)	Four Square Physicians
Department	ORG (second part)	org (second part)	Medical
Telephone			**(All the phone numbers the vCard includes. Any numbers with labels iPod doesn't recognize are lumped in with Office.)**
Home	TEL;HOME	tel;type=home	510-555-1212
Work	TEL;WORK	tel;type=work	415-555-1212
Mobile	TEL;CELL	tel;type=cell	415-555-1234
E-mail			**(All the e-mail addresses the vCard includes, default address first)**
Default e-mail	EMAIL;PREF; INTERNET	email;type=internet;type=pref	test1@example.com
Other e-mail 1	EMAIL;INTERNET	email;type=internet	test2@example.com
Other e-mail 2	EMAIL;INTERNET	email;type=internet	test3@example.com
Web			
Home URL	URL;HOME	url;type=home	http://www.example.com/ ~moi
Office Address			
Office address	ADR;WORK	adr;type=work	1, Four Square Oakland, CA 94610 USA
Home Address			
Home Address	ADR;HOME	adr;type=work	728 Maine Street Alameda, CA 94501 USA
Notes	**NOTE**	**note**	**(Contents of the Notes field)**

TABLE 10-1   vCard Fields That Your iPod Can Use (in Order of Use)

10

to create a basic note using any text editor (for example, Notepad in Windows or TextEdit in Mac OS X). Here's an example:

```
BEGIN VCARD
VERSION:2.1
N:How to Create a vCard Note, Shopping List, or Whatever
ORG:Use the N field to name the vCard. Then type the ORG field
and enter the text you want to appear on the vCard note.
End your note with the END:VCARD statement.
END:VCARD
```

This bargain-basement vCard works fine if you copy it to the Contacts folder on your iPod. But as you'll see in Chapter 12, there are much better ways of getting text into your iPod.

If you find it handy to create vCards from a text editor, create a template file—a skeleton file that contains just the BEGIN VCARD, VERSION, N, ORG, and END VCARD lines. To create a vCard, double-click this file to open it, enter the text on the N line and the ORG line, and then save the file under a different name.

Create vCards from Your Contacts

If you're feeling energetic and punctilious, you can create your own vCards manually by typing the appropriate text (and, for version 3.0 vCards, spaces) smartly into a text editor. If you pore through the earlier part of this chapter once again, you'll find that I've just about given you enough information to create your own vCards in this way—but only just, because I'd prefer you find more creative ways of squandering your time.

On the other hand, if you're normal, you'll create vCards the easy way—by exporting them from whichever address book or contact manager you use. This section discusses the main tools for creating vCards on the Mac and then talks about the most prominent Windows tools.

If you have Mac OS X, you can use iSync to put your contacts on your Mac iPod without creating vCards manually. Go straight to the section "Use iSync to Put Contacts and Calendars on Your iPod Automatically from the Mac," later in this chapter.

Create vCards on the Mac

On the Mac, you can create your own vCards with minimal effort from Address Book, Microsoft Entourage, and Palm Desktop.

With each of these applications, you can create contacts directly on your iPod. Open a Finder window to show the Contacts folder on your iPod, and then drag the contacts to that folder to create vCards from them.

Create a vCard from Address Book

To create a vCard from Address Book, drag an item from the Address Book to another application or location. For example, to create a vCard on the desktop, drag a vCard to the desktop. Address Book names the vCard using the contact's name and applies the .vcf extension.

> **TIP**
>
> *Normally, a vCard contains the data for one person or organization. But the Mac OS X Address Book can create a single vCard that contains multiple entries. To create such a vCard, select multiple cards and then export them. Alternatively, export an entire group. You can drag any group to the desktop except for the All group. Alternatively, you can export any group (including the All group) by selecting it, issuing an Export Group vCard command from the File menu or the shortcut menu, specifying the filename and location in the Save dialog box, and then clicking the Save button.*

Create a vCard from Microsoft Entourage

To create a vCard from Microsoft Entourage, follow these steps:

1. Click the Address button in the upper-left pane to display your address book.
2. Select the contact or contacts from which you want to create vCards.
3. Drag the selected contact or contacts to the folder in which you want to create the vCards, or to the desktop.

> **CAUTION**
>
> *You can export all your Entourage contacts to a tab-delimited text file by opening the Address Book, choosing File | Export Contacts, using the Save dialog box to specify the filename and location, and then clicking the Save button. But the resulting file isn't vCard compatible.*

> **TIP**
>
> *To export all your Entourage information to your iPod, use the iPod It utility. See the "iPod It" section, in Chapter 12, for details.*

Create a vCard from Palm Desktop

You can create a vCard from Palm Desktop by dragging a contact to the folder in which you want to create the vCard. But you can also create vCards by using the Export: Palm Desktop dialog box. To do so, follow these steps:

1. In the Address List window, select the contact from which you want to create a vCard.
2. Choose File | Export to display the Export: Palm Desktop dialog box (shown here with settings chosen):

The Addresses item will be selected in the Modules drop-down list by default.

3. Use the Save As text box to specify the filename and the Where drop-down list to specify the location under which to save the file.

4. In the Items drop-down list, select the appropriate item—for example, All *NN* Addresses.

5. In the Format drop-down list, select the vCard item.

6. Click the Export button to export the contacts to the specified file.

Create vCards in Windows

This section discusses how to create vCards from the most widely used sources in Windows: Address Book, Outlook Express, and Palm Desktop.

Create a vCard from Address Book

Address Book, an applet that comes built into Windows, is the default location for storing contact information in Windows. You can launch Address Book by choosing Start | Programs | Accessories | Address Book or by clicking the Address Book button in an application such as Outlook Express, Outlook, or Microsoft Word.

You can create vCards from Address Book in two ways. The easier and faster way is to select the contacts you want to export to vCards, drag them to the desktop or the folder in which you want to create the vCards, and drop them there. This technique lets you create multiple vCards at once.

TIP   *For speed, open a window to display the Contacts folder on your iPod. Then drag the vCards directly into it from Address Book.*

To create a vCard from Address Book the harder and slower way, follow these steps:

1. Select the contact from whose entry you want to create a vCard. (You can export only one contact at a time to a vCard.)

2. Choose File | Export | Business Card (vCard) to display the Export As Business Card (vCard) dialog box. (This is a Save As dialog box in disguise.)

3. Specify the filename and location for the file, and then click the Save button.

Create a vCard from Outlook Express

The contacts in the Windows Address Book appear in the Contacts pane in Outlook Express, but you can't export them directly from there. Instead, click the Addresses button to display Address Book, and then create vCards as described in the previous section.

Create vCards from Palm Desktop

To create one or more vCards from Palm Desktop, follow these steps:

1. Click the Addresses button or choose View | Addresses to display the Addresses pane.

2. Select the contact or contacts from which you want to create vCards.

How to ... Create vCards from CSV Files

All these means of creating vCards are fine—provided your addresses are stored in one of those applications. But if the application in which your addresses are stored can't export them as vCards, you'll need to take a couple of extra steps to get the addresses onto your iPod. For example, if you use the Yahoo! address book, you won't be able to create vCards directly from it.

The first step is to export the addresses from the application into a text file. Most applications can create a CSV file, so that's usually the best format to use. Other applications create tab-separated values (TSV) files, which will usually work as well.

Once you've created the CSV or TSV file, import it into an address book that can handle CSV or TSV files *and* can create vCards. On Windows XP, both Address Book and Palm Desktop can handle CSV imports, so use whichever you prefer.

On the Mac, the news isn't so good. The Address Book in Mac OS X can import only vCards and LDAP Interchange Format (LDIF) files. (Before you ask, LDAP is the abbreviation for Lightweight Directory Access Protocol, a standard protocol for accessing directory information.) Palm Desktop can't import CSV or TSV files either, but Microsoft Entourage can import just about anything in sight.

Once you've found the appropriate Import command (usually File | Import), the tricky part about importing is assigning each field in the CSV or TSV file to the corresponding field in the address book. The following illustration shows a couple of examples of the dialog boxes used for mapping data to fields. The Specify Import Fields dialog box (on the left) is from Palm Desktop for Windows; the Import Contacts dialog box (on the right) is from Entourage, which can usually map some of the fields automatically.

The second step is to export the vCards from the address application, as described earlier in the chapter.

3. Choose File | Export vCard to display the Export As dialog box.

4. Enter the filename in the File Name text box, specify the destination, and then click the Export button.

Use iSync to Put Contacts and Calendars on Your iPod Automatically from the Mac

If you have Mac OS X 10.2.3 or later, the easiest and quickest way to put your contacts and calendars on your iPod is to use iSync. If you don't yet have iSync, download it from the iSync area of the Apple web site (www.apple.com/isync). Install iSync, and then work your way through the following sections.

NOTE *Apple keeps updating iSync and iCal, so if you're trying to use them for the first time, check the requirements. If you're using Jaguar, you'll probably do best to update to the latest version of Jaguar available. If you're using Panther, you should be in good shape for using iSync and iCal—but updating to the latest version of Panther available is unlikely to hurt.*

Set iSync to Synchronize with Your iPod

First, you need to add your iPod to the list of devices iSync synchronizes. To do so, follow these steps:

1. Run iSync by whichever means you prefer.

2. Connect your iPod to your Mac via the FireWire cable as usual.

3. Press COMMAND-N or choose Devices | Add Device to display the Add Device dialog box (shown here with a device already identified):

4. If iSync doesn't scan automatically for devices, click the Scan button to force a scan.

5. Double-click the icon for your iPod to add it to the iSync window.

6. Click the close button on the Add Device window.

Figure 10-1 shows an iPod added to the iSync window.

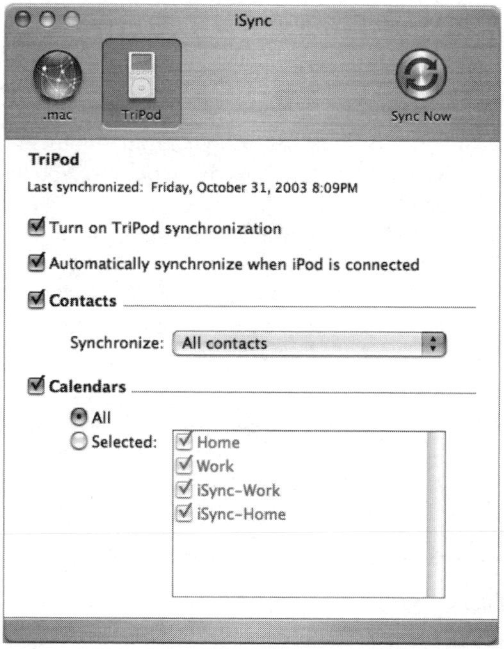

FIGURE 10-1   After adding your iPod to the iSync list of devices, you're ready to choose synchronization options.

Choose Synchronization Options for Your iPod

Once you've added your iPod to the list of devices that iSync can synchronize with, choose the appropriate synchronization options (shown in Figure 10-1):

■ **Turn On *iPod* Synchronization**   Controls whether iSync synchronizes with your iPod (identified by *iPod*). Normally, you'll want to keep this check box selected, as it is by default.

■ **Automatically Synchronize When iPod Is Connected**   Controls whether iSync automatically synchronizes your contacts and calendar (as appropriate) whenever you plug your iPod into your Mac. If you don't select this check box, you can force a synchronization by clicking the Sync Now button.

■ **Contacts**   Controls whether iSync synchronizes your contacts.

■ **Synchronize**   Controls which of your contacts iSync synchronizes. The default setting for the iPod is All Contacts.

■ **Calendars**   Controls whether iSync synchronizes your calendars. Select the All option button (the default) to synchronize all your calendars. To synchronize only some of your calendars (for example, just your Home calendar, not your Work calendar), select the Selected option button, and then select the check boxes for the calendars you want to synchronize.

How to ... Synchronize Only Some Contacts with Your iPod

If you keep a lot of contacts in your Address Book, synchronizing them all to your iPod can make the Contacts folder on your iPod difficult to navigate because you have to scroll endlessly to find the people you're interested in.

To get around this problem, you can synchronize only some of your contacts from Address Book to your iPod. To do so, follow these steps:

1. In Address Book, create a new group by clicking the Add New Group button (the + button below the Group pane), pressing COMMAND-SHIFT-N, or choosing File | New Group.

2. Type the name for the group and press RETURN.

3. Select the All group (or whichever group contains the contacts you want to add to the group you'll synchronize) to display its contents.

4. Select the contacts, and then drag them to the new group you created.

5. In iSync, select the new group in the Synchronize drop-down list.

6. Synchronize your iPod as usual.

Synchronize Your Contacts and Calendar

If you chose to have iSync automatically synchronize your iPod when you connect it, all you need do to start a synchronization is to connect your iPod. If you opted for manual synchronization, connect your iPod, run iSync, and then click the Sync Now button.

TIP *To synchronize quickly, or run iSync easily, you can add an iSync icon to the menu bar. To do so, choose iSync | Preferences or press COMMAND-COMMA and then select the Show iSync In Menu Bar check box in the Preferences dialog box. You can then click the icon and choose Open iSync (to open iSync so that you can synchronize) or simply select Sync Now from the menu (to synchronize immediately).*

iSync displays the Data Change Alert dialog box (two examples of which are shown in Figure 10-2) or the Safeguard dialog box (the Jaguar incarnation of the same feature) to make sure you understand how the synchronization will affect the data on your iPod. Click the Proceed button if you want to go ahead with the synchronization. Select the Do Not Show This Dialog Again check box first if you want iSync to skip alerting you in the future.

Data Change Alert			
Your contacts on this computer will be changed by this synchronization			
The following changes will be made if you proceed:	Add	Delete	Modify
This computer	18	–	1
⑦ ☐ Do not show this dialog again		Cancel	Proceed

Data Change Alert			
Your calendars and To Do items on this computer will be changed by this synchronization			
The following changes will be made if you proceed:	Add	Delete	Modify
This computer	32	–	–
⑦ ☐ Do not show this dialog again		Cancel	Proceed

FIGURE 10-2   The Data Change Alert dialog box warns you of the extent of changes that synchronization will cause.

TIP   *To turn off the Data Change Alert warnings or Safeguard warnings, choose iSync | Preferences, and then clear the Show Data Change Alert check box or the Show The Safeguard Panel check box in the Preferences dialog box. To change the threshold for which the warnings appear, leave this check box selected, but choose Any, More Than 1%, More Than 5%, or More Than 10% in the drop-down list. When the specified amount of data will be changed, iSync displays the warning to make sure you know the changes will occur.*

Revert to Last Sync

If synchronizing your data with iSync gives you an undesirable result (for example, you lose contacts or calendar information you weren't intending to get rid of), you should be able to repair the damage by reverting to the last synchronization. To do so, choose Devices | Revert To Last Sync, and then click the Revert To Last Sync button in the confirmation dialog box that iSync displays:

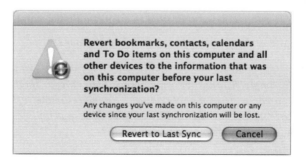

> **Revert bookmarks, contacts, calendars and To Do items on this computer and all other devices to the information that was on this computer before your last synchronization?**
>
> Any changes you've made on this computer or any device since your last synchronization will be lost.
>
> (Revert to Last Sync)   (Cancel)

iSync then restores the data from a copy it made of your data at the last synchronization.

10

TIP
You can also force iSync to make a backup of your data at any time by choosing Devices |
Back Up My Data.

Stop Synchronizing Your iPod

You can stop synchronizing your iPod either temporarily or permanently:

- To stop synchronization temporarily, select your iPod in the iSync window, and then clear the Turn On *iPod* Synchronization check box (where *iPod* is the name of your iPod).

- To stop synchronization permanently, select your iPod in the iSync window, choose Devices | Remove Device, and then click the Remove button in the confirmation dialog box that appears. To make your iPod synchronize again, add your iPod once more as described in the section "Set iSync to Synchronize with Your iPod," earlier in this chapter.

Put Your Contacts on Your iPod Manually Using the Mac

If you choose not to use iSync to put your contacts and calendar on your iPod automatically, you can create contacts from mainstream Mac OS X applications (as described in "Create vCards on the Mac," earlier in this chapter) and transfer them to your iPod manually.

To transfer contacts to your Mac manually, follow these steps:

1. Export your contacts to vCard files.

2. Connect your iPod to your Mac (if it's not currently connected). If iTunes is set to synchronize automatically on connection, let synchronization take place.

3. If disk mode isn't enabled on your iPod, enable it. (See "Enable Disk Mode," in Chapter 14, for instructions.)

4. Double-click the desktop icon for your iPod to display a Finder window of its contents.

5. Drag the vCard files to the Contacts folder and drop them there.

TIP
The first time you put contacts on your iPod manually, you may want to get rid of the
Instructions and Sample vCards that come preinstalled on your iPod. To do so, delete
the files ipod_created_instructions.vcf and ipod_created_sample.vcf. Alternatively, you
might want to store the samples in a folder on your Mac as templates in case you ever
want to create vCards manually.

6. Close the Contacts folder.

7. Eject your iPod by selecting it and pressing COMMAND-E, issuing an Eject "*iPod*" command (where *iPod* is the name of your iPod) from the Controls menu or the shortcut menu, or dragging the iPod icon to the Trash.

How to ...

Prevent Your iPod from Showing Duplicate Contacts and Calendar Information

If you use iSync to put contacts and calendar information on your iPod automatically, you can get duplicate entries for contacts and calendar information you've already copied to your iPod manually (or that you subsequently copy to your iPod manually).

This happens because iSync doesn't delete any data from the iPod that iSync itself hasn't put there. So if you want to synchronize your contacts and calendar information automatically, you need to commit fully to iSync. To do so, follow these steps:

1. Connect your iPod to your Mac.

2. Enable disk mode if it's not currently enabled. (In iTunes, select the icon for your iPod in the Source pane, click the Display Options for Player button, select the Enable Disk Use check box in the iPod Properties dialog box, and click the OK button.)

3. From the Contacts folder on your iPod, import into Address Book the vCards for any contacts it doesn't yet contain. Make sure you don't add existing contacts to Address Book—it'll happily create duplicate entries that you'll then need to weed out manually.

4. From the Calendars folder on your iPod, import into iCal any calendar information it doesn't already contain.

5. Drag the Contacts folder and the Calendars folder on your iPod to the Trash. iSync will automatically create these folders if they don't exist. Alternatively, drag the contents of each folder to the Trash.

6. Run iSync and synchronize your calendars and contacts.

10

Put Contacts on Your Windows iPod

To put contacts on your Windows iPod, you must enable your iPod for use as a hard disk and assign a drive letter to it. (In some cases, you may find that Windows treats your iPod as a hard disk and assigns it a drive letter without your intervention.) If you've already done this, you're set to go; if not, follow these steps:

1. Connect your iPod to your PC as usual. If you have your iPod set to synchronize automatically, let it do so.

2. In iTunes, right-click the iPod's entry in the Source pane and choose iPod Options from the shortcut menu to display the iPod Preferences dialog box:

3. Select the Enable Disk Use check box. iTunes displays a dialog box warning you that you'll need to unmount your iPod manually before disconnecting it:

4. Click the OK button. iTunes returns you to the iPod Preferences dialog box.

5. Click the OK button to close the iPod Preferences dialog box.

Once you've enabled disk mode, you can copy the contact files directly onto your iPod. To do so, follow these steps:

1. Choose Start | My Computer to open a My Computer window that lists the drives on your computer. Your iPod should now appear as a drive with its own drive letter in the Devices With Removable Storage category.

2. Double-click the icon for your iPod to open it in a Windows Explorer window. You'll see it contains the folders Calendars and Contacts. If Windows Explorer is set to display hidden files and folders as well, you'll see an iPod_Control folder, too.

TIP

To control whether Windows Explorer displays hidden files and folders, choose Tools | Folder Options from a Windows Explorer window. In the Folder Options dialog box, display the View tab, select the Show Hidden Files And Folders option button, and then click the OK button.

3. Open another Windows Explorer window and display the folder that contains the vCard files for the contacts you want to put on your iPod.

4. Select the vCard files, drag them to the Contacts folder, and drop them there. Windows copies the vCard files to the Contacts folder.

Because you're copying the contact files directly to the iPod, you don't need to synchronize to make the files appear on your iPod.

View Your Contacts on Your iPod

To view your contacts on your iPod, follow these steps:

1. Choose Extras | Contacts from the main menu to display the Contacts submenu (shown on the left in Figure 10-3).

2. Scroll to the contact you want to view, and then press the Select button. Your iPod displays the contact's information. The right screen in Figure 10-3 shows an example. You may need to scroll down to view all the data about the contact.

3. To display the previous contact, press the Previous button. To display the next contact, press the Next button.

To specify how your iPod should sort your contacts' names and display them on screen, scroll to the Contacts item on the Settings screen, and then press the Select button to display the Contacts screen.

To change the sort order, scroll (if necessary) to the Sort item, and then press the Select button to toggle between the First Last setting (for example, *Joe Public*) and the Last, First setting (for example, *Public, Joe*).

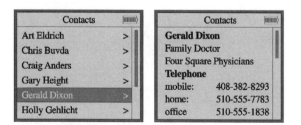

FIGURE 10-3   From the Contacts submenu (left), select the contact you want to view, and then press the Select button to display the contact's information (right).

10

How to ... Force a Contact Missing from the Contacts List to Appear on Your iPod

If a contact fails to appear in the Contacts list on your iPod even if you're sure it has been copied to the iPod's Contacts folder, check that the vCard is correctly formatted. The vCard must be formatted using either the vCard 2.1 format or the vCard 3.0 format for it to appear on your iPod.

In most cases, the easiest way to make sure the vCard is correctly formatted is to export it from a compatible application, as described in "Create vCards from Your Contacts," earlier in this chapter. There's no sense in poring over the spaces in a vCard file by eye unless you have no alternative.

To change the display format, scroll (if necessary) to the Display item, and then press the Select button to toggle between the First Last setting and the Last, First setting.

Most people find using the same sort order and display format best, but you may prefer otherwise. For example, you might sort by Last, First but display by First Last.

Chapter 11

Put Your Calendars on Your iPod or iPod mini

How to...

■ Understand vCalendar and iCalendar

■ Create iCalendar and vCalendar files from your calendars

■ Use iSync to put your calendars on your iPod automatically using a Mac

■ Put your calendars on your iPod manually using a Mac

■ Put your calendars on your iPod manually using Windows

This chapter shows you how to put your calendars on your iPod or iPod mini so you can keep your appointments handy along with your music and contacts.

> **NOTE** *Apple added calendar capabilities to the iPod software in version 1.2. If your iPod doesn't have calendar capabilities, download the latest iPod Updater for it using Mac OS X's Software Update utility or directly from the Apple web site (www.apple.com/swupdates/). Remember that first-generation and second-generation iPods use different updaters than the third-generation iPods and the iPod mini.*

If you're using Mac OS X 10.2.2 or later and iCal 1.0.2 or later, you can synchronize your calendars automatically with your iPod or iPod mini by using Apple's free iSync software. If you're using Windows, you'll need to transfer calendar files to your iPod or iPod mini manually.

> **NOTE** *If you've worked your way through Chapter 10 (which covers putting your contacts on your iPod), you'll be able to skip quickly through parts of this chapter, as some of the steps involved in putting calendars on your iPod are similar to those for contacts.*

This chapter covers both the regular (full-size) iPod models and the iPod mini. Where either the regular iPod or the iPod mini behaves differently, I'll point out the differences. Otherwise, I'll use the term *iPod* to cover both.

Understand vCalendar and iCalendar

vCalendar and iCalendar are standards for storing information about calendar events and to-do items, and for transferring this information from one vCalendar/iCalendar-aware application to another. vCalendar and iCalendar are platform-independent, so your Mac calendaring application can use the vCalendar and iCalendar formats to schedule meetings or other events with vCalendar/iCalendar-aware applications on other platforms, such as Windows, Linux, or Unix.

Typically, calendaring applications (such as iCal, Microsoft Outlook, or Microsoft Entourage) use vCalendar and iCalendar files in the background to transmit the details of events, appointments, and invitations. Under normal circumstances, you won't need to work directly with vCalendar or iCalendar files yourself. But sometimes, when you need to put your calendar on an iPod, you'll need to create vCalendar files or iCalendar files by exporting them from your calendaring software.

Where vCalendar and iCalendar Came From

As you learned in Chapter 10, Apple, IBM, AT&T, and Siemens set up the versit Consortium to streamline PDI. As well as vCards, versit worked on the vCalendar format for exchanging electronic calendaring and scheduling information. Then, in December 1996, the IMC took over vCard and vCalendar; it kept the vCard name but changed the name of vCalendar to iCalendar (short for Internet Calendaring and Scheduling Core Object Specification) when it updated vCalendar to version 2.0.

iCalendar files contain more information than vCalendar files, so they're "better" in that sense. Sooner or later, pretty much every calendaring application will likely use iCalendar files, and vCalendar will fall by the wayside. But at the time of writing, vCalendar is still more widely used than iCalendar and is supported by a wider range of applications.

What's Inside a vCalendar/iCalendar File?

Like vCards, vCalendar and iCalendar files are text files that contain information tagged to fields. A vCalendar file or iCalendar file can contain the details of one appointment or multiple appointments. vCalendar files use the .vcs extension, while iCalendar files use the .ics extension.

The following is an example of a vCalendar file created by Palm Desktop for Windows. The file contains one event.

```
BEGIN:VCALENDAR
VERSION:1.0
PRODID:PalmDesktop Generated
BEGIN:VEVENT
SUMMARY:Birthday lunch for Ulla at Charlie's
DESCRIPTION:Card, present, champagne
DTSTART:20030612T120000Z
DTEND:20030612T143000Z
DALARM:20030610T120000Z
END:VEVENT
END:VCALENDAR
```

Here's an example of an iCalendar file created by iCal on Mac OS X. The file contains two events.

```
BEGIN:VCALENDAR
CALSCALE:GREGORIAN
X-WR-TIMEZONE;VALUE=TEXT:USA/San Francisco
METHOD:PUBLISH
PRODID:-//Apple Computer\, Inc//iCal 1.0//EN
X-WR-RELCALID;VALUE=TEXT:FD2F3300-279F-11D7-8BC2-000393DB77DE
X-WR-CALNAME;VALUE=TEXT:Home
VERSION:2.0
```

11

```
BEGIN:VEVENT
SEQUENCE:2
DTSTART;TZID=USA/San Francisco:20030401T114500
DTSTAMP:20030110T125940Z
SUMMARY:Lunch with Peggy
UID:FD2F1A7C-279F-11D7-8BC2-000393DB77DE
DTEND;TZID=USA/San Francisco:20030401T140000
DESCRIPTION:Zza's
END:VEVENT
BEGIN:VEVENT
SEQUENCE:1
DTSTAMP:20030110T125920Z
SUMMARY:Meeting at Jake's
UID:FD2F1CA0-279F-11D7-8BC2-000393DB77DE
DTSTART;TZID=USA/San Francisco:20030401T094500
DURATION:PT1H
DESCRIPTION:Bring project reports\, laptop\, speakers\, iPod\n\nDiscuss:
 \n\t* New developments\n\t* Reconstitute project team?\n\t* Bill:
 progress since last meeting
END:VEVENT
END:VCALENDAR
```

Just glance through those examples, then note these highlights:

- Each vCalendar file and iCalendar file begins with a BEGIN:VCALENDAR statement and ends with an END:VCALENDAR statement.

- After the BEGIN:VCALENDAR statement comes a VERSION declaration of the vCalendar standard used: 1.0 for the vCalendar file, 2.0 for the iCalendar file.

- The PRODID (product ID) statement identifies the application that created the file: PalmDesktop Generated for the Palm Desktop file, -//Apple Computer\, Inc//iCal 1.0//EN for the iCal file. (If you're wondering which mad slasher attacked the statement, the forward slashes are separators, while the backslash is used to escape out nonalphanumeric characters, such as the comma.)

- The version 2.0 file contains several other items of general calendaring information: the calendar used (Gregorian), the time zone (USA/San Francisco), the calendar name (Home), and more.

- Each event begins with a BEGIN:VEVENT statement and ends with an END:VEVENT statement.

- The SUMMARY field contains the name assigned to the event in your calendaring application—the text the calendar displays for the event.

■ The DESCRIPTION field contains any notes you've entered for the event.

■ The DTSTART field and DTEND field give the starting and ending dates and times for the event in the format *YYYYMMDDTHHMMSSZ*. For example, 20030612T120000U represents noon on June 12, 2003, in the U (or "Uniform"—military letter-speak) time zone, better known as Pacific Standard Time (PST). In version 2.0, these fields include TZID (time zone ID) information as well.

Create iCalendar and vCalendar Files from Your Calendars

Because vCalendar and iCalendar files are text files, in theory you could create them by typing in a text editor if you were desperate enough. But if you keep your appointments in a calendaring application, you should be able to create vCalendar files or iCalendar files much more easily by exporting either your whole calendar or particular events from it.

As you'll see in the following sections, some calendaring applications provide better features for creating vCalendar and iCalendar files easier than other applications do. But most major calendaring applications let you create files in one format or the other.

NOTE   *If you're using iCal (preferably the latest version) on Mac OS X (likewise), you don't need to create iCalendar files or vCalendar files directly. Instead, you can synchronize your calendars with your iPod by using iSync. Turn straight to the section "Use iSync to Put Your Calendars on Your iPod Automatically from Mac OS X," later in this chapter.*

Create iCalendar and vCalendar Files on the Mac

The following sections show you how to create iCalendar and vCalendar files from iCal, Microsoft Entourage, and Palm Desktop for the Mac.

Create iCalendar Files from iCal

Unlike many other applications, iCal doesn't support creating calendars by dragging to the desktop or another location. Instead, to create iCalendar files from iCal, follow these steps:

1. In the Calendars pane, select the calendar you want to export.

2. Choose File | Export to display the iCal: Export dialog box.

3. Enter the filename in the Save As text box.

4. Use the Where drop-down list to specify the folder in which to save the calendar. If your iPod is docked and mounted, you could save the file directly to your iPod's Calendars folder.

5. Click the Export button.

11

Create iCalendar Files from Microsoft Entourage

To create iCalendar files from Microsoft Entourage, select the appointment or event you want to export, drag it to the desktop or the folder in which you want to create the file, and then drop it there.

TIP   *To export all of your Entourage information to your iPod, use iPod It. See "iPod It," in Chapter 12.*

Create vCalendar Files from Palm Desktop

Palm Desktop provides two ways to create vCalendar files.

To create a vCalendar file that consists of a single Date Book item, select the item, drag it to the desktop or the folder in which you want to create the file, and then drop it there. If your iPod is connected to your Mac and disk mode is enabled, you can drag the item directly to a Finder window displaying your iPod's Calendars folder.

But usually, you'll want to put more than a single Date Book item on your iPod—you'll want to load the entire contents of your Date Book. To do so, export your Date Book to a vCalendar file by following these steps:

1. Choose File | Export to display the Export: Palm Desktop dialog box:

2. Use the Save As text box to specify the filename and the Where drop-down list to specify the location under which to save the file. For example, if your iPod is docked and mounted, you could save the file directly to your iPod's Calendars folder.

3. Ignore the Items drop-down list. It appears to offer you the choice of exporting some Date Book items or all of them, but in fact the only choice is All Datebook Items. Similarly, ignore the Columns button, because Palm Desktop makes this unavailable when you select the vCal format.

4. In the Format drop-down list, select the vCal item.

5. Click the Export button.

Create vCalendar Files on Windows

This section shows you how to create vCalendar files from Palm Desktop for Windows as well as iCalendar and vCalendar files from Microsoft Outlook.

Create vCalendar Files from Palm Desktop

To create a vCalendar file from Palm Desktop, follow these steps:

1. Click the Date button or choose View | Date Book to display your calendar.

2. If your calendar isn't already displayed in Day view or Week view, click the Day button or the Week button to display the calendar in one of those views.

3. Select the event you want to export.

4. Choose File | Export vCal to display the Export As dialog box.

5. In the File Name text box, enter the filename under which you want to save the file.

6. Specify the folder in which to save the file.

7. In the Export Type drop-down list, make sure Palm Desktop has selected the vCal File item.

8. Click the Export button to export the event.

Create vCalendar or iCalendar Files from Microsoft Outlook

To create a vCalendar or iCalendar file from Microsoft Outlook, follow these steps:

1. Click the Calendar button in the Outlook bar to display your calendar if it's not already displayed.

2. Select the appointment from which you want to create the vCalendar file or iCalendar file.

3. Choose File | Save As to display the Save As dialog box.

4. Specify the location in which to save the iCalendar file or vCalendar file.

> **TIP**   *If your iPod is currently connected to your computer and disk mode is enabled, you can save the file directly into your iPod's Calendars folder. Otherwise, save your calendar files to a folder from which you can then copy them to your iPod's Calendars folder once you connect your iPod.*

5. In the Save As type drop-down list, select the iCalendar Format item or the vCalendar Format item, as appropriate.

6. Click the Save button to save the appointment to a file.

Put Your Calendars on Your iPod from Mac OS X

As with your contacts, you can put your calendars on your iPod either automatically (by using iSync) or manually. Again, doing so automatically is easier, so I'll show you how to do that first.

11

How to ...

Export Multiple (or All) Appointments from Outlook

As explained in "Create vCalendar or iCalendar Files from Microsoft Outlook," Outlook lets you export only one appointment at a time to a vCalendar or iCalendar file. Unless your calendar is very sparsely populated or you have commendable reserves of patience, exporting your appointments will be a time-consuming and tedious process.

Good news: other people have run into this problem before you, and some of them decided to try to fix it. The following are three of the utilities you can use to export multiple appointments from Outlook:

■ iPodSync ($12.99; iccnet.50megs.com/iPodSync/) is a powerful shareware application that can export contacts to vCard files and appointment information to iCalendar files. You can choose a wide variety of options, such as whether to synchronize only certain fields, whether to include notes, and even whether to add birthday and anniversary dates to notes. The following illustration shows iPodSync's Calendar page, on which you can choose which appointments to synchronize. You can download a 15-day trial version of iPodSync from the preceding URL. iPodSync works with Outlook XP and Outlook 2000 on Windows XP, Windows 2000, and Windows Me.

■ iAppoint (freeware; www.xs4all.nl/~hagemans/) has a simple interface, shown below, that lets you choose the calendar to work with, specify the range of dates from which you want to export appointments, and tell iAppoint where to store the file. (If your iPod is connected and disk mode is enabled, you can save the file directly to the Calendars folder.) The Contacts button displays a window with controls for exporting your contacts. iAppoint is currently at version 0.5 but seems stable.

■ OutPod (freeware; www.stoer.de/ipod/ipod_en.htm) lets you export multiple appointments into a single vCalendar or iCalendar file. OutPod, shown here, also can export multiple contacts at once:

Use iSync to Put Your Calendars on Your iPod Automatically from Mac OS X

If you have Jaguar or Panther, the easiest and quickest way to put your calendars on your iPod is to use iSync. iSync is free, so there's no reason not to try it. If you don't have iSync yet, use Software Update (choose Apple | System Preferences, and then click the Software Update item) to download it, or download it manually from the iSync area of the Apple web site (www.apple.com/isync) and install it.

Introduce your iPod to iSync by following the procedure described in "Set iSync to Synchronize with Your iPod," in Chapter 10. Then configure iSync to synchronize with your iPod as described in "Choose Synchronization Options for Your iPod," in Chapter 10. Make sure the Calendars check box is selected. If you want to synchronize all of your calendars, select the All option button. If you want to synchronize only some of your calendars, select the Selected option button, and then select or clear the check boxes beside the calendars that you want to synchronize.

NOTE   *If you find duplicate events in your calendars, see the sidebar "Prevent Your iPod from Showing Duplicate Contacts and Calendar Information," in Chapter 10.*

After synchronizing with iSync, remember to unmount your iPod manually. (If you forget, you may lose or corrupt your data.)

Put Your Calendars on Your iPod Manually from Mac OS X

If you can't use iSync or you prefer (for whatever reason) to synchronize your calendars manually, you can transfer your calendars to your Mac manually.

To transfer contacts manually, disk use must be enabled on your iPod. If it's not enabled, follow the steps described in "Enable Disk Mode on Your iPod Using a Mac," in Chapter 14, to enable it.

Once you've enabled disk mode, you can put the calendar files directly onto your iPod. Connect your iPod to your Mac as usual, and then double-click the icon for your iPod to display a Finder window of its contents.

- If you haven't yet created the calendar files, you can simply create them in your iPod's Calendars folder. For example, select the Calendars folder in the iCal: Export dialog box or the Export: Palm Desktop dialog box. Or drag an event from Microsoft Entourage or Palm Desktop directly to the Calendars folder.

- Alternatively, export your contacts to vCalendar or iCalendar files in another folder, and then copy them from there to your iPod's Calendars folder. Using this method, you can export the contacts when your iPod isn't connected to your Mac.

After adding your calendar files to your iPod, eject your iPod in any of these ways: select it and press COMMAND-E, issue an Eject command from the File menu or the shortcut menu, or drag the iPod icon to the Trash.

Put Your Calendars on Your iPod from Windows

At the time of writing, there's no version of iSync for Windows—but there is iPodSync (discussed in the "Export Multiple (or All) Appointments from Outlook" sidebar, earlier), an equivalent for putting your calendar information on your iPod from Windows. If you prefer not to use iPodSync, you can do things the hard way, as described in this section.

First, enable disk mode on your iPod. Doing so causes Windows XP to assign a letter to it. If you've already done so (for example, so you could put your contacts on your iPod, as described in Chapter 10), you're ready to load your calendar files. If not, follow the steps described in "Enable Disk Mode on Your iPod Using Windows," in Chapter 14, to enable it.

Once you've enabled disk mode, and after Windows has assigned a letter to your iPod's hard disk, you can copy the calendar files directly onto your iPod. To do so, follow these steps:

1. Choose Start | My Computer to open a My Computer window that lists the drives on your computer. Your iPod should now appear as a drive with its own drive letter in the Devices With Removable Storage category.

2. Double-click the icon for your iPod to open it in a Windows Explorer window. You'll see it contains the folders Calendars and Contacts. If Windows Explorer is set to display hidden files and folders as well, you'll see an iPod_Control folder, too.

TIP   *To control whether or not Windows Explorer displays hidden files and folders, choose Tools | Folder Options from a Windows Explorer window. In the Folder Options dialog box, display the View tab, select the Show Hidden Files and Folders option button, and then click the OK button.*

3. Open another Windows Explorer window to the folder that contains the iCalendar files for the events you want to put onto your iPod.

4. Select the iCalendar files, drag them to the Calendars, and drop them there. Windows copies the iCalendar files to the Calendars folder.

Because you're copying the calendar files directly to the iPod, you don't need to synchronize to make the files appear on your iPod.

View Your Calendar on Your iPod

To view your calendar on your iPod, follow these steps:

1. Choose Extras | Calendar to display the Calendars screen.

2. If you synchronize multiple calendars, the first Calendars screen contains a list of available calendars, as shown here. Scroll down to the calendar you want (or to your To Do list), and then press the Select button to display it.

Calendars	▯▯▯▯
All	>
Home	>
iSync-Home	>
iSync-Work	>
Work	>
To Do	>

11

3. If you synchronize only one calendar, your iPod automatically displays the calendar for the current month (the first time you access the calendar) or the last month you accessed (thereafter):

4. Scroll backward or forward to the day you're interested in.

    ■ To access the next month or the previous month, press the Next button or the Previous button, respectively.

    ■ If you're happier scrolling, you can scroll back past the beginning of the month to access the previous month, or scroll forward past the end of the month to access the next month.

5. Press the Select button to display your schedule for that day:

6. To view the details for an appointment, scroll to it and press the Select button. The following illustration shows a sample appointment. From there, you can press the Next button to display the next appointment or the Previous button to display the previous appointment.

7. Once you've accessed a day, you can press the Next button to access the next day or the Previous button to access the previous day.

Chapter 12

Create Notes and Put Other Information on Your iPod or iPod mini

How to...

- Understand the basics of putting text on your iPod or iPod mini
- Use the Notes feature to put text on your iPod from a Mac or Windows
- Put text on your iPod from a Mac
- Put text on your iPod from Windows

This chapter discusses how to store other information on your iPod or iPod mini so you can display it on the screen. Essentially, that means text information—at the time of writing, the iPod screen can display only text and its system graphics (such as the battery symbols and the Apple symbol). For the future, iPod enthusiasts dream of video iPods with color displays or holographic displays...but I digress.

By using your iPod as a hard drive (as discussed in Chapter 14), you can store any type of file on your iPod. But unless the file is in a text format that your iPod's software can handle, you won't be able to display the file on the iPod's interface—you'll be able to work with the file only when you've connected your iPod to your computer.

Third-generation iPods and the iPod mini include a Notes feature specifically designed for putting text files on your iPod in a readable format, and for accessing and reading those files. First- and second-generation iPods lack the Notes feature, so you have to disguise the text files as contact records. As you'll see, developers have addressed this limitation so neatly that you can quickly land yourself with a huge list of contacts—some real, some text.

TIP *Two great places for finding utilities such as those discussed in this chapter are VersionTracker.com (www.versiontracker.com) and iPodLounge.com (www.ipodlounge.com). You'll also find Mac-related utilities at Apple's Mac OS X Downloads page (www.apple. com/macosx/downloads).*

Limitations to Putting Information on Your iPod

If you have an iPod and you're reading this book, you probably have a pretty favorable impression of the iPod—and so do I. But before you start putting huge chunks of text onto your iPod, it's a good idea to be clear about the iPod's limitations as a text-display device.

The main limitation is obvious: the screen is small enough to make even the screens on low-resolution Palm devices seem spacious. A regular iPod can display a heading plus seven or eight lines of text of up to about 30 characters each; an iPod mini can display a line or so less. This is enough to be useful for compact information such as recipes, memos, driving directions, or even winsome love poetry, but so small as to make reading any lengthy document more of a chore than a joy. You can see why Apple hasn't succumbed to any temptation it may have felt to incorporate an e-book reader in the iPod.

Still, if you've been reading Tolstoy on your mobile phone's display on the bus, reading text on your iPod might seem—or even be—a significant step up in the world. Besides, the iPod has enough battery power to let you read for a while in the dark; you can play music at the same time; and putting the text on your iPod can save you from needing to tote multiple devices.

If you're using a first- or second-generation iPod, there's a second and less obvious limitation: each text file you want to put on your iPod needs to go into a contact record for you to be able to display it on your iPod. Each contact record is limited to 2000 characters—enough for about 300 average-length words. So if a file is longer than that, it needs to be divided among two or more contact records. (As you'll see in "Mac Utilities for Putting Information on Your iPod" and "Windows Utilities for Putting Information on Your iPod," both later in this chapter, some applications get around this limitation.)

What Text Can You Put on Your iPod?

With the right utilities, you can put on your iPod any text file you have on your computer. That text could be anything from a parts list to part of a novel, from a thesis to a section of a thesaurus. Each text file has a maximum size of 4KB, which limits it to 600 to 700 words of average length, but you can use utilities to split up longer files into iPod-size bites automatically. The iPod can hold up to 1000 notes at a time, and the notes can be linked together to make them easy to navigate.

As you'll see in the following sections, apart from text files, utility designers have concentrated on types of text that are widely useful and can be downloaded easily from sources on the Internet. For example:

- **News headlines** Various iPod utilities can download news headlines from news sites; most of these utilities let you choose the sites (other utilities are limited to one site). Many people find news headlines more or less useless when their accompanying stories aren't available. However, you may find the headlines useful as a means of determining which sites you need to visit and which stories you want to read. But this still pales in comparison to AvantGo on Palms and Pocket PCs, which delivers both the headlines and the full stories.

- **Weather reports** Various iPod utilities can download weather reports from online sites. You specify the city (or ZIP code) and the type of weather reports (for example, today's forecast or a five-day report), and the utility downloads the relevant information.

- **Stock quotes** Several utilities can download stock quotes. You specify the stock symbols and (in some cases) choose the frequency of updates.

- **Lyrics** Some utilities can look up the lyrics to songs you specify.

- **Horoscopes** Some utilities can download horoscopes.

All the items are created as contacts, so your Contacts folder on your iPod can get jammed. But apart from your needing to scroll further than usual, accessing the information is easy. On third-generation iPods and the iPod mini, the Notes feature, discussed next, keeps the notes in a separate category from contacts, so both notes and contacts remain easy to access.

12

Use the Notes Feature on a Third-Generation iPod or an iPod mini

If you have a third-generation iPod or an iPod mini, you can use its built-in Notes feature to put text files on it and read them. This feature works effectively only with plaintext files. You *can* transfer other documents, such as rich-text format documents or Word documents, by using the Notes feature, but the text displayed on the iPod will include formatting codes and extended characters. These make the text nearly impossible to read, especially given the small size of the iPod's screen.

To put notes on your iPod or iPod mini, enable disk mode (see Chapter 14 for details), connect your iPod, and then copy or move (as appropriate) the note to the Notes folder on your iPod using the Finder (on Mac OS X) or Windows Explorer.

NOTE   *The first time you open the Notes folder on your iPod, you may want to delete the Instructions file to prevent it from continuing to appear in your listings.*

On your iPod, you can then read the file by choosing Extras | Notes, scrolling down to the file, and pressing the Select button.

Use iPod Scripts to Create and Manage Text Notes on the Mac

If you use the Notes feature extensively on the Mac, consider downloading the iPod Scripts collection that Apple provides for creating and managing text notes. These scripts require Mac OS X 10.2 or later.

At the time of writing, the iPod Scripts collection contains the following scripts:

■ The List Notes script provides an easy way of opening one of the scripts stored on your iPod for editing on your Mac. This script displays a dialog box that lists the notes stored on your iPod. You select the appropriate script and click the Open button to open it:

Please make your selection:

BASE Jumping for Amateurs.txt
Description of Roman Candles.txt
Dopamine Receptors.txt
Ebola Symptoms.txt
Explanations for SARS.txt
Instructions
Sericulture.txt
Skeleton Manipulation.txt
Skeletons – edit 2.txt
Stimulating Fast-Twitch Fibers.txt
Theories for Industrial Diseases in Tibet.txt

Cancel   Open

■ The Clear All Notes script deletes all the notes in the Notes folder on your iPod and lets you choose whether to delete subfolders in the Notes folder as well. This script displays these two dialog boxes:

■ The Eject iPod script checks that you want to eject the currently mounted iPod, and then ejects it if you click the Continue button. In normal use, you'll find it easier to eject the iPod using either iTunes or the desktop icon (if the iPod is in disk mode) rather than running this script.

■ The Clipboard To Note script creates a note from the current contents of the Clipboard. This script is great for quickly grabbing part of a document or a web page, and generating a note from it. Select the text, issue a Copy command, and then run the script. Click the Continue button in the first dialog box (shown on the left in the next illustration), enter the name for the note in the dialog box shown on the right in the next illustration, and click OK. The script then displays a message box telling you that it has created the note.

■ The Note From Webpages folder contains two scripts: MacCentral and Printer Friendly. The MacCentral script is for extracting an article from the MacCentral web site from the foremost browser window. The Printer Friendly script follows the same theme but is less specialized, extracting the contents of the foremost browser window to a note. For best effect, set the foremost window ready to print without ads and without other HTML items that will otherwise mess up the text of the note.

To use the iPod Scripts collection, follow these steps:

1. Download the iPod Scripts collection from www.apple.com/applescript/ipod/.

2. Move the downloaded file to your ~/Library/Scripts folder, and then expand the disk image.

12

NOTE   *If you haven't used any scripts before, you'll need to create the Scripts folder manually under the Home:Library folder.*

3. Connect your iPod to your computer.

4. Use the Script menu to run the script. If you haven't installed the Script menu, do so as described next.

Put the Script Menu on the Mac OS X Menu Bar

You can run the iPod scripts directly from the Scripts folder, but doing so is slower and more awkward than it needs to be. The better way to run scripts is from the Scripts menu that Mac OS X can display on your menu bar.

If you haven't used scripts before, you'll probably need to add the Script menu to the menu bar manually. To do so, follow these steps:

1. From the Finder, choose Go | Applications to display your Applications folder.

2. Double-click the AppleScript folder to open it in the window.

3. Drag the ScriptMenu.menu icon to the menu bar in the upper-right corner of your screen and drop it there. Mac OS X adds an icon that you can click to display the script menu, shown here with the iPod scripts expanded:

You can then run scripts easily from the desktop by using the Script menu.

Mac Utilities for Putting Information on Your iPod

The Notes feature is great if you have a third-generation iPod or iPod mini and if you have the information in a text file. To put text on other iPods, you need to use third-party utilities. This section discusses some utilities for putting information on your iPod from a Mac, starting with the most useful. The next section discusses utilities for putting information on your iPod from Windows.

iSpeakIt

iSpeakIt ($9.95; www.zapptek.com/ispeak-it/) is a versatile utility that enables you to load news headlines and summaries (from Google), weather forecasts, web pages, and text onto your iPod. iSpeakIt can load not only plaintext files but also the text from other applications installed on your Mac. To transfer the text, choose *Application* | Services | Add Book To iPod (where *Application* is the application's name).

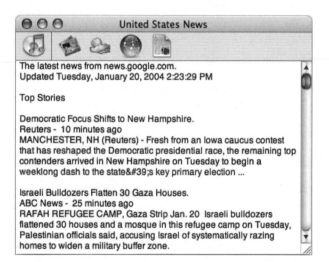

iSpeakIt's name comes from its other leading capability—it lets you have your Mac's text-to-speech capability read text files to audio files and load them into iTunes (and thus onto your iPod). You can have iSpeakIt make audio files of the information it downloads from the Internet.

If you have severe sight problems, the Mac's text-to-speech capability can be a great boon. But for most people, the computerized delivery (even of the clearest voices, such as Vicki) lies somewhere between a curiosity and a perversion. You'll know if you want to make audio files from text files— and if you do, iSpeakIt is the application to use.

iPod It

iPod It ($14.95; www.zapptek.com) is a utility that enables you to copy contacts, notes, tasks, e-mail, and calendar information from Microsoft Entourage, or from Mail, Stickies, Address Book, and iCal, to your iPod. iPod It also supports downloading news headlines from Google, weather forecasts, and directions.

Pod2Go

Pod2Go (freeware; www.kainjow.com/pod2go/website) lets you put news, weather, stock quotes, text files, horoscopes, and driving directions on your iPod. Once you've specified the details of the information you want, Pod2Go downloads the information automatically when you synchronize. Pod2Go can also put your Address Book contacts, Safari bookmarks, Stickies, and iCal calendars onto your iPod.

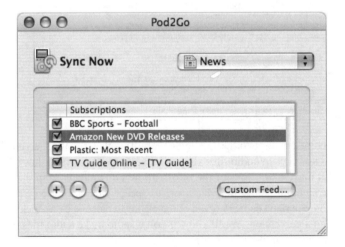

If you have iPod Software 2.0 or later, Pod2Go lets you choose whether to put the text on your iPod as contacts or as notes. If you're using an earlier version of iPod Software, you can use contacts only.

Book2Pod

Book2Pod (freeware; www.tomsci.com/book2pod or www.ipodlounge.com) is a tool for splitting up a text file into pieces the right size for iPod notes. Book2Pod embeds links at the start and end of each note-size section so that you can navigate to the next section by pressing the Select button. Book2Pod enables you to get around the 1000-note limitation by letting you load and unload books even after you've split them up into pieces. Book2Pod requires Mac OS X 10.2 and iPod firmware 2.0 or higher.

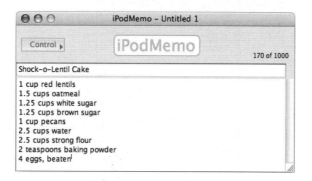

iPodMemo

iPodMemo (freeware; various sites including www.versiontracker.com and www.ipodlounge.com) is a text editor with which you can create memos of up to 1000 characters and put them on your iPod as contacts. iPodMemo is basic but functional—and the price is right.

12

PodWriter

PodWriter (freeware; www.steigerworld.com/doug/podwriter.php) is a small text editor that you can use to put text files on your iPod. At the time of writing, PodWriter is limited to 1000 characters in a file, so it pales in comparison to some of the previously discussed utilities. But PodWriter is free, has a straightforward interface, and works well, so you may want to consider it, particularly for creating memos and other short notes.

Windows Utilities for Putting Information on Your iPod

Because the iPod came to Windows much later than to the Mac, there are still fewer Windows utilities than Mac utilities for the iPod—but Windows is catching up at a good pace.

EphPod

EphPod (freeware; www.ephpod.com) is a mature utility originally designed, in the days before Windows iPods were released, to enable Windows users to use Mac-formatted iPods. EphPod still performs that function (for which you need to have the non-freeware application MacOpener installed on your PC), but it also works without MacOpener for Windows-formatted iPods.

Among its other features, discussed in "EphPod" in Chapter 16, EphPod lets you download news feeds.

GoogleGet

GoogleGet (freeware; mesmerized.org/teki/extra/googleget/index.html) is a compact utility for downloading news from www.google.com. At this writing, you may find you have to download and install Visual Basic component files from the GoogleGet web site before GoogleGet will run—but once it's running, it's straightforward to use.

iPod Library

iPod Library (freeware; home.btconnect.com/enduser/ipodlibrary) is a utility for dividing text files, HTML text files, and PDF files into note-sized sections and loading them on the iPod. At the time of writing, you may have to download and install extra Windows DLL (dynamic link library) files from the iPod Library web site in order to get iPod Library running.

12

Part IV

iPod Care: Advanced Topics and Troubleshooting

Chapter 13

Keep Your iPod or iPod mini in Good Working Shape

How to...

- Understand what your iPod or iPod mini consists of
- Get the maximum life possible from the battery
- Avoid doing things that make your iPod unhappy
- Keep your iPod's operating system up-to-date
- Carry and store your iPod safely
- Clean your iPod

This chapter covers how to keep your iPod or iPod mini in good working shape. It starts by discussing what your iPod contains, then moves along to tell you how to maximize battery life. From there, this chapter walks you through things that make your iPod unhappy; how to keep your iPod's operating system up-to-date; and how to carry, store, and clean your iPod.

As in earlier chapters, I'll use *iPod* to refer to all iPods, *regular iPods* to refer to full-size iPods, and *iPod mini* to refer to the iPod mini.

What You Might Want to Know About Your iPod's Internals

Unless your background is in consumer electronics, you probably don't need to know much detail about what's inside your iPod to appreciate the massive amount of songs it can store (or, if you have an iPod mini, the more modest number of songs) and the audio quality it delivers. But you'll find it helps to have a general idea of what your iPod contains and how it's constructed, because this knowledge can help you use your iPod more effectively and either head off or troubleshoot problems. (See Chapter 17 for a full discussion of troubleshooting your iPod.)

CAUTION   *Your iPod or iPod mini isn't user-upgradeable—in fact, it's designed to be opened only by trained technicians. If you're not such a technician, don't try to open your iPod: you're unlikely to achieve anything positive, and if your iPod is still under warranty, you'll void the warranty.*

Your iPod is based around a hard drive that takes up the bulk of the space inside the case. The hard drive in a regular iPod is similar to those used in the smaller portable PCs; the hard drive in an iPod mini is even smaller, and is similar to those used in consumer electronics such as the more ambitious mobile phones.

Some of the remaining space is occupied by a rechargeable battery that provides up to ten hours of playback. (Typically, third-generation iPods and the iPod mini manage more like eight hours.) The length of time the battery provides depends on how you use it (more on this in the following section). Like all rechargeable batteries, the iPod's battery gradually loses its capacity—but if your music collection grows, or if you find the iPod's nonmusic capabilities useful, you'll probably want to upgrade to a higher-capacity iPod, or even a higher-capacity iPod mini, in a couple of years anyway.

Your iPod includes a 32MB memory chip that's used for running the iPod's operating system and for caching music from the hard drive. The cache reads up to 20 minutes of data ahead from the hard drive for two purposes:

■ Once the cache has read the data, your iPod plays back the music from the cache rather than from the hard disk. This lets the hard disk *spin down* (stop running) until it's needed again. Because hard disks consume relatively large amounts of power, the caching spares the battery on your iPod and prolongs battery life.

NOTE   *After the hard disk has spun down, it takes a second or so to spin back up—so when you suddenly change the music during a playlist, there's a small delay while your iPod spins the disk up and then accesses the song you've demanded. If you listen closely (put your ear to your iPod), you can hear the disk spin up (there's a "whee" sound) and search (you'll hear the heads clicking).*

■ The hard disk can skip if you joggle or shake your iPod hard enough. If your iPod were playing back audio directly from the hard disk, such skipping would interrupt audio playback, much like bumping the needle on a turntable (or bumping a CD player, if you've tried that). But because the memory chip is solid state and has no moving parts, it's immune to skipping.

The length of time for which the caching provides audio depends on the compression ratio you're using and whether you're playing a playlist (or album) or individual songs. If you're playing a list of songs, your iPod can cache as many of the upcoming songs as it has available memory. But when you switch to another song or playlist, your iPod has to start caching once again. This caching involves spinning the hard disk up again and reading from it, which consumes battery power.

Your iPod's skip protection is impressive compared to some other hard disk–based digital audio players, some of which read directly from disk the whole time (and thus run down the battery very quickly). Compared to many portable CD players, your iPod's skip protection is amazing; even compared to solid-state players, which are essentially skip-proof because they contain no moving parts, the iPod's skip protection is very impressive.

Maximize Your iPod's Battery Life

Chapter 2's "Recharge Your iPod's Battery to Keep the Songs Coming" section ran you through the basics of recharging your iPod's battery. But if you're reading this chapter, you probably want to know how the battery works, what you can do to shoehorn in as much power as possible, and how you can squeeze out as much battery life as possible.

Your iPod's battery is a lithium polymer that's rated for 500 or more charging cycles. (A *charging cycle* is a full discharge—running the battery all the way down until it has no charge left—followed by a full charge.) Lithium polymer batteries have no memory effect, so you don't need to discharge them fully before recharging them. That means you can recharge your iPod at any time that's convenient.

13

NOTE Memory effect *is a phenomenon that occurs with older battery technologies. If you don't fully discharge a battery based on such a technology, when you start charging the battery, it may figure that it was fully discharged at that point after all. In other words, the battery resets its zero-charge level to the level at which you started charging it. By doing so, it squanders that part of its capacity that's below the new zero-charge level, and so reduces the amount of power it can provide.*

If you recharge your iPod's battery every other day, 500 charges should last you the best part of three years. If you recharge your iPod's battery less frequently than that, there's a good chance the battery will outlast the hard drive.

Don't Let the Battery Discharge Fully

To get the most life out of your battery, don't let it discharge fully. However little you use your iPod, recharge it fully at least once every three weeks to prevent the battery from going flat. This means if you go on vacation for a month, you should take your iPod with you and recharge it during that time. (But you were going to take your iPod with you on your vacation anyway, weren't you?)

Reduce Demands on the Battery

To get the longest possible playback time from your iPod, reduce the demand on the battery as much as possible. Here are three ways to do so:

- Play your music by album or by playlist rather than hopping from one track to another. Remember that your iPod can cache ahead on an album or playlist to minimize the time the hard disk is spinning. But when you ask your iPod to produce another track it hasn't cached, it has to spin up the hard disk and access the song.

- Use AAC files or MP3 files on your iPod rather than WAV file or AIFF files. Because they're uncompressed and therefore much bigger than compressed files, WAVs and AIFFs prevent your iPod from using its cache effectively, so the hard disk has to work much harder. This chews through battery life.

- Minimize your use of the backlight. It's anything but a searchlight, but even so, it uses up battery life that you'd probably rather spend on playing songs.

Understand Apple's Battery-Replacement Policy

Batteries have proved such a weak chink in the iPod's armor that Apple has reversed its initial policy of not replacing iPod batteries at all. At the time of writing, Apple will replace defective iPod batteries for free if the iPod is still under warranty, and for $99 (plus $6.95 shipping and handling) if the iPod is out of warranty—but only if neither you nor anyone else unqualified have messed with it. (If anyone *has* messed with your iPod, Apple reserves the right to refuse to repair it.) $99 is kinda steep, especially as you get only a 90-day warranty on the materials and workmanship, but it pales in comparison with the $249 that Apple charges for other repairs to the iPod. Many people figure that if you're paying that much, you might as well get a brand new iPod instead—and in case anyone asks for repairs without having that thought pop into their head, Apple staff have been known to suggest it to them unprompted.

CAUTION   *When you send in your iPod for battery replacement or any other repairs, Apple sends you back a different iPod, not your original one. If your iPod contains vital files, you'll lose them.*

If you're planning to use your iPod extensively, you might look at the battery as a potential Achilles heel and consider it worth buying the AppleCare Protection Plan for iPod. This plan extends the hardware coverage from one year to two years, extends telephone support from 90 days to two years, costs $59, and is not available to consumers in Florida. Given that many users report that their batteries have barely made it out of the warranty period before declining rapidly, buying AppleCare might be good insurance. You can buy AppleCare while your iPod is still under its original warranty.

Replace the Battery Yourself

If your iPod or iPod mini is out of warranty, you don't have AppleCare for it, and you're sure that you won't want to send the iPod to Apple for a battery replacement, you can find replacement batteries for less money elsewhere. (Make sure your iPod is out of warranty, because opening it voids the warranty.)

At this writing, Laptops for Less (www.ipodbattery.com) offers iPod batteries for $49, together with a delicate screwdriver and instructions for fitting the batteries yourself. PDASmart (www.pdasmart.com/ipodpartscenter.htm) offers a DIY battery kit for $59 and mail-in service for $68. ipodminibattery (www.ipodminibattery.com) offers batteries for second- and third-generation iPods for $49. As the iPod market matures and continues to expand, expect to see more companies offering replacement batteries and installation.

NOTE   *The first- and second-generation iPods use different batteries from the third-generation iPods. The iPod mini uses a smaller battery. When ordering a replacement battery, get the right type for your iPod.*

13

Understand What Makes Your iPod Unhappy

This section discusses four items that are likely to make your iPod unhappy: unexpected disconnections, fire and water (discussed together), and punishment. None of these should come as a surprise, and you should be able to avoid all of them most of the time.

Disconnecting Your iPod at the Wrong Time

If you've ever performed a successful synchronization with your iPod, you'll know the drill for disconnecting your iPod from its FireWire cable or USB cable: Wait until your iPod has stopped displaying the *Do not disconnect* message and is showing the *OK to disconnect* message. Then—and not before—you can safely unplug the cable.

The main danger in disconnecting your iPod from the FireWire cable at the wrong time is that you may interrupt data transfer and thus corrupt one or more files. Typically, you'll know when data is being transferred, because iTunes displays status information and progress messages as it updates your iPod and transfers data to it. Similarly, if you're using your iPod in disk mode, you'll know when you're copying or moving data to it, because you'll have instigated the copy or move operation. Where you're more likely to trip up is when you open various files from the iPod in different applications, work with the files, and perhaps hide some of the applications without closing the files.

In theory, you could scramble the data on your iPod's hard drive badly enough that you'd need to restore your iPod before you could use it. A restoration would lose any data on the iPod that you didn't have on your computer—so a badly timed disconnection could cost you valuable data.

In practice, however, disconnecting your iPod during data transfer is likely to corrupt only those files actually being transferred at the moment you break the connection. If those files are valuable, and if you're moving them to your iPod rather than copying them, corrupting them could cause you problems. But in most cases, you won't need to restore your iPod.

Disconnecting the cable without warning when no data is being transferred should do nothing worse than annoy your computer. If you disconnect your iPod from your Mac at the wrong time, your Mac displays the following warning dialog box, telling you that you should have ejected it properly and that data may have been lost or damaged. Bow your head in contrition, and then click the OK button:

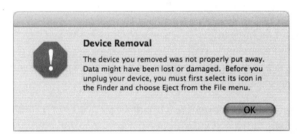

At the time of writing, iTunes for Windows doesn't notice if you disconnect an iPod when it's telling you not to. If you find your iPod's entry is showing up in the Source pane in iTunes for Windows long after the iPod has bolted, shut the stable door by right-clicking the iPod's entry in the Source pane and choosing Eject iPod from the shortcut menu.

After an unexpected disconnection, your iPod simply figures out there's a problem, dusts itself down, and displays its main screen.

Your iPod Doesn't Like Fire or Water

Apple reckons iPods work at temperatures of up to 158 degrees Fahrenheit (70 degrees Celsius). You're unlikely to endure temperatures this high voluntarily (unless you're in a sauna or steam room), so scratch any plans you may have had for using your iPod in such locations. The danger is more that you'll leave your iPod in a confined space, such as the glove box of a car parked in the sun, which might reach searing temperatures. If you live in sunny climes, take your iPod with you when you get out of the car.

CAUTION *If your iPod gets much too hot or much too cold, don't use it. Give it time to return to a more normal temperature before trying to find out if it still works.*

Further, your iPod isn't waterproof, so don't expect to use it for swimming or in the bath. You can get various water-resistant cases for iPods (see Chapter 15), but they're all intended to keep out rain and splashes rather than to go deep-sea diving.

Your iPod Isn't Indestructible

Apple has built the iPod to be tough, so it'll survive an impressive amount of rough handling. Macworld columnist Chris Breen has written about how he eventually destroyed an iPod by dropping it from a bicycle traveling at 30 mph. (This was after the iPod survived a 25-mph drop from the bicycle, a drop while jogging, and a stationary drop from waist height—each of which caused some damage to the iPod and probably weakened it.) Even the diminutive iPod mini is strongly built.

I haven't destroyed an iPod for your edification (or mine) but have no doubt that I could do so if I needed to. Running the iPod over with a Hummer, hitting it squarely with an eight-pound sledgehammer, or playing Sinatra uninterrupted for a couple of days should do the trick. In the meantime, my three iPods have traveled the equivalent of halfway around the world and taken a few falls that would have damaged me, so I reckon they're doing pretty well. My iPod mini has yet to take any punishment.

Keep Your iPod's Operating System Up-to-Date

To get the best performance from your iPod, it's a good idea to keep its operating system (or *firmware*) up-to-date. To do so, follow the instructions in this section to update your iPod on Mac OS X or Windows.

But before you start, here's one thing you must be clear on: the first- and second-generation iPods use different iPod software (versions 1.*x*) from the third-generation iPods (versions 2.*x*), and the iPod mini uses a different version yet (iPod mini versions 1.*x*). When updating your iPod or iPod mini, you must get the right version of Updater for it. Apple makes the iPod Software Updaters smart enough not to let you install the wrong version of firmware on an iPod, but you can give yourself a short course in frustration by trying to do so. If the iPod Software Updater keeps telling you to "plug in an iPod to update it" even after iTunes is showing the iPod to be connected, you may be using the wrong iPod Software Updater.

Update Your iPod on Mac OS X

The easiest way to update your iPod on Mac OS X is to use the Software Update feature: Choose Apple | System Preferences, click the Software Update icon, and then click the Check Now button to check for updates. Mac OS X checks for iPod updates along with all other updates and presents them to you in the Software Update dialog box. Figure 13-1 shows an example of an iPod Software update.

13

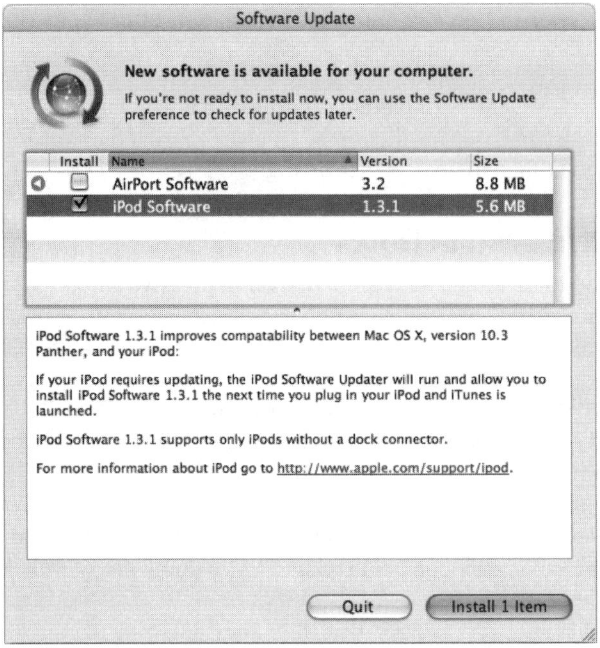

FIGURE 13-1 Use Mac OS X's Software Update feature to keep your iPod's software up-to-date.

Click the Install button (it's called Install 1 Item, Install 2 Items, and so on, depending on how many updates you're installing) to proceed. You'll need to authenticate yourself by entering an administrative password in the Authenticate dialog box to show the installer that you have authority to install the software. Mac OS X then downloads the update and installs it to your Utilities folder.

NOTE *If you choose not to use Software Update, you can download the Updater from the Apple Software Downloads web site (www.apple.com/swupdates/). Double-click the disk-image file to mount the disk image, double-click the disk image to display its contents in a Finder window, double-click the iPod Software Updater folder to display its contents in the Finder window, and then double-click the iPod.pkg file to open it. Follow through the resulting installation routine.*

After downloading and installing the update, you need to apply it to your iPod. iTunes may prompt you to apply the update automatically, but usually you'll have to apply it manually. To do so, follow these steps:

1. Connect your iPod to your Mac via the FireWire cable.

2. With the Finder active, press COMMAND-SHIFT-U or choose Go | Utilities to open a Finder window to your Utilities folder.

3. Double-click the folder that contains the Updater that you downloaded. (The folder will be named iPod Software *N.N* Updater, where *N.N* is a number such as 2.1 or 1.3.1.)

4. Double-click the iPod Software Updater icon to launch the iPod Software Updater:

5. When the iPod Software Updater notices your iPod, it displays its details:

6. Check that the Software Version readout says "needs update."

7. Click the lock icon to display the Authenticate dialog box:

8. Enter your password and click the OK button. The iPod Software Updater makes the Update and Restore buttons available:

 If the Update button remains unavailable, your iPod doesn't need this update. Either the iPod's firmware is already up-to-date or you're trying to use the wrong iPod Software Updater.

9. Click the Update button and wait for the update to take place.

At this point, the current version of the iPod Software Updater switches to telling you to "plug in an iPod to update it" while the iPod itself performs the update. Wait for a minute or two, and then your iPod should reestablish communication with the iPod Software Updater.

If you're updating a first- or second-generation iPod, you have to unplug it at this point, wait a few seconds, and then plug it back in. The iPod Software Updater tells you when to unplug your iPod, and the iPod itself tells you when to plug it back in.

10. When the iPod Software Updater displays the details about your iPod again, check that the Software Version readout says "up to date," as shown here:

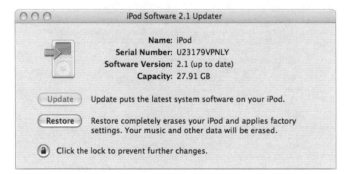

11. Press COMMAND-Q or choose iPod Updater | Quit iPod Updater to quit the iPod Software Updater.

12. At this point, iTunes should display the iPod Setup Assistant page:

In some cases, you may need to quit iTunes and restart it to force it to detect the iPod.

13. Enter the name for your iPod in the The Name Of My iPod Is text box.

14. Choose whether to clear the Automatically Update My iPod check box or leave it selected.

15. Click the Done button to close the iPod Setup Assistant. If you left the Automatically Update My iPod check box selected, iTunes then synchronizes your iPod.

Update Your iPod on Windows

Apple hasn't yet managed to insinuate iPod software updates into Microsoft's Windows Update process, but iTunes does check for updates, and displays a message box such as that shown here if it finds an update. (You can also force a check by choosing Help | Check For iTunes Updates in iTunes.) Click the Run Updater button to run the updater.

13

Alternatively, you may prefer to check for and download updates manually from the Apple Software Downloads web site (www.apple.com/swupdates/). Double-click the distribution file to launch the setup routine, and then follow through the installation process. Then choose Start | All Programs | iPod | System Software | Updater to run the iPod Software Updater.

Whichever way you run the iPod Software Updater, it looks like this:

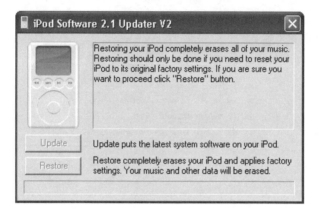

Click the Update button to update your iPod's software. If you're using a FireWire cable for synchronizing a third-generation or later iPod with iTunes on Windows, the iPod Software Updater and your iPod take care of the rest of the update between them.

If you're using a USB cable, the iPod Software Updater then displays the following iPod Updater dialog box, asking you to disconnect your iPod from your PC and connect it to the external power supply to allow the iPod's firmware (the programs stored in your iPod's read-only memory) to be reflashed:

Disconnect your iPod from the FireWire cable or USB cable, suppress the temptation to shout "Clear!" in the best medical-TV tradition, and plug the iPod into the iPod Power Adapter. The power adapter applies current that wakes up your iPod, which then applies the update to its firmware. (This is called *reflashing*. Put images of men in raincoats from your mind.) You'll see a progress bar crawl across the screen as the reflash happens. When your iPod reboots itself and displays the Apple logo, disconnect it from the iPod Power Adapter and connect it to your PC again.

After you plug your iPod back in, the iPod launches or activates iTunes.

How to ... Restore Your iPod to an Earlier Version of the iPod Software on Windows

If you install an update that produces an effect you don't like, you can run an earlier Updater again to restore your Windows iPod to the previous version of the iPod software—provided that you have a copy of the earlier Updater.

Sometimes, a new Updater that you install overwrites its predecessor automatically, presumably to spare you the indignity of installing an older version of the iPod software by mistake. Similarly, Apple tends to remove older updaters from the Apple Software Downloads web site to encourage people to download the latest versions. For this reason, it's a good idea to keep copies of the Updaters that you download in case you need them again.

Apple has designed the Mac Updaters to refuse to overwrite their successors, so you can't use this method to restore a Mac iPod to an earlier version of the software.

NOTE   *Typically, a "Can't lock iPod" message indicates that another application is trying to access the iPod while the iPod Software Updater is attempting to update it. Make sure that iTunes and MUSICMATCH Jukebox Plus (if you're using it) are closed. Also close any Windows Explorer windows that are displaying My Computer (because these will show the iPod as a removable drive) and any Windows Explorer windows that are open to the drive letter representing the iPod.*

Carry and Store Your iPod Safely

Carrying and storing your iPod safely is largely a matter of common sense.

■ Use a case to protect your iPod from scratches, dings, and falls. The more expensive models of the regular iPod include a sturdy case that offers good protection. You can buy a wide variety of other cases, from svelte-and-stretchy little numbers designed to hug your body during vigorous exercise, to armored cases apparently intended to survive Schwarzenegger movies, to waterproof cases good enough to take sailing. See "Cases," in Chapter 15, for more information on cases.

■ If your iPod spends time on your desk or another surface open to children, animals, or moving objects, use the iPod Dock to keep it in place. If your iPod doesn't have an iPod Dock, or if you live in a truly active environment, consider investing in a stand to keep it in place. A stand should also make your iPod easier to control with one hand. For example, if you patch your iPod into your stereo, you might use a stand to keep it upright so you could push its buttons with one hand. Some stands can also supply power via your iPod's FireWire cable. See "Stands, Docks, and Mounting Kits" in Chapter 15, for more information on stands.

13

Clean Your iPod

To keep your iPod looking its best, you'll probably need to clean it from time to time. Before doing so, unplug it to reduce the chance of short disagreements with the basic principles of electricity. If it's a second-generation iPod, close the cover of the FireWire port to help avoid getting liquid in the port.

Various people recommend different cleaning products for cleaning iPods. You'll find various recommendations on the Web—but unless you're sure the people know what they're talking about, proceed with great care. In particular, avoid any abrasive cleaner that may mar your iPod's acrylic faceplate or its polished back and sides.

Unless you've dipped your iPod in anything very unpleasant, you'll do best to start with Apple's recommendation: simply dampen a soft, lint-free cloth (such as an eyeglass or camera-lens cloth) and wipe your iPod gently with it.

But if you've scratched your iPod, you may need to resort to heavier duty cleaners. I've read good reports of the Novus plastic polishes (www.oldphones.com/novus.html) and the Nu-Life polishing kit (which includes a cleaner/polish solution and a scratch remover/surface restorer solution, and is available from various sources), though I can't vouch for either.

Chapter 14

Use Your iPod or iPod mini As a Hard Drive

How to...

- Decide whether or not to use your iPod or iPod mini as a hard drive
- Enable disk mode on your iPod using a Mac
- Enable disk mode on your iPod using Windows
- Transfer files to and from your iPod
- Start up your Mac from your iPod
- Back up your iPod so you don't lose your music or data
- Optimize your iPod's hard disk to improve performance

Apple sells iPods primarily as portable music players—and, as you know by now, they're arguably the best portable music players around. But, as you also know by now, an iPod or iPod mini is essentially an external FireWire or USB hard drive with sophisticated audio features. This chapter shows you how to use your iPod or iPod mini as a hard drive for backup and portable storage. If your computer is a Mac, you can even boot from your iPod (but not from an iPod mini) for security or to recover from disaster.

NOTE   *One hard-drive feature this chapter* doesn't *show you is how to transfer song files from your iPod's music database onto your computer. "Transfer Song Files from Your iPod's Music Library to Your Computer," in Chapter 16, covers this subject.*

Why Use Your iPod As a Hard Drive?

If all you want from your iPod is huge amounts (or, if it's an iPod mini, more modest amounts) of music to go, you may never want to use your iPod as a hard drive. Even so, briefly consider why you might want to do so:

- Your iPod provides a great combination of portability and high capacity. You can get smaller portable-storage devices (for example, CompactFlash drives, Smart Media cards, and Memory Sticks), but they're expensive and have much lower capacities.

- You can take all your documents with you. For example, you could take home that large PowerPoint presentation you need to get ready for tomorrow. You could even put several gigabytes of video files on your iPod if you needed to take them with you (for example, to a studio for editing) or transfer them to another computer.

- You can use your iPod for backup. If you keep your vital documents down to a size you can easily fit on your iPod (and still have plenty of room left for music), you can quickly back up the documents and take the backup with you wherever you go.

- You can use your iPod for security. By keeping your documents on your iPod rather than on your computer, and by keeping your iPod with you, you can prevent other people from accessing your documents. If your computer is a Mac (and if it's the right kind of Mac—more on this later), you can even boot your Mac from a regular iPod, thus preventing anyone else from using your computer at all.

The disadvantages to using your iPod as a hard disk are straightforward:

- Whatever space you use on your iPod for storing non-music files isn't available for music. This disadvantage is particularly acute on an iPod mini because of its smaller capacity.

- If you lose or break your iPod, any files stored only on it will be gone forever.

Enable Disk Mode

To use your iPod as a hard drive, you need to enable disk mode. (Disk mode used to be called "FireWire disk mode" in the days before iPods learned to connect to PCs via USB as well as FireWire.) In disk mode, your computer uses your iPod as an external hard disk. You can copy to your iPod any files and folders that will fit on it.

NOTE   *You can copy song files and playlists to your iPod in disk mode, but you won't be able to play them on the iPod. This is because when you copy the files, their information isn't added to the iPod's database the way it's added by iTunes and other applications (for example, EphPod or XPlay) designed to work with the iPod. So your iPod's interface doesn't know the files are there, and you can't play them.*

Did you know?

iPods Have Been Used to Steal Software

iPods have been used to steal software from stores. For example, enterprising thieves have plugged iPods into Macs in computer stores such as CompUSA and copied application software (such as Microsoft Office) from the Mac onto the iPod.

This approach usually works only on the Mac. This is because software installations on Windows not only typically place files in multiple folders (as opposed to a single folder on the Mac), but they also rely on system files installed by the installation routine.

Of course, stealing software like this is horribly illegal. But you can use the same technique legally to move an application from one Mac to another if you don't have a means of connecting them. For example, if you scratch your Microsoft Office CD so it won't work in a CD drive anymore, and you need to migrate to a new Mac, you might need an alternative means of transferring Office from your old Mac to your new one. (Yes, this is a stretch, but such emergencies do occur.) More likely, you might copy your Microsoft Office installation to your iPod so you could restore it easily if the copy on your hard drive became corrupted when you were on the road without your Office CD.

14

From the computer's point of view, a FireWire hard disk works in essentially the same way as any other disk. The differences are that the disk

- is external.

- may draw power along the FireWire cable (as the iPod and iPod mini do) rather than being powered itself (as high-capacity and high-performance external disks tend to be).

When you use your iPod as a FireWire disk, it draws power from the computer provided that the FireWire controller and FireWire cable supply power. If the controller doesn't supply power (for example, because it's a PC Card controller and can't muster the required wattage), or if the cable can't transmit the power (for example, because it's a four-pin cable rather than a six-pin cable), your iPod has to rely on its battery power. If you need to use your iPod extensively with a four-pin cable, buy a third-party add-on that delivers power through a sleeve that you attach where the four-pin cable connects to the iPod's six-pin cable.

CAUTION *Using your iPod as an external disk with a controller or cable that can't supply power may run down the battery quickly. Bear in mind that your iPod can't use its caching capabilities when you use it as an external disk. (Caching works only for playlists and albums, when your iPod knows which files are needed next and so can read them into the cache.) If your iPod isn't receiving power, check the battery status periodically to make sure your iPod doesn't suddenly run out of power.*

Much the same goes for a USB hard disk, except that USB's lower power specifications don't usually deliver enough power to drive a demanding peripheral such as a hard disk—even such an economical one as a regular iPod—or a CD drive. So if you're using a regular iPod as an external disk connected to your PC via USB, be sure to plug the FireWire end of the V-shaped cable into a power source so that you don't run down your iPod's battery.

In this area, the iPod mini outdoes the regular iPod. Because the tiny hard disk in the iPod mini is very frugal in its power consumption, you can both drive it and recharge it via USB. The disadvantage of using the iPod mini like this is that its lower capacity makes it that much less useful as an external disk than a regular iPod.

Enable Disk Mode on Your iPod Using a Mac

To enable disk mode on your iPod using a Mac, follow these steps:

1. Connect your iPod to your Mac via the FireWire cable.

2. Launch iTunes (for example, click the iTunes icon in the dock) if iTunes doesn't launch automatically.

3. In the Source pane, select the icon for your iPod.

4. Click the Display Options For Player button, in the lower-right corner of the iTunes window, to display the iPod Preferences dialog box.

5. Select the Enable Disk Use check box. iTunes displays the following warning dialog box, telling you that using disk mode requires you to unmount the iPod manually before each disconnect, even when synchronizing songs (instead of being able to have iTunes unmount the iPod automatically):

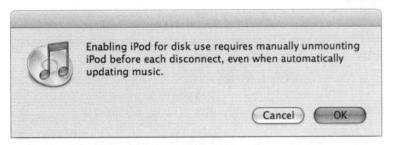

6. Click the OK button if you can live with this limitation. Otherwise, click the Cancel button to cancel your use of disk mode.

7. If you clicked the OK button in the warning dialog box, click the OK button again in the iPod Preferences dialog box to close it. If you clicked the Cancel button in the warning dialog box, click the Cancel button in the iPod Preferences dialog box to dismiss it.

Once you've enabled disk mode on your iPod, you'll need to unmount your iPod manually after synchronizing your music library or transferring files to or from your iPod. To unmount your iPod, take any of the following actions:

■ In the Source pane in iTunes, select the icon for your iPod, and then click the Eject iPod button in the lower-right corner of the iTunes window.

■ In the Source pane in iTunes, right-click the icon for your iPod, and then choose Eject *iPod,* where *iPod* is the name assigned to your iPod.

■ Select the icon for your iPod on the desktop, and then issue an Eject command from the File menu or the shortcut menu. (Alternatively, press COMMAND-E.)

■ Drag the desktop icon for your iPod to the Trash.

When your iPod displays the *OK to disconnect* message, you can safely disconnect it.

Enable Disk Mode on Your iPod Using Windows

To use your iPod as an external hard disk on a PC, you need to enable disk mode—in theory, at least. In practice, you may find you don't need to enable disk mode to use your iPod with your PC. On the PCs I've used with Windows XP and Windows 2000 Professional, Windows Explorer

14

always assigns the iPod a drive letter even when it's *not* in disk mode. But you may find that your iPod behaves differently with your PC—or you may choose to explicitly enable disk mode in any case. (Enabling disk mode certainly won't do any harm.)

To enable disk mode on the PC, follow these steps:

1. Connect your iPod to your PC as usual.

2. Launch iTunes if it doesn't launch automatically.

3. In the Source pane, select the icon for your iPod.

4. Click the Display Options For Player button, in the lower-right corner of the iTunes window, to display the iPod Preferences dialog box.

5. Select the Enable Disk Use check box. iTunes displays the following warning dialog box, telling you that using disk mode requires you to manually unmount the iPod before each disconnect, even when you're automatically updating music:

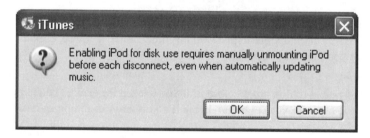

6. Click the OK button. iTunes returns you to the iPod Preferences dialog box.

7. Click the OK button to close the iPod Preferences dialog box.

Once you've enabled disk mode, your iPod appears to Windows Explorer as a removable hard drive (if it wasn't appearing as a removable hard drive already). Windows Explorer automatically assigns a drive letter to the drive, so you can access it as you would any other drive connected to your computer.

To eject your iPod, take any of the following actions:

■ In the Source pane in iTunes, select the icon for your iPod, and then click the Eject iPod button in the lower-right corner of the iTunes window.

■ In the Source pane in iTunes, right-click the icon for your iPod, and then choose Eject *iPod,* where *iPod* is the name assigned to your iPod.

■ Choose Start | My Computer to open a Windows Explorer window to My Computer view, right-click the icon for your iPod, and choose Eject from the shortcut menu to eject it.

When your iPod displays the *OK to disconnect* message, you can safely disconnect it.

How to ... **Force Disk Mode**

If your FireWire or USB port is unpowered (or underpowered), you may need to force your iPod to enter disk mode. To do so, follow these steps:

1. Connect your iPod to the FireWire cable or USB cable.

2. Hold down the Menu button and the Play button on your iPod for about five seconds to reboot your iPod. (For an iPod mini, toggle the Hold switch on and off, then hold down the Select and Menu buttons for about five seconds.)

3. When your iPod displays the Apple logo, hold down the Previous button and Next button briefly. Your iPod sends the computer an electronic prod that forces the computer to recognize it.

Transfer Files to and from Your iPod

When your iPod is in disk mode, you can transfer files to it by using the Finder (on the Mac), Windows Explorer (on Windows), or another file-management application of your choice. (You can transfer files by using the command prompt, if you so choose.)

CAUTION *If your iPod appears in the My Computer window as a drive named Removable Drive, and Windows Explorer claims the disk isn't formatted, chances are you've connected a Mac-formatted iPod to your PC. Windows Explorer can't read the HFS Plus disk format that Mac iPods use, so the iPod appears to be unformatted. (HFS Plus is one of the disk formats Mac OS X can use. HFS Plus is also called the Mac OS Extended format.) To use the iPod with Windows, you'll need to restore it; see the section "Restore Your iPod," in Chapter 17.*

You can create and delete folders on your iPod as you would any other drive. But be sure you don't mess with the iPod's system folders, such as the Calendars folder, the Contacts folder, and the iPod_Control folder.

NOTE *As mentioned earlier, don't transfer music files to your iPod by using file-management software if you want to be able to play the files on your iPod. Unless you transfer the files by using iTunes or another application designed to access the iPod's music database, the details about the files won't be added to the iPod. You won't be able to play those files on your iPod because their data hasn't been added to its database of contents.*

The exception to transferring files from your iPod is transferring song files that you've put on your iPod by using iTunes or another application that can access the iPod's music database. The section "Transfer Song Files from Your iPod's Music Library to Your Computer," in Chapter 16, shows you how to do this.

14

Start Up Your Mac from Your iPod

You can start up, or *boot,* your Mac from your iPod by turning a regular iPod into a bootable FireWire disk. See the special project "Start Up Your Mac from Your iPod" for details.

Back Up Your iPod So You Don't Lose Your Music or Data

If you synchronize your complete music library with your iPod, and perhaps load your contacts and some calendar information on your iPod as well, you shouldn't need to worry about backing up your iPod. That's because your computer contains all the data that's on your iPod. (Effectively, your iPod is a backup of part of your hard disk.) So if you lose your iPod, or it stops functioning, you won't lose any data you don't have on your computer.

If your computer's hard disk goes south, you might need to recover your music library, contacts, and calendar data from your iPod onto another computer or a new hard disk. You can transfer contacts and calendar data by enabling disk mode and using the Finder (Mac) or Windows Explorer (PC) to access the contents of the Contacts folder and the Calendars folder. For instructions on recovering song files from your iPod, see the section "Transfer Song Files from Your iPod's Music Library to Your Computer," in Chapter 16.

So, normally, your iPod will be the vulnerable member of the tag team. But if you store files directly on your iPod, you should back them up to your computer to make sure you don't lose them if your iPod vanishes or its hard disk gives up the ghost.

To back up files, either use a file-management utility (for example, the Finder or Windows Explorer) to simply copy the files or folders to your computer, or use custom backup software to create a more formal backup. For example, you might use the Backup Utility included with Windows XP (Start | All Programs | Accessories | System Tools | Backup) to back up your Windows iPod. On Mac OS X, you might use the Backup application to back up your files to your .Mac iDisk (which you can access via any Internet connection), use iDisk Utility to mount your .Mac iDisk via WebDAV (a protocol for transferring information to web servers), or use a commercial alternative such as Dantz Retrospect (www.dantz.com).

Optimize Your iPod's Hard Disk to Improve Performance

If you've been using a Windows computer for a while, you'll know you need to optimize your computer's hard disk every now and again to keep it performing well. This is because each file of any size beyond the smallest files occupies multiple clusters of the sectors into which a hard disk is divided. If the clusters are close to one another, the hard disk's read head can read the clusters without needing to travel back and forth unnecessarily across the disk. But if the clusters are spread out all over the disk, the read head needs to travel farther to do the reading. Traveling farther makes the reading take longer.

Ideally, of course, your operating system writes each file into a nice, neat series of contiguous clusters, the sun shines, and you don't get parking tickets when you overstay your welcome in a tightly patrolled area. But when your hard disk grows full, your operating system is forced to break files across whichever clusters are available on the disk rather than being able to put them all together. The disk's read head has to travel farther, and so reads take longer; fog settles or snow falls; and you get parking tickets or a free Denver boot.

Breaking files across various clusters is called *fragmentation.* To reduce fragmentation and improve performance, you can *defragment* (or *defrag*) a drive. The defragmentation utility rearranges and rewrites the data so that files are written onto contiguous clusters wherever possible. As a result, your disk's read head can access any given file more quickly and with less effort, performance improves, and the sun clears the fog so you see the traffic warden coming in time to move your car.

Apple takes a relatively robust view of fragmentation, stating "the file system used on Macintosh computers is designed to work with a certain degree of fragmentation.... You should not need to frequently defragment the computer's hard disk." But even Apple concedes that "if you create

How to ...   Decide Whether to Defragment Your iPod

If you're not using your iPod as a hard drive, you may not need to defragment it at all. This is for a couple of reasons.

First, under normal use, your iPod's hard disk won't become fragmented quickly or to a severe degree. What will typically happen is that you'll load a relatively large number of song files at first, and then gradually add to them, perhaps removing those you don't like. The files for your contacts, calendars, notes, and so on may change more frequently than your music files, but typically these text files will be fairly small. But if you're loading an iPod mini (or a regular iPod) with frequently changing playlists (rather than your entire music library), or if you manage your music manually and often change your songs, its hard disk may become fragmented.

Second, when you're using your iPod only for music, contacts, and calendars, you won't necessarily need the ultimate performance that its hard drive can deliver. Performance is more important when you're using your iPod as an external disk. However, having your song files defragmented may help you squeeze a little more playing time out of your iPod's battery, so this may give you the motive to defragment it.

On the other hand, if you use your iPod extensively as a hard drive, it may become fragmented relatively quickly. If this happens, defragmenting it is a good idea.

14

and delete a large number of files, your hard disk may become fragmented to the point that you may see a slight slow-down of file system performance."

Interestingly enough (or trivially enough, depending on your point of view), this line of Apple's is very close to what Microsoft used to claim in the early days of its Windows NT operating system: essentially, the file system didn't get fragmented—or, if it did, the fragmentation didn't really matter. Reality subsequently intruded on this vision of a maintenance-free file system to such an extent that Windows XP (which is based on Windows NT) includes a Disk Defragmenter, which Microsoft recommends you run regularly to keep your disks in good shape.

This little history lesson might lead you to suspect that defragmenting Mac drives would be a good idea as well—and most people agree that it is. Apple doesn't specifically recommend any single defragmentation utility, but most people find that utilities such as Norton Utilities for the Mac's Speed Disk from Symantec Corporation (www.norton.com) or PlusOptimizer from Alsoft, Inc., (www.alsoft.com) get the job done.

Defragmenting utilities reshuffle the files on your hard disk so that files are stored on contiguous clusters wherever possible. Depending on the efficiency of the defragmenter, you may need to run it twice or more to get the files arranged as well as possible.

CAUTION *Before defragmenting a drive, it's always a good idea to back up the data on it just in case anything goes wrong. (And it's a good idea to back up your data regularly in any case.) It's especially important to back up your data if you decide to defragment all your drives at once, including your iPod. If your iPod contains a partial backup of your hard disk, it's a much better idea to defragment them separately (in case you need to recover files from one to the other) than to defragment them at the same time.*

Run the Windows XP Disk Defragmenter

To run the Disk Defragmenter included with Windows XP, choose Start | All Programs | Accessories | System Tools | Disk Defragmenter. Alternatively, follow these steps:

1. Choose Start | My Computer to open a My Computer window.

2. In the Devices With Removable Storage area, right-click the drive that represents your iPod, and then choose Properties from the shortcut menu to display the Properties dialog box.

3. Click the Tools tab to display it.

4. Click the Defragment Now button to display the Disk Defragmenter window (Figure 14-1).

The Disk Defragmenter utility is straightforward to use. You select the drive you want to defragment, and then click the Analyze button to analyze it or the Defragment button to defragment it. If you click the Analyze button, Disk Defragmenter displays a summary of the state of the drive and tells you whether or not you need to defragment it.

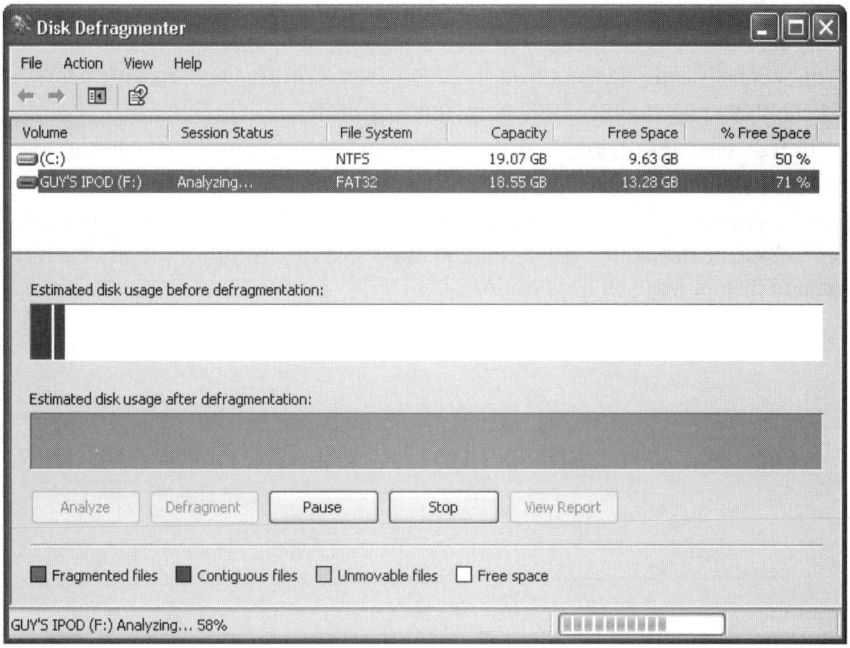

FIGURE 14-1   You can use the Disk Defragmenter utility included with Windows XP to defragment your iPod.

Defragment Your iPod or iPod mini the Cheap and Easy Way

If you prefer not to pay for a defragmenter for your Mac, you don't need to: you can defragment your iPod easily by moving all the files off it, optionally reformatting it, and then putting the files back on it. When you put the files back on your iPod, they're written in contiguous clusters as much as possible.

> **NOTE**   *You can defragment your iPod by using this technique on Windows, as well. In many cases, it's a toss-up whether to use this technique or to use Disk Defragmenter. Your decision will probably depend on exactly which files you store on your iPod and how difficult it would be to replace them after restoring your iPod.*

The cleanest way to perform defragmentation this way is to restore your iPod's operating system (as described in "Restore Your iPod," in Chapter 17) and then synchronize your iPod with your computer. Restoring the iPod removes all the files, leaving the disk in great shape. This synchronization will take much longer than normal synchronizations because your computer will have to transfer every file to your iPod.

14

Before you defragment your iPod in this way, make sure you have a copy of all the files on it:

■ If your iPod contains only a copy of your iTunes music library and synchronized copies of your contacts and calendars, you shouldn't need to worry about making copies of the files—your computer already contains copies of them.

■ If your iPod contains files other than your iTunes music library, your contacts, and your calendars, you may need to copy them to (or back them up to) your computer.

■ If you've installed Mac OS X or System 9 on your iPod, don't restore your iPod unless you want to lose the operating system. Instead, move the files from your iPod to a different disk, and then move them back again.

Chapter 15

Enhance Your iPod or iPod mini with Accessories

How to...

- Select alternative cases for your iPod or iPod mini
- Learn about power adapters and car adapters for your iPod
- Investigate headphone accessories for your iPod
- Choose iPod stands
- Learn about strange accessories you might possibly want
- Connect your iPod to your home stereo or car stereo

Like many a consumer product that's been a runaway success, the iPod has spawned a huge market for accessories—from cases to stands, from microphones for input to speakers for output, from handbags to a custom jacket. (That's a jacket for the iPod user, not for the iPod itself.)

Some of these accessories are widely useful (although you may not need any of them yourself). Others are niche products, to put it kindly. Others are—well, weird. Sure, you *could* figure out a way to use them, but would you want to buy them?

This chapter discusses the major categories of accessories (leaving you to choose the types that you need) and highlights some of the less obvious and more innovative accessories that you might want to know about for special needs.

NOTE   *For some types of accessories, such as power adapters and cassette adapters, you don't need to restrict your horizons to iPod-specific accessories—you can choose generic accessories as well. Often, generic accessories are substantially less expensive than custom accessories, give you much more flexibility, or both. So this chapter mentions generic accessories as well as custom accessories where appropriate.*

Cases

Your iPod is built to be carried, so it's hardly surprising that a wide variety of cases has been developed for iPods—everything from bifold cases to armband cases to armored cases and waterproof cases.

Many people find the case that comes with most of the regular iPod models to be fine and functional for everyday use; it attaches firmly to a belt or a stiff waistband, and it keeps your iPod securely in place unless you undertake extreme activity (for example, skateboard stunts or gymnastics) or attempt to renegotiate your relationship with gravity. The case is open at the top and so lets you access your iPod's FireWire port, headphone socket, and Hold switch. It doesn't let you access your iPod's front-panel controls, but the remote control included with many iPods duplicates the key functions of the front-panel controls for playing music, so you don't need to use the front-panel controls once you've started playing an album or playlist.

The iPod mini doesn't include a case. Instead, it includes a plastic belt clip that snaps onto the player and holds it firmly to your belt, exposing it proudly to the world and to damage. To keep your iPod mini pristine, you may well choose to invest in a case.

Choosing an iPod case is as fiercely personal a choice as choosing comfortable underwear or a car. Different aspects of cases are important to different people, and while one size (read: the standard iPod case) may suit many, it doesn't fit all. As with underwear (or a car), you may prefer not to use a case at all—but your iPod's shiny surfaces will tend to get scratched, and you'll need to be careful not to drop your iPod onto any unforgiving surface.

But as with underwear (and, to a lesser extent, a car), one point is vital: to make sure the case you choose is the right size for the model of iPod you have. Obviously, the iPod mini has significantly different dimensions than the regular iPod, and the third-generation iPods have a slimmer design than the first- and second-generation iPods—but even same-generation iPods of different capacities have different dimensions from each other. So if you put a second-generation 10GB iPod in a second-generation 20GB case, it may rattle around a bit (depending on the design of the case). If you try to stuff that second-generation 20GB iPod in a skintight second-generation 10GB case, the iPod or the case will probably become unhappy. (And you may too.)

Beyond getting the size right, the remaining choices are yours. The following paragraphs summarize the key ways in which the cases differ. You get to decide which points are important for you.

- ■ **How the case attaches to you (if at all)**   Many cases attach to your belt, while some hook onto a lanyard that goes around your neck or a strap that goes over your shoulder (for example, the DLO Podsling). Still others attach to an armband, which some people find better for performing vigorous activities. (Other people find a regular iPod a little heavy for wearing on an arm.) Some cases come with a variety of attachments—for example, a belt clip and an armband, or a mounting for sticking your iPod to a flat surface. Other cases are simply protective, designed to be carried in a pocket or a bag.

NOTE *Examples of armband cases include the Action Jacket from Netalogic, Inc. ($29.99; www. everythingipod.com). The Action Jacket is made of thick neoprene with holes that let you see the screen and access the front-panel controls. It attaches to either a belt clip or an armband.*

- ■ **The amount of protection the case provides**   In general, the more protection a case provides, the larger and uglier it is, the more it weighs, and the more it costs. Balance your need for style against your iPod's need for protection for when gravity gets the better of your grip.

TIP *If you have a rugged lifestyle and want your iPod to share it, consider the iPod Armor case from Matias Corporation ($49.95; halfkeyboard.com/ipodarmor/index.php). The iPod Armor cradles your iPod in a full metal jacket made of anodized aluminum padded with open-cell EVA foam. If you land on this case, you're more likely to damage yourself than your iPod.*

- ■ **Whether or not the case is waterproof**   If you plan to take your iPod outdoors for exercise, you may want to get a case that's water-resistant or waterproof. Alternatively, carry a sturdy plastic bag in your pocket for weather emergencies. Either way, it's a good idea to protect the Dock Connector port with its plug.

15

- **Whether or not the case lets you access your iPod's controls**   On the face of it, access to the controls might seem a compelling feature in a case—and in some cases (literally, for once, in both senses), it is. But if you have a remote control for your iPod, your need to access your iPod's controls once you've set the music playing will be much less. Generally speaking, the more waterproof the case, the less access it offers to your iPod's controls.

- **Whether or not the case can hold your iPod's headphones and remote control**   If you'll be toting your iPod in a bag or pocket, a case that can hold your iPod's ear-bud headphones and remote control as well as the player itself may be a boon. You may even want a case that can accommodate the FireWire cable and power adapter for traveling. But if you're more interested in a case that straps firmly to your body and holds your iPod secure, you probably won't want the case to devote extra space to store other objects.

TIP   *If you're looking for a case that'll take your iPod's complete entourage, consider the type of case designed for portable CD players and built into a padded belt.*

- **Whether or not you need to take your iPod out of the case to dock or recharge it**   Some cases are designed to give you access to your iPod's FireWire port and front panel controls, so you can leave your iPod in the case unless you need to admire it. Some cases for third-generation iPods and iPod minis provide access to the Dock Connector, while others don't. With more protective cases, usually you need to remove your iPod more often.

- **What the case is made of and how much it costs**   Snug cases tend to be made of neoprene. Impressive cases tend to be made of leather. Leather and armor cost more than lesser materials.

TIP   *When shopping for a case, look for special-value bundles that include other iPod accessories you need—for example, a car cassette adapter or a car adapter.*

Stands, Docks, and Mounting Kits

Cases are (or can be) great, but you won't always want to carry your iPod. Sometimes, you'll want to park it securely so you can use it without worrying about knocking it down, or so you can contemplate its lustrous beauty. If you have a third-generation iPod that came with an iPod Dock, you're all set. (If your third-generation iPod came without an iPod Dock, or you need an extra iPod Dock, you can buy one for $39 from the Apple Store.) Otherwise, you can get a third-party stand, dock, or mount kit, depending on where you're trying to position your iPod and how firmly you want it to stay there.

Here are some of your options:

- **PodStand** The PodStand from Marware, Inc. ($14.95; www.marware.com) is a simple acrylic stand barely wider than your iPod. The PodStand holds a first-, second-, or third-generation iPod upright, does nothing else, and comes in white and clear models.

- **DVBase** The DVBase from the ThinkDifferent Store (thinkdifferentstore.com) costs $50 and is a sleek stand made of polished aluminum to match the polished nickel stainless steel on your iPod's back and sides. The base holds your iPod at a jaunty angle to the universe and looks beautiful but has no other function. The ThinkDifferent Store comments, "Frankly, it is a product that reeks of overkill." You'll know if you need one.

- **iPodCradle** The iPodCradle from BookEndz ($29.95; www.bookendzdocks.com/bookendz/dock_cradle.htm) is a simple white cradle that holds your first- or second-generation iPod firmly in an almost-upright position. It has no other function.

- **iPodDock** The iPodDock, also from BookEndz ($44.95; www.bookendzdocks.com/bookendz/dock_cradle.htm) is a stand that holds your first- or second-generation iPod upside down so it connects with audio and FireWire ports built into the unit. The iPodDock connects to your stereo and computer, allowing you to charge your iPod and play back music. The problem, as you'd imagine, comes with trying to navigate your iPod's display upside down.

- **FlipStand** The FlipStand from Speck Products ($29.95; www.speckproducts.com) is a protective hard case for your iPod that also acts as a stand when you flip the door fully open. The FlipStand fits the third-generation iPods.

- **Gripmatic** The Gripmatic from Netalog, Inc. ($29.99; www.everythingipod.com) is a multiangle mount designed for use in the car. You can mount the Gripmatic either with screws or with adhesive (both of which are provided).

- **Cup Holder Car Mount**   The Cup Holder Car Mount ($34.99; www.everythingipod.com) enables you to mount your iPod securely in your car's cup holder.

- **TuneDok Car Holder**   The TuneDok Car Holder for iPod from Belkin ($29.99; www. belkin.com) lets you mount any regular iPod in your car's cup holder. The TuneDok includes large and small bases to fit securely in any cup holder.
- **PodHolder**   The PodHolder ($15; thinkdifferentstore.com) is a clear acrylic stand for supporting your iPod at an angle on a flat surface.
- **Bike Holder Accessory**   The Bike Holder Accessory ($7.95; thinkdifferentstore.com) from Marware works with cases such as the iPod SportSuit Convertible, iPod SportSuit Basic, and the iPod Leather C.E.O. The Bike Holder Accessory lets you strap your iPod to your bike's handlebars so that you can manipulate the music when you have a hand free.

In a category all of its own is the PocketDock FireWire Adapter for third-generation iPods. This adapter is a short tube with a Dock Connector at one end and a standard six-pin FireWire jack on the other, allowing you to connect your third-generation iPod to any FireWire cable instead of requiring a cable with a Dock Connector built in. The PocketDock FireWire Adapter costs $18.95 and is available from thinkdifferentstore.com.

Power Adapters

Your iPod should have come with a power adapter for recharging from the mains instead of recharging along the FireWire cable from your Mac or PC. But you may want to supplement the standard adapter with a more specialized adapter. You may also want to prolong your AC-free playing time by using a backup battery pack.

Backup Battery Pack for iPod

The Battery Backup Pack for iPod from Belkin ($69.99; www.belkin.com) is a clip-on battery pack for third-generation iPods. The Backup Battery Pack runs off four AA batteries, connects through the Dock Connector, and provides up to 20 hours of additional playing time.

Basic AC Power Adapters

If you break or lose your power adapter, or simply want a second adapter so you can keep one upstairs and one downstairs, you can buy another iPod Power Adapter (that's the formal name) from the Apple Store (store.apple.com) or from an authorized reseller. The iPod Power Adapter costs $49.

You can also get equivalent power supplies from other sources. For example, Netalog, Inc. (www.everythingipod.com) offers the DLO A/C Power Adapter for first- and third-generation iPods for $14 at the time of this writing. The prongs aren't removable, but the price is great.

Powered FireWire Adapters for Unpowered FireWire Ports

If your computer has an unpowered FireWire port (for example, a four-pin port on a PC or a six-pin port on a CardBus or PC Card device), one option is to get a powered FireWire adapter to attach to your FireWire cable so you can recharge your iPod by plugging it into your computer. The adapter sits between the unpowered port and your power-capable FireWire cable and "injects" power into the cable. Examples of such adapters include the FireCable from CompuCable Manufacturing Group (www.compucable.com) and the FireJuice 6 and FireJuice 4 from SiK, Inc. ($25; www.sik.com/firejuice.php).

The disadvantage to such an adapter is that you have to plug it into an AC socket for it to have any power to supply to your iPod. Most people find it easier to use their iPod's power adapter to recharge the iPod directly from the AC. But if you want to make synchronization and recharging a one-stop option, you might want to try such an adapter.

Power-Only FireWire Cable for Playing While Charging from a Computer

The HotWire from SiK, Inc. ($13; www.sik.com/hotwire.php) is a FireWire cable that transfers power but not data. By using this cable, you can charge your iPod from a computer while continuing to use your iPod to play music, instead of having your iPod become a slave to your computer the moment you plug it in.

15

TIP *If your computer has only one FireWire port (as most PowerBooks and iBooks do) or you have too many FireWire peripherals for however many FireWire ports your computer has, consider getting a FireWire hub that will allow you to plug in multiple FireWire devices at once.*

Car Adapters

If you drive extensively (or live in a vehicle), you may find even your iPod's impressive battery life isn't enough for your lifestyle. To recharge your iPod in your car, you need a power adapter that'll run from your car's 12-volt accessory outlet or cigarette-lighter socket. Technically, such an adapter is an *inverter,* a device that converts DC into AC, but we'll stick with the term *adapter* here.

You can choose between a generic car adapter, a FireWire car adapter, and a custom car adapter for the iPod. The following subsections discuss these options.

Generic Car Adapter

The simplest and most versatile option is to get a generic car adapter that plugs into your car's 12-volt accessory outlet or cigarette-lighter socket. Models vary, but the most effective types give you one or more conventional AC sockets. You plug your iPod's power adapter into one of these AC sockets just as you would any other AC socket, and then plug the FireWire cable into your iPod's power adapter.

The advantage to these adapters is that you can run any electrical equipment off them that doesn't draw too heavy a load: a portable computer, your cell phone charger, a portable TV, or whatever. The disadvantage is that such adapters can be large and clumsy compared with custom adapters.

Cost usually depends on the wattage the adapter can handle; you can get 50-watt adapters from around $20 and 140-watt adapters for around $50, whereas 300-watt adapters cost more like $80. A 50-watt adapter will take care of your iPod and portable computer easily enough.

FireWire Car Adapters

Your next option is to get a car adapter that provides a FireWire port into which you can plug your iPod's cable. The adapter draws power through the 12-volt accessory socket or cigarette-lighter socket and provides power to the FireWire port.

An example of such an adapter is the FirePod charger from CompuCable Manufacturing Group (www.compucable.com). The FirePod provides one FireWire port and one USB port, so it's not an iPod-only product.

iPod-Specific Adapters

If the only thing you want to power from your car is your iPod, you can get a car adapter designed specially for the iPod. You'll find an impressive number of different models available, including the following:

- Belkin iPod Car Charger ($19.95; www.belkin.com) is a charger for iPods with the Dock Connector.

- Griffin PowerPod ($24.99; www.griffintechnology.com) is an adapter with a FireWire socket into which you plug your FireWire cable. Griffin makes a PowerPod that works with first-, second-, and third-generation iPods.

- XtremeMac Premium iPod Car Charger ($19.95; www.xtrememac.com/foripod/car_charger.shtml) is an adapter with a springy coil of FireWire cable built in. You plug the other end of the FireWire cable into your iPod, and you're in business. There's a different model for the third-generation iPods than for the first- and second-generation iPods.

- The AutoPod charger from Netalog, Inc. ($19.99; www.everythingipod.com) is similar to the iPod Car Charger—an adapter with a built-in, coiled FireWire cable. You can choose between black and white models.

> NOTE   *The ultimate iPod-specific power adapter is the TransPod, a power adapter built into an iPod holder and an RF transmitter for sending your iPod's output to your car radio. See "Connect Your iPod to Your Car Stereo," later in this chapter, for a more detailed discussion of the TransPod.*

World Travel Adapters

If you travel abroad with your iPod, the lightest and easiest way to recharge it is from your PowerBook, iBook, or portable PC (if that PC has a six-pin FireWire port rather than a four-pin port, which can't transfer power). You have to have your computer with you, of course, and you need a way to plug in your computer to the mains so you don't deplete its battery charging your iPod. But even that tends to be better than having to plug in your iPod separately.

If you need to recharge your iPod directly from the mains, get an adapter that lets you plug your iPod's power adapter into the mains. The adapter can handle multiple voltages, so you can plug it in safely, even in countries that think 240 volts is just a refreshing tingle.

As in so many things in life, you can choose between a set of cheap and ugly adapters and a set of stylish and sophisticated adapters. The cheap and ugly adapters you can get from any competent electrical-supply shop; they consist of an assortment of prong-converter receptacles

15

into which you plug your iPod's U.S. prongs. The resulting piggyback arrangement is clumsy and vaguely obscene looking, and sometimes you have to jiggle the adapters to get a good connection. But these adapters are inexpensive (usually from $5 to $10) and functional, and they work for any electrical gear that can handle the different voltages.

The stylish and sophisticated adapters are designed by Apple and are (collectively) called the World Travel Adapter Kit. The kit costs $39.95 from the Apple Store (store.apple.com) or an authorized reseller. You slide the U.S. prongs off your iPod adapter and replace them with a set of prongs suited to the country you're in. The kit includes six prongs that'll juice up your iPod in continental Europe, the United Kingdom, Australia, Hong Kong, South Korea, China, and Japan, as well as in the United States. These adapters also work with the white power adapters that come with the PowerBook G4 and the iBook, but they won't help you plug in any of your other electrical equipment.

TIP	*If you're going somewhere sunny that lacks electricity, or you live somewhere sunny that suffers frequent power outages, or if you lost all your money investing in Enron and will do anything to reduce your next electric bill, one option for powering your laptop is a portable folding solar panel such as the Note Power 20 (www.cetsolar.com/notepower20.htm). Compared to batteries and a mains supply, a solar panel is an unwieldy form of power, but it can be useful when a mains supply isn't available and batteries won't last you long enough. Your iPod can take its power from your laptop—again, provided the laptop has a six-pin FireWire port.*

Headphones and Enhancers

You can connect pretty much any standard type of headphones to your iPod—over-the-ear (circumaural) headphones, on-the-ear (supra-aural) headphones, or in-the-ear headphones (ear buds), such as Apple's iPod In-Ear Headphones ($39). If the headphones have a quarter-inch jack, you'll need a miniplug converter (make sure its quality is high enough for your headphones). And if you want to enhance sound quality, you might want to try a headphone amplifier (see Chapter 2).

Choosing headphones should be a straightforward matter of balancing sound quality, comfort, cost, style, and special needs, such as excluding other noises or keeping your ears warm. I'll let you make the choice on your own; but in the next three sections, I'll quickly mention three headphone-related products that may be of interest. Okay, the first product is actually a pair of headphones, but it's an unusual pair that you might care to know about.

Zip Cord Retractable Earbuds

Getting the headphone cord tangled is a perennial problem with ear-bud headphones, particularly when you need to stuff them into your pocket or pack quickly. The Zip Cord Retractable Earbuds from Netalog, Inc. ($26.95; www.everythingipod.com) feature an integrated spool onto which you can quickly retract the cord when you need to stow them.

Speaker and Headphone Splitters

Headphones are great for solitary listening, but if you find there are times when you want to share your music without using speakers, you need a headphone splitter. A typical splitter is a Y-shaped cable or device with a stereo miniplug at one end and two stereo jacks on the other end. The miniplug goes into your iPod or other audio source, and then each set of headphones plugs into one of the stereo jacks.

You can find splitters at Radio Shack and most other electronics stores at prices starting from a few bucks. When buying a splitter, make sure it has high-quality contacts so that it won't degrade the audio signal. It's also a good idea to check that the splitter balances the sound between the jacks so that each listener receives the same signal level. Different signal levels tend to be more of a problem when you daisy-chain splitters to share the signal with two or more people. Some splitters, such as the iShare Earbud Splitter ($12.95; www.xtrememac.com/foripod/ishare.shtml), are explicitly designed for daisy-chaining, but most aren't.

Splitters are best used in static situations such as on a plane, in a car, or on the sofa reacquainting yourself with the baser parts of heavy metal after your sensitive neighbors have twitched their way to bed. (On the street, splitter users run the risk of garroting children, lassoing lampposts, and suffering unexpected sharp tugs at their ears.) You can also use a splitter to connect an iPod or other sound source to multiple receivers or speakers instead of headphones, or to a mixture of output devices. For example, when DJing, you might run one pair of headphones and a receiver.

Koss eq50 Three-Band Equalizer

If your iPod's graphic equalizer settings don't always suit you, or you want to be able to change the equalizer settings manually while you're playing music, try a portable graphic equalizer such as the Koss eq50 ($19.99; various retailers). You plug the eq50 into your iPod, and then plug your headphones or other listening gear into the eq50.

The eq50 is a pocket-size unit that runs on two AAA batteries. It offers three frequency sliders, giving you reasonable, but not fine, control over the equalization of your music. For best effect, use the eq50 in concert with your iPod's built-in equalizations.

Remote Control

If you connect your iPod to your stereo (as discussed in "Connect Your iPod to Your Stereo," later in this chapter), you'd probably appreciate being able to control your iPod from across the room. You can do so using the NaviPod wireless remote control from Ten Technologies ($49.95; available from thinkdifferentstore.com and www.everythingipod.com) The NaviPod uses an infrared transmitted from its remote control to the receiver that connects to the iPod. It comes in different models, one for first- and second-generation iPods, and one for third-generation iPods.

15

Input Devices for the iPod

In its original incarnation, the iPod's only input device was the computer, feeding it data along the FireWire cable. But with the iPod's tearaway success have come demands for additional input devices for the iPod—and the market has supplied them in the form of iPod microphones and a media-card reader. Most of these devices work with third-generation iPods only—they don't work with first- and second-generation iPods, nor do they work with the iPod mini (which has different firmware than the third-generation iPod).

Voice Recorder for iPod

The Belkin Voice Recorder for iPod ($59.99; www.belkin.com) is a microphone with an integrated tiny speaker that plugs into the headphone socket and remote-control socket of third-generation iPods. (The Voice Recorder doesn't work with the first- and second-generation iPods, which lack not only the third-generation's remote-control socket but also the firmware features that support recording.)

Plugging in the Voice Recorder switches your iPod to its Voice Memo screen—which you can also access manually by choosing Extras | Voice Memos | Record Now—from which you can start recording by pressing the Select button with the Record item selected. Once the recording is running, you can pause it by using the Pause command, or stop the recording and save it by using the Stop And Save command. Your iPod saves the recording under a name that consists of the date and time—for example, 6/25 4:45 PM.

You can play back and delete the memos from the Extras | Voice Memos screen. When you synchronize your iPod with iTunes, your voice memos are transferred to your computer and added to the Voice Memos playlist.

iTalk

On the face of it, the Griffin iTalk ($40; www.griffintechnology.com) is very similar to the Voice Recorder for iPod, but it outdoes the Voice Recorder in several important ways. First, the iTalk lets you connect an external microphone, while the Voice Recorder doesn't. Second, the iTalk has a pass-through headphone jack so that you can play back your recordings or your music without disconnecting it; you can also monitor the recording you're making, which can be useful when you're using an external microphone. Third, the iTalk costs a third less than the Voice Recorder.

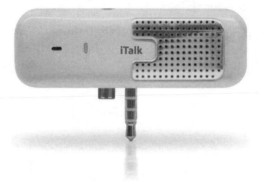

Belkin Media Reader for iPod

The Belkin Media Reader for iPod ($99.99; www.belkin.com) is a compact unit that enables you to transfer pictures from media cards (including CompactFlash cards, Secure Digital cards, and Memory Stick cards) to your iPod.

The Media Reader is discussed at length in Special Project 1. (To find the Special Project, look for the colored pages.)

Portable Speakers for the iPod

You can use your iPod as the sound source for just about any stereo system, as you'll see in "Connect Your iPod to Your Stereo," later in this chapter. But if you travel with your iPod, or simply prefer a compact lifestyle, you may want portable speakers that will treat your iPod as the center of their universe. Luckily, manufacturers have seen your need and catered to it.

NOTE   *Apart from the two sets of speakers mentioned here, another possibility is the Groove Bag Tote Speaker Purse, discussed in the "Weird Stuff" section, a little later in this chapter.*

Creative TravelSound Portable Speakers

The Creative TravelSound ($99; store.apple.com or www.creative.com) is a foldable pair of amplified portable speakers. The TravelSound isn't designed specifically for the iPod, so it will work with any audio source that you connect (for example, your laptop).

The TravelSound has a total power output of 4W—enough for a few people to listen to, but not nearly enough for a party—and runs off four AAA batteries or an AC adapter.

Altec Lansing inMotion Portable iPod Speakers

The Altec Lansing inMotion ($149; store.apple.com or www.alteclansing.com) is an ultraportable stereo system designed for third-generation iPods. The iPod connects through a Dock Connector that enables you to recharge it from the inMotion.

Because of the Dock Connector, the inMotion can't charge first- or second-generation iPods or the iPod mini, but you can connect these other iPods (or indeed any other sound source) through an auxiliary input. The inMotion delivers 4W RMS.

Weird Stuff

This section mentions a short handful of oddball accessories determined not to fit into the previous categories.

Burton Amp Jacket

Burton Snowboards and Apple teamed up to produce the Burton Amp ($499.95; www.burton.com/gear/pr_amp_jacket.asp), a waterproof GORE-TEX snowboarding jacket designed to house an iPod. The iPod fits into a secure chest pocket from which wires run to a remote control built into a fabric data strip on the left forearm. From the remote control, wires run to the neck of the jacket, where you plug in your headset.

If you're a fanatical snowboarder, you own an iPod, you're short a waterproof jacket, and you happen to have $500 burning a hole in your upper thigh, the Burton Amp may seem an unmissable opportunity. For most of the rest of the world, though, the jacket is a fair illustration of the triumph of style over sense.

Most boarders will achieve the same effect at no cost by attaching their iPod's own remote control to their torso or sleeve, padding or reinforcing an internal pocket, and perhaps running the wires under the fabric (or taping them down) to avoid tangling in aerial maneuvers. If they have $500 in urgent need of a new home, they'll buy a new board or a second iPod for the rest of their music collection, or perhaps put down a deposit on a 17-inch PowerBook.

Burton Amp Pack

The Burton Amp Pack ($199; store.apple.com or www.burton.com) is a laptop backpack with a special storage pocket for the iPod and a remote control pad built into the shoulder strap. The Amp Pack is designed for iPods with the Dock Connector.

Groove Bag Tote Speaker Purse

The Groove Bag Tote Speaker Purse from Felicidade ($144.95; www.drbott.com) is a bizarre anti-fashion accessory—a soft, faux-leather bag containing amplified speakers and a pocket for your iPod. The iPod pocket is see-through, giving you access to your iPod's controls and enabling you to flash your iPod at passersby.

Connect Your iPod to Your Stereo

Connecting your iPod to your stereo is easy. In most cases, all you need is a cable with a miniplug at one end for your iPod's headphone socket and two RCA plugs at the other end to go into your amplifier or boom box. (For some cassette players, you'll need a miniplug at each end of the cable.)

If you have a high-quality receiver and speakers, get a high-quality cable to connect your iPod to them. After the amount you've presumably spent on your iPod and your stereo, it'd be a mistake to degrade the signal between them by sparing a few bucks on the cable.

15

TIP

You can find various home-audio connection kits that contain a variety of cables likely to cover your needs. These kits are usually a safe buy, but unless your needs are peculiar, you'll probably end up with one or more cables you don't need. So if you do know which cables you need, make sure a kit offers a cost saving before buying it instead of the individual cables.

When you connect your iPod to your stereo, turn the volume all the way down on the iPod and on the amplifier before making the connection. Connect the RCA plugs to one of the inputs on your amplifier or boom box—for example, the AUX input. Then increase the volume on the two controls in tandem until you reach a satisfactory sound level. Too low a level of output from your iPod may produce noise on the wire as your amplifier boosts the signal. Too high a level of output from your iPod may cause distortion.

CAUTION *Don't connect your iPod to the Phono input on your amplifier. This is because the Phono input is built with a higher sensitivity to make up for the weak output of a record player. Putting a full-strength signal into the Phono input will probably blow it.*

Connect Your iPod to Your Car Stereo

You can connect your iPod to your car stereo in any of the following ways:

- Use a cassette adapter to connect your iPod to your car's cassette player.
- Use a radio-frequency device to play your iPod's output through your car's radio.
- Wire your iPod directly to your car stereo and use it as an auxiliary input device.

Each of these methods has its merits and disadvantages. The following subsections tell you what you need to know to choose the best option for your car stereo.

Use a Cassette Adapter

If your car stereo has a cassette player, your easiest option is to use a cassette adapter to play audio from your iPod through the cassette deck. You can buy such adapters for between $10 and $20 from most electronics stores.

The adapter is shaped like a cassette and uses a playback head to input analog audio via the head that normally reads the tape as it passes. A wire runs from the adapter to your iPod.

A cassette adapter can be an easy and inexpensive solution, but it has a couple of disadvantages. First, the audio quality tends to be poor, because the means of transferring the audio to the cassette player's mechanism is less than optimal. If the cassette player's playback head is dirty from playing cassettes, audio quality will be that much worse. (Clean the cassette player regularly using a cleaning cassette.)

Second, many autoreverse cassette players can't play input from a cassette adapter for more than 30 minutes or so without deciding they need to change directions and look for more music on the other side of the adapter—which can't supply it. So if you use a cassette adapter, you may have to reset the direction of play every once in a while. This isn't difficult, but it gets tedious fast.

CAUTION *If you use a cassette adapter in an extreme climate, try to make sure you don't bake it or freeze it by leaving it in your car.*

Use a Radio-Frequency Adapter

If your car stereo doesn't have a cassette deck, your easiest option for playing music from your iPod may be to get a radio-frequency adapter or mobile FM transmitter. This device plugs into a sound source (your iPod in this case) and broadcasts a signal on an FM frequency to which you then tune your radio to play the music. Better radio-frequency devices offer a choice of frequencies to allow you easy access to both the device and your favorite radio stations.

Radio-frequency devices can deliver reasonable audio quality. If possible, try before you buy by asking for a demonstration in the store (take a portable radio with you, if necessary).

The main advantages of these devices are that they're relatively inexpensive ($25, give or take $10) and they're easy to use. They also have the advantage that you can put your iPod out of sight (for example, in the glove compartment—provided it's not too hot) without any telltale wires to help the light-fingered locate it.

On the down side, most of these devices need batteries (others can run off the 12-volt accessory outlet or cigarette-lighter socket), and less expensive units tend not to deliver the highest sound quality. The range of these devices is minimal, but at close quarters, other radios nearby may be able to pick up the signal—which could be embarrassing, entertaining, or irrelevant, depending on the circumstances.

If you decide to get a radio-frequency adapter, you'll need to choose between getting a model designed specifically for the iPod and getting one that works with any audio source. Radio-frequency adapters designed for the iPod typically mount on the iPod, making them a neater solution than general-purpose ones that dangle from the headphone socket.

Examples of radio-frequency adapters designed for the iPod include the Belkin TuneCast Mobile FM ($39.99; www.belkin.com) and the Griffin iTrip. The iTrip ($34.95; available from various retailers including store.apple.com) comes in different models for first- and second-generation iPods, and for third-generation iPods. The iTrip is a strong contender because it draws power from the iPod rather than using batteries of its own.

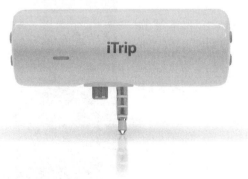

15

TIP *As you'd guess, a radio-frequency adapter works with radios other than car radios, so you can use one to play music through your stereo system (or someone else's).*

Wire Your iPod Directly to Your Car Stereo

If neither the cassette adapter nor the radio-frequency adapter provides a suitable solution, or if you simply want the best audio quality you can get, connect your iPod directly to your car stereo. How easily you can do this depends on how the stereo is designed:

- If your car stereo is one of the few that has a miniplug input built in, get a miniplug-to-miniplug cable and you'll be in business.

- If your stereo is built to take multiple inputs—for example, a CD player (or changer) and an auxiliary input—you may be able to simply run a wire from unused existing connectors. Plug your iPod into the other end, press the correct buttons, and you'll be ready to rock-and-roll down the freeway.

- If no unused connectors are available, you or your local friendly electronics technician may need to get busy with a soldering iron.

If you're buying a new car stereo, look for an auxiliary input that you can use with your iPod.

An Integrated Solution for the Car: the TransPod

The TransPod from Netalog, Inc. ($99.99; www.everythingipod.com) is a one-stop solution for using your iPod in your car. TransPod combines a cradle for holding the iPod with a power adapter and a wireless transmitter to pipe the iPod's output to your car radio. The TransPod comes in different models for the different generations of iPod.

A third-generation iPod slides down into the cradle so that its Dock Connector connects, whereas a first- or second-generation iPod slides up into the cradle so the miniplug and FireWire plug in the top of the sleeve go into its headphone port and FireWire port. You then plug the charger plug into your 12-volt accessory outlet or cigarette-lighter socket, which supports the cradle and provides power to the iPod and the TransPod. You can play back music as your iPod charges, so you can keep the tunes going continuously.

The only drawback to the TransPod (apart from the price) is that it makes your iPod highly visible to the covetous—so you'd be well advised to remove it when you park.

Chapter 16

Master Advanced iPod Skills

How to...

- Move your iPod from the Mac to Windows and back
- Change the computer to which your iPod is linked
- Synchronize several iPods with the same computer
- Load your iPod from two or more computers
- Transfer song files from your iPod's music library to your computer
- Manage your iPod with EphPod, MUSICMATCH Jukebox, Anapod Explorer, or XPlay
- Use your computer to play songs directly from your iPod

This chapter shows you how to perform a variety of advanced maneuvers with your iPod or iPod mini. The chapter starts by walking you through the processes of moving an iPod from a Mac to a PC and vice versa. Then it shows you how to change the computer to which your iPod is linked—a useful skill when you upgrade your computer. The chapter explains the nuances of synchronizing several iPods with the same computer, and it walks you through loading your iPod from two or more computers at the same time.

Next, you'll see how to transfer song files from your iPod's music library to your computer, a skill that can save your music library when your computer has disk trouble, and how to use Windows applications other than iTunes to manage your iPod. The chapter ends by showing you how to play songs from your iPod through your computer.

Move Your iPod from Mac to Windows—and Back

As you learned in Chapter 1, the iPod started off (in its first generation) as a Mac-only product. Enough Windows users craved the iPod for Ephpod (discussed later in this chapter) to be created. Apple then released second-generation iPods in separate versions for the Mac and for Windows; the iPods for the two platforms started off separate, but you could convert them from one to the other. Currently, the third-generation iPod and the iPod mini come in a single version for both the Mac and Windows.

Now that iTunes is available for Windows as well as for the Mac, iPods work seamlessly with both Windows and the Mac as long as their hard disks are formatted with the FAT32 file system, the format used by the iPod Software Updater running on Windows. If a third-generation iPod or iPod mini's disk is formatted with the Mac OS Extended file system (which is the format used by the iPod Software Updater running on Mac OS X), you'll need to reformat the iPod before it will work with Windows.

CAUTION   *If you reformat your iPod, you'll lose all its contents—every file you've stored on it. If your iPod contains valuable files, back them up to your Mac or PC before reformatting your iPod.*

Move Your iPod from the Mac to Windows

To move an iPod from the Mac to Windows, follow these steps:

1. Make sure the PC has iTunes and the iPod Software—preferably the latest version of each—installed. Make sure it's the right iPod Software for the type of iPod: version 1.x of the iPod Software for first- and second-generation iPods, version 2.x of the iPod Software for third-generation iPods, and version 1.x of the iPod Software for iPod mini for the iPod mini.

2. If nobody has used iTunes on that computer, run iTunes and get the iTunes Setup Assistant out of the way.

3. Connect the iPod to the PC. If the iPod's hard disk is formatted with the Mac OS Extended file system, the iPod Software displays the iPod Not Readable dialog box. If so, follow steps 3 and 4. Otherwise, go to step 5.

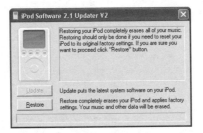

4. Click the Update button to launch the iPod Software Updater:

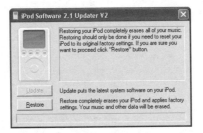

NOTE   *If the iPod Software Updater displays the error message "Updater can't install firmware on connected iPod. The iPod's hardware and the Updater firmware are not compatible," see the section "'Updater Can't Install Firmware on Connected iPod' Message," in Chapter 17.*

16

5. Click the Restore button to format the iPod using the FAT32 file system and to reinstall the iPod firmware on it. Unplug your iPod from the PC when the iPod Software Updater tells you to, plug it into the iPod Power Adapter to complete the firmware reflash, and then plug it back into the PC.

6. iTunes displays the following dialog box, warning you that your iPod is linked to another iTunes music library and asking if you want to change the link to the iTunes music library on this computer:

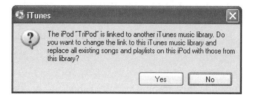

7. Click the Yes button. iTunes then replaces the music library on the iPod with the contents of the music library on the new computer you've attached it to.

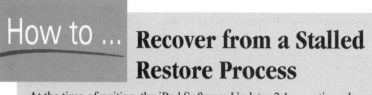

Recover from a Stalled Restore Process

At the time of writing, the iPod Software Updater 2.1 sometimes hangs while telling you to wait for the iPod to complete the restore process. It's usually pretty clear when this has happened; the iPod Software Updater tells you to wait, and the iPod tells you not to disconnect it…and several minutes pass without completion occurring.

If you've waited several minutes, recover by taking as many of the following steps as necessary:

1. Disconnect your iPod from your PC.

2. Let your iPod recover from any confusion caused by your unplugging it. If all is well, your iPod displays the Language screen.

3. Select your preferred language and press the Select button. (If the Select button on a third-generation iPod isn't working, move the Hold switch to the On position, and then back to the Off position. If that doesn't make the Select button work, connect your iPod to the iPod Power Adapter, and then repeat the trick with the Hold switch.)

4. Connect your iPod to your PC again.

5. If the iPod Software Updater is still telling you to hold your horses, try to close it by clicking its Close button (the X button). Usually, it then tells you it can't be interrupted. Right-click the taskbar and choose Task Manager to display Windows Task Manager. On the Applications tab, select the iPod Software Updater entry, and then click the End Task button. Windows will display the End Program dialog box. Click the End Now button.

If the iPod Software Updater displays the iPod Updater error message box saying that it can't mount the iPod, restart your computer.

Move Your iPod from Windows to the Mac

To move your iPod from Windows to the Mac, follow these steps:

1. For best results, update iTunes to the latest version available. (The easiest way to check that iTunes is up-to-date is to choose Apple | System Preferences, click the Software Update icon in System Preferences, and then click the Check Now button on the Update Software tab of Software Update.)

2. Connect the iPod to the Mac. When iTunes detects the iPod, it displays a dialog box such as that shown here, pointing out that the iPod is linked to a different music library and asking if you want to replace that music library:

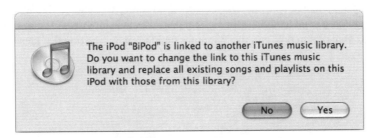

3. Click the Yes button. iTunes replaces the music library on the iPod with the music library on the Mac. This may take some time if the music library is extensive.

16

At this point, you've set up your iPod to work with your Mac, but you've left it using the FAT32 file system. FAT32 works fine with Mac OS X but is marginally less efficient than the Mac OS Extended file system, so you won't be able to fit quite as many files on your iPod with FAT32 as with Mac OS Extended.

If you intend to use your iPod with the Mac for the long term, and if your iPod doesn't contain any valuable files that you want to keep, you may choose to convert it to Mac OS Extended to pack on as many songs as possible. To do so, restore your iPod by following the process described in "Restore Your iPod on Mac OS X," in Chapter 17.

Change the Computer to Which Your iPod Is Linked

Apple has designed the iPod so that it can synchronize with only one Mac or one PC at a time. This computer is known as the *home* computer—home to the iPod, not necessarily in your home. However, you can use two or more computers to load files onto the same iPod. See the section "Load Your iPod from Two or More Computers at Once," later in this chapter, for details.

CAUTION *Linking your iPod to another computer replaces all the songs and playlists on your iPod with the songs and playlists on the other computer. Be sure you want to change the link before you proceed. You can restore your previous music library by linking again to the first computer, but, even with FireWire file-transfer speeds, you'll waste a good deal of time if your music library is large.*

To change your iPod's home computer, follow these steps:

1. Make sure the other computer contains an up-to-date version of iTunes and the latest version of the appropriate iPod Software for the iPod. If necessary, set up iTunes and install any relevant updates.

NOTE *If you're moving an iPod formatted with the Mac OS Extended file system to Windows, you'll need to restore it as described in "Move Your iPod from the Mac to Windows," earlier in this chapter.*

2. Connect your iPod via the FireWire cable to the other Mac or PC, or via the USB cable to the other PC.

3. iTunes displays a dialog box warning you your iPod is linked to another iTunes music library and asking if you want to change the link to the iTunes music library. The next illustration shows the Mac dialog box, but the Windows dialog box is functionally identical.

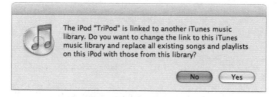

4. If you're sure you want to replace your music library, click the Yes button.

Because changing your iPod to a different home computer replaces the entire music library, the initial synchronization may take a long time (depending on how big the music library is and whether it's stored on a local drive or a network drive).

Synchronize Several iPods with the Same Computer

As you've seen earlier in this book, usually a computer and an iPod have a mutually faithful relationship. As discussed in the previous section, the iPod can decide to leave its home computer and set up home with another computer. It can even switch to the other platform (Mac or PC) if it wants OS-reassignment as well as a new home.

For most people, such fidelity (or serial fidelity) works fine. But if you have several iPods and one computer—for example, if several music-lovers in a household share the same computer—what happens? Can your computer practice polyPodry (or perhaps poliPodry)?

Briefly—yes. While your iPod is wired not to sync around, the computer in the partnership has no such restrictions and can sync with as many iPods as you have. Here are the points to keep in mind:

- Even if your computer has plenty of FireWire ports, it's best not to plug in more than one iPod at once. That way, you don't get confused, and synchronization can take place at full speed.

- Each iPod has a unique ID number that it communicates to your computer on connection, so your computer knows which iPod is connected to it. You can even give two or more iPods the same name if doing so amuses rather than confuses you.

- You can configure different updating for each iPod by choosing options in the iPod Preferences dialog box when the iPod is connected.

Load Your iPod from Two or More Computers at Once

As you read earlier in this chapter, you can synchronize your iPod with only one computer at a time—your iPod's home computer. You can change your iPod's home computer from one computer to another, and even from one platform (Mac or PC) to the other, but you can't actively synchronize your iPod with more than one computer at once.

But you *can* load tracks onto your iPod from computers other than the home computer. If your iPod is formatted using the FAT32 file system, you can use a mixture of Macs and PCs to load files onto your iPod. If your iPod is formatted using the Mac OS Extended file system, you can use only Macs.

All the computers you use must have iTunes and the appropriate iPod Software installed and configured, and you must configure the iPod for manual updating on each computer involved—on the home computer as well as on each other computer. Otherwise, synchronizing the iPod with the home computer after loading tracks from other computers will remove those tracks (because they're not in the home computer's music library).

16

How to ... Synchronize a Full—Different—Music Library onto Different iPods from the Same Computer

Synchronizing two or more iPods with the same computer works well enough provided that each iPod user is happy using the same music library or the same set of playlists. But if you want to synchronize the full music library for each iPod, yet have a different music library on each, you need to take a different approach.

In most cases, the easiest solution is to have a separate user account for each separate user who uses an iPod with the computer. (Most computer experts and software designers recommend that each user have a separate user account anyway to prevent one user from trashing another user's work or settings. But frequently, reality refuses to correspond to their edicts.)

Place the music files that users will share in a folder that each user can access. In iTunes, make sure that the Copy Files To iTunes Music Folder When Adding To Library check box on the Advanced sheet of the Preferences dialog box (on the Mac) or on the Advanced tab of the iTunes dialog box (on Windows) is cleared so iTunes doesn't consolidate the files for the music library.

If you have enough free space on your hard disk, users can set up their own music libraries under their own user accounts and store all their music files in them. But unless your hard disk is truly gigantic, sharing most of the files from a central location is almost always preferable.

Configure Your iPod for Manual Updating

The first step in loading your iPod from two or more computers is to configure it for manual updating. You'll need to do this on your iPod's home computer first, and then on each of the other computers you plan to use.

To configure your iPod for manual updating, follow these steps:

1. Connect your iPod to your Mac or PC. Allow synchronization to take place.

2. Right-click your iPod in the Source pane and choose iPod Options from the shortcut menu to display the iPod Preferences dialog box.

3. Select the Manually Manage Songs And Playlists option button. iTunes displays the warning dialog box telling you that you'll need to unmount your iPod manually before disconnecting it.

4. Click the OK button to return to the iPod Preferences dialog box. iTunes selects the Enable Disk Use check box (if it wasn't already selected) and makes it unavailable, so that you can't clear it manually.

5. Click the OK button to close the iPod Preferences dialog box.

Load Files onto Your iPod Manually

After you've configured your iPod for manual updating, you can load files onto it manually by following these general steps:

1. Connect your iPod to the computer that contains the files you want to load. Your iPod will appear in the Source pane in iTunes.

2. Drag song files from your iTunes library, or from a Finder window or a Windows Explorer window, and then drop them on your iPod or on one of its playlists.

3. After loading all the songs you want from this computer, unmount your iPod by issuing an Eject command before you disconnect it. For example, right-click the iPod's entry in the Source pane and choose Eject *iPod* (where *iPod* is the name of your iPod).

You can then disconnect your iPod from this computer, move it to the next computer, and then add more song files by using the same technique.

NOTE   *From this point on, to add further song files to your iPod from your home computer, you must add them manually. Don't synchronize your iPod with your home computer, because synchronization will delete from the iPod all the song files your music library doesn't contain.*

Transfer Song Files from Your iPod's Music Library to Your Computer

For copyright reasons, your iPod's basic configuration prevents you from copying music files (for example, AAC files or MP3 files) from your iPod's music library to your computer. This restriction prevents you from loading files onto your iPod on one computer via iTunes, and then downloading them onto another computer. Otherwise, you could use your iPod to copy files from one computer to another, most likely violating copyright left, right, and in stereo by making unauthorized copies of other people's copyrighted material.

This restriction is about as effective as the "Don't steal music" admonition on the sticker you peeled off your iPod the moment you unpacked it. This is because, as you saw in Chapter 14, by turning on disk mode, you can use your iPod as a portable hard drive. In disk mode, you can copy music files onto your iPod from one computer, attach your iPod to another computer, and copy or move the files from the iPod to that computer. The only limitation is that the files you copy this way aren't added to your iPod's music database, so you can't play them on the iPod. But if you want to use your iPod for copying or moving the files, that shouldn't concern you too much.

So you can use your iPod to violate copyright easily if you want to. You can also use many other technologies and devices to violate copyright in this way—anything from a CD burner to a parallel cable to an Internet connection can make illegal copies of files.

16

But what concerns us here is that, once you've added song files to your iPod's music library, you can't get them back immediately. Normally, you shouldn't need to get them back, because they'll be redundant copies of the song files stored on your computer's hard drive or other drives.

But there may come a time when you need to get the song files out of your iPod's music library for legitimate reasons. For example, if you dropped your iBook, or your PC's hard disk died of natural causes, you might need to copy the music files from your iPod to a replacement computer. Otherwise, you might risk losing your entire music collection. If I dared moralize at you for a moment, I'd point out that this is why you should always back up your valuable files, especially the songs you've bought from the iTunes Music Store or other online music stores.

iPod enthusiasts have developed several utilities for transferring music files from an iPod's hidden music storage to a computer. This section discusses some of the possibilities. First, though, let's look at where the song files are stored on your iPod, how you can access them through conventional file-management utilities (such as the Finder or Windows Explorer), and why copying the files using conventional means yields unsatisfactory results.

Where—and How—Your iPod Stores Song Files

As you saw in Chapter 14, when you turn on disk mode, you can access the contents of your iPod's hard drive by using the Finder (on the Mac) or Windows Explorer (on Windows). Until you create other folders there, though, you'll find only the Calendars and Contacts folders on a first- or second-generation iPod, and these folders plus a Notes folder on a third-generation or later iPod—there's no trace of your song files.

> **NOTE**   *You can also use other file-management utilities (if you have them) for manipulating files on your iPod, but in this chapter, I'll assume you're sticking with the Finder and Windows Explorer.*

This is because the folders in which the song files are stored are formatted to be hidden on Windows and to be invisible on the Mac. Before you can see the folders or the files they contain, you need to change the Hidden attribute on the Windows folders or the Visible attribute on the Mac folders.

> **TIP**   *If you're comfortable with Unix commands, you can open a Terminal window on Mac OS X and use the* ls *command to list the folders and files, even though they're invisible to the Finder.*

Make the Hidden Folders Visible on the Mac

To make hidden folders visible on your Mac running Mac OS X, download and install TinkerTool from www.bresink.de/osx/TinkerTool.html. TinkerTool is a free configuration utility that lets you perform a variety of tweaks on Mac OS X, including making hidden folders visible.

After installing TinkerTool, follow these steps to make hidden folders visible:

1. Run TinkerTool from wherever you installed it (for example, your Applications folder).

2. On the Finder sheet (which is displayed by default and shown here), select the Show Hidden And System Files check box in the Finder Options area:

3. Click the Relaunch Finder button in TinkerTool to relaunch the Finder. (You need to relaunch the Finder to make it read the now-visible folders.)

4. Navigate back to TinkerTool if necessary (relaunching the Finder may have moved the focus to a Finder window), and then press COMMAND-Q or choose TinkerTool | Quit TinkerTool to quit TinkerTool.

After the Finder relaunches, you can examine the song folders. To do so, follow these steps:

1. Connect your iPod to your Mac via the FireWire cable as usual.

2. If you haven't yet enabled disk mode, enable it.

3. Double-click your iPod's icon on the desktop to display its contents in a Finder window. The contents will include the Calendars folder and the Contacts folder, as before, but you'll also be able to see the previously hidden files and folders: the iPod_Control folder, the .Trashes folder, and the .DS_Store, .VolumeIcon.cns, Desktop DB, Desktop DF, and Icon files.

4. Double-click the iPod_Control folder to open it.

5. Double-click the Music folder to open it.

6. Double-click one of the F folders to open it. Here's an example of the structure of the iPod's music folders in Column view:

16

How to ...   Make the Hidden Folders Visible the Hard Way

The hard way to make the hidden folders visible is to use the SetFile command. The SetFile command is one of the tools included in the Mac OS X Developer Tools package.

Most likely, if you're the kind of person who'll use the SetFile command, you'll know at least some Unix commands, and you'll have installed the Mac OS X Developer Tools package already so as to tweak and play with your system. If neither of the above applies, you may be better off with a tool such as TinkerTool, which automates the process of making the folders visible (and offers various other features as well—all at no cost).

If you'd like to try the SetFile command, and you haven't installed the Mac OS X Developer Tools, install them now. If Mac OS X 10.2 or later came preinstalled on your computer, install them by opening the Applications:Installers:Developer Tools folder and double-clicking the Developer.mpkg icon. If you bought Mac OS X and then installed it, install the Developer Tools from the Developer Tools CD that came with Mac OS X.

The installation routine for the Developer Tools is straightforward: an Introduction screen, forcible acceptance of the license agreement if you want to proceed, and choosing the disk on which to install the tools. If you're interested only in the SetFile command and don't have disk space to burn, choose a Custom install and install only the Developer Tools Software item (about 110MB), not the Mac OS X SDK (Software Development Kit; about 240MB), the Developer Documentation (about 480MB), the Developer Example Software (about 30MB), or the BSD SDK (about 30MB). BSD is the Berkeley Software Distribution, a family of Unix versions.

After installing the Developer Tools package, choose Go | Applications | Utilities | Terminal to open a Terminal window. Then navigate to your iPod and issue a `SetFile -a v` command for the iPod_Control folder:

```
/Developer/Tools/SetFile -a v iPod_Control
```

Repeat the command for other folders as necessary to make them visible.

Before the files show up in the Finder, you need to restart it. To do so, do either of the following:

- Log out and then log back in. (Alternatively, restart your Mac.)
- Press COMMAND-OPTION-ESC or choose Apple | Force Quit to display the Force Quit Applications dialog box. Select the Finder item, click the Relaunch button, and then click the Relaunch button in the resulting confirmation dialog box.

Once the Finder has relaunched, the folders you made visible appear in the Finder.

Making the Hidden Folders Visible on Windows

To display hidden files and folders on Windows XP, follow these steps:

1. Choose Start | My Computer to open a My Computer window.

2. Choose Tools | Folder Options to display the Folder Options dialog box.

3. Click the View tab:

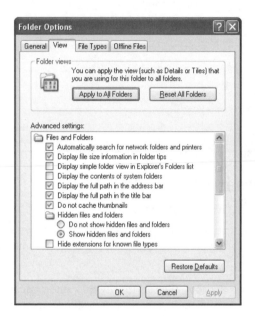

4. Select the Show Hidden Files And Folders option button.

5. Click the OK button to apply the change and to close the Folder Options dialog box. Windows Explorer now displays hidden files and folders as well as normal, unhidden files and folders.

To see the song folders on your iPod, follow these steps:

1. Double-click the icon for your iPod in the My Computer window. Windows Explorer displays the contents of your iPod: the Calendars and Contacts folders as before, and the Notes folder on a third-generation or later iPod, but also an iPod_Control folder that was previously hidden.

2. Double-click the iPod_Control folder to display its contents: a Device folder, an iTunes folder, and a Music folder.

16

3. Double-click the Music folder to display its contents: a series of folders named F*NN,* where *NN* is a two-digit number: F00, F01, F02, and so on.

4. Double-click one of these F folders to display its contents:

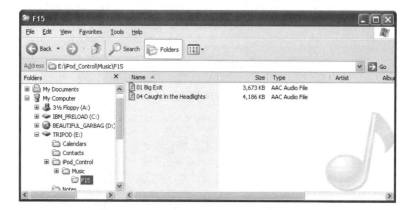

Transfer Song Files from Your iPod Using the Finder or Windows Explorer

If you looked closely at the illustrations of the song files in the previous two sections, you'll probably have noticed that the way in which your iPod stores the song files isn't immediately useful to most humans for two reasons:

- First, your iPod lumps the song files arbitrarily into automatically named folders (F01, F02, and so on) at its convenience. As long as your iPod's internal database knows which folder a particular song is in, that's fine. But if you want to find a particular file, you'll need to go spelunking for it or search for it.

- Second, your iPod truncates and mashes the names of the song files. It truncates longer filenames down to 27 characters, plus the extension. So the track "Pink Floyd – Get Your Filthy Hands Off My Desert.mp3" becomes "Pink Floyd _ Get Your Filth.mp3"—a more interesting title, perhaps, but not how you want the file represented in your file system. And it substitutes extended characters with alternative formulations. For example, "Alizée" becomes "Aliz_e". Again, such machinations confuse humans, and you'll find it tedious renaming such files.

So if you copy (or move) song files from your iPod's song folders to your computer (or another computer), you'll need to perform some heavy-duty sorting and renaming afterward. Even this will likely be preferable to losing your entire music collection (if you've lost your music library)—but you'll probably feel there's got to be a better way.

There is. Read on.

Mac OS X Utilities for Transferring Song Files from Your iPod to Your Mac

iPod enthusiasts have created an impressive array of utilities for transferring song files from your iPod (or someone else's iPod) to your Mac (or someone else's Mac). This section discusses some of the leading utilities for doing so, starting with the shareware and commercial utilities (which tend to offer the fullest features) and then proceeding to the best of the free utilities.

> **NOTE** *If you don't like the look (or performance) of these utilities, search sites such as iPodLounge. com (www.ipodlounge.com), VersionTracker.com (www.versiontracker.com), MacUpdate (www.macupdate.com), and Apple's Mac OS X Downloads page (www.apple.com/macosx/ downloads) for alternatives.*

Different utilities work in different ways. The most basic utilities simply assemble a list of the filenames in the iPod's music folders, which leaves you with truncated filenames. The best utilities read the database the iPod maintains of the tracks it holds, while other utilities plow painstakingly through each file on your iPod and extract information from its ID3 tags. Reading the iPod's database gives much faster results than assembling what's essentially the same database from scratch by scouring the tags. But if the database has become corrupted, reading the tags is a good recovery technique.

PodWorks

PodWorks from Sci-Fi Hi-Fi ($5.99; www.scifihifi.com/podworks) is a neat utility for transferring music files from your iPod to your Mac. PodWorks requires Mac OS X 10.2 or later. You can download an evaluation version that limits you to 30 days, copying 250 songs, and copying one song at a time—enough limitations to persuade you to buy the full version.

16

iPod Access

iPod Access from Findley Designs (www.findleydesigns.com) also simplifies the process of transferring music files from your iPod to your Mac. iPod Access costs $10, but you can download a limited evaluation version to see if the application works for you. You can also use iPod Access to play back tracks directly from your iPod.

iPodRip

iPodRip from The Little App Factory PTY Ltd. ($9.00; www.thelittleappfactory.com) integrates with iTunes and enables you to play back songs from either your music library or your iPod. iPodRip comes in a trial version that you can use ten times before it cripples itself. iPodRip's SmartSync feature enables you to automatically copy to your music library songs that you've loaded onto your iPod using a different computer.

iPod.iTunes

iPod.iTunes, from www.crispsofties.com, is shareware costing $19.99. iPod.iTunes synchronizes the songs and playlists from your iPod or iPods to your Mac(s), allowing you to load songs from multiple Macs and have them all be integrated automatically into your music library.

Pod 2 Pod

Pod 2 Pod, which you can find at www.ipodlounge.com, is an impressive freeware package that enables you to clone one iPod to another iPod. This capability is great if you have two iPods and want to make sure that they contain the same songs and other files.

Pod 2 Pod also enables you to back up your iPod easily to your hard drive so that you don't lose your songs or data if you lose or damage your iPod.

16

iPod Viewer

iPod Viewer (homepage.Mac.com/initgraf/iPodViewer/) is a freeware utility that focuses on copying files from your iPod back to your Mac. iPod Viewer lets you specify the folder structure in which it should place the files, but it doesn't let you rename the files (for example, from the tags) during the copy. At this writing, iPod Viewer works with MP3 files and WAV files but not with AAC files.

Windows Utilities for Transferring Song Files from Your iPod to Your PC

At this writing, there are several Windows utilities for transferring song files from your iPod to your PC. All of the main contenders—Ephpod, Anapod Explorer, and XPlay—also enable you to transfer song files to, and generally manage, your iPod, so they're discussed in the next section. Ephpod is freeware, while Anapod Explorer and XPlay are commercial software—so if you're interested only in rescuing song files from an iPod, Ephpod is the best place to start.

Control Your iPod with Other Software on Windows

At this writing, iTunes for Windows is still at a relatively early stage of development (version 4.2, having started with version 4.0) and suffers by comparison with iTunes for Mac OS X. iTunes for Windows' current problems include very slow startup, sporadic failure to notice new CDs you've inserted, frequent failure to notice when you've connected an iPod, and generally lethargic behavior.

If you find iTunes for Windows slow or balky, you have several alternatives. This section discusses the four leading contenders: Ephpod, MUSICMATCH Jukebox, Anapod Explorer, and XPlay. Of these, MUSICMATCH Jukebox is the only one that can rip and encode audio from CD and burn CDs. With Ephpod, Anapod Explorer, and XPlay, you need to use other software for these tasks. iTunes will perform both tasks, as will Windows Media Player with an MP3 codec added to it.

EphPod

EphPod (pronounced *eefpod* rather than *effpod,* and downloadable from www.ephpod.com and other sites) is a free and very full-featured application for managing iPods on Windows. (More accurately, EphPod is donationware—the author invites you to contribute to his beer fund, and even allows you to request that a donation be spent on something better than beer.)

EphPod was originally built, in the days the iPod was Mac only, to enable you to use Mac iPods with Windows PCs. Since then, Apple first teamed up with MUSICMATCH to deliver the version of MUSICMATCH Jukebox Plus that works with Windows iPods and the Updaters with which you can change Mac iPods to Windows iPods, and then later released iTunes for Windows.

These days, EphPod works with Windows iPods as well. EphPod still lets you use Mac iPods with Windows, but you need to use MacOpener, a $40 product from DataViz, Inc. (www.dataviz.com), to enable Windows to read an iPod formatted with the Mac OS X Extended file system. Few users want to spend good music money on MacOpener when they can reformat their iPod's hard disk to FAT32 and manage it for free from Windows.

If you're finding iTunes for Windows awkward to use, you may want to try EphPod and see how it suits you. EphPod offers features for downloading news, weather, and RSS (Really Simple Syndication) web feeds to your iPod.

But even if you find iTunes fine for managing your iPod, you may need EphPod to recover music from your iPod after your computer has a disaster. EphPod not only makes this process easy, but it allows you to specify the conventions to use for naming the files that it recovers.

To download song files using EphPod, follow these steps:

1. Click the Configure EphPod button on the toolbar, or choose Extras | Configuration, to display the Configuration dialog box.

2. Click the Advanced Options tab:

3. Make sure the Preserve MP3 Filename In Copy check box is cleared.

4. Make sure the Use Internal Copy Routines option button is selected.

5. To improve performance, increase the size of the Internal Copying Buffer Size drop-down list from its default setting of 1024KB to 4096KB.

6. In the Naming Convention For Copied Songs text box, enter the format EphPod should use for creating folders and naming the MP3 files it saves to your hard disk. You can use the variables shown in the following list to use information from the tags on the MP3 files. For example, you might use %A\%L\%A – %T.mp3 to create folders and files such as Artist\Album\Artist – Song Title.mp3. If you're copying files in formats other than MP3, put a period at the end but don't include the mp3 extension.

Variable	Explanation
%A	Artist name
%L	Album title
%T	Song title
%N	Track number
%Y	Year
%G	Genre
%C	Comment

7. Click the OK button to close the Configuration dialog box.

8. Navigate through the EphPod interface to the songs you want to export.

9. Select the songs and press CTRL-ALT-C; or right-click, and then choose Copy Songs To Directory from the shortcut menu, as illustrated here:

10. In the Browse For Folder dialog box, select the folder in which you want EphPod to create the folders and files.

11. Click the OK button. EphPod copies the files and folders and names them according to the convention you specified.

EphPod seems happy enough to work alongside iTunes, but it's a good idea to choose iPod Tools | Make EphPod Default iPod Manager App to make EphPod the default application for managing your iPod.

MUSICMATCH Jukebox Basic and Plus

MUSICMATCH Jukebox Plus is the software that Apple included with the Windows-formatted versions of the second-generation iPods and then with the third-generation iPods until it released iTunes for Windows in late 2003. MUSICMATCH Jukebox Plus works with second- and third-generation iPods and with iPod minis. It offers strong features for ripping and encoding to MP3, burning CDs,

MUSICMATCH Jukebox comes in two versions. The Basic version is free but lacks many of the attractive features included in the Plus version, which costs $19.99 for lifetime upgrades. The Basic version includes ripping, CD burning, synchronizing with portable devices, listening to MUSICMATCH radio, and downloading song files from the MUSICMATCH online music service. The Plus version adds faster ripping, faster burning, stronger tagging features, the ability to record audio via a line-in input (which enables you to rip from analog sources), CD label printing, and more.

MUSICMATCH Jukebox can encode audio files in MP3, mp3PRO, WAV, and WMA formats. Almost invariably, you'll want to stick with MP3 files so that you can use them with your iPod. mp3PRO files offer higher audio quality than MP3 at the same file size, but your iPod can read only the MP3-compatible part of the mp3PRO file, so the mp3PRO files sound disappointing when you play them back on the iPod.

Before you can use MUSICMATCH Jukebox with your iPod, you must install the iPod for Windows plug-in. If your iPod came with MUSICMATCH Jukebox, the iPod for Windows plug-in should be on the CD as well. Otherwise, go to www.musicmatch.com/info/plug-ins/ and download the right plug-in for your iPod. At the time of this writing, there's a different plug-in for first- and second-generation iPods (which MUSICMATCH refers to as "iPod") and third-generation and later iPods (which MUSICMATCH refers to as "iPod 2").

Before you can install the iPod for Windows plug-in successfully, usually you need to uninstall iTunes for Windows and the iPod Software from your PC. Problems almost always occur when you install iTunes for Windows and the iPod Software *after* installing MUSICMATCH Jukebox, because the iPod Software corrupts MUSICMATCH Jukebox's iPod for Windows plug-in, but these problems also tend to occur if you install MUSICMATCH Jukebox after iTunes for Windows. Bottom line: usually the town ain't big enough for the two of them.

Once you've got the plug-in installed and running, you should be able to plug in your iPod and have the iPod Manager detect it. The iPod Manager lets you choose among your iPods when you have two or more attached to your computer. Less esoterically, it lets you enable and disable

16

disk mode, specify a home application (for example, MUSICMATCH Jukebox) for the iPod and choose whether to run the home application when you plug in your iPod, and whether to display the iPod Manager icon in the system tray (which is usually convenient).

Once you've introduced your iPod to MUSICMATCH Jukebox and launched MUSICMATCH Jukebox itself, use the MUSICMATCH Portables Plus window to load songs onto your iPod and remove songs from it.

Anapod Explorer

Anapod Explorer, from Red Chair Software, Inc. (www.redchairsoftware.com), is a full-fledged utility for managing your iPod or iPods on Windows. Anapod Explorer comes in a Trial Edition that's free but has limited features and a Full Edition that costs $25.00. Anapod Explorer runs as a plug-in to Windows Explorer, so you work in a largely familiar interface (see Figure 16-1), and you can use drag-and-drop to perform file transfers.

Anapod Explorer installs easily enough (there's a wizard), but its activation regime is enough to try the patience of even a doctor. You have to activate Anapod Explorer for each iPod you want to use. The activation process involves generating an ID for the iPod, supplying that ID to Red Chair Software via the company's web site, and waiting to receive an activation key via e-mail. The process can take up to 24 hours.

Anapod Explorer uses a controller named Anapod Manager to establish communication with and control the iPod. Anapod Manager runs by default when you launch Windows and displays an icon in the notification area. You can right-click this icon to launch Anapod Explorer or configure Anapod Manager.

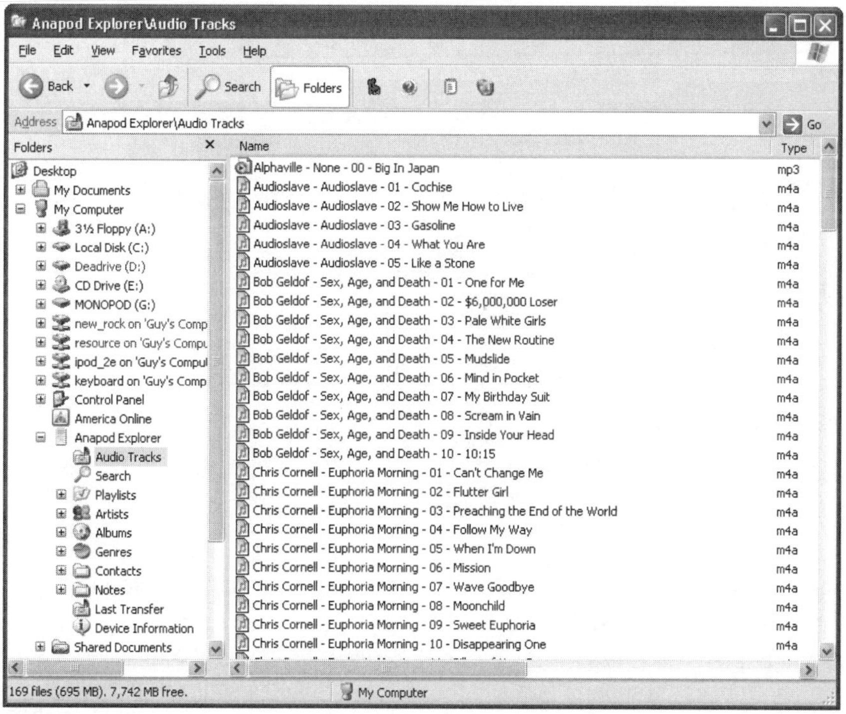

FIGURE 16-1   Anapod Explorer works as a plug-in to Windows Explorer.

16

Once you've got it working, Anapod Explorer offers strong features:

■ Anapod Explorer launches much faster than iTunes for Windows.

■ Anapod Explorer's AudioMorph feature lets you automatically convert song files in the MP3, WAV, OGG (Ogg Vorbis), and WMA formats to a particular bitrate when loading them on your iPod. For example, you might choose to load all song files on your iPod at the 128 Kbps bitrate if you felt that bitrate delivered the optimum balance of audio quality versus file size. Anapod Explorer then converts song files encoded at other bitrates (usually higher bitrates) to your specified bitrate before transferring them to the iPod. To get AudioMorph working, you may need to download and install the LAME encoder, the AudioMorph Ogg Components, and some Windows Media Encoder 9 components. Anapod Explorer walks you through the process.

■ Anapod Explorer can transfer files from your iPod back to your computer.

■ Anapod Explorer has some well-thought-out user features. For example, the Transferring To Device dialog box not only lets you see which file Anapod Explorer is working on, the overall progress, and the transfer performance, but it also lets you compare the transfer performance to that of other users.

■ Anapod Explorer's SpeedSync feature lets you quickly synchronize specific folders between your iPod and your PC.

■ Anapod Explorer includes a miniature web server that allows you to access your iPod remotely from any computer on the network. You can play songs in formats that your browser's plug-ins can play, or you can download any song to your local hard disk.

XPlay

XPlay from Mediafour Corporation (www.mediafour.com) was originally developed to let Windows users synchronize Mac-formatted iPods with their PCs. XPlay now works with Windows-formatted iPods as well. XPlay costs $29.95, making it the most expensive of these options for managing your iPod or recovering music from it. You can download a 15-day trial version of XPlay to find out how you like it.

XPlay (see Figure 16-2) uses Windows Explorer as its interface, displaying your iPod as a drive and using an XPlay Music folder to represent the contents of the iPod's music database. Within the XPlay Music folder, you can drill down to view playlists, albums, and artists. You can use the Songs item to view all the songs on your iPod.

Having your iPod appear as a drive in Windows Explorer makes management and file transfers easy:

- To copy song files to your iPod, drag them and drop them on it.

- To copy song files from your iPod to your PC using XPlay, drill down to the appropriate song or folder on the iPod. Then either drag the song or folder to a folder on your PC, or click the Copy To button on the toolbar and use the Browse For Folder dialog box to specify the destination.

- To add contacts to your iPod, drop them on the Contacts folder. Similarly, to add data files, drop them on your iPod.

- You can play songs directly from your iPod using players such as Winamp, MUSICMATCH Jukebox, or Windows Media Player. (The player must support the format used by the song file. Almost any player supports MP3 files, but relatively few support AAC files.)

16

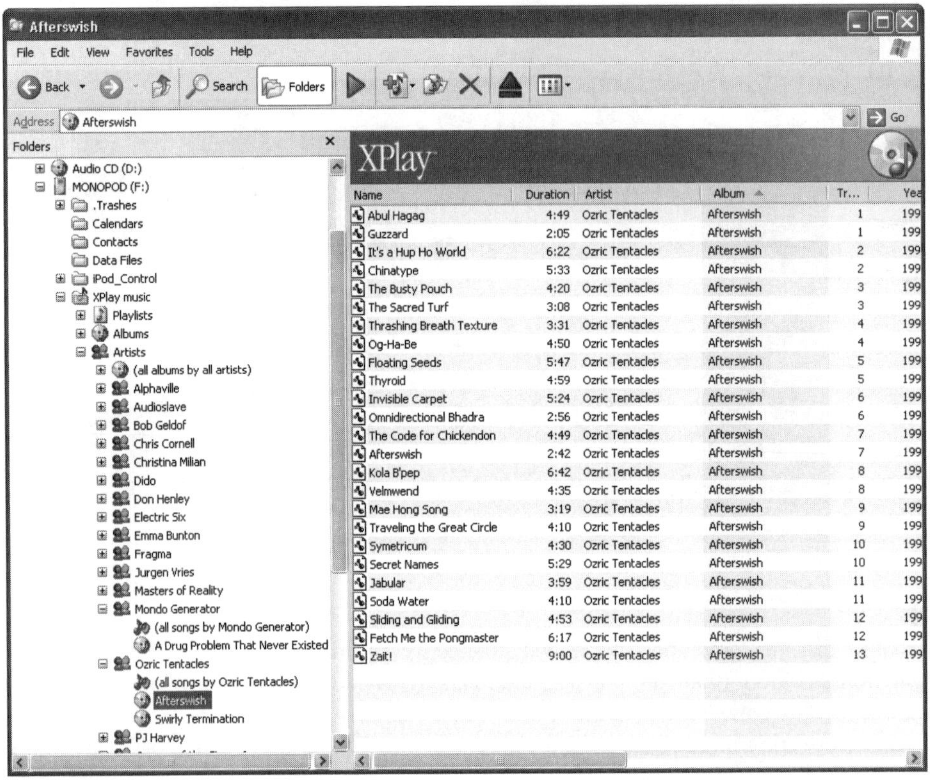

FIGURE 16-2   XPlay uses Windows Explorer as its interface, giving you access to your songs in a familiar format.

Play Songs from Your iPod Through Your Computer

Another capability of the iPod that's not immediately obvious is that you can play music from your iPod through your computer's speakers by setting the music playing from iTunes. iTunes reads the track information off the iPod via the FireWire cable or USB cable and plays it through its sound system, treating your iPod as a local hard drive (which it is, in effect).

Depending on what kind of speakers your computer has and how much you enjoy listening to them, this item may be anything from a curiosity to an indispensable part of your listening.

This capability tends to be most useful when your iPod contains tracks that the computer you're using doesn't contain. (If the computer contains the tracks, it's easier to play the tracks directly from the computer.) If the computer is the one with which you use your iPod, the only reason to use this capability (beyond curiosity) is if you've configured your iPod for manual updating because it contains a music library larger than your computer can hold. More likely, you'll want to use this capability with a computer other than your own—for example, when you're visiting a friend, and you want them to hear the great music they've been missing.

To play songs from your iPod through your computer, you must configure it for manual management of songs and playlists. To do so, right-click the iPod's entry in the Source pane in iTunes and choose iPod Options to display the iPod Preferences dialog box, select the Manually Manage Songs And Playlists option button, click the Yes button in the confirmation dialog box, and then click the OK button to close the iPod Preferences dialog box.

Once you've done that, you can play songs from your iPod using your computer. Follow these steps:

1. Connect your iPod to the computer through which you want to play the music. If this computer isn't your iPod's home computer, iTunes may offer to synchronize with this computer (depending on the settings currently in effect). Click the No button.

2. Select your iPod's icon in the Source pane to display the contents of your iPod.

3. Select the song or songs you want to play.

4. Press SPACEBAR or click the Play button.

Use the iTunes controls to pause play, apply equalizations, or change the volume. As usual when connected to a computer via the FireWire or USB cable, your iPod is acting as a slave drive, so its controls won't respond.

Before disconnecting your iPod, remember to reset your synchronization preference, if appropriate.

16

Chapter 17

Troubleshoot iPod and iTunes Problems

How to...

- ■ Avoid voiding your warranty
- ■ Know the best approach for troubleshooting your iPod
- ■ Learn key troubleshooting maneuvers
- ■ Use your iPod's built-in diagnostic tools to pinpoint problems
- ■ Troubleshoot common and less-common problems

It goes without saying that Apple has built the iPod and iPod mini to be as reliable as possible—after all, Apple would like to sell at least one iPod or iPod mini to everyone in the world who has a computer, and they'd much prefer to be thwarted in this aim by economics than by negative feedback. But even so, iPods go wrong sometimes. This chapter shows you what to do when it's *your* iPod that goes wrong.

This chapter pursues a two-pronged approach to troubleshooting. First, it shows you some standard troubleshooting maneuvers you may need to perform to resuscitate your iPod or rope its operating system back under control, and some diagnostics you may want to try when you think something is really wrong (or you want to see what—if anything—the diagnostic tests do). Second, it presents problems as they'll typically manifest themselves, and then walks you through troubleshooting the problems and (with any luck) solving them.

Before we get our—*your*—hands grubby, let's talk briefly about the warranty your iPod should have included and how you can avoid voiding it.

NOTE   *As in previous chapters, this chapter uses* iPod *as a generic term to refer to both regular (full-size) iPods and the iPod mini. Where the iPod mini or a particular generation of regular iPod behaves differently, this chapter points out the difference.*

Your Warranty and How to Void It

Like most electronics goods, your iPod almost certainly came with a warranty. Unlike with most other electronics goods, your chances of needing to use that warranty are relatively high. This is because you're likely to use your iPod extensively and carry it with you.

Even if you don't sit on your iPod, rain or other water doesn't creep into it, and gravity doesn't dash it sharply against something unforgiving (such as the sidewalk), your iPod may suffer from other problems—anything from critters or debris jamming the FireWire port or Dock Connector port to its hard drive getting corrupted or its operating system getting scrambled. Perhaps most likely of all is that your iPod's battery will lose its potency, either gradually or dramatically. If any of these misfortunes befalls your iPod, you'll probably want to get it repaired under warranty—provided you haven't voided the warranty.

The first iPods carried a 90-day warranty, which inspired little confidence in their durability. However, Apple then moved to a one-year warranty both for newer iPods and for those already sold. The iPod Service Page (depot.info.apple.com/ipod/index.html) contains details of which iPods are still under warranty and the prices you'll pay for repairs if your iPod is out of warranty.

Most of the warranty is pretty straightforward, but the following points are worth noting:

- You have to make your claim within the warranty period, so if your iPod fails a day short of a year after you bought it, you'll need to make your claim instantly.

- If your iPod is currently under warranty, you can buy an AppleCare package for it to extend its warranty to two years. Most extended warranties on electrical products are a waste of money, because the extended warranties largely duplicate your existing rights as a consumer to be sold a product that's functional and of merchantable quality. But given the attrition rate among hard-used iPods, AppleCare may be a good idea. Similarly, CompUSA offers a Technology Assurance Program (TAP) for iPods that provides two years of service and a one-time replacement of your iPod if you break it.

- Apple can choose whether to repair your iPod using either new or refurbished parts, exchange it for another iPod that's at least functionally equivalent but may be either new or rebuilt (and may contain used parts), or refund you the purchase price of your iPod. Unless you have valuable data on your iPod, the refund is a great option, because you'll be able to get a new iPod—perhaps even a higher-capacity one.

- Apple takes no responsibility for getting back any data on your iPod. This isn't surprising, as Apple may need to reformat your iPod's hard drive or replace it. But this means that you must back up your iPod if it contains data you value that you don't have copies of elsewhere.

You can void your warranty more or less effortlessly in any of the following easily avoidable ways:

- Damage your iPod deliberately.

- Open your iPod or have someone other than Apple open it for you. As discussed in "What You Might Want to Know About Your iPod's Internals," in Chapter 13, your iPod isn't designed to be opened by anyone except trained technicians. Unless you're highly skillful, very careful, and you have the right tools, all you'll achieve by opening your iPod is damage.

- Modify your iPod. Modifications such as installing a larger drive in the iPod would necessarily involve opening your iPod anyway, but external modifications can void your warranty, too. For example, if you choose to trepan your iPod so as to screw a holder directly onto it, you would void your warranty. (You'd also stand a great chance of drilling into something sensitive inside the case.)

Approach Troubleshooting Your iPod

17

When something goes wrong with your iPod, take three deep breaths before you do anything. Then take another three deep breaths if you need them. Then try to work out what's wrong.

Remember that a calm and rational approach will always get you further than blind panic. This is easy to say (and if you're reading this when your iPod is running smoothly, easy to nod your head at). But if you've just dropped your iPod onto a hard surface from a significant height, left it on the roof of your car so it fell off and landed in the perfect position for you to reverse over it, or gotten caught in an unexpectedly heavy rainfall, you'll probably be desperate to find out if your iPod is alive or dead.

So take those three deep breaths. You may well *not* have ruined your iPod forever—but if you take some heavy-duty troubleshooting actions without making sure they're necessary, you might lose some data that wasn't already lost or do some damage you'll have trouble repairing.

Any of the following can go wrong:

- The iPod's hardware—anything from the FireWire port (which is surprisingly vulnerable) to the Dock Connector port (less so) to the battery or the hard disk
- The iPod's software
- The iPod's power adapter
- The FireWire cable or USB cable
- Your computer's FireWire port or FireWire controller, or its USB port or USB controller
- iTunes or the other software you're using to control your iPod

Given all these possibilities, be prepared to spend some time troubleshooting any problem.

Learn Troubleshooting Maneuvers

This section discusses several maneuvers you may need to use to troubleshoot your iPod: resetting your iPod, draining its battery, restoring its operating system on either Mac OS X or Windows, running a disk scan, and using its built-in diagnostic tools to pinpoint problems.

Reset Your iPod

If your iPod freezes so it doesn't respond to the controls, you can reset it by connecting it to a power source (either a computer that's not sleeping or an electrical socket) and then holding down the Menu button and the Play/Pause button for several seconds. When your iPod displays the Apple logo, release the buttons, and then give your iPod a few seconds to finish booting.

Resetting an iPod mini is a little different. First, toggle the Hold switch on and off. Then hold down the Select button and the Menu button for about five seconds until your iPod mini displays the Apple logo.

If your iPod freezes when you don't have a power source available, try resetting it by using the above technique without the power source. Sometimes it works; other times it doesn't. But you've nothing to lose by trying.

TIP   *If the Select button on a third-generation iPod stops working, but all the other buttons and the Scroll wheel are working, move the Hold switch to the On position and then back to the Off position. If that doesn't clear the problem, connect the iPod to the iPod Power Adapter and repeat the maneuver with the Hold switch.*

Drain Your iPod's Battery

If you can't reset your iPod, its battery might have gotten into such a low state that it needs draining. (This supposedly seldom happens—but the planets might have decided that you're due a bad day.) To drain the battery, disconnect your iPod from its power source and leave it for 24 hours. (Yes, this is a painful length of time to be without your music.) Then try plugging your iPod into a power source. After your iPod has received power for a few seconds, hold down the Menu button and the Play/Pause button to reset it. (For an iPod mini, hold down the Select button and the Menu button.)

If draining the battery and recharging it revives your iPod, update your iPod's software with the latest update from Apple Software Updates to try to prevent the problem from occurring again. See the section "Keep Your iPod's Operating System Up-to-Date," in Chapter 13, for details on how to update your iPod's operating system. (Briefly, if you're using Mac OS X, use Software Update to download the latest version. If you're using Windows, visit www.apple.com/swupdates/ and download the latest version manually.)

Restore Your iPod

If your iPod is having severe difficulties, you may need to restore it. Restoring your iPod replaces its operating system with a new copy of the operating system that has Apple's factory settings.

CAUTION *Restoring your iPod deletes all the data on your iPod's hard disk—the operating system, all your music, all your contacts, and calendar information—and returns your iPod to its original factory settings. So restoring your iPod is usually a last resort when troubleshooting. If possible, back up all the data you care about that's stored on your iPod before restoring it. (Only "if possible"? Yes—if your iPod is so messed up that you need to restore it, you may not be able to back up the data.)*

To restore your iPod, you need the iPod Software Updater. You should have installed a version of it with your iPod, but for best results, download the latest version of the iPod Software Updater:

- On Mac OS X, use Software Update: choose Apple | System Preferences, click the Software Update icon, and then click the Check Now button.

- On Windows, go to www.apple.com/swupdates/ and follow the iPod link to find iPod-related updates. If there's a new version of the iPod Software Updater, download it, and then double-click the resulting file to install it.

Quick reminder: The first- and second-generation iPods use the iPod Software Updater versions numbered 1 (for example, 1.3), while the third-generation iPods use the iPod Software Updater versions numbered 2 (for example, 2.1), and the iPod mini uses the iPod Software Updater for iPod mini versions numbered 1 (for example, 1.0). You can't use the version 2 updaters with first- and second-generation iPods, nor can you use the version 1 updaters with third-generation iPods. The iPod mini needs its own updaters, and you can't use them for regular iPods.

17

Restore Your iPod on Mac OS X

To restore your iPod on Mac OS X, follow these steps:

1. Connect your iPod to your computer via the FireWire cable. If your iPod is set to synchronize automatically with iTunes, allow it to do so.

2. Press COMMAND-SHIFT-U or choose Go | Utilities from the Finder menu to display the contents of your Applications/Utilities folder.

3. Open the folder that contains the latest version of the iPod Software Updater. Apple has named most of the iPod Software Updater versions consistently, using folders such as iPod Software 1.3 Updater, iPod Software 1.3.1 Updater, iPod Software 2.0 Updater, and iPod Software 2.0.1 Updater, but the iPod Software 2.1 Updater unhelpfully bucks the convention by using a folder named iPod Software Updater.

4. Double-click the iPod Software Updater to run it.

5. Run the iPod Software Updater. (You should find it in the Applications/Utilities/iPod Software Updater folder unless you've moved it or someone else has moved it.) Your Mac displays an iPod Software Updater window such as this:

6. If the lower-left corner of the Updater window contains a lock icon and the text "Click the lock to make changes," click the lock icon to display the Authenticate dialog box:

Enter your password in the Password or Phrase text box, and then click the OK button. If you entered the correct password, the Updater returns you to the Update window and enables the Update button (if you can install an updated version of the iPod software) and the Restore button.

7. Click the Restore button to start the restore process. The Updater displays a final warning to make sure you understand you're about to lose all the data on your iPod:

8. Click the Restore button if you're absolutely sure you want to proceed. The iPod Software Updater restores your iPod's operating system and deletes the files on it.

9. What happens next depends on the generation of iPod you're updating.

- With a third-generation iPod or an iPod mini, the iPod Software Updater and the iPod complete the update without your needing to disconnect your iPod and plug it back in.

- With a first- or second-generation iPod, the iPod Software Updater displays a window telling you that it has restored your iPod to factory settings and asking you to unplug and replug your iPod to complete the restore process. Unplug your iPod from the FireWire cable, and then plug it back in when it displays a FireWire cable and socket. Your iPod displays an Apple logo and a progress bar as it completes the restoration process.

NOTE   *At this point, the iPod Software Updater window implies that you need to click the lock icon if you want to prevent anyone else from restoring your iPod. In fact, you don't need to do so; when you quit the iPod Software Updater, it automatically locks your iPod against changes.*

10. Press COMMAND-Q or choose iPod Updater | Quit iPod Updater to close the iPod Software Updater window.

11. Your iPod should then appear on your desktop under the default name "iPod." If it doesn't, you may need to reset it by holding down the Menu button and the Play/Pause button for several seconds.

17

12. When iTunes notices your iPod, it displays this iPod Setup Assistant page:

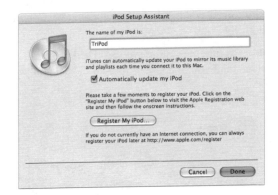

NOTE *If iTunes doesn't notice your iPod, launch iTunes manually.*

13. Enter the name for your iPod in the text box. Select or clear the Automatically Update My iPod check box as appropriate, then click the Done button. iTunes then synchronizes your iPod with the music library if you left the check box selected. If you cleared the check box, iTunes configures your iPod for you to manage your songs and playlists manually.

NOTE *After you next disconnect your iPod, you'll need to specify the language for it to use.*

Restore Your iPod on Windows XP

To restore your iPod on Windows XP, follow these steps:

1. Connect your iPod to your PC via the FireWire cable or the USB cable. Allow iTunes to synchronize with your iPod if it's set to do so.

2. Choose Start | All Programs | iPod | Updater or a similar command (for example, Start | All Programs | iPod | System Software | Updater) to display the iPod Software Updater window:

CAUTION *Unlike the iPod Software Updater for the Mac, the iPod Software Updater for Windows doesn't double-check if you're sure you know what you're doing when you click the Restore button.*

3. Click the Restore button. The iPod Software Updater formats your iPod's hard disk:

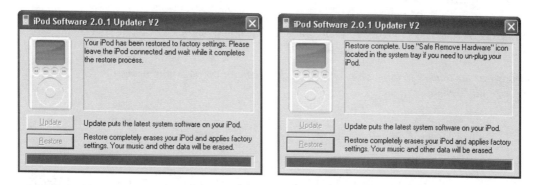

4. What happens next depends on which generation of iPod you're restoring and how it's connected to your PC:

■ If you're restoring a third-generation iPod, and it's connected via a FireWire cable or via a USB cable whose other fork is plugged into the iPod Power Adapter, the iPod Software Updater displays the screen shown on the left below, asking you to leave your iPod connected and wait while it completes the restore process. When the restore process is complete, the iPod Software Updater displays the screen shown on the right below. The process is similar for an iPod mini connected via FireWire or USB.

17

TIP *If you're restoring a third-generation iPod via a USB cable, plug the other fork of the cable into the iPod Power Adapter. Doing so simplifies the update process over having to disconnect and then reconnect it.*

■ If you're restoring a third-generation iPod, it's connected via a USB cable, and the other fork of the cable isn't plugged into the iPod Power Adapter; or if you're restoring a first- or second-generation iPod (which will always be connected via FireWire), the iPod Software Updater prompts you to disconnect your iPod and connect it to the iPod Power Adapter:

Disconnect your iPod as instructed and wait for it to display a iPod Dock Connector symbol indicating that you should plug it in. Then connect the iPod to the iPod Power Adapter using the FireWire-to–iPod Dock Connector cable. Wait until the progress bar has made its way across the screen, and then connect your iPod to the USB cable as usual.

5. Click the Close button (the X button) in the upper-right corner of the iPod Software Updater window to close the iPod Software Updater.

After you disconnect your iPod, you'll need to set the language it uses.

 If the iPod Software Updater hangs after you plug your iPod back in, follow the steps described in "Recover from a Stalled Restore Process," in Chapter 16, to recover.

Run a Disk Scan

If you think there might be something wrong with your iPod's hard disk, you can run a disk scan to find out. A scan takes roughly 15 to 30 minutes, depending on the capacity of your iPod's hard disk, so set aside plenty of time to run the scan.

At the time of writing, you can't run a disk scan for an iPod mini using this technique.

To run a disk scan, follow these steps:

1. Hold down the Menu button and the Play/Pause button for a few seconds to reset your iPod.

2. When your iPod displays the Apple logo, hold down the Previous, Next, Select, and Menu buttons for a second or two. (Guitarists can usually perform this maneuver more easily than other people. If you're not a guitarist, put down your iPod on a flat surface first.)

3. Your iPod them performs a disk scan, displaying a magnifying glass poring over a hard disk and a progress bar as it does so:

4. When the scan has finished, check the icon your iPod is displaying:

■ A check mark on a disk icon means the disk is fine.

■ An exclamation mark on a disk icon means the disk scan failed.

■ An arrow on a disk icon means that the scan fixed some problems it found. The scan may have fixed all problems, but the iPod doesn't tell you that. Restore your iPod as described in "Restore Your iPod," earlier in this chapter, to resume normal service. (If your iPod contains valuable files that you don't have copies of elsewhere, try to rescue those files before restoring your iPod.)

■ An exclamation point in a warning triangle on a picture of an iPod with a sad face means the hard disk isn't working. Go directly to Apple Support. Do not pass Go. Collect $200 from the ATM if your iPod's out of warranty.

5. Press the Play button to exit the disk-scan mode.

NOTE *If your iPod runs a disk scan automatically when you start it, your iPod suspects there's a problem with the hard drive. It's best to allow the scan to continue, but in extreme circumstances, you may need to cancel the scan. To cancel it, hold down the Select button for a few seconds. Your iPod then displays a disk icon with a cross mark on it, which means it'll repeat the disk scan the next time you turn it on.*

Use Your iPod's Diagnostics to Pinpoint Problems

Next along the line of troubleshooting tools are the diagnostic tools built into your iPod's operating system. To access the diagnostic tools, follow these steps:

1. Hold down the Menu and Play/Pause buttons for a few seconds to reset your iPod. For an iPod mini, toggle the Hold switch on and off, and then hold down the Select button and the Menu button for a few seconds.

2. When your iPod displays the Apple logo, hold down the Previous, Next, and Select buttons together for a couple of seconds. On an iPod mini, hold down the Previous and Select buttons for a few seconds until your iPod mini displays a reversed Apple logo.

17

3. When the screen goes blank, release the buttons. Your iPod momentarily displays a screen of scattered text that details the version number of the diagnostic tools. Then it displays a list of diagnostic tests:

```
A . 5  I N  1
B . R E S E T
C . K E Y
D . A U D I O
E . R E M O T E
F . F I R E W I R E
G . S L E E P
H . A 2 D
```

Different generations of iPods have different diagnostic tests to reflect their capabilities and aspirations. Table 17-1 lists the tests and which generations they're available on. The table follows the iPods' convention of listing the tests by a letter.

CAUTION *Sometimes Apple changes the diagnostic tests in iPod firmware updates, so your iPod may show you different diagnostics than those listed here.*

Letter	First- and Second-Generation iPod	Third-Generation iPod	iPod mini
A	5 IN 1	5 IN 1	5 IN 1
B	RESET	RESET	RESET
C	KEY	KEY	KEY
D	AUDIO	AUDIO	CHGRCUR
E	REMOTE	REMOTE	REMOTE
F	FIREWIRE	FW ID	HP STAT
G	SLEEP	SLEEP	SLEEP
H	A2D	A2D	BATT A2D
I	OTPO CNT	OTPO CNT	A2D STAT
J	LCM	LCM	FIREWIRE
K	RTC	CHG STATUS	HDD R/W
L	SDRAM	USB DISK	SMRT DAT
M	FLASH	CHK SUM	SMRT SCAN
N	WHEELA2D	CONTRAST	DRV TEMP
O	HDD SCAN	HDD SCAN	DISKMODE
P	RUN IN	RUN IN	WHEEL
Q	—	—	CONTRAST
S	—	—	AUDIO
T	—	—	STATUS

TABLE 17-1   Diagnostic Tests on the Different Generations of iPods and the iPod mini

To use the diagnostic tests, use the following keys:

- Press the Next and Previous buttons to navigate through the list of tests.
- Press the Select button to run the highlighted test.
- Press the Play button to return from the results of a test to the diagnostic screen.
- Reset your iPod by using the RESET diagnostic or the techniques described earlier in this chapter to leave the diagnostic screen.

The following sections discuss the diagnostic tests you'll most likely want to perform.

Check the FireWire Port

To check the FireWire port on your iPod, run the FIREWIRE test (on first- or second-generation iPods or the iPod mini) or the FW ID test (on third-generation iPods). If your iPod displays FW PASS, your FireWire port is working. (Third-generation iPods display the FireWire ID as well.) If your iPod displays FW FAIL, seek professional assistance.

The iPod mini gives a readout such as the following for a successful FireWire connection:

```
FW TEST
CONNECT
SPD S400
CHIP OK
FW PASS
```

If the test diagnoses no connection, the iPod mini displays NOCONECT.

Check the Audio Subsystem

To check your iPod's audio subsystem, connect a pair of headphones or speakers and run the AUDIO test. You'll hear six thumping electronic beats in rapid succession if all is well. After managing this test, first- and second-generation iPods display 0X00000001 DONE. Third-generation iPods simply display PLAY TEST.

The AUDIO test on the iPod mini is a little different. When you enter the test, your iPod mini displays AD GAIN and a number (for example, 120). You can press the Previous button to decrease the gain or the Next button to increase it. Press the Select button to play the audio test and check that you hear fast-paced electronic beats. The iPod mini then displays END TEST.

Check the RAM

To check your iPod's RAM (the 32MB chip used for buffering audio) on first- and second-generation iPods, run the SDRAM test. If all is well, your iPod displays SDRAM PASS. If there's a problem, your iPod displays SDRAM FAIL.

Check the iPod's Buttons

If one of the buttons on your iPod seems to stop working, you'll probably be able to tell without diagnostics. But before you call for backup, you may want to check that your iPod agrees with you that there's a problem. To do so, run the Key test. Your iPod gives you five seconds to press all the buttons on your iPod's front panel. It lists each button you press, starting off with HOLD, which you don't need to press. (The iPod mini doesn't list HOLD.) The Select button is listed as ACTION. If you press the buttons within the five seconds, and your iPod registers the presses, your iPod displays KEY PASS. If you miss a button, or if one or more of the buttons isn't working, your iPod displays KEY FAIL.

Check the Remote Control

To check the remote control, plug in the remote control, and then run the REMOTE test. Press each button on the remote control: Volume Up, Volume Down, Next, Previous, and Play/Pause. (You don't need to move the Hold button on the remote control.) As you do so, the screen displays a shaded block for each key registered rather than displaying words. If you register presses on all five buttons in time, your iPod displays RMT PASS. If you miss a button, or if one or more of the buttons isn't working, your iPod displays RMT FAIL.

This test is a little different on the iPod mini: You press the buttons the same way, but the iPod mini screen displays text for the buttons: + and – for Volume Up and Volume Down, Next and Pre for the Next and Previous buttons, and Play for the Play button. The iPod mini describes the test as UARTTEST and rewards it with UARTPASS or UARTFAIL. (UART is the acronym for *universal asynchronous receiver/transmitter*.)

Check the Scroll Wheel

To check the Scroll wheel on any regular iPod but a first-generation iPod, run the OTPO CNT test. (OTPO is a typo—it should be OPTO.) When you do so, your iPod displays the text OPTO TEST, OPT, and the value of the current position of the Scroll wheel in hexadecimal (for example, 0XFFFFFFFD). To check the Scroll wheel is working, scroll in either direction and watch the value change.

The OTPO CNT test is for a nonmoving Scroll wheel, which is why it doesn't work for first-generation iPods. To test the Scroll wheel on a first-generation iPod, use the WHEEL A2D test. If your iPod has a nonmoving Scroll wheel, the WHEEL A2D test doesn't work.

To test the Scroll wheel on an iPod mini, run the WHEEL test. The iPod mini screen displays WHELTEST and a value that changes as you move your finger around the Scroll wheel. Reset your iPod to escape from this test.

Check That Sleep Mode Is Working

To check that Sleep mode is working on your iPod, run the SLEEP test. If the test works, you'll need to reset your iPod to get it working again. If your iPod doesn't go to sleep, the test has failed.

Change the Default Contrast on a Third-Generation iPod or iPod mini

To change the default contrast on a third-generation iPod, run the CONTRAST diagnostic and scroll clockwise (to increase the contrast) or counterclockwise (to decrease the contrast). When you've reached the degree of contrast you want the iPod to have after you reset it, press the Play button to exit the diagnostic test.

On an iPod mini, run the CONTRAST diagnostic but use the Play button to move from screen to screen, and the Previous and Next buttons to increase or decrease the contrast on each screen. Press the Menu button to toggle the backlight. At the end, you reach a screen that invites you to press Action (in other words, the Select button) to quit or Play to continue.

Check How Your Third-Generation or Later iPod Is Getting Charged

To check how a third-generation or later iPod is getting charged, run the CHG STUS test. You'll see something like this:

```
STATUSTEST
USB 0
FW 1
HP 0
BAT CHR 1
CHGR 00000
```

An entry of 0 means that the iPod has not been receiving charge from the device—for example, third-generation iPods return "USB 0" because they don't receive charge along the USB cable and "FW 1" because they receive charge along the FireWire cable.

Check How Hot Your iPod mini Is Running

To check how hot your iPod mini is running, run the DRV TEMP test. You'll see a screen that gives the current temperature, together with minimum and maximum temperatures.

What About the Other Diagnostic Tests?

Okay—so those were the diagnostic tests that are most likely to be directly useful to you. But what are the others for?

The brief answer is that you really don't need to know. But since you're curious (or perhaps strange), Table 17-2 explains the remaining diagnostic tests briefly.

Troubleshoot Specific Problems

This section discusses how to troubleshoot specific problems with the iPod, starting with the more common problems and moving gradually toward the esoteric end of the spectrum.

Your iPod Won't Respond to Keypresses

If your iPod won't respond to keypresses, follow as many of these steps, in order, as are necessary to revive it:

1. Check that neither the Hold switch on your iPod nor the Hold switch on the remote control (if you're using it) is on.

2. Check that the battery is charged. When the battery is too low to run the iPod (for example, for playing back music), your iPod will display a low-battery symbol—a battery icon with an exclamation point—for a few seconds when you press a key. (You may miss this icon if you're using the remote or you're pressing your iPod's buttons without looking at the screen.) Connect the iPod to a power source (either an electrical outlet or a computer that's not asleep), give it a few minutes to recharge a little, disconnect it again, and then try turning it on.

17

Test	Explanation
5 IN 1	Runs the following tests: LCM, RTC, SDRAM, FLASH, and WHEEL A2D. Press the Select button to move through the LCM test; if you don't, your iPod will appear to have hung with a blank screen.
RESET	Resets your iPod.
A2D	Tests your iPod's power system.
LCM	Checks the liquid crystal display by showing different patterns on it. (Press the Select button to display the next pattern.)
RTC	Displays the current output of your iPod's real-time clock.
FLASH	Displays a hexadecimal number identifying your iPod's current version of ROM (read-only memory).
HDD SCAN	Starts a hard-disk scan. As you saw in "Run a Disk Scan," earlier in this chapter, you can start a hard-disk scan without visiting the diagnostics screen. Running the scan from the diagnostics screen skips the graphics and displays the result in text (for example, HDD PASS if all is well).
RUN IN	Runs a looping battery of tests: LCM, RTC, OTPO CNT, HDD, and AUDIO. Reset your iPod to escape from the loop.
CHK SUM	Verifies that the signature of the Firmware is valid. If the firmware has been compromised in any way (for example, if there's a change in the file size of the installed firmware), the CHK SUM test will fail.
CHG STUS	Displays information on how the iPod is connecting to a PC (via USB or via FireWire).
HDD R/W	Performs a read-write test on the hard disk. You must plug the iPod mini into a power source before the scan will start.
SMRT DAT	Displays a readout of drive-related data.
SMRT SCAN	Performs a scan of the hard disk. You must plug the iPod mini into a power source before the scan will start.
HP STAT	Displays a screen that lets you check whether the iPod mini has detected a device plugged into its headphone socket (HP 1) or not (HP 0), and whether the Hold switch is on (HOLD 1) or off (HOLD 0).
DISKMODE	Forces disk mode on the iPod mini.
CHGRCUR	Displays a screen on which you can check and set charging and suspend levels for USB.

TABLE 17-2   Brief Explanations of the iPod's Other Diagnostic Tests

3. Reset your iPod (see the section "Reset Your iPod," earlier in this chapter).

4. Enter diagnostic mode and run the Key test (see the section "Check the iPod's Buttons," earlier in this chapter).

Your Remote Control Stops Working

If your iPod's remote control suddenly stops working without having suffered any obvious accident (such as you sitting on it or the dog chewing it into tinsel and confetti), check that its plug is pushed in fully. This is a particular problem on second-generation iPods, on which the remote control connects in a recessed ring around the headphone socket; you may need to twist the plug a little to improve the connection. (Don't twist the plug on a third-generation iPod or an iPod mini, because you'll stand a good chance of breaking it.)

If the plug is firmly seated, enter diagnostic mode and run the Remote test. See the section "Check the Remote Control," earlier in this chapter, for details.

Your Computer Doesn't React When You Plug In Your iPod

If your computer (Mac or PC) doesn't react when you plug in your iPod, any of several things might have gone wrong. Try the actions described in the following subsections.

Unplug Any Other FireWire Devices in the FireWire Chain

If you're connecting via FireWire and you've plugged in another FireWire device, try unplugging it. The problem may be that your FireWire controller can't supply power to another unpowered device as well as to your iPod.

Check That the FireWire Cable Is Working

Check that the FireWire cable is working. Make sure the cable is firmly plugged into both the FireWire port on the computer and the port on your iPod.

NOTE *If possible, use the cable that came with your iPod rather than a third-party cable; some third-party cables may not work with the iPod.*

If you're not sure the cable is working, you can run a partial check by plugging the FireWire cable into your iPod and its power adapter, and then plugging the power adapter into an electrical socket. If your iPod starts charging, you'll know that at least the power-carrying wires on the FireWire cable are working.

Check That the FireWire Port on the Computer Is Working

Check that the FireWire port on the computer is working. In most cases, the easiest way to check is by plugging in another FireWire device that you know is working.

Check That the FireWire Port on the iPod Is Working

Once you've verified that the FireWire cable and the FireWire port on the computer are both working, the FireWire port on your first- or second-generation iPod may be the guilty party. Clean out any dirt or other detritus that's worked its way into the port (this can happen if the port's cover gets loose) and make sure that the cable is securely connected.

You can run a partial check of whether this port is working by plugging your iPod into its power adapter and the adapter into an electrical socket. If your iPod starts charging, you'll know that at least the power-carrying wires in the FireWire socket are working. Chances are the other four wires are okay as well.

But if your iPod *doesn't* start charging, as is more likely, you'll have reason to believe the FireWire port on your iPod is damaged. Enter diagnostic mode and run the FireWire test as described in the section "Check the FireWire Port," earlier in this chapter.

If the FireWire port isn't working, you'll need to get your iPod repaired by an Apple technician (if it's under warranty) or a third-party repair service (if it's not). Broken FireWire ports are a problem that a fair number of users have encountered with first- and second-generation iPods, because pulling out the FireWire cable too hard or too abruptly can easily disconnect the FireWire socket from its connection to the iPod's motherboard. PDASmart.com (www.pdasmart.com) charges $55.00 to repair a broken FireWire port, which compares well to Apple's charge of $249.00 for most iPod repairs other than the battery.

Your iPod Says "Do Not Disconnect" for Ages When Connected to Your Computer

As you saw in Chapter 2, when you connect your iPod to your Mac or PC via the FireWire cable or USB cable, your iPod displays the "Do not disconnect" message while it synchronizes with iTunes. When synchronization is complete, your iPod should display the charging indicator for as long as it's taking on power via the FireWire cable (assuming the FireWire port is powered) or the power fork on the USB cable (assuming that fork is connected to the iPod Power Adapter).

But sometimes it doesn't. If your iPod displays the "Do not disconnect" message for long after synchronization should have finished, first try to remember if you've enabled disk mode on your iPod. If so, you need to unmount your iPod manually, so nothing has gone wrong. Issue an Eject command (for example, right-click the iPod's icon on your Mac desktop and choose Eject from the shortcut menu, or right-click the iPod's drive icon in a My Computer window and choose Eject from the shortcut menu), and your iPod should display the "OK to disconnect" message.

If you haven't enabled disk mode on your iPod, your iPod's hard drive may have gotten stuck spinning. If you pick up your iPod to scrutinize it further, you'll notice it's much hotter than usual if the drive has been spinning for a while. When this happens, eject it in one of the following ways:

■ On the Mac, from iTunes, click the Eject iPod button, press COMMAND-E, or choose Controls | Eject *iPod,* (where *iPod* is the name of your iPod).

■ On the Mac, from the Finder, drag the iPod to the Trash, or right-click it and choose Eject from the context menu.

■ On the Mac or on the PC, right-click the iPod's entry in the Source pane in iTunes and choose Eject *iPod* (where *iPod* is the name of your iPod) from the shortcut menu.

■ On the PC, open a My Computer window (for example, choose Start | My Computer), right-click the drive that represents your iPod, and choose Eject from the shortcut menu.

Your iPod should then display the "OK to disconnect" message, and you can disconnect it safely.

If that doesn't work, you may need to reset your iPod by holding down the Menu and Play/Pause buttons for a few seconds. (For an iPod mini, toggle the Hold switch on and off, and then hold down the Select and Menu buttons for a few seconds.) After your iPod reboots, you should be able to eject it by taking one of the actions listed above.

TIP *If you experience this problem frequently, try updating your iPod to the latest software version available. If there's no newer software version, or if an update doesn't help, use the AC adapter to recharge your iPod rather than recharging it from your computer.*

Your iPod Displays a Disk Icon with Magnifying Glass, Arrow, Check Mark, X, or Exclamation Point

If your iPod displays a disk icon on startup, it suspects there's a problem with its hard disk. See the section "Run a Disk Scan," earlier in this chapter, for details.

Your iPod Displays Only the Apple Logo When You Turn It On

If, when you turn on your iPod, it displays the Apple logo as usual but goes no further, there's most likely a problem with the iPod software. Try resetting your iPod first to see if that clears the problem. Failing that, on a third-generation iPod, move the Hold switch to the On position and then back to the Off position.

If neither of these basic maneuvers works, usually you'll need to restore your iPod as described in "Restore Your iPod," earlier in this chapter.

Songs in Your Music Library Aren't Transferred to Your iPod

If songs you've added to your music library aren't transferred to your iPod even though you've synchronized successfully since adding the songs, there are two possibilities:

- First, check that you haven't configured your iPod for partial synchronization or manual synchronization. For example, if you've chosen to synchronize only selected playlists, your iPod won't synchronize new music files not included on those playlists.

- Second, check that the songs' tags include the artist's name and song name. Without these two items of information, iTunes won't transfer the songs to your iPod, because your iPod's interface won't be able to display the songs to you. You can force iTunes to transfer song files that lack artist and song name tags by adding the song files to a playlist, but in the long run, you'll benefit from tagging all your song files correctly.

Mac OS X Displays the SBOD and Then Fails to Recognize Your iPod

If, when you connect your iPod to your Mac, OS X displays the Spinning Beachball of Death (SBOD) for a while (usually several minutes) and then refuses to recognize your iPod even though your iPod is displaying the "Do not disconnect" message, it may mean you've plugged a Windows iPod into your Mac.

Troubleshooting iTunes

As you've seen in the previous sections, some of the problems with the iPod involve iTunes as well—which is hardly surprising, given how closely they work in partnership. This section focuses on problems that are primarily related to iTunes or that manifest themselves on the iTunes side of the partnership.

"The iPod *'iPod'* Is Linked to Another iTunes Music Library" Message

If, when you connect your iPod to your computer, iTunes displays the message "The iPod *'iPod'* is linked to another iTunes music library," chances are that you've plugged the wrong iPod into your computer. The message box also offers to change this iPod's allegiance from its current computer to this computer. Click the No button and check which iPod this is before synchronizing it.

NOTE *For details about moving your iPod from one computer to another, see "Change the Computer to Which Your iPod Is Linked," in Chapter 16.*

Letting iTunes Copy All Song Files to Your Music Library Runs You Out of Hard-Disk Space

As you saw in the sections "Choose Whether to Store All Song Files in Your Music Library," in Chapter 4 (on the Mac) and Chapter 5 (on Windows), iTunes can copy to your music library folder all the files you add to your music library. Adding all the files to your music library means you have all the files available in one place. This can be good when (for example) you want your PowerBook's, iBook's, or Windows laptop's hard disk to contain copies of all the music files stored on network drives so you can listen to them when your computer isn't connected to the network. But it can take up brutal amounts of disk space—perhaps more space than you have.

If your song files are stored on your hard drive in folders other than your music library folder, you have three choices:

- You can have iTunes copy the files to your music library, doubling the amount of space they take up. In almost all cases, this is the worst possible choice to make. (Rarely, you might want redundant copies of your song files in your music library so you could experiment with them.)

- You can have iTunes store references to the files rather than copies of them. If you also have song files in your music library folder, this is the easiest solution. To do this, clear the Copy Files To iTunes Music Folder When Adding To Library check box on the Advanced sheet of the Preferences dialog box on the Mac or the Advanced tab of the iTunes dialog box on Windows.

- You can move your music library to the folder that contains your song files. This is the easiest solution if your music library is empty.

On the Mac, you usually notice you've got a problem with consolidation when iTunes displays this message box, telling you there isn't enough room on your computer for all the files:

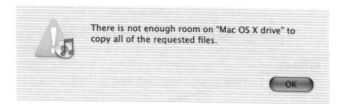

There is not enough room on "Mac OS X drive" to copy all of the requested files.

OK

You may also identify the problem when consolidation appears to be taking halfway until eternity.

Clearly, not having enough space to copy the files *isn't* okay—but iTunes offers only an OK button. But when you click OK to dismiss this message box, iTunes goes ahead and tries to copy all the files anyway.

Much the same thing happens on Windows, except that the error message is marginally more helpful—at least iTunes tells you that it's going to copy as many files as possible:

iTunes

There is not enough room on "IBM_PRELOAD" to copy all of the requested files. iTunes will copy as many files as possible.

OK

Clearly, *this* isn't okay either, but again, iTunes doesn't let you cancel the operation. (Perhaps this is intended to be a learning experience and to build character.)

Unless you're consumed by morbid curiosity to see exactly how many files iTunes can pack on your hard disk before it's stuffed to the gills, and the exact order of the alerts and error messages that Mac OS X and Windows XP hurl at you to warn you of the impending disaster, stop the copying process as soon as you can:

- On the Mac, quit iTunes by pressing COMMAND-Q or choosing iTunes | Quit iTunes. If you can't quit iTunes gently, force quit it: OPTION-click the iTunes icon in the Dock and choose Force Quit from the shortcut menu. (Failing that, press COMMAND-OPTION-ESC to display the Force Quit dialog box, select the entry for iTunes, and click the Force Quit button.)

- On Windows, quit iTunes by pressing ALT-F4 or choosing File | Exit. If iTunes doesn't respond, right-click the taskbar and choose Task Manager to display Windows Task Manager. On the Applications tab, select the iTunes entry and click the End Task button.

Once you've done this, you may need to remove the tracks you've just copied to your music library from the folder. You can do this effectively on Windows by using the Date Created information

17

about the files and folders, because Windows treats the copy made by the consolidation as a new file. To search for the new files on Windows XP, follow these steps:

1. Choose Start | Search to display a Search Results window.

2. On the What Do You Want To Search For? screen, click the Pictures, Music, Or Video link. (If Search Companion displays the Search By Any Or All Of The Criteria Below screen instead of the What Do You Want To Search For? screen, click the Other Search Options link to display the What Do You Want To Search For? screen. Then click the Pictures, Music, or Video link.)

3. On the resulting screen, select the Music check box in the Search For All Files Of A Certain Type, Or Search By Type And Name area.

4. Click the Use Advanced Search Options link to display the remainder of the Search Companion pane.

5. Display the Look In drop-down list, select the Browse item to display the Browse For Folder dialog box, select your iTunes Music folder, and then click the OK button. (If you're not sure where your iTunes Music is, switch to iTunes, press CTRL-COMMA, and check on the Advanced sheet of the iTunes dialog box.)

6. Click the When Was It Modified? heading to display its controls, and then select the Specify Dates option button. Select the Created Date item in the drop-down list, and specify today's date in the From drop-down list and the To drop-down list. (The easiest way to specify the date is to open the From drop-down list and select the Today item. Windows XP then enters it in the To text box as well.)

7. Click the Search button to start the search for music files created in the specified time frame.

8. If the Search Results window is using any view other than Details view, choose View | Details to switch to Details view.

9. Click the Date Created column heading twice to make Windows Explorer sort the song files by reverse date, so that the files created most recently appear at the top of the list.

10. Check the Date Modified column to identify the files created during the consolidation, and then delete them without putting them in the Recycle Bin. (For example, select the files and press SHIFT-DELETE.)

Unfortunately, Mac OS X maintains the Date Created information from the original files on the copies made by the consolidation, so you can't search for the files this way on the Mac. Your best bet is to search by date created to identify the folders that iTunes has just created in your music library folder, so that you can delete them and their contents. This approach will get all of the consolidated songs that iTunes put into new folders, but it will miss any songs that were consolidated into folders that already existed in your music library. For example, if the song file Mary's In India.m4a is already stored in your music library with correct tags, your music library will contain a Dido/White Flag folder. If you then consolidate in the file Life For Rent.mp3, it'll go straight into the existing folder, and your search will miss it. The date-modified attribute of the White Flag folder will change to the date of the consolidation, but you'll need to drill down into each modified folder to find the song files that were added.

To search for the new folders on the Mac, follow these steps:

1. Press COMMAND-F or choose File | Find from the Finder to display the Find window.

2. In the Search In drop-down list, choose the Specific Places item.

3. Click the Add button and use the resulting Choose A Folder dialog box to specify your iTunes Music folder. (If you're not sure where your iTunes Music folder is, check on the Advanced sheet of the Preferences dialog box in iTunes.)

4. In the list box, make sure the check box for your iTunes Music folder is selected.

5. In the Search For Items Whose group box, specify a first condition of Date Created Is Today and a second condition of Kind Is Folder.

6. Click the Search button. Mac OS X displays a list of the folders created today.

7. Sort the folders by date created, identify those created during the consolidation by the time on the date, and then delete them.

8. Empty the Trash.

After deleting the files (or as many of them as possible), you'll need to remove the song references from iTunes and add them again from their preconsolidating location before iTunes can play them. When iTunes discovers that it can't find a song's file where it's supposed to be, it displays an exclamation point in the first column. Delete the files with exclamation points, and then add them to your music library again.

Troubleshooting iTunes on the Mac

This section shows you how to troubleshoot a handful of problems that you may run into when running iTunes on the Mac.

Troubleshooting: Ejecting a "Lost" CD

Sometimes Mac OS X seems to lose track of a CD (or DVD) after attempting to eject it. It's as if the eject mechanism fails to get a grip on the CD and push it out, but the commands get executed anyway, so that Mac OS X believes it has ejected the CD even though the CD is still in the drive.

When this happens, you probably won't be able to eject the disc by issuing another Eject command from iTunes, but it's worth trying that first. If that doesn't work, use Disk Utility to eject the disc. Follow these steps:

1. Press COMMAND-SHIFT-U or choose Go | Utilities from the Finder menu to display the Utilities folder.

2. Double-click the Disk Utility item to run it (see Figure 17-1).

3. Select the icon for the CD drive or the CD itself in the list box.

4. Click the Eject button.

5. Press COMMAND-Q or choose Disk Utility | Quit Disk Utility to quit Disk Utility.

17

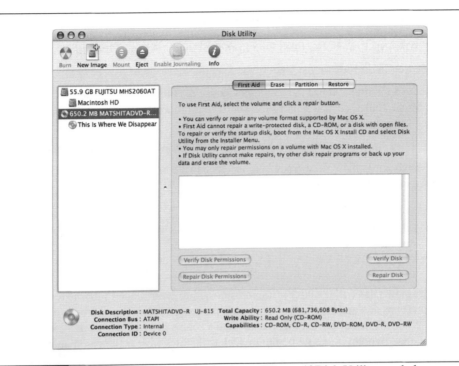

FIGURE 17-1   If you're having trouble ejecting a CD, see if Disk Utility can help.

If that doesn't work, you may need to force your Mac to recognize the drive. If it's a hot-pluggable external drive (for example, FireWire or USB), try unplugging the drive, waiting a minute, and then plugging it back in. If the drive is an internal drive, you may need to restart your Mac to force it to recognize the drive.

iTunes Won't Start

If iTunes displays the following dialog box, saying that you can't open iTunes because another user currently has it open, it means that your Mac is using Fast User Switching, and that someone else is logged on under another account and has iTunes open:

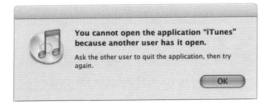

Click the OK button to dismiss the dialog box, and then either log on as that user (if you know that user's password, or if they have no password) and quit iTunes, or have the user log on and quit iTunes. When you switch back to your account, you'll be able to run iTunes.

"You Do Not Have Enough Access Privileges" When Importing Songs

The following error occurs when you've moved the iTunes music folder to a shared location and the user doesn't have Write permission to it:

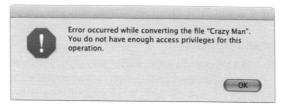

To fix this problem, an administrator needs to assign Write permission for the music folder to whoever received this error.

Troubleshooting iTunes on Windows

This section shows you how to troubleshoot a handful of problems that you may run into when running iTunes on Windows.

At the time of writing, the current version of iTunes (4.2) suffers from a variety of minor bugs that are annoying if you use iTunes all the time. Because iTunes started with version 4.0, and 4.2 is still an early release, it seems likely that Apple will fix these problems soon. In the meantime, following are some suggestions on how to deal with them.

iTunes Won't Start on Windows

If iTunes displays this Cannot Open iTunes dialog box saying that you can't open iTunes because another user currently has it open, it means that Windows XP is using Fast Switching, and that someone else is logged on under another account and has iTunes open:

Click the OK button to dismiss the dialog box. If you know the other user's password, or if you know they have no password, switch the user to their account by choosing Start | Log Off | Switch User and clicking their entry on the Welcome screen, close iTunes, and then switch back to your own account.

17

If you don't know the other user's password, either induce them to log on and close iTunes for you, or use Task Manager to close iTunes (right-click the taskbar and choose Task Manager from the shortcut menu to display Windows Task Manager, select the iTunes entry on the Applications tab, and then click the End Task button).

iTunes Starts Very Slowly

At this writing, iTunes starting excruciatingly slowly is a fact of life. The more songs your music library contains, the worse this problem is. Having to look up a CD's information across a slow Internet connection also slows down iTunes' starting.

iTunes Starts but Doesn't Appear

Sometimes you may find that iTunes doesn't appear after you launch it—even when you give it more than its usual length of time (see the previous section) to get going. When this happens, you'll usually need to track down iTunes and kill it ("kill" is the technical term, believe it or not) so that you can start it again. Follow these steps:

1. Right-click the taskbar and choose Task Manager from the shortcut menu to display Windows Task Manager:

2. Check on the Applications tab (shown above) whether iTunes is listed. If it is, try selecting it and clicking the Switch To button to display it. If that works, start using iTunes. If not, continue with these steps.

3. If iTunes appears on the Applications tab, select it and click the End Task button to close it.

4. If iTunes doesn't appear on the Applications tab, click the Processes tab:

5. Click the Image Name heading to sort the processes by name if necessary.

6. Select the iTunes.exe entry.

7. Click the End Process button. Windows displays a Task Manager Warning dialog box like this:

8. Click the Yes button to close iTunes.

9. Press ALT-F4 or choose File | Exit Task Manager to close Windows Task Manager.

Once you've done this, you should be able to start iTunes again as usual. If you're still not able to start iTunes, restart Windows and try again.

iTunes Doesn't Recognize Your iPod

If your iPod doesn't appear in the Source pane in iTunes, take as many of the following steps as necessary to make it appear there:

1. Check that your iPod is okay. If you find it's displaying an exclamation point or the Sad iPod symbol, you'll know iTunes isn't guilty this time.

2. Check that your iPod knows it's connected to your PC. Your iPod should be displaying the Do Not Disconnect message. If it's not, fix the connection so that it does display this message.

3. Check that Windows is recognizing your iPod. Choose Start | My Computer to display a My Computer window that shows all the drives and devices that Windows thinks are connected to your PC. Your iPod should show up as a drive, even if you haven't specifically enabled disk mode.

   ■ If your iPod doesn't appear as a drive in My Computer, restart your iPod by holding down the Play button and the Menu button together for several seconds. Wait for a few seconds, and then press F5 or choose View | Refresh to refresh the view in the My Computer window.

   ■ If restarting your iPod doesn't make it appear in My Computer, restart it again. This time, when your iPod displays the Apple symbol, hold down the Previous button and the Next button for a moment to send a request to the computer to mount your iPod as a drive.

4. If Windows is recognizing your iPod, but iTunes isn't, restart iTunes.

5. If restarting iTunes doesn't make it recognize your iPod, restart Windows, and then restart iTunes.

iTunes Doesn't Notice When You Insert Another CD

If iTunes doesn't notice when you remove one CD and insert another, usually you'll need to quit iTunes and restart it to make it reread the CD.

If you're familiar with Windows, you may be disappointed to find that a couple of maneuvers you might expect to help with this problem don't help:

■ First, using the Show Songs Using iTunes item in the Autoplay dialog box for the CD (which you can display by right-click the Audio CD entry in a My Computer window and choosing Autoplay from the shortcut menu) merely makes iTunes list the CD it thinks is in the drive. (The Play CD Using iTunes item has even less effect—it doesn't even start the CD playing.)

■ Second, ejecting the CD from iTunes itself (instead of from Windows Explorer or by using the manual eject button on your CD drive) doesn't make iTunes realize that you've removed the CD and that it might want to check if you've put in another CD.

■ Third, choosing Advanced | Get CD Track Names doesn't make iTunes check which CD is in the drive—instead, this command makes iTunes check CDDB for information on the CD it thinks is in the drive.

So usually you'll need to quit iTunes and restart it to make it notice the new CD. If even that doesn't work, you'll need to restart Windows.

Your PC Cannot Read Your iPod

The iPod Not Readable dialog box indicates that you've plugged a Mac-formatted iPod into your PC:

If you did so by mistake, click the Cancel button, and then disconnect the iPod. If you plugged in the iPod intentionally, you'll need to reformat the iPod before you can use it with Windows. Click the Update button to launch the iPod Software Updater, and then follow through the restore process to reformat the iPod. See "Restore Your iPod," earlier in this chapter, for details.

"Updater Can't Install Firmware on Connected iPod" Message

This error message indicates that you're trying to use the wrong version of the iPod Software Updater for your iPod (for example, you can't use the iPod Software Updater versions 2.0 and above on first- and second-generation iPods):

To solve this problem, open your browser to www.apple.com/swupdates/ and download the latest version of the iPod Software Updater for the type of iPod that you have.

NOTE *At this writing, the latest version of the iPod Software Updater for the earlier iPods is 1.3.1. Versions 2.0 and higher of the iPod Software Updater are for the third-generation and later iPods. The iPod mini uses iPod Software Updater for iPod mini versions 1.x.*

17

Index

INTERNATIONAL CONTACT INFORMATION

AUSTRALIA
McGraw-Hill Book Company
Australia Pty. Ltd.
TEL +61-2-9900-1800
FAX +61-2-9878-8881
http://www.mcgraw-hill.com.au
books-it_sydney@mcgraw-hill.com

CANADA
McGraw-Hill Ryerson Ltd.
TEL +905-430-5000
FAX +905-430-5020
http://www.mcgraw-hill.ca

GREECE, MIDDLE EAST, & AFRICA
(Excluding South Africa)
McGraw-Hill Hellas
TEL +30-210-6560-990
TEL +30-210-6560-993
TEL +30-210-6560-994
FAX +30-210-6545-525

MEXICO (Also serving Latin America)
McGraw-Hill Interamericana Editores
S.A. de C.V.
TEL +525-1500-5108
FAX +525-117-1589
http://www.mcgraw-hill.com.mx
carlos_ruiz@mcgraw-hill.com

SINGAPORE (Serving Asia)
McGraw-Hill Book Company
TEL +65-6863-1580
FAX +65-6862-3354
http://www.mcgraw-hill.com.sg
mghasia@mcgraw-hill.com

SOUTH AFRICA
McGraw-Hill South Africa
TEL +27-11-622-7512
FAX +27-11-622-9045
robyn_swanepoel@mcgraw-hill.com

SPAIN
McGraw-Hill/
Interamericana de España, S.A.U.
TEL +34-91-180-3000
FAX +34-91-372-8513
http://www.mcgraw-hill.es
professional@mcgraw-hill.es

UNITED KINGDOM, NORTHERN,
EASTERN, & CENTRAL EUROPE
McGraw-Hill Education Europe
TEL +44-1-628-502500
FAX +44-1-628-770224
http://www.mcgraw-hill.co.uk
emea_queries@mcgraw-hill.com

ALL OTHER INQUIRIES Contact:
McGraw-Hill/Osborne
TEL +1-510-420-7700
FAX +1-510-420-7703
http://www.osborne.com
omg_international@mcgraw-hill.com